Periods in Pop Culture

Periods in Pop Culture

Menstruation in Film and Television

Lauren Rosewarne

LEXINGTON BOOKS
Lanham • Boulder • New York • Toronto • Plymouth, UK

Published by Lexington Books
A wholly owned subsidiary of The Rowman & Littlefield Publishing Group, Inc.
4501 Forbes Boulevard, Suite 200, Lanham, Maryland 20706
www.rowman.com

10 Thornbury Road, Plymouth PL6 7PP, United Kingdom

Copyright © 2012 by Lexington Books

All rights reserved. No part of this book may be reproduced in any form or by any electronic or mechanical means, including information storage and retrieval systems, without written permission from the publisher, except by a reviewer who may quote passages in a review.

British Library Cataloguing in Publication Information Available

Library of Congress Cataloging-in-Publication Data Available
ISBN 978-0-7391-7000-7 (cloth : alk. paper)—ISBN 978-0-7391-7001-4 (electronic)

™ The paper used in this publication meets the minimum requirements of American National Standard for Information Sciences Permanence of Paper for Printed Library Materials, ANSI/NISO Z39.48-1992.

Printed in the United States of America

Contents

Acknowledgments		vii
Introduction: Blood Hunting		1
1	Women Bleeding Secretly: The Gender, Place, and Segregation of Menstruation	7
2	Red Tents and Moon Lodges: Menstruation and the Rites of Passage	39
3	The Curse of Eve: Cramped Stomachs and Cramped Lifestyles	67
4	The Menstrual Mess: The Disgust, Horror, and Fear of Menstruation	93
5	I Want to Suck Your Blood: Sex, Sexiness, and Menstruation	121
6	Bleeding Out Proud: Menstruation and Empowerment	151
7	You Don't Know What You've Got 'Til It's Gone: Absent Menstruation	177
8	Where Have All the Menstruators Gone?: Rereading Missing Menstruation	203
Conclusion: A Strange Phenomenon		223
Media References		227
Bibliography		233
Index		247
About the Author		259

Acknowledgments

With thanks to the Center for Public Policy and Administration at the University of Massachusetts, Amherst, where I was based during much of the writing of this book; special thanks to Professor Lee Badgett and Kathy Colón for making me feel so welcome. Thanks to Michelle Lague—my best American friend—who made geographic and social isolation much more bearable! Appreciation to Lenore Lautigar and Johnnie Simpson from Lexington Books as well as the anonymous referees whose advice proved invaluable. Last, thanks to Simon for helping me all to find a very fitting illustration of menstrual-themed irony.

Introduction

Blood Hunting

My parents' version of the story was that I talked so much that they were compelled to outsource managing me to the education system. The less mean-spirited reality was that in 1985, students where I lived in Australia could start primary school at four if they seemed ready and if they would turn five before July. Starting school early scarcely impacted on me; perhaps delaying driving or purchasing cigarettes and alcohol, although I didn't mind too much about that. One time it did matter was in high school. At eleven, I watched my friends, one by one, get their periods in Year 7; I had to wait a good year to join them (and by then, everyone's interest had long faded). I don't remember feeling particularly envious—the vivid "squeezing extra blood out" accounts from one friend quelled that yen—but it did make me feel different. Not younger necessarily, but certainly outside of *something*.

Myself, I don't have a fascinating first period story. It was a Tuesday. 1993. It was a month or so before my thirteenth birthday and it was wonderfully untraumatic. It wasn't in public, I didn't think I was dying, and there was no fear that life as I knew it was over. It was a drop of blood in my underwear after school on a Tuesday. I do however, have a favorite menstruation memory centered on my then best friend's first period. She disclosed it through a scrap of paper pushed toward me during an English class: "I got it." She needn't have written anything further; as early high schoolers *it* only ever meant one thing. Eschewing a congratulations—something even a decade into my out-and-proud feminism would still feel weird—my first thought was to call her "Rambo": an allusion to the first Rambo film, *First Blood* (1982). To say that she was unamused would be thoroughly downplaying proceedings: I don't remember how she phrased her rebuke or how long

1

her iciness lasted, but I remember her scowl and how she dismissed me as immature. I actually still find the comment funny, albeit acknowledge my timing stumble.

That my Rambo quip stands out as my favorite menstruation memory is testimony to a number of things. Notably it nicely demonstrates that popular culture has always played a pivotal role in my making sense of the world. My first exposure to every human experience has always been vicariously through film and television. Every big-ticket social, sexual and sentimental issue on the screen served as my introduction: abortion in *Dirty Dancing* (1987), AIDS on *Life Goes On*, homosexuality in *My Own Private Idaho* (1991), mortality in *Cocoon* (1985). And yet, even at eleven, I knew it seemed very strange that the only menstrual screen reference I could conjure was from a war film I hadn't even seen.

My menstrual education in fact was gleaned completely *off* screen. I read *Are You There God? It's Me, Margaret* at eight years old. I rifled through the tame contents of a polystyrene chest labelled "Health Box" in my primary school library. I rolled my eyes at my high school math teacher who felt a peculiar need to constantly clarify the difference between mesuration and *menstruation*. I listened to those friends' all too willing to divulge their own viscous details. When the screen abandoned me, when my world was one to be navigated before Google, I scavenged for tidbits wherever they lay. While I never felt lacking in information, I was long stuck on the idea that something so widely discussed amongst my friends, something so common and so seemingly *normal*, was absent from film and television. Just where were all the menstruators?

Gleaned from a lifetime of voracious media consumption, my assumption when embarking on this book was that nearly all of the blood sloshed around on screen came from orifices *other* than vaginas. This hypothesis, of course, proved largely accurate. For all the incalculable women on screen, for all the adolescent narratives and pregnancy quest storylines and so very many sex scenes, menstruation is strikingly absent. Predictably, the vast majority of on-screen blood comes from violence. That said, it wasn't too hard to find *some* portrayals. In fact, *some* portrayals would grow to *many* and at completion I would tally close to 200 scenes from film and television discussed across eight chapters. There may not be *thousands* of scenes, menstruation may seldom get a *starring* role, and a lot of the presentations discussed may be completely awful—if not thoroughly *misogynist*—but examples do exist. From the shock of a first period, the sting of a PMS accusation, the joy of an eagerly awaited late period or a boyfriend's midnight tampon run, menstruation is indeed identifiable. My primary motivation for this book was to examine what transpired on those rare occasions when producers dared eschew the popular taboo and allowed women to do *on* screen what they so frequently do *off* screen and menstruate.

I have chosen to focus on screen representations in this book over other types of popular culture primarily because film and television are the most persistent disseminators of cultural messages. Our heavy consumption of screen content presents, as well as *reinforces*, a cavalcade of ideas—often contradictory—about politics and society and most notably about *the female body*. In the case of menstruation, the downplaying, if not *demonizing*, of menstruation helps to reinforce popular ideas related to taboo, stigma, and secrecy, and in doing so presents a wide range of topics for academic analysis.

There are several aims of *Periods in Pop Culture*. The first is, in line with the objective of feminist media studies, to examine the way women are portrayed on screen. Feminist film theorist Laura Mulvey noted that crucial to the women's movement was identifying that women's "exclusion from the *public* voice and the language of culture and politics" was a *political* issue.[1] As applied to a menstruation discussion, the frequent exclusion of menstruation from the public sphere as well as the stereotyped ways it often gets portrayed makes analysis of this situation a salient feminist project. The second task of this volume is to provide a taxonomy of menstruation portrayals. Drawing from scenes sourced from television dramas and sitcoms, movies, and advertising, I classify presentations according to narrative themes. Each chapter of this book is devoted to exploring a specific cluster of portrayals: those associated with the gendered nature of place and space; as a rite of passage; as something disrupting life; as disgusting; as connected to sexuality; as empowering, and as absent. More than simply categorizing, however, as a feminist and as a social scientist, I was also interested in *dissecting* those portrayals. How do they relate to existing academic work on menstruation? On women's portrayal in the media? What social and sexual messages are being conveyed in each scene? If girls *did* get their first experience of menstruation vicariously from film and television, what impression would they glean? What role does gender play? What about sexuality? Politics? Space, place, and time? What role do the unreal and even *surreal* narratives play?

And what about all those glaring *omissions*?

In an episode of the television drama *Californication* (2007–), Becca (Madeleine Martin) got her first period. Later in the episode she fronted her band with a cover of Alice Cooper's "Only Women Bleed" (1975). While Cooper has long denied that his song is about menstruation,[2] evidently Becca made the link on the day of her menarche, and in my adolescence, I too assumed it was about menstruation. Whether intended by Cooper or not, the lyrics encapsulate a fascinating—if ridiculously simple—reality: that menstruation is one of very few things experienced *exclusively* by biological women. More than this, it is something experienced by virtually *all women*.[3] Whereas many women won't ever get pregnant or breastfeed, menstruation traverses class and race, sexual preference, politics, religion, and personal choice: nearly *every woman* will get a period at some point in her life, and most of us will end up with many more. That of the deluge of things that make women socially, sexually, and aesthetically disparate, menstruation exists as a common experience: as Helen (Isabelle Adjani) remarked in *Possession* (1981): "There is nothing in common among women except menstruation." This female universality of menstruation positions it as the archetype women's story and as an important subject for feminist, and more broadly social and political inquiry.

As my bloated media references list demonstrates, my research unearthed many more menstruation scenes than I could have ever anticipated. While rarely at the forefront of a narrative as in *Carrie* (1976), I was nonetheless able to draw together a large sample of menstrual allusions, accusations, conversations, and calamities. Menstruation indeed has a role in sitcoms, dramas, cartoons, reality television, and also in a significant number of films: it is there if we look hard enough. Less pleasing, however, is the deluge of *negative* portrayals. Men blaming women's moods on their menstruation; *women* blaming moods on menstruation; of synced periods causing *men* grief; of periods ruining sex lives: overwhelmingly the screen presents menstruation as not only a dramatic event, but as a pretty awful plight for *everybody*. Over fifty years of supposed feminist enlightenment, of female and *feminist* filmmaking, of feminist media theory and with women's stories increasingly at the forefront of screen narratives, and such routine and intense negativity seemed peculiar. Peculiar and certainly worthy of analysis. Why, when menstruation is so very normal and when so many women manage their periods without fanfare or catastrophe, is its appearance on screen so frequently connected to slurs, derision, and disaster? This situation is put under the microscope in this volume.

Fortunately, however, it is not all stained skirts and maniacal mood swings: some positive representations were also detected. Girls cunningly use menstruation to get out of gym class. Mothers warmly welcome their daughters into a sisterhood of bleeders. Fathers throw menarche parties and load up trolleys with menstrual supplies. Friends help conceal blood stains and cheer on reluctant bleeders. Many screen examples do indeed buck stereotypes, challenge taboo, and eschew the secrecy imperative. Such scenes were probed in this volume as vigorously as the negative depictions.

Perhaps most interesting were scenes when menstruation was controversially presented as *sexy*. Scenes when men find the menstruator sexy, when the menstruating woman finds *herself* sexy, and where sex during a period is portrayed as simply part of life. While I analyze the burgeoning genre of menstrual porn where blood is explicitly eroticized—if not also *fetishized*—

the sexy menstruator is also a portrayal identifiable in mainstream narratives and advertising, examined here in the context of issues including consent and self-esteem.

Periods in Pop Culture presents an interdisciplinary analysis of menstruation scenes sourced from the screen and also examined alongside those found in art, literature, and online, to explore how an incredibly normal offscreen reality features in our popular culture. Psychology and anthropology, cultural studies, political science, gender studies, social work, and feminist theory are each called upon to help dissect these presentations and to unravel the very strange role menstruation plays both in our lives and on our screens.

NOTES

1. Laura Mulvey, *Visual and Other Pleasures* (London: Macmillan, 1989), viii.

2. According to Alice Cooper, the song is "a tribute to a woman's mental state—not an anthem for menstruation" (in Alice Cooper, *Alice Cooper, Golden Monster: A Rock 'n' Roller's Life and 12 Steps to Becoming a Gold Addict* (New York: Crown Publishers, 2007), 171).

3. While I contend that nearly all women menstruate, gender researcher Chris Bobel articulates some useful disclaimers: "not all women menstruate, and not only women menstruate. Postmenopausal women, women posthysterectomy, and some athletes, for example, do not menstruate, and some preoperative transmen do menstruate (as do many intersexuals)." (Chris Bobel, *New Blood: Third-Wave Feminism and the Politics of Menstruation* (New Brunswick, NJ: Rutgers University Press, 2010), 11–12).

Chapter One

Women Bleeding Secretly

The Gender, Place, and Segregation of Menstruation

Women's physical and emotional separation from men is explored in this chapter with specific attention devoted to the role of the bathroom: a space that facilitates physical and gender segregation. The female nature of menstruation is explored through an examination of narratives specifically concerned with menstrual bonding and synchrony. Also examined are the roles men are left to occupy, notably with their relegation to caricatures such as menstrual dolts, as menstrually emasculated and as menstrually creepy.

A TIME FOR SEPARATION

In her self-help book *The Wild Genie: The Healing Power of Menstruation*, Alexandra Pope contended that it is quite common for women to want time alone during menstruation.[1] In psychologist Jane Ussher et al.'s research on women's health, one woman claimed that during her period, "I become very *drawn*. . . . I just *don't* want to be with anybody else."[2] While these are rare published examples documenting a yen for physical separation, they indeed relate research on menstruation being excluded from the public sphere more broadly. Sociologist Laura Fingerson, for example, in her book *Girls in Power*, wrote that our society views menstruation "as a private event not to be talked about in public."[3] Psychologist Judith Daniluk similarly contended: "[t]here are few experiences in a girl's life subjected to as much secrecy and privacy as menstruation."[4] Psychologist Joan Chrisler wrote that "[t]he emphasis on secrecy reinforces the idea that menstruation is a negative, stigmatizing, and embarrassing event,"[5] and Ussher identified a Western cultural mandate of "concealment through secrecy and shame."[6] The widespread acceptance of menstruation as a private sphere experience was in fact at the crux of a 2007 Tampax advertising campaign boasting the slogan, "Keep your period private with Tampax." One commercial showed a girl standing up in a cafeteria, shouting out "I'm menstruating" and then proceeding to do the "period dance" on the tops of lunch tables. In another version a woman in a shoe store was followed by a mariachi band singing "she's on her period." The humor in these commercials centers on two key ideas: one, that society considers it thoroughly inappropriate for anybody to know about a woman's menstruation, and two, that it is inconceivable that any woman would *want* anybody else to know about it.

While there exists a general cultural imperative to keep menstruation hidden, there is an even more specific demand to keep it hidden *from men*. This idea was discussed in sociologist Sophie Laws' research: "[t]he one thing British girls at menarche are always told is that men must not know."[7] Gender researcher Chris Bobel made a similar point: "[girls] are often congratulated for entering womanhood, and they are instructed to keep it a secret."[8] Germaine Greer in her seminal feminist text, *The Female Eunuch*, also referenced the privacy mandate in a discussion of her own menstrual experiences: "I used to creep into the laundry and crouch over a bucket of foul clouts, *hoping my brother would not catch me* at my revolting labours."[9] In artist Zannette Lewis's puberty recollections, she too alluded to the ideas of secrecy and gender separation: "I remembered my sister's disgust that my mother needed to share this event with my dad."[10] On screen both the secrecy imperative and the mandate for gender separation are clearly apparent in the film *To Sir With Love* (1967). Following the burning of a menstrual product in a classroom, teacher Mark Thackeray (Sidney Poitier) reprimanded the female students who he believed were responsible: "A decent woman keeps certain things private. Only a filthy slut would have done this!" Encapsulated in Mr. Thackeray's words is the derogatory perception of women who eschew cultural mandates of secrecy and dare let men discover their periods.[11] In this chapter I explore the privacy imperative as manifested in two types of screen narratives centered on one, women's desire for physical separation from men, and two, the more subtle menstrual concealment narratives complicit with the secrecy mandate.

In the film *The Blue Lagoon* (1980), on being frightened at the appearance of her first period, Emmeline (Brooke Shields) called out for help to her island companion Richard (Christopher Atkins). As Richard approached, Emmeline suddenly retreated, pleading, "Go away, don't look at me!" In the sequel, *Return to the Blue Lagoon* (1991), after Lilli (Milla Jovovich) got her first period, she abruptly moved her bed to another part of the hut that she shared with her own secluded island companion, Richard (Brian Krause). In

My Girl (1991), when Vada (Anna Chlumsky) got her first period, she responded to a visit from her best friend, Thomas J (Macaulay Culkin), by saying, "Get out of here! And don't come back for five to seven days." While each example illustrated the character's embarrassment and shame, they also showed girls seeking *physical separation* from the men closest to them. A number of factors may explain this response, notably that in each instance it was the girl's *first* period: she had no education about it, no understanding of it, and potentially simply likened it to any other private bodily function, presumably conceiving of it as a "sanitary event,"[12] and something done *away* from men. A second explanation is that each example complies with an *essentialist* view of menstruation whereby women are assumed to instinctively *know* that menstruation is private and thus each harbors an innate yen to retreat and tend to it in isolation. A third explanation relates to self-policing and menstruation being just one of many aspects of women's bodies under ongoing patrol. Feminist philosopher Sandra Bartky, for example, wrote about women's self-surveillance as manifested in an internalized mandate to always be suitably feminine, presentable, if not *desirable*, because their appearance, unlike men's, is always being judged.[13] The menstrual secret is therefore kept through vigilance about concealment: of blood, of odor, of products.

While Emmeline and Lilli in the *Blue Lagoon* films didn't have many external influences—both girls came of age on a deserted island, after all—that each girl exhibited shame and a yen for privacy exploits the *audience's* knowledge of cultural expectations; these scenes have resonance because of viewers' *own* frames of reference and internalized social mores. For Vada, while her desire for privacy may have been based on intuition or on the explanations provided by her father's girlfriend, Shelly (Jamie Lee Curtis), it may also be attributable to her empirical observations. In their book *Period*, for example, psychotherapist JoAnn Loulan and Bonnie Worthen contended, "How we feel about it [menstruation] depends on what our mothers, friends, older sisters, grandmothers or aunts have said."[14] For Vada, that no woman around her had ever spoken about menstruation in her earshot made her infer that it was something to be kept private.[15]

Another way menstrual privacy is presented on screen is in the "don't tell Dad" secret-keeping manner alluded to in Lewis's recollections discussed earlier. In *A Walk on the Moon* (1999), for example, on the day of her first period, Alison (Anna Paquin) begged her mother, "Please don't tell Daddy." In an episode of the television series *7th Heaven* (1996–2007), while eagerly awaiting her first period, twelve-year-old Lucy (Beverley Mitchell) ordered her mother to "keep Dad out of this." In a later season of the series, younger daughter Ruthie (Mackenzie Rosman) didn't want either of her parents knowing because she knew "there'll be tears, crying, [and] a special dinner that ends with Dad buying me feminine products." One interpretation of these scenes is that—as in the physical separation examples discussed—keeping the secret from dad reflects the internalized dictum that menstruation is a *woman's* problem and having fathers know about it would be embarrassing. While each girl's secrecy in these scenes complies with cultural expectations, interestingly, such secrecy actually appears motivated by some *unexpected* reasons. Alison, Lucy, and Ruthie's sentiments stemmed not necessarily from them being embarrassed about their fathers finding out about their changing bodies or that their fathers might mock them (chapter 4), or even that their fathers might be embarrassed,[16] *rather*, each girl appeared worried that her father might make her menarche a "big deal"; that her period might be made into a production whereas she just wanted to quietly get on with it (chapter 8). The fathers in these examples actually *were* very happy for their daughters and while celebrations weren't as grandiose as the girls feared, nonetheless the fathers *did* take an interest. Each of these examples presents a standard narrative about culturally normalized secrecy—if not also embarrassment—but interestingly, presents fathers acting in sharp contrast to the ways that men are often presented; these fathers were proud rather than disgusted or offended (chapter 4).

BATHROOMS: THE PLACE FOR MENSTRUATION

A particularly interesting element of the menstrual experience on screen is the bathroom existing as the standard backdrop: a space achieving both privacy *and* separation from men. In gender researchers Mariamne Whatley and Elissa Henken's book on sexuality-based folklore, the authors discussed a common misunderstanding about menstruation as related to bathrooms; a misunderstanding which interestingly links with popular perceptions of menstruation as primarily a sanitary event:

> It is also common to believe that menstruation is like urination or defecation, in that there is a feeling that "you have to menstruate," at which point the woman excuses herself to go to the bathroom to put on a pad or insert a tampon.[17]

This toilet-trip/sanitary idea was particularly well illustrated in the comedy *Superbad* (2007). At a party, Seth (Jonah Hill) discovered blood on his jeans and exclaimed, "someone period-ed on my fucking leg!" In the scene, Seth construed menstruation as like urination or defecation and as something that could be actively *done*. While of course menstruation is not like this, the bathroom does frequently serve as the place for it; periods may not actually be *done* there, but on screen they are frequently *experienced* there.

While bathrooms might not seem an obvious subject for academic inquiry, in recent years their usage has come under close scrutiny. The *where* of use has been analyzed from a feminist perspective in terms of inadequate stalls for women and disproportionately long queues,[18] as well as the *who* of use related to race[19] and sexuality.[20] In this section, I analyze the pivotal role of bathrooms in menstruation stories in real life and notably on screen.

Anthropologist Emily Martin described the bathroom as "the place that women depend on to take care of their bodily functions including menstruation."[21] In Fingerson's research, female adolescents identified the too-short gaps between classes as something that made trips to the bathroom problematic and thus rendered menstruation difficult: "They have to negotiate their time, their menstrual supplies, and the adult world telling them when they may go to the bathroom."[22] Historian Lara Freidenfelds identified the bathroom as a site for many different menstrual milestones: as a site where women learned about menstruation from their mothers through observation[23]; where menstrual products came to be stored in modern cabineted bathrooms[24]; where fathers became aware of their daughters' menstruation through increased supplies[25]; and where, as discardable products became more common, disposal occurred.[26] Certainly the importance of the bathroom to menstruation in real life pre-empts its central role in popular culture. American artist Judy Chicago's installation "Menstruation Bathroom" (1972), for example, depicted a scene of a bathroom, the focal point being a bin overflowing with bloodied menstrual products. This work is considered one of the first examples of menstruation—particularly of seemingly *used* menstrual products—leaving the private sphere and entering the public space of galleries. While certainly not as explicit as Chicago's work, there are indeed numerous mainstream examples whereby the starring role of bathrooms in the menstrual story is identifiable on screen.

In her book *The Curse*, Karen Houppert described the bathroom as "one of the few places where girls and women can relax their artifices for a while."[27] This idea was well illustrated in an episode of the sitcom *Community* (2009–). Shirley (Yvette Nicole Brown) had invited classmate Britta (Gillian Jacobs) to join her on a restroom trip. Britta declined, seemingly unaware of the unwritten rules of the journey (as classmate Jeff (Joel McHale) explained: "Girls go in groups. Did you learn *nothing* from stand-up comedy in the 90s?"). Britta eventually joined Shirley and afterward the following conversation transpired:

> **Britta:** Apparently I failed yesterday's try-outs for the position of bathroom companion.
>
> **Shirley:** Oh Britta, I wasn't trying to hurt your feelings.

> **Britta:** You didn't hurt my feelings, Shirley. I don't *need* to go to the bathroom with other people. I was just trying to throw you a bone because I like you.
>
> **Shirley:** Oh? You can keep that bone. Listening to a story about a stranger pissing me off and taking the stranger's side. And then you can't talk about your own business but you insinuate my mama's a robot because she and I want make-overs. *That* is the *ladies* room, Britta. A place where ladies go to share, listen, support each other and discreetly eliminate waste. I like you too, I even like that you're a little hard. But if you can't learn to be soft in there, you need to pee on your own.

Shirley's summary of the ladies' room—as a "place where ladies go to share, listen, support each other and discreetly eliminate waste"—provides not only an outline of the feminized nature of the bathroom experience but also spotlights that the chatter and support actually occurs in the *very same place* as the elimination of waste.[28] That, potentially, the sharing, listening, and support occurs *because* the bathroom is such a social leveler: as the tagline for Charmin toilet paper reminds us, "we all go."

For this discussion, my interest in bathrooms—both public and private—relates to their on-screen presentation as the one place where menstruation can be experienced both socially with other women and in isolation from men. For most women, menstrual products will be removed and changed in bathrooms: in an episode of *Californication*, for example, Marcy (Pamela Adlon)—in dialogue very unusual for the screen—declared that she was going upstairs to change her tampon: she went, of course, to the bathroom. While such events may transpire because menstruation has been *confined* to the bathroom because of widespread taboo and disgust[29] (chapter 4), more simply, bathrooms are just the place where women are likely to *already* be engaged with intimate bodily functions like urination and defecation. Bathrooms are also usually the place where menstrual product storage and disposal is.

On screen one of the key functions of the bathroom is as the site for menstrual *discovery*.

Bathrooms and Menarche Discovery

As most health and hygiene books—and in fact as the experience of most women testifies—first periods are often discovered in the bathroom: likely through stained underwear; presumably because the crotch is rarely looked at elsewhere (chapter 8). Judy Blume's novel *Are You There God? It's Me, Margaret* exists as the most famous menstruation narrative, and even forty years after its publication is one of a few popular narratives with menstruation at the core. Protagonist Margaret's long-pined-for period arrived at the end of the novel, discovered in the bathroom when she found blood on her underwear. Earlier in the novel, Margaret's friend Gretchen described discovering her own period similarly.[30] Menarche discovery scenes set in bathrooms are identifiable in a broad range of screen examples. In *A Walk on the Moon*, for example, Alison called out to her grandmother from the family bathroom to reveal her newly stained underpants. In *My Girl*, Vada ran from the family bathroom shrieking that she was hemorrhaging. In the Australian film *Puberty Blues* (1981), Debbie (Nell Schofield), seated on the toilet, looked down at her underpants, smiled, and threw her head back in delight. In *Towelhead* (2007), while also on the toilet, Jasira (Summer Bishil) noticed a small blood spot on her underpants; the same thing transpired in the German film *Hungerjahre* (*Years of Hunger*) (1980), for Ursula (Sylvia Ulrich). In the cartoon sitcom *King of the Hill* (1997–2010), Connie emerged from a prolonged session in the bathroom at her neighbor Hank's house with a note confessing that she had gotten her first period. In the Canadian television series *Ready or Not* (1993–1997), Busy (Lani Billard) exited a school toilet cubicle and told two classmates that she had to go to the hospital: "I'm bleeding, I'm really sick"; Busy had just gotten her first period. In the sitcom *Curb Your Enthusiasm* (2000–), girl scout Kyra (Kaitlyn Dever) suspected—while selling cookies to Larry (Larry David)—that she might have gotten her first period. Larry ushered her to the bathroom where her suspicions were confirmed. One feminist criticism of staging these scenes in bathrooms is that in doing so menstruation is portrayed as "dead blood,"[31] like excrement, and relegated to a segregated, waste-disposal site. An alternate interpretation, however, is that the bathroom is simply where it is most practical to tend to a period: the space is sanitary[32], there is running water, a flushing toilet, and soap, thus making the bathroom an obvious place for menstrual activities both on screen and off.

In films from the horror genre such as *Carrie* (1976) and the Chinese film *Feng kuang de dai jia* (*The Price of Frenzy*) (1989), the bathroom, while again functioning as a place for menarche discovery, also served a more sinister function by exploiting the aesthetics of the space. Considered the most famous of menstrual-themed films, *Carrie* opened with the title character (Sissy Spacek) getting her first period in the high school gym shower. As in *The Blue Lagoon*, *Return to the Blue Lagoon*, and *My Girl*, Carrie was confused and horrified by the sight of her blood. The fusion of a naked girl, shower stream, screaming, and blood harked back to cinema's most famous shower horror scene, from *Psycho* (1960). Even though the audience presumably recognized that Carrie was *only* menstruating,[33] the character's terror was contagious for the audience: wet skin and water spread the blood, making it appear more gory and plentiful. A similar horror-themed shower/menarche discovery occurred in *Feng kuang de dai jia* (*The Price of Frenzy*). When teenage Lan Lan (Jing Li) got her first period in a public shower, the horror of the scene was based on the character's isolation and vulnerability;

something which helped establish the shock of her rape afterward. While these scenes can be assumed to be set in bathrooms for the practical and sanitary reasons outlined earlier, another explanation relates to the visual nature of film: a bathroom is a place that is supposed to be sanitary, where there is frequently much white (in terms of surfaces and tiles), and is a place where people are often naked, vulnerable and where blood appears most stark and out of place (even if easily explained). *Carrie* and *Feng kuang de dai jia* (*The Price of Frenzy*) are made much more frightening because menstruation is unexpected in such a public site.

While menarche connotes the beginning of a woman's fertility, for sexually active women, periods notably function as *the* demonstration of *not being pregnant*: menstruation, as explored in chapter 7, may enter a narrative when connected to a pregnancy possibility storyline. Whether pregnancy is desired and thus a period is feared, or whether a woman is terrified of having conceived and thus is desperate for blood, inevitably the bathroom is where her fate is delivered. In *Where the Heart Is* (2000), for example, Novalee (Natalie Portman), fearing she might be pregnant, went into a gas station bathroom and, once inside the stall, shouted "Yes!" and "Thank you Lord! Thank you so much." In the television series *Beverly Hills 90210* (1990–2000), Brenda (Shannen Doherty) also feared she was pregnant and, while preparing to give a urine sample at her gynecologist's office, got her period: "What a relief!" she exclaimed. We didn't see blood in either example, but neither did we need to: each character's reaction provided the answer. While the screen's disproportionate focus on the negative aspects of menstruation (chapters 3 and 4) perpetuates the idea that menstruation is something horrible,[34] Novalee and Brenda's reactions in these scenes demonstrate one storyline when menstruation is presented as a godsend: when it connotes *not* being pregnant. (Other portrayals centered on the positives of menstruation are explored in chapter 6.)

Just as the bathroom is typically the place where periods are discovered, it is also the one place where they can be experienced *socially*.

Social Menstruation

In Gwen Macsai's novel *Lipshtick*, she described receiving advice in bathrooms from other women such as: "Always pee *before* you change your tampon, or you could end up peeing on your hand." Macsai concluded, "This is the way bathrooms are. Halls of higher learning."[35] Sociologist Harvey Molotch presented a similar idea in his chapter on public restrooms:

> Some women report that the ladies' room is where they learned as girls to do their hair, hold their bodies, use menstrual products, and adjust their clothes— with pals and relatives fussing around them in real time.[36]

In Freidenfelds's cultural history of menstruation, she discussed girls learning to use menstrual products from observations made in bathrooms. This idea of bathrooms serving as impromptu classrooms is identifiable in a number of screen examples. In *Pups* (1999), for example, Rocky (Mischa Barton) got her first period while she and a male companion robbed a bank; Rocky forced a female customer into the bathroom to assist her. When Becca (Madeleine Martin) got her first period on *Californication*, her father, Hank (David Duchovny), took her to a gas station to purchase tampons. Inside, another woman (Christen Sussin) retrieved the last box from the shelf. Hank attempted to buy the tampons from the woman, she refused, and a physical fight ensued between Hank and the woman's husband (Charlie Mattera). As the men fought, the woman spotted Becca and took her to the bathroom to help her with the tampons. *The Runaways* (2010) opened with Cherie (Dakota Fanning) wiping blood from her thigh: she had just gotten her first period. Her sister (Riley Keough) took her to a gas station bathroom to help her. Early into the Australian film *Hey Hey It's Esther Blueburger* (2008), while in the school bathroom, Esther (Danielle Catanzariti) realized that her first period had arrived. Another girl from her school, Sunni (Keisha Castle-Hughes), helped her retrieve a tampon. A similar scene transpired in the *Ready or Not* episode discussed earlier when Busy's assumption of sickness was corrected; a classmate even attempted to buy her a pad in the scene. In an episode of the Canadian series *Degrassi: The Next Generation* (2001–), Emma (Miriam McDonald) got her first period while at school. While alone in a bathroom stall, her usually surly classmate Paige (Lauren Collins) handed her a pad and provided her an explanation of the menstrual process. The role of the bathroom in these scenes provides wide scope for analysis. As identified earlier, the bathroom is where women commonly tend to intimate matters: it is private, often sanitary, and there is fresh water and toilet paper. More interestingly, these scenes present the bathroom as a place which allows—if not *encourages*—women to "relax their artifices,"[37] to let their guard down and to show solidarity.[38] In the *Community* episode discussed earlier, Shirley expected Britta to intuitively *know* that women are expected to be less guarded in bathrooms. Certainly as apparent in the scenes discussed in this section, bathrooms do encourage uncharacteristic softness: in *Pups*, a bank robber had to soften enough to allow a stranger—*her hostage*—to help her; in the *Degrassi: The Next Generation* and *Ready or Not* scenes, classmates who were normally portrayed as mean and mocking mellowed when called to assist. A third reading—in line with Macsai, Molotch, and Freidenfelds's comments—is the informal health class created in the bathroom. Just as school health classes are routinely gender segregated (chapter 3), the bathroom functioned in these scenes to provide a space separated from men to facilitate a more personalized and more intimate education experience. The bathroom is a place where women can both lower their guard and exhibit vulnerability, exposing themselves as menstruating and seeking assistance if needed.

MENSTRUATION AND FEMALE BONDING

As alluded to in many of the examples discussed thus far in this chapter, menstruation can function as something that facilitates bonding between women. In this section I discuss bonding over shared menstrual products as well as the specific kinds of bonding—bonding between mothers and daughters, sisters and friends—that can be motivated by menstruation.

Menstrual Product Bonding

In *The Curse*, Houppert wrote that "asking to borrow a tampon or some ibuprofen can almost be an overture of friendship, entrusting a colleague or acquaintance with your secrets."[39] The same idea is referenced in Ani DiFranco's song "Blood in the Boardroom" (1993): a woman whose period arrived early exited a meeting in search of a tampon. The woman approached a secretary who both commiserated with her about her early period and then gave her a tampon. The sharing of menstrual products is often used on screen to convey intimacy between women; even between women with few connections beyond biology, as in the DiFranco song. The sharing of menstrual products demonstrates women comfortable enough with their "sisters" to divulge their bleeding; something particularly interesting given cultural mandates that menstruation be kept secret: in such circumstances biological similarities evidently hold more sway than other, more divisive factors.

In an episode of *The Sopranos* (1999–2007), Carmela (Edie Falco) and her daughter Meadow (Jamie-Lynn Sigler) were at a museum when Carmela quietly asked, "Do you have a tampon? I'm spotting." In an episode of *Grey's Anatomy* (2005–), while George (T. R. Knight) showered, his housemate Izzie (Katherine Heigl) entered the bathroom and angrily rummaged for a tampon. The third housemate, Meredith (Ellen Pompeo), entered also looking for one. That George had "forgotten" (read: passive aggressively refused) to purchase tampons united the women in their anger toward him. In a scene from *Sex and the City* (1998–2004), after Carrie (Sarah Jessica Parker) hands a friend a tampon, the following conversation transpires with her friends Charlotte (Kristin Davis) and Miranda (Cynthia Nixon):

> **Charlotte:** Do you have another?
>
> **Carrie:** Ladies, I am not Tampax Central. Put on list: buy tampons.

Charlotte: Well, I have them at home but they won't fit in my Kate Spade purse.

Miranda: Wow. Kate must have a tiny vagina.

These three scenes present an intimacy between women which is based, at least partly, on shared biology, and more practically, on the leveler that bleeding and being without product creates. While women may know the cultural mandate to keep their menstruation private, in the company of other women artifices can be relaxed and needs articulated in a compassionate environment; that confessing menstruation to another woman will always be preferable to exposing it to men. These scenes also allude to bonding on another level: through menstrual synchrony, addressed later in this chapter.

Just as the sharing of menstrual products connotes intimacy between women, the sharing of the menstrual experience more broadly can showcase female bonds; that both on screen and off the depth of women's connections can be conveyed through this shared bodily function.

Mother-Daughter Menstrual Bonding

It seems almost a truism that in real life a mother will guide a daughter through menarche and function as the central figure in a girl's menstrual experience. Freidenfelds discussed this idea in a historic context[40] and it is similarly identifiable in Fingerson's contemporary research. Fingerson quoted teenager Kasey, for example, who fondly mused that both she and her mother craved chocolate during their periods: "[I]t's this mother-daughter thing . . . we always have chocolate in our house for a least two weeks a month."[41] Leslie in the same study commented, "my mom and I are on the same cycle now, so she's, like, 'Leslie, we're getting close to our period.' I'm like, 'Thanks mom.' She like, circles it on the calendar."[42] In Daniluk's research on female sexuality, she identified that most girls divulged their first period to their mothers, with the girls fearing that telling their fathers would embarrass them both.[43] On screen the mother's role is presented as pivotal: as communications scholar Elizabeth Kissling wrote in her work on menstruation on screen, "it is a mother's role, and sometimes an older sister's supporting role, to facilitate the transition to womanhood."[44] Scenes of first periods divulged to mothers are notably identifiable in *I Could Never Be Your Woman* (2007) and on the sitcom *Roseanne* (1988–1997).

In *I Could Never Be Your Woman*, at the end of her school day, Izzie (Saoirse Ronan) divulged the arrival of her period to her mom, Rosie (Michelle Pfeiffer):

Izzie: Ma, you know what happened today? I went to the bathroom and there was this brownish spot but it wasn't from you know where.

> **Rosie:** Honey, that's your period. Oh, congratulations, you're a woman.
>
> **Izzie:** Let the games begin.

In an episode of *Roseanne*, Roseanne (Roseanne Barr) watched her daughter Darlene (Sara Gilbert) pack sporting goods into garbage bags:

> **Roseanne:** Oh, I get it. You think you've gotta leave this stuff behind you now. Like women have to give up baseball gloves and start wearing aprons and stuff.
>
> **Darlene:** All I know is I'm not shaving my legs or wearing pantyhose like Becky.
>
> **Roseanne:** You think I make Becky put on make-up and wear perfume?
>
> **Darlene:** No.
>
> **Roseanne:** No. She does it 'cos she's always liked that kind of stuff. That's the kind of woman she wants to be.
>
> **Darlene:** Well that's not the kind of woman I want to be.
>
> **Roseanne:** Well then why are you throwing all your stuff away? These are girls' things, Darlene, as long as a girl uses them. You love all this stuff. That's reason enough to keep it.

While we don't know much about Izzie and Rosie's relationship prior to Izzie's menarche, we do know—from previous episodes—that Roseanne and Darlene's relationship had been strained. Darlene was a tomboy who had an easier relationship with her father. Darlene's first period—while creating a gender role conflict for her (chapter 2)—also provided her an opportunity to bond with her mother. In this scene, Roseanne convinced her daughter that womanhood doesn't have to manifest in the ultra-feminine form that Darlene's sister had modeled; that being a woman might be biological but the rest can be as gender appropriate as a girl wants it to be.

In these examples, menstruation is presented as a bonding experience and as an illustration of the central role of mothers in menarche. In narratives where the mother was absent, however—such as in *My Girl* and in the sitcom *Blossom* (1990–1995)—the absence of the mother is both noticeable and outlier. In *My Girl*, for example, Vada's mother is dead and when Vada got her first period, only her father's new girlfriend Shelly was home. Like Darlene's pre-menarche relationship with Roseanne, Vada's relationship with Shelly had been difficult. In this scene, however, Shelly assumed the mother role to guide Vada; as in *Roseanne*, menstruation existed to bond two women who previously had little to connect them. In the pilot episode of *Blossom*, the title character (Mayim Bialik) got her first period. Blossom, whose mother lived overseas, lamented to her best friend, Six (Jenna von Oÿ), "I just wish my mom lived here sometimes. . . . I know the technical stuff. . . . I just, really wish my mom was here to talk to. You know, I have questions." Blossom pined for the kind of mother/daughter menarche experience that she had idealized; the kind of relationship that is in fact often *normalized* on screen. Blossom's menarche fantasy, interestingly, was actually based around Phylicia Rashad, who played Clair Huxtable in the sitcom *The Cosby Show* (1984–1992) and who, in one episode, guided her own daughter Rudy (Keshia Knight Pulliam) through her menarche, declaring it a "Woman's Day." While of course, had Blossom's mother actually been present there is no guarantee that she would have acted like Clair Huxtable,[45] nonetheless, Blossom—in line with an essentialist view of motherhood—presumed that a mother would instinctively know how best to handle—if not also celebrate—her daughter's menarche, predicated, apparently, on gender. While this presumption has many flaws—for example, just because a woman *has* a period doesn't mean she is comfortable with it or in discussing it[46]—it nonetheless is an undercurrent present in most menstruation narratives: that periods are *women's* business, that there is something intrinsically feminine about them, and that a *normal* menarche experience will involve a girl's mother.

As Kissling alluded, sometimes—in lieu of a mother figure—the older sister will provide menstrual guidance; the experience thus facilitating bonding between siblings. Just as a frosty mother/daughter relationship can be thawed by menarche, an age difference between sisters can shrink based on this new shared "adult" experience. Teenager Cindy quoted in Fingerson's study illustrated this well:

> I was excited at first, hey, hey, 'cause both my older sisters had already started their periods and they were always, like, talking about it. And I was like, well, we can't wait 'til I'm big enough to have my period, and you know. And then I started it and I was like really excited.[47]

In *The Runaways*, discussed earlier, sisterly bonding was presented through an impromptu menstruation lesson; however, sisterly menstrual intimacy is also conveyed through a variety of other narratives, notably: menstrual synchrony, the supernatural and sibling rivalry. In the Korean horror film *Janghwa, Hongryeon* (*A Tale of Two Sisters*) (2003), for example, two sisters woke realizing they each got their period overnight; their menstrual synchrony was presented as one of numerous weird and otherworldly things that happened while they resided in a haunted house. This synced-sister/supernatural idea was also apparent in the television series *Charmed* (1998–2006): in one episode the witches discussed their aligned periods, identifying how they made Phoebe (Alyssa Milano) more emotional, Paige (Rose McGowan) more jumpy, and Piper (Holly Marie Combs) more "pissy": "The good news is we all get over it at the same time," chimed Paige. While a stereotypical PMS presentation can be detected in this scene, notable is menstrual synchrony used to illustrate that the sisters are closer than normal; that having coordinated biological functions underpins this. Menstruation as presented through a sibling rivalry storyline is identifiable in an episode of the sitcom *According to Jim* (2001–2009). Sisters Gracie (Billi Bruno) and Ruby (Taylor Atelian) had quarreled for three consecutive days before their father, Jim (James Belushi), discovered—through a maxi-pad wrapper—that the youngest daughter, Gracie, had gotten her period while Ruby still waited for hers; their bickering was centered on Ruby's jealousy. Menstrual moodiness is, predictably, a distinct theme of this scene, but as relevant to sibling rivalry, Ruby wanted her period. She wanted—like Cindy in Fingerson's study—to be part of her sister's comparably *adult* world; she felt that she was owed reaching menarche first by virtue of being the older sister.

Family Matriarchs and Menstrual Bonding

While thus far I have discussed bonding between mothers, daughters and sisters, it is worthwhile noting that it can also occur between grandmothers and granddaughters. In research on menstrual education in non-Western cultures, the role of grandmothers is often noted;[48] likely attributable to a grandmother's greater presence in the family and the potentially shorter age gaps between generations. While perhaps not as common, grandmothers in Western cultures can also function in this role, notably, when a mother is absent. Pediatricians Kelly Orringer and Sheila Gahagan, for example, noted that for most women in their study, knowledge about menstruation came from other women in their household, presumably including grandmothers.[49] In the Loulan and Worthen book discussed earlier, the attitude of grandmothers to menstruation was presumed to affect girls' attitudes to their periods. Freidenfelds presented a case study of a woman born in the early 1950s who was raised by her grandmother and recalled "being so glad my grandmother had prepared me for [menstruation], because some of my friends, this did happen to them at school, where a teacher would have to carry them home."[50] On screen a grandmother occupying the maternal guide role is evident in scenes from *A Walk on the Moon* and *My Louisiana Sky* (2001). In both narratives a girl divulged her first period to her grandmother. In *A Walk on the Moon*, Alison's grandmother, Lillian (Tovah Feldshuh) was jubilant; in contrast, in *My Louisiana Sky*, Tiger Ann's (Kelsey Keel) grandmother Jewel (Shirley Knight) expressed muted disappointment, "You got the curse," she said. "From now on, you can look forward to it every month til' you're too old like me. Then, thank the Lord, it's over." Interestingly, in both scenes the girls' mothers were *also* present and both exhibited pride and celebration, but it was the grandmother who was portrayed as the most knowledgeable; both mothers allowed the older women to have center stage. That the girls divulged their periods to their grandmothers in these scenes conveys intergenerational intimacy. The disparate reactions of these grandmothers, however, are notable because they can be interpreted as indicative of how the grandmother herself was introduced to menstruation, in line with Loulan and Worthen's comments quoted earlier: Lillian, for example, slapped Alison in the Jewish celebratory custom she had experienced; Jewel's sour reaction may have stemmed from her being taught that menstruation was arduous and unpleasant, thus informing how she responded to Tiger Ann's menarche.

Given that many menstruation narratives are staged in school contexts, for young female protagonists their friends are often central to the experience, with periods functioning to bond peers.

Friends and Menstrual Bonding

The female friend can function in a number of different capacities in a menstruation narrative: one, she is often the obvious choice as confidante given that she is likely similarly aged and if she hasn't already will soon menstruate; two, she can function as a female guide in place of an absent mother, and three, she can cheerlead for a reluctant menstruator.

In Fingerson's study, she explored the role of menstruation in the lives of young women, noting that:

> [M]enstruation is not simply a private bodily event. Rather, they use menstruation as a resource in social interaction: for telling stories and for making connections with others through shared experience.[51]

The girls in Fingerson's study identified a distinct role for friends in their menstrual experience; something nicely encapsulated by comments made by teenager Marcia: "I had a friend in middle school; she kept making me check her butt to make sure she wasn't leaking through."[52] Marcia's comments closely resemble the *Degrassi: The Next Generation* episode discussed earlier; in one scene, Manny (Cassie Steele) escorted her best friend Emma to the toilet by holding a book over her-blood stained white skirt. Similar menstrual camaraderie occurred in the *Blossom* pilot. After a failed solo trip to purchase tampons, Blossom's best friend, Six, brought her a box: "If you hadn't brought those over here, I don't know what I would have done," thanked Blossom. Ever the optimist, Six tried to reassure her friend, "Oh come on, you don't need a mother to deal with your first period, I mean everything you need to know is printed right on the box." Here, Six functioned as a guide for Blossom, physically assisting her by bringing her Tampax as well as joking to lighten the moment. Just as Six attempted to ease what might have been a depressing moment for Blossom,[53] in *Ready or Not*, something similar transpired when Busy's best friend Amanda (Laura Betram) tried to compensate for Busy's lack of enthusiasm during a phone call:

> **Amanda:** What do you mean no big deal? This is incredible. I can't believe this. Oh, what's today date? We have to remember this. Okay. I am so jealous. I can't believe you got it before I did. Tell me everything. I want to know.
>
> **Busy:** I knew you would do this. You're acting as if everything's changed.
>
> **Amanda:** Oh, but it has. I have to come over.
>
> **Busy:** No, you can't.
>
> **Amanda:** Why not? This is the most important day of your life.
>
> **Busy:** It's no big deal. It's nothing. It's gross.
>
> **Amanda:** Oh, how can you say that? You're a woman now. You can have a baby.
>
> **Busy:** Yeah right.
>
> **Amanda:** Oh, this is a huge thing. Do you look any different? Are you wearing a tampon? Tell me everything. I want to know.
>
> **Busy:** I have homework to do. I have to clean my room.

In this scene, Busy—at least *verbally*—considered her period as "nothing" and as "gross." Interestingly, her response mirrors the anti-climactic reactions of many women in real-life about their first periods (chapter 2). Amanda, however, provided a contrast: her excitement buffered Busy's lack of enthusiasm. Given the likely youth audiences of *Blossom* and *Ready or Not*, it is unsurprising that the narratives offered both a girl anxious about menstruation—reflecting audience fears—as well as a girl presented as excited about it in order to mitigate anxiety.

Alluded to in *Janghwa, Hongryeon* (*A Tale of Two Sisters*), as well as in episodes of *Charmed*, *Sex and the City*, and *Grey's Anatomy* was menstrual synchrony. The menstrual synchrony narrative is perhaps the strongest example of on-screen menstrual bonding, presenting women not merely united by menstruation, but by the experience of bleeding *simultaneously*.

MENSTRUAL SYNCHRONY

In an episode of the sitcom *30 Rock* (2006–), Jack (Alec Baldwin) offhandedly remarked, "Oh, sure. Then we can sit around and braid each other's hair until we get our periods at the same time." In an episode of the sitcom *The*

Big Bang Theory (2007–), Howard (Simon Helberg) conceded to watching *Sex and the City*, sarcastically saying, "Fine, let's watch it. Maybe all our periods will synchronize." In an episode of the sitcom *The Office* (2005–), Dwight (Rainn Wilson) claimed that women meeting on their own would be a bad idea: "If they stay in there too long, they're gonna get on the same cycle. Wreak havoc on our plumbing." In an episode of *Community*, Pierce (Chevy Chase) responded to the surly behavior of his female classmates by jeering, "I guess it's true what they say about the sync-up." While Jack and Howard are being facetious and Dwight and Pierce are being derisive, the idea of synchrony—"women who live in the same apartment or house often notice that they begin to cycle together"[54]—is a common vehicle by which menstruation is used on screen to connote female bonds deeper than mere friendship or kinship. In this section, the various incarnations of the menstrual synchrony storyline are explored, notably through narratives centered on shared products, shared woes, the pregnancy question, and as something apparently compounding men's suffering.

In the *Grey's Anatomy* episode discussed earlier, that Izzie and Meredith both sought tampons at the same time indicated that they were *both* bleeding. They were united by bleeding at the same time *and* by their annoyance at George for failing to purchase tampons (and ultimately failing to understand their needs as women). In the *Sex and the City* tampon-sharing scene, the synchrony idea was also alluded to through menstrual products: that three of the four women each needed tampons at the same time demonstrated synchrony and worked to subtly convey the strength of the friends' bonds. While these narratives present menstrual synchrony as normal and simply as another layer of female closeness, in other examples, the subject matter is portrayed less innocuously and with a greater emphasis on demonizing women. Two other ways that synchrony is presented are, one, through synced woes, and two, as something that significantly inconveniences men. In the comedy *I'm Gonna Git You Sucka* (1988), Cheryl (Dawnn Lewis), a diner waitress, looked pained as she tended to her demanding customers. Eventually she slammed a pot of coffee down and another waitress approached her:

Waitress: Cheryl, are you okay?

Cheryl: I think I better go home. It's my *time*.

Waitress: Girl, me too.

Cheryl: I'm gonna go and lay down, okay?

Waitress: I know exactly how you feel, Cheryl. Be strong.

The fact that it is both women's *time* illustrates the synchrony theme but also spotlights one element of the shared experience: shared pain. In the romantic comedy *No Strings Attached* (2011), this theme was exacerbated when Emma (Natalie Portman) and her two female housemates were synced and shown lying in their loungeroom with hot water bottles and suffering together (a fourth housemate—a gay male—joined in sympathy with them). This same scenario was depicted in an episode of the television series *Rescue Me* (2004–): the women in protagonist Tommy's (Denis Leary) house were having their periods together and each exhibited various kinds of moodiness and self-loathing. Such narratives are very much indicative of a misery-loves-company idea whereby individual woes are exacerbated through group whining.[55] While in these examples the pain and suffering is largely centered on the menstruators themselves, in other narratives the focus is on the pain that synchrony causes *men*. In an episode of the sitcom *Married with Children* (1987–1997), for example, on a camping trip, Peggy (Katey Sagal), daughter Kelly (Christina Applegate), and neighbor Marcy (Amanda Bearse) had synced periods: their whining and nagging was presented as proof that the camping trip should have been a male-only excursion:

Kelly: Oh, I need a back rub.

Marcy: I need a foot rub.

Peggy: I need someone to yell at. Where are the men?

In an episode of the sitcom *My Wife and Kids* (2001–2005), mother Jay (Tisha Campbell-Martin) and her daughter Claire (Jennifer Freeman) both had their periods while on a family trip. The two bickered constantly; something that father, Michael (Damon Wayans), referred to as "DefCon Two." In an episode of the sitcom *The New Adventures of Old Christine* (2006–2010), Barb (Wanda Sykes) warned her gym business partner Christine (Julia Louis-Dreyfus) about the state of their restroom:

> Um, Christine, you've got to get out there. There's a group of ladies in the bathroom who are about to riot. Everyone who works out on Wednesday is on the same cycle, and you're out of maxi-pads. It's like a CSI crime scene in there.

In an episode of the medical drama *House* (2004–), Dr. Masters (Amber Tamblyn), reflected on her relationship with her cousin: "When our menstrual cycles synced, it was like gladiator school." In *Charmed*, when the witch sisters discussed their synced periods, Paige explained, "The good news is we all get over it at the same time," to which her sister Piper responded, "As long as we don't kill each other in the process." In these scenes, while the narratives explored menstruation through predictable references to moodiness and women's supposed high-level emotional instability (chapter 4), another reading is that they reflect and explain the female catfight.[56] I have written previously about the media preoccupation with showing women in conflict and competition with one another[57]: one interpretation of the synchrony narrative is to provide a biological explanation that synced periods amplify this.

One final manifestation of the synchrony narrative addressed in this chapter relates to the pregnancy possibility storyline. In the aforementioned *Sex and the City* episode, Carrie, Charlotte, and Miranda discussed their periods. It was discovered during this conversation that Samantha—who was normally synced with her friends—hadn't had a period in 35 days; her friends questioned pregnancy. The same fears were also referenced via the synchrony storyline in an episode of the drama series *Brothers and Sisters* (2006–2011): Kitty (Calista Flockhart) suspected her sister Sarah (Rachel Griffiths) was pregnant; her suspicion was premised on the theory that given that *she* was bleeding so too should Sarah be. This storyline was also used in an episode of *Degrassi: The Next Generation*: Manny asked Emma for a tampon; that Emma didn't have one caused Manny to suspect Emma was pregnant based on their normally synced periods. In these episodes a late period and the *disruption* of synchrony was the catalyst for female confidantes—who were each presented as very tuned to the intricacies of each other's bodies—to speculate on what a missed period might mean. Such narratives highlight the capacity for female closeness, something presented as markedly distinguishing women from men.[58]

THE MEN IN MENSTRUATION

While menstruation might only be physically experienced by women, men who share their lives—as fathers and husbands and brothers and colleagues—exist on the periphery. At various junctures in this book the role of men in menstruation narratives is discussed; in this section I focus on three male caricatures identified on screen with men frequently portrayed as foolish, emasculated, and creepy.

Men as Menstrual Dolts

In Fingerson's research, she asked young men about their menstrual knowledge and got a wide range of peculiar explanations: fourteen-year-old Brian, for example, commented that menstruation is "[w]hen girls get really mean and they bleed everywhere."[59] Laws similarly reported a widespread lack of knowledge amongst men.[60] In John Scalzi's essay about menstrual products, he attempted to explain men's ignorance:

> [T]here is no parallel in the male experience. . . . We can't even imagine it. Suggest to a man that his equipment should hemorrhage for five out of every 28 days, and he will instantly drop to a fetal position.[61]

Men's comparative lack of knowledge is routinely presented on screen as a source of humor. In the British comedy *Red Dwarf* (1988–) for example, the following conversation transpired between Lister (Craig Charles) and colleague Kryten (Robert Llewellyn):

> **Lister:** What's that?
>
> **Kryten**: Oh, it's just a present to help cheer up Miss Kochanski.
>
> [Kryten holds up a calendar]
>
> **Lister:** What, a calendar?
>
> **Kryten:** Mmm. A couple of days ago she was looking at the old calendar and she said it was the wrong time of the month, so I got her a new one. I'm going to tell her the calendar people made a mistake, but let's just leave this whole 'wrong month' thing behind us; they were stupid, it was careless, but being grumpy and tearful about it is getting it way out of proportion.
>
> **Lister:** A little word in your audio receiver:
>
> [Kryten leans closer and Lister whispers into his ear. The men separate].

A similar scene was evident in another British comedy, *The Young Ones* (1982–1984), where a number of characters were seated in a loungeroom and Rick (Rik Mayall) took Rhiannon's (Cindy Shelley) handbag to look for cigarettes:

> **Rick:** Oh what a great bag! [Grabs her handbag] Oh, it's really great, isn't it? In here, are they? Oh, it's tinted—amazing! You've bought me a present. [Brings out an applicator tampon] What is it? What do you do with it? No, don't tell me, don't tell me. I'll guess. [Opens it] It's a telescope—a telescope with a mouse in it—brilliant! Bouncy bouncy bouncy bounce! Hello Rhiannon. Are you glad you could come to the party? Here, have a drink, mousy. Bouncy bouncy bounce! [Dips the tampon into Rhiannon's drink]. Oh, it's gone all big. I'll get a tissue, it's all right. Oh, you've got a whole box of them in here! They're called. . . . [Look of realization and horror]. I think I'd better go to the lavatory. [Rick rushed upstairs.]

In these scenes, the men actually do appear to have some very cursory knowledge of menstruation: while Kryten seemingly wasn't familiar with the "wrong time of the month" expression, when told, he exhibited predictable embarrassment; while Rick evidently hadn't handled or even seen a tampon before, when he read the word on the box he evidently also knew to be embarrassed. Interestingly, while initially presented as foolish, once Kryten and Rick experienced clarity, they exhibited embarrassment centered less on their lack of knowledge and more on menstruation as *an entity*; they were embarrassed to have spoken about and touched menstrual products. This interestingly reflects how men in our culture are not expected to have *any* understanding of menstruation at all, in fact, are considered *more* masculine when they aren't associated with or know anything about it, an idea returned to later in this chapter.

While the men in these scenes were portrayed as foolish, an element of menstrual disgust is also detectable in *The Young Ones* as well as in the aforementioned episode of *Californication* (and a topic expanded on in chapter 4). In *The Young Ones*, Rick was perfectly happy to play with the tampons *until* he found out what they were for and suddenly appeared horrified. A stronger example occurred in the *Californication* episode referred to earlier: during Hank's argument with the woman in the gas station, he rationalized:

> If I was in the market for say, I don't know, adult diapers and some poor incontinent soul walked by who obviously needed them a lot more than I did, I would surrender those diapers.

Hank—while trying to be a good father—inadvertently alluded to male contempt for menstruation: he likened menstruation to *incontinence*, and menstrual products to *diapers*, illustrating a lack of understanding and even loathing. In this scene, Hank showcased another way men are portrayed as menstrual dolts: via their presentation as foolish fathers. In the episode of *King of the Hill* discussed earlier, after Connie revealed that she had just gotten her first period, Hank drove her to the hospital. In an episode of the sitcom *Something So Right* (1996–1998), when his stepdaughter Sarah (Emily Ann Lloyd) revealed that she had just gotten her first period, Jack (Jere Burns) awkwardly high-fived her. In *Roseanne*, when Darlene got her first period, her father, Dan (John Goodman), said, "Good job." In the *According to Jim* episode discussed earlier, Jim tried to console his oldest daughter, Ruby, about not yet getting her period with a bizarre series of suggestions:

> Maybe we can figure something out to kinda help it along, like you do with pregnant women. Have you tried eating steak? Jumping rope? Hanging out with older girls? You can drink from their cup and maybe their hormones will rub off on you.

In *Californication, Something So Right* and *According to Jim*, each father *explicitly* acknowledged that how they responded would be remembered for the rest of their daughter's life; each *tried* to do the right thing, albeit within a narrative designed to be funny. Such narratives aren't seemingly deliberately misogynist, but nevertheless are indicative of men's discomfort with menstruation and also potentially their lack of understanding, ideas routinely presented as humorous on screen. Another reading of these menstrual dolt scenes relates to feminist analyses of menstruation and of periods being widely construed as abject and repellent.[62] In such a reading, the feminine nature of menstruation—discussed throughout this chapter—may discourage men from taking too much of an interest, fearing that too much understanding may somehow link them too closely to women, too closely to femininity, and thus emasculate them, or alternatively, render them perverted (addressed later in this chapter).

Men and Menstrual Emasculation

The *Red Dwarf* and *The Young Ones* episodes discussed earlier presented men wanting to distance themselves from menstruation and menstrual products: they seemingly feared that too much connection may rub off; that through some kind of *osmosis* they would become feminized. Men presented as fearful of feminization is a standard male caricature on screen; something routinely presented through the "tampon run" storyline. A 2007 Dr Pepper television commercial, for example, perfectly illustrated this theme: soundtracked by the Meat Loaf song "I'd Do Anything for Love" (1993), the advertisement opened with a man purchasing tampons for his girlfriend, the premise being that for a man to do something *so emasculating* must demonstrate true love (discussed further in chapter 4). In the *Grey's Anatomy* episode discussed earlier, George's own fears of emasculation underpinned his opposition to purchasing tampons for his female housemates:

> **George:** You don't understand. Me gonads, You ovaries!
>
> **Izzie:** Oh, that reminds me, we are out of tampons.
>
> **George:** You're parading through the bathroom in your underwear when I'm naked in the shower.
>
> **Izzie:** Will you add it to your list please?
>
> **George:** What?
>
> **Izzie:** Tampons. To the list. It's your turn.
>
> **George:** I am a man! I don't buy girl products.

Later in the episode, when Izzie reprimanded George for not having purchased tampons, he responded: "Men don't buy tampons" and later, "I am not your sister." Evidently being compelled to purchase tampons offended George much more than the women's actual menstruation; perhaps, given that he is a doctor, he can accept the biology of menstruation but still justify his disinclination to actively participate. As further explored in chapter 4, men's on-screen battles with gender routinely play out in the feminine hygiene aisle at the supermarket.

While, as in the Dr Pepper advertisement, it may appear endearing for a man to do the tampon run, on screen there is a very fine line between men's admirable behavior regarding menstruation and menstruation-related behavior construed as *weird*.

Men as Menstrually Creepy

Cultural theorist David Linton reflected on his research on menstruation contending that "[w]hen a man appears "excessively" curious about menstrual matters (which means curious at all) he crosses the menstrual line."[63] Linton's ideas are certainly detectable in both academic research and on screen whereby too much interest or knowledge can be construed as creepy or perverted. In Laws's research on men's attitudes to menstruation, she quoted one man's story about a former colleague which distinctly highlights a crossed line:

> [A] married man but in a hospital situation where there are a lot of young girls around, young nurses, young women . . . there was a female toilet just outside the lab so we could always see the women going to the toilet and he actually used to time them and if they were taking a long time he used to say, "Oh well, they've got the rags up, there's no point in chatting her up." It's like trying to impress people by being weird, I don't know.[64]

This man's behavior is weird not only because he appeared eerily conscious of the (possible) menstruation happening around him, but more sinisterly, was seemingly *documenting* the bleeding. This kind of invasive behavior is, in varying degrees, also detectable on screen. Earlier, I discussed the *7th Heaven* episode where Lucy eagerly awaited her period. In that episode, her father, Eric (Stephen Collins), strangely seemed as anxious and excited as Lucy; so much so, in fact, that his wife, Annie (Catherine Hicks), had to explain to him that menstruation *isn't* always so wonderful. While Eric's behavior is potentially more akin to the other fathers discussed in this chapter who were each trying to do the "right thing," his high-level enthusiasm can also be construed as *somewhat* peculiar,[65] particularly given the inextricable link between menstruation and sexuality. In an episode of the sitcom *Friends* (1994–2004), Monica (Courteney Cox) expressed skepticism about Joey

(Matt LeBlanc) and Chandler's (Matthew Perry) allegations that they knew her and Rachel (Jennifer Aniston) better than the women knew them. The men's claims were tested by their attempts to guess the contents of one of Rachel's grocery bags. Chandler whispered a guess in Joey's ear and Joey responded: "No, not for like another two weeks." Joey's knowledge of the women was demonstrated through his awareness of their menstrual cycles; perhaps not with formal menstrual monitoring, but Joey nonetheless seemed surprisingly aware of their bleeding patterns. Similar weirdness was apparent in an episode of *The Big Bang Theory*: when Sheldon (Jim Parsons) went grocery shopping with Penny (Kaley Cuoco), he noticed that she only bought one month's supply of tampons at a time. He suggested that buying in bulk would save her money because "they don't spoil." Later, Sheldon began marking her periods on his calendar which, while perhaps understandable given Sheldon's nerdiness, was nonetheless presented—and interpreted by Penny—as strange. In an episode of *Community*, Abed (Danny Pudi) was exposed as having charted the menstrual cycles of his female classmates. He justified this as a method of keeping track of the women's moods so he could respond accordingly: he is shown, for example, to have tissues and chocolates ready to placate a moody Annie. While these examples can each, variously, be considered weird, conversely they can simply illustrate men's *actual* interest in the women around them and their efforts to be sensitive and understanding.

Moving along the weirdness spectrum is one of Grace's (Debra Messing) boyfriends on the sitcom *Will and Grace* (1998–2006). In one season, Grace dated Josh (Corey Parker), a man presented as an exaggeratedly "sensitive new age guy," something demonstrated aptly in a scene where the two returned to Grace's office to find Karen (Megan Mullally) reading a magazine:

> **Josh:** I had a really good time. I'm glad we could meet for lunch. Hey, did you get the lumbar pillow I left with your doorman?
>
> **Grace:** I did. Thank you. That was . . . that was so sweet of you.
>
> **Josh:** It's filled with tea. The lady at the nature store said it's very soothing, particularly if you're cramping during menses.
>
> **Grace:** I had a really nice time. [Hugs Josh] Don't say menses.
>
> **Josh:** Bye. You'll call me later?
>
> **Grace:** I will.
>
> [Josh kisses Grace's forehead then exits.]
>
> **Karen:** He should be killed.
>
> **Grace:** He happens to be the sweetest, most thoughtful, most sensitive guy I have ever gone out with. I think he's great.

Karen: He makes me wanna barf. I wanna kick him til' he's dead, honey.

Grace and Karen continued to argue about Josh, with Grace contending that "He truly loves and understands women" and Karen remaining unconvinced. Later in the episode, Josh told Grace that he planned to pick her up some wild yam essence because, "It helps with breast tenderness brought on by water retention." In a later scene, he tried to teach her how to do pelvic floor exercises—which he described as "sit-ups for love's sweet flower"—to which Grace responded, "Wow. Almost brought up a little yam there." While Josh's behavior was indeed much sweeter and more sensitive than Grace had previously experienced, it was also construed by her—and most certainly by Karen and the audience (evidenced through the laugh track)—as peculiar. Josh's knowledge of menstruation—while initially construed as endearing—was ultimately interpreted as repellent.

Further along the weirdness spectrum was Dr. House's (Hugh Laurie) behavior in *House*. A continuing narrative theme in the series was the sexual tension between Dr. House and his boss Dr. Cuddy (Lisa Edelstein). In one episode, the following conversation occurred:

> **House:** You don't have cancer.
>
> **Cuddy:** You don't have dwarfism.
>
> **House:** You have no proof of that. I, on the other hand, have this. [He handed her a results sheet.]
>
> **Cuddy:** You ran a PCR on me without my consent?
>
> **House:** Hey, it's good news.
>
> **Cuddy:** Really? It's just hard to access because of this overwhelming sense of personal violation.
>
> **House:** Deal with it on your own time. Bad news, estrogen is too high.
>
> **Cuddy:** No matter how many people you tell otherwise, I am and always have been a woman. Estrogen is normal.
>
> **House:** Not this much, not for at least for another week. That's when you ovulate.
>
> **Cuddy:** You monitor my periods? Based on when I get bitchy or—
>
> **House:** Once a month, when you leave the kids' cancer ward, your eyes glisten. About three days later, you break your ban on sugar and chow down a bucket of frozen yogurt in the cafeteria, sprinkles included. Based on the last yogurt sighting, you've got another week before you ovulate.

While in this scene House did run the PCR (polymerase chain reaction) test because he was concerned about Cuddy's health, his actions also construed "personal violation." While House's behavior is somewhat mitigated based on the obvious *mutual* sexual attraction between the characters, this is not the case for criminals on screen whereby their menstrual monitoring is only presented as sinister. In an episode of *Law and Order: Special Victims Unit* (1999–), for example, a serial rapist monitored women to keep track of their menstrual cycle to pinpoint the best time to rape them for impregnation. In the film *Kiss the Girls* (1997) something similar occurred when the serial killer Nick Ruskin (Cary Elwes) boasted about all that he could find out about a woman from her trash: "What a lady eats, how often she shaves. He can even tell a lady's time of the month." In these examples, a male stranger's knowledge of something as intimate as menstruation is portrayed as the *ultimate* invasion of privacy.

One way to read each of these scenes is men's attempts to control the seemingly uncontrollable. Fingerson, for example, reflected on the gaps in men's knowledge and alluded to their concerns with powerlessness:

> Menstruation is a place where males do not have the experience and the boys do not understand what is happening, so they are in a threatened position. It is the girls, in this case, who have the power.[66]

The behavior of the rapist in *Law and Order* and the serial killer in *Kiss the Girls*—and even to certain degrees the behavior of Sheldon, Joey, House, and Abed—may be construed as male attempts to control a situation that is normally *beyond* their control: this theme is expanded on in chapter 4 in the context of men only viewing tampon runs as palatable if the run can be construed as a mission, that is, when the act is less about menstruation and more about project management.

Another way menstrual monitoring manifests is when men are shown as aware of a woman's menstrual cycle, albeit incorrectly. While the sexist assumption of PMS is discussed in later chapters, for this section it is worthwhile spotlighting men *purporting* to have calendar-knowledge of menstruation, albeit grounded in pure—and sexist—stereotype. In an episode of the sitcom *Murphy Brown* (1988–1998), for example, when Murphy (Candice Bergen) was grouchier than usual, colleague Miles (Grant Shaud) asked, "Is it the eighteenth already?" In an episode of *According to Jim*, after his wife Cheryl (Courtney Thorne-Smith) snapped at him, Jim looked at his watch and said, "It's the fifteenth, isn't it?" While Miles and Jim's awareness of the menstruation of women around them may simply be read as reflecting their interest and compassion, realistically these characters *weren't* actually aware of anything: each month is not the same length and thus the women *can't* have the same symptoms on the same date each month. Clearly the comic effect is much more important than accuracy (discussed further in chapter 4).

The narrative themes identified in this chapter highlight some predictable menstruation storylines as well as some surprising and outlier portrayals. Perhaps the most unexpected finding of this chapter not yet discussed is the unexpectedly high number of non-white menstruators discussed. While this book focuses more on a feminist analysis of menstrual images rather than a race-based or identity politics analysis, it is most certainly worth spotlighting the non-white portrayals. Western media are frequently criticized as being dominated by portrayals of white women.[67] Given the general infrequency of menstruating characters in Western film and television, it might then be assumed that it would be rare to see *any* ethnic minorities in menstrual narratives. While it is rare, there are indeed some notable examples as this chapter has illustrated: the mothers and daughters in *The Cosby Show* and *My Wife and Kids*, as well as the women in *I'm Gonna Git You Sucka*, were all African-American. In *No Strings Attached*, Emma's synced housemate Shira (Mindy Kaling) was seemingly of Indian descent, and Jasira in *Towelhead* was an Arab-American. While, as briefly addressed in chapter 8, there may be many reasons why non-white women are largely *not* portrayed menstruating, that a significant number of the characters discussed in this chapter were of traditionally marginalized ethnicities can be construed as a kind of mainstreaming of ethnic minorities: in such examples, the characters' sex appears much more important to the storyline than race.

This chapter explored female bonding over periods, shared products and synced bleeding and also investigated some of the roles that men are left to occupy amidst such a female experience. Chapter 2 builds on this issue, delving deeper into the issue of menstruation as a rite of passage and exploring real-life and on-screen menarche narratives.

NOTES

1. Alexandra Pope, *The Wild Genie: The Healing Power of Menstruation* (Bowral, New South Wales: Sally Milner, 2001).
2. In Jane M. Ussher, Myra Hunter, and Susannah J. Brown, "Good, bad or dangerous to know: Representations of femininity in narrative accounts of PMS," in *Culture in Psychology*, ed. Corinne Squire (Philadelphia: Taylor and Francis, 2000), 91. [Emphasis in original.]
3. Laura Fingerson, *Girls in Power: Gender, Body and Menstruation in Adolescence* (Albany: State University of New York Press, 2006), 94.
4. Judith C. Daniluk, *Women's Sexuality Across the Life Span: Challenging Myths, Creating Meaning* (New York: Guilford Press, 1998), 69.

5. Joan C. Chrisler, "The menstrual cycle in a biopsychosocial context," in *Psychology of Women: A Handbook of Issues and Theories*, ed. Florence L. Denmark and Michele A. Paludi (Westport, CT: Praeger, 2008), 418.

6. Jane M. Ussher, *Managing the Monstrous Feminine: Regulating the Reproductive Body* (New York: Routledge, 2006), 19.

7. Sophie Laws, *Issues of Blood: The Politics of Menstruation* (Houndmills, Basingstoke, Hampshire: Macmillan, 1990), 19.

8. Chris Bobel, *New Blood: Third-Wave Feminism and the Politics of Menstruation* (New Brunswick, NJ: Rutgers University Press, 2010), 31.

9. Germaine Greer, *The Female Eunuch* (London: Paladin, 1971), 50. [My emphasis.]

10. Zannette Lewis, "Loss and Gain of Responsibility, 1969," in *My Little Red Book*, ed. Rachel Kauder Nalebuff (New York: Twelve, 2009), 40.

11. In *To Sir With Love*, a class theme was central to the plot, with the students' bad behavior viewed as low-class. The same idea of the class connotations of failing to conceal menstruation was discussed by historian Lara Freidenfelds where she explored the class-based acts of washing and deodorizing during menstruation (Lara Freidenfelds, *The Modern Period: Menstruation in Twentieth-Century America* (Baltimore: Johns Hopkins University Press, 2009)). This idea was also presented in philosopher Jami Anderson's work on prisons where she discussed the connotations of female prisoners requesting menstrual products: "Just what are we to make of that woman who unashamedly asks [a] male guard for a sanitary pad or tells all and sundry about her menstrual cycle? She's a vulgar hussy—no wonder she's in prison" (Jami Anderson, "Bodily privacy, toilets and sex discrimination: The problem of "manhood" in a woman's prison," in *Ladies and Gents: Public Toilets and Gender*, ed. Olga Gershenson and Barbara Penner (Philadelphia: Temple University Press, 2009), 99).

12. The idea of thinking of menstruation as a "sanitary event" comes from Hope Edelman's book *Motherless Daughters: The Legacy of Loss* where she quoted psychologist Naomi Lowinsky who commented, "Without a mother, a first menstruation is just a big sanitary event." (Hope Edelman, *Motherless Daughters: The Legacy of Loss* (Cambridge, MA: Da Capo Press, 2006), 218).

13. Sandra Lee Bartky, "Foucault, femininity and the modernization of patriarchal power," in *Feminism and Foucault: Reflections on Resistance*, ed. Irene Diamond and Lee Quimby (Boston, MA: Northeastern University Press, 1988).

14. JoAnn Loulan and Bonnie Worthen, *Period: A Girl's Guide* (Minnetonka, MN: Book Peddlers, 2001), 51.

15. A rare screen example of concealment of a menstrual product occurs in the film *Carnage* (2011), when Penelope (Jodie Foster) quickly puts her tampons in the cupboard so that her visitors don't see them.

16. Judith C. Daniluk in her book on women's sexuality noted that few girls tell their fathers about the menstruation "due to the 'embarrassment' that this may cause for both father and daughter" (Judith C. Daniluk, *Women's Sexuality Across The Life Span: Challenging Myths, Creating Meanings* (New York: Guilford Press, 1998), 55).

17. Mariamne H. Whatley and Elissa R. Henken, *Did You Hear About the Girl Who? Contemporary Legends, Folklore, and Human Sexuality* (New York: New York University Press, 2000), 63.

18. See Kathryn H. Anthony, *Designing for Diversity: Gender, Race, and Ethnicity in the Architectural Profession* (Urbana: University of Illinois Press, 2001); Clara Greed, *Inclusive Urban Design: Public Toilets* (Jordan Hill, Oxford: Architectural Press, 2003).

19. See Sherrie Tucker, *Swing Shift: "All-Girl" Bands of the 1940s* (Durham, NC: Duke University Press, 2000).

20. See Judith Halberstam, *Female Masculinity* (Durham, NC: Duke University Press, 1998); Lori B. Girshick, *Transgender Voices* (Lebanon, NH: University Press of New England), 2008.

21. Emily Martin, *The Woman in the Body: A Cultural Analysis of Reproduction* (Boston: Beacon, 1987), 94.

22. Fingerson, *Girls in Power: Gender, Body and Menstruation in Adolescence* (Albany: State University of New York Press, 2006), 49.

23. Lara Freidenfelds, *The Modern Period: Menstruation in Twentieth-Century America* (Baltimore, MD: The Johns Hopkins University Press, 2009), 72.

24. Freidenfelds noted that prior to the 1950s bathrooms rarely had cabinets and thus menstrual products were stored in bedrooms (Lara Freidenfelds, *The Modern Period: Menstruation in Twentieth-Century America* (Baltimore, MD: The Johns Hopkins University Press, 2009), 147).

25. Lara Freidenfelds, *The Modern Period: Menstruation in Twentieth-Century America* (Baltimore, MD: The Johns Hopkins University Press, 2009), 148.

26. Lara Freidenfelds, *The Modern Period: Menstruation in Twentieth-Century America* (Baltimore, MD: The Johns Hopkins University Press, 2009), 149–150.

27. Karen Houppert, *The Curse: Confronting the Last Unmentionable Taboo: Menstruation* (New York: Farrar, Straus and Giroux, 1999), 93.

28. In his chapter on public restrooms, sociologist Harvey Molotch spotlighted the interesting situation of "intensely private acts" happening in what is at least nominally a *public* space (Harvey Molotch, "Introduction: Learning from the Loo," in *Public Restrooms and the Politics of Sharing*, ed. Laura Noren and Harvey Molotch (New York: New York University Press, 2010), 1).

29. In sociologist Sophie Laws's book *Issues of Blood: The Politics of Menstruation*, she alluded to the shame and disgust associated with menstrual products: "[m]enstrual products remain a necessary part of life for women. Women are expected to buy, store and use them without men noticing." (Sophie Laws, *Issues of Blood: The Politics of Menstruation* (Houndmills, Basingstoke, Hampshire: Macmillan, 1990), 45).

30. Judy Blume, *Are You There God? It's Me, Margaret* (New York: Random House, 1970).

31. In response to a question about the absence of menstruation in her books, *Twilight* series author Stephenie Meyer described Bella's blood as "dead blood" and thus as not appealing to Edward. (See Danielle Dick McGeough, "Twilight and Transformations of Flesh: Reading the Body in Contemporary Youth Culture," in *Bitten by Twilight: Youth Culture, Media and the Vampire Franchise*, ed. Melissa A. Click, Jennifer Stevens Aubrey, and Elizabeth Behm-Morawitz (New York: Peter Lang, 2010), 94).

32. In social scientist Frances Pheasant-Kelly's discussion of bathrooms, she contrasts the presentation of male and female toilets on screen, noting: "the women's toilet is simultaneously most commonly signalled as a communal, friendly place, with a focus on appearance and cosmetics. It lacks the dangerous frisson of 'the men's' and, more significantly, is likely to be a clean space." (Frances Pheasant-Kelly, "In the men's room," in *Ladies and Gents: Public Toilets and Gender*, ed. Olga Gershenson and Barbara Penner (Philadelphia: Temple University Press, 2009), 205).

33. While a depiction of menstruation may appear obvious to most people, such images aren't always construed this way. This situation is well illustrated in gender researcher Chris Bobel's discussion of Judy Chicago's photolitograph "Red Flag" (1971), which showed a close-up of the artist removing a bloodied tampon from her vagina. Bobel noted that at the time, many people appeared unsure what the red object was, with some thinking it was a bloodied penis (Chris Bobel, *New Blood: Third-Wave Feminism and the Politics of Menstruation* (New Brunswick, NJ: Rutgers University Press), 2010).

34. In Elizabeth Kissling's research on menstruation on screen she observed: "Compare, for instance, how much more common it is to see a female character in a film or television show represented as having PMS rather than as actually menstruating." (Elizabeth A. Kissling, "On the rag on screen: Menarche in film and television," *Sex Roles* 46, nos. 1–2 (January 2002): 5–12).

35. Gwen Macsai, *Lipshtick* (New York: HarperCollins, 2000), 44.

36. Harvey Molotch, "Introduction: Learning from the Loo," in *Public Restrooms and the Politics of Sharing*, ed. Laura Noren and Harvey Molotch (New York: New York University Press, 2010), 7.

37. Karen Houppert, *The Curse: Confronting the Last Unmentionable Taboo: Menstruation* (New York: Farrar, Straus and Giroux, 1999), 93.

38. In his chapter on public restrooms, sociologist Harvey Molotch similarly described the bathroom as a place where women "can let their hair down and exercise solidarity" (Harvey Molotch, "Introduction: Learning from the Loo," in *Public Restrooms and the Politics of Sharing*, ed. Laura Noren and Harvey Molotch (New York: New York University Press, 2010), 7).

39. Karen Houppert, *The Curse: Confronting the Last Unmentionable Taboo: Menstruation* (New York: Farrar, Straus and Giroux, 1999), 92.

40. Lara Freidenfelds, *The Modern Period: Menstruation in Twentieth-Century America* (Baltimore, MD: The Johns Hopkins University Press, 2009).

41. In Laura Fingerson, *Girls in Power: Gender, Body and Menstruation in Adolescence* (Albany: State University of New York Press, 2006), 53.

42. Laura Fingerson, *Girls in Power: Gender, Body and Menstruation in Adolescence* (Albany: State University of New York Press, 2006), 19.

43. Judith C. Daniluk, *Women's Sexuality Across the Life Span: Challenging Myths, Creating Meanings* (New York: The Guilford Press, 1998), 55.

44. Elizabeth A. Kissling, "On the rag on screen: Menarche in film and television," *Sex Roles* 46, 1–2 (January 2002): 5–12.

45. The flawed idea of assuming absent mothers would have acted perfectly in a menarche situation is discussed in Hope Edelman's book on motherless daughters (Hope Edelman, *Motherless Daughters: The Legacy of Loss* (Cambridge, MA: Da Capo Press, 2006)). This issue is also alluded to in an episode of *Party of Five* (1994–2000) in the context of miscarriage: Julia (Neve Campbell) miscarried and her brother Charlie (Matthew Fox) apologized for not having handled the situation better: "You probably would have been a lot better off if Mom had been here. 'Cos she would have known the exact way to talk to you about all this stuff." Here, Charlie alleged that their mother—presumably simply by virtue of her being a woman—would have known how to handle Julia's grief.

46. In Tina Fey's memoir *Bossypants*, the author discussed the menstruation education she received from her mother which involved being handed two Modess booklets, one which was actually a set of guidelines intended for *mothers* on explaining menstruation to their daughters; evidently something Mrs. Fey wanted to avoid (Tina Fey, *Bossypants* (New York: Little, Brown, 2011)).

47. In Laura Fingerson, *Girls in Power: Gender, Body and Menstruation in Adolescence* (Albany: State University of New York Press, 2006), 50.

48. For example, public health researcher Sabina Faiz Rashid discussed menstruation education in Bangladesh being delivered by female relatives including grandmothers (Sabina Faiz Rashid, "Providing sex education to adolescents in rural Bangladesh: experiences from BRAC," in *Gender and Lifecycles*, ed. Caroline Sweetman (Oxford: Oxfam, 2000)).

49. Kelly Orringer and Sheila Gahagan, "Adolescent girls define menstruation: A multiethnic exploratory study," *Health Care for Women International* 31 (2010): 831–847.

50. Lara Freidenfelds, *The Modern Period: Menstruation in Twentieth-Century America* (Baltimore, MD: The Johns Hopkins University Press, 2009), 59.

51. Laura Fingerson, *Girls in Power: Gender, Body and Menstruation in Adolescence* (Albany: State University of New York Press, 2006), 94.

52. Laura Fingerson, *Girls in Power: Gender, Body and Menstruation in Adolescence* (Albany: State University of New York Press, 2006), 18.

53. The idea of menstruation becoming just a "sanitary event" for a motherless daughter—and thus potentially being depressing—is discussed in Hope Edelman's book on motherless daughters (Hope Edelman, *Motherless Daughters: The Legacy of Loss* (Cambridge, MA: Da Capo Press, 2006), 218). A similar point was made in historian Joan Brumberg's research, where she identified that for women in the Victorian Age, menstruation was primarily a *hygiene* event (Joan Jacobs Brumberg, *The Body Project: An Intimate History of American Girls* (New York: Random House, 1997)).

54. Janell L. Carroll, *Sexuality Now: Embracing Diversity* (Belmont, CA: Wadsworth, 2010), 129.

55. Laura Fingerson in fact discussed this idea as being a result of the medicalization of menstruation: "some boys talk about girls using menstruation and menstrual symptoms as an excuse to avoid certain activities. This is one result for the medicalization of menstruation and PMS, where menstruation is seen as a chronic medical condition with symptoms." (Laura Fingerson, *Girls in Power: Gender, Body and Menstruation in Adolescence* (Albany: State University of New York Press, 2006), 135). A slightly different analysis of the same idea was presented by feminist philosopher Kate Millet. Millet discussed the idea of self-fulfilling prophesy in relation to women's bodies: "Patriarchal circumstances and beliefs seem to have the effect of poisoning the female's own sense of physical self until it often truly becomes the burden it is said to be." As related to menstrual synchrony, the argument would be that women *think* they are suffering because patriarchy has taught them that menstruation is an ordeal. (Kate Millet, *Sexual Politics* (New York: Doubleday, 1970), 47).

56. This idea is alluded to in Fingerson's study where she discussed the moon lodge rituals of other cultures with the girls in her study:

Erin: Yeah. I see cat fight.

Laura: *Really? Why?*

Briana: Okay, seriously though. You're kind of moody during that time. Maybe even before, usually for me before. It's like I don't want to deal with other people before that –

Marcia): – when you get that many women with those many different opinions and that bad mood in a small, confided area—oh no.

Laura: *Sitting on moss.*

Briana: Only one will come out alive.

Marcia: Exactly. (pause) With a handful of hair. (In Laura Fingerson, *Girls in Power: Gender, Body and Menstruation in Adolescence* (Albany: State University of New York Press, 2006), 152–153.

57. See for example, Lauren Rosewarne, "Sweet charity, sleazy catfight," *The Drum*, November 9, 2010, www.abc.net.au/unleashed/40896.html (accessed September 6, 2011); Lauren Rosewarne, "Women can critique each other without the catfight," *The Punch*, March 1, 2011, www.thepunch.com.au/articles/women-can-critique-each-other-without-a-catfight (accessed September 6, 2011).

58. This is something Fingerson spotlighted when she reflected on the intimacy between the girls in her interviews: "I generally have no idea when my friends and co-workers are menstruating, what their symptoms are, and we generally do not share our everyday menstrual status. Yet these girls are highly in tune with not only their friends' cycle timing, but also their friends' symptoms and management strategies" (Laura Fingerson, *Girls in Power: Gender, Body and Menstruation in Adolescence* (Albany: State University of New York Press, 2006), 88).

59. In Laura Fingerson, *Girls in Power: Gender, Body and Menstruation in Adolescence* (Albany: State University of New York Press, 2006), 1.

60. See Sophie Laws, *Issues of Blood: The Politics of Menstruation* (Houndmills, Basingstoke, Hampshire: Macmillan, 1990).

61. John Scalzi, "Best personal hygiene products of the millennium," in *Your Hate Mail Will Be Graded: A Decade of Whatever, 1998–2008* (New York: Tom Doherty Associates, 2008), 349.

62. Film theorist Barbara Creed's discussion of the "monstrous feminine," for example, proposes that monsters in films are feminized by the elements that make women repellent: i.e., that they are moist, that they bleed: "Menstruation and childbirth are seen as the two events in woman's life which have placed her on the side of the abject." (Barbara Creed, *The Monstrous-Feminine: Film, Feminism, Psychoanalysis* (Routledge: London, 1993), 50).

63. David Linton, "Crossing the menstrual line," in *Embodied Resistance: Challenging the Norms, Breaking the Rules*, ed. Chris Bobel and Samantha Kwan (Nashville, TN: Vanderbilt University Press, 2011), 220.

64. In Sophie Laws, *Issues of Blood: The Politics of Menstruation* (Houndmills, Basingstoke, Hampshire: Macmillan, 1990), 76. Biologist Karen Messing relayed a similar story in her research on gender in the workplace when she discussed a male lab technician who proudly told her that he "could always tell when a woman was menstruating by the fact that she carried her purse to the bathroom at those times" (Karen Messing, *One-Eyed Science: Occupational Health and Women Workers* (Philadelphia: Temple University Press, 1998), 147).

65. It should be noted that while I have presented Eric's actions as possibly being construed as weird, this might not actually be the dominant reading. Sociologist Jean Elson, for example, discussed the role of fathers in guiding daughters through their first periods and in her examples—fathers teaching their daughters how to use sanitary belts and fathers convincing their wives to let their daughters use tampons—Elson noted, "None of the women who talked about their fathers' involvement in their menarche interpreted this as inappropriately intrusive." (Jean P. Elson, *Am I Still A Woman? Hysterectomy and Gender Identity* (Philadelphia: Temple University Press, 2004), 77).

66. Laura, Fingerson, *Girls in Power: Gender, Body and Menstruation in Adolescence* (Albany: State University of New York Press, 2006), 114.

67. See Lauren Rosewarne, *Sex in Public: Women, Outdoor Advertising and Public Policy* (Newcastle: Cambridge Scholars Publishing, 2007).

Chapter Two

Red Tents and Moon Lodges

Menstruation and the Rites of Passage

This chapter focuses on screen presentations of menarche and offers a discussion of celebration narratives as well as those associated less with jubilation and more so with the depressing end of childhood. Also examined are issues of gender identity as illustrated through the feminine performances assumed by, and expected of, the newly menstruating girl on screen, expectations which frequently conflict with tomboy identities. Depictions of other changes occurring in the life of the newly bleeding female—notably entry to the adult world of love and romance—are also explored.

A COMING OF AGE CELEBRATION

Western culture is often considered as one which neglects to appropriately commemorate menstruation as a coming of age milestone for girls.[1] The fact that it is not celebrated and rarely publicly even *discussed* conveys the impression that there is something wrong with it, or at the very least, there exist reasons to feel uncomfortable about it. Whereas anthropologists have extensively documented the coming of age rituals apparent in *other* cultures,[2] the West is often thought to downplay the event, rendering it a private event, a sanitary event, alternatively, as a *non-event* (this latter idea is further examined in chapter 8). While menstruation in the West may not have any specific rituals attached,[3] research does document micro-level celebrations occurring in the lives of some girls. Sociologist Laura Fingerson, for example, quoted teenager Andrea who described her mother as having bought her a present when she got her first period. Rebecca in the same study reported that her mom "made up a song" and sang it to her father.[4] Kassie similarly spoke about her mom being so happy that she phoned all her friends.[5] On screen menstrual celebrations transpire most commonly as verbal congratulations and much less frequently as formal festivities.

Parents and Menarche Celebrations

In this section I explore some of the on screen attempts made by parents—and less frequently *grandparents*—to acknowledge a girl's menarche. An obvious way this manifests—in line with the stories shared by the girls in Fingerson's study—is through a mother's verbal commemoration; something apparent in films *I Could Never Be Your Woman* (2007), *A Walk on the Moon* (1999), *My Louisiana Sky* (2001), and in the sitcom *Roseanne* (1988–1997). In *I Could Never Be Your Woman*, when Izzie (Saoirse Ronan) disclosed her first period, her mother Rosie (Michelle Pfeiffer) exulted, "Congratulations, you're a woman." In *A Walk on the Moon*, when Alison (Anna Paquin) got her first period she called her grandmother Lillian (Tovah Feldshuh) into the bathroom:

> **Lillian:** What is it, my shainehkuh, huh? What is it, darling?
>
> [Alison lifted her dress to reveal her stained underpants]
>
> **Lillian:** Oh, my God. Mazel tov.
>
> [Lillian slapped Alison]
>
> **Alison:** Why'd you hit me?
>
> **Lillian:** It's a tradition. My mother, your great-grandmother, Sonia—may she rest in peace—she did the same thing to me.
>
> **Alison:** It's a stupid tradition.
>
> **Lillian:** It's the stupidest goddamn tradition. It's true. You know what I did? I slapped her right back.
>
> [Alison slapped Lillian]
>
> **Lillian:** Bandeet!
>
> [Alison's mother, Pearl, entered]
>
> **Pearl:** What's going on in here?
>
> **Lillian:** Pearl . . .
>
> **Pearl:** What?
>
> **Lillian:** I got news. Today Alison became a woman.
>
> [Pearl hugged Alison]

A similar scene occurred in *My Louisiana Sky* when Tiger Ann's (Kelsey Keel) period was commemorated by her mother, Corrina (Amelia Campbell) and, to a lesser extent, by her grandmother, Jewel (Shirley Knight):

Tiger Ann: I'm bleedin' from inside.

Jewel: Go get yourself some rags. You got the curse.

Tiger Ann: I got a curse?

Jewel: From now on, you can look forward to it every month til' you're too old like me. Then, thank the Lord, it's over. That's the only good thing I can think of about getting' older.

Corrina: What's wrong, Tiger?

Tiger Ann: I got the curse, Mama.

Corrina: Oh, Tiger, I'm so happy for you!

Tiger Ann: It's a curse! Grandma just said so. It's a curse.

Corrina: It's not a curse! It's beautiful! Oh, it's a little messy and sometimes your tummy hurts, but I couldn't have you til' I was bleedin' every month, and havin' a baby, havin' you, was the best thing that ever happened to me.

When Darlene (Sara Gilbert) got her first period on *Roseanne*, a similar conversation transpired with her mother, Roseanne (Roseanne Barr):

Darlene: Oh God, why me?

Roseanne: 'Cos you're lucky.

Darlene: Right.

Roseanne: Now you get to be a part of the whole cycle of things. You know, the moon and the water and the seasons. It's almost magical, Darlene. You should be really proud today 'cos this is the beginning of a lot of really wonderful things in your life.

Darlene: Yeah, cramps.

Roseanne: Well I'll admit that's one of the highlights, but I'm talking about a part that's even better than that.

Darlene: Name one good thing that could come out of this whole mess.

Roseanne: Okay, I'll name three. Becky, DJ, and . . . what's that other kid's name?

Jewel's negativity in *My Louisiana Sky* aside, these scenes each showcased women—*mothers*—verbally congratulating a young girl at menarche. In each scene, the girl was explicitly welcomed into a sisterhood of women. While implied in *A Walk on the Moon* (by the presence of three generations in the scene) and made more explicit in *My Louisiana Sky* and *Roseanne*, is the acknowledgment—and celebration—of the girl being *fertile*: menstruation is celebrated not just as a generic developmental milestone, but one with *life-giving* properties; the girl is being welcomed into a community of those who can procreate, notably by the woman who gave her life. Roseanne referenced the moon and the seasons and while perhaps lofty assertions, she connected Darlene's menarche to something bigger than herself and certainly more momentous than Darlene's evident anxiety. In line with spiritual feminist and womanist analyses of menstruation, Roseanne presented menstruation as something with momentous significance: periods were considered as important for Roseanne herself as a menstruator, for her daughter as a new and reluctant menstruator, and also for the audience. Given Barr's well-documented feminist politics,[6] her character's welcoming of her daughter into a sisterhood can be construed as a concerted effort to offer an explicitly *feminist* presentation of menstruation in contrast to dominant negative portrayals.

Celebrations become slightly more elaborate, if not ritualistic, in sitcom *The Cosby Show* (1984–1992) and in the Canadian comedy-horror film *Ginger Snaps* (2000). Contemporary parenting manuals routinely advise mothers to celebrate their daughter's menstruation as way to demystify it, to boost self-esteem, and to create a sense of community.[7] Such suggestions appear to have informed the episode of *The Cosby Show* centered on Rudy's (Keshia Knight Pulliam) menarche. In the episode, mother Clair (Phylicia Rashad) dubbed the occasion a "Woman's Day," a day designed to create an environment of accurate information sharing; similar occasions had been held for Clair's older daughters. In *Ginger Snaps*, Ginger's (Katharine Isabelle) first period was commemorated by her mother, Pamela (Mimi Rogers), through the presentation of a large strawberry cake. While in *The Cosby Show* Rudy was seemingly not interested in the celebration and Ginger in *Ginger Snaps* was embarrassed about the cake, in both narratives—as in *Roseanne*—menarche was presented as bigger than the individual bleeder and as something connecting the girl to entities—a sisterhood, fertility, nature, and so on—bigger than herself; her enthusiasm (or lack thereof) therefore was completely irrelevant. The girls' lack of enthusiasm in these scenes potentially also functions to mirror the widespread anxiety and negative views about menstruation held by the audience: the girls on screen weren't quite convinced that bleeding from their genitals was worth celebrating; their mothers thus worked to assuage character (as well as audience) fears. Another reading is that such low-key—if not *negative*—responses from the girls can be interpreted as grounded in internalized cultural attitudes about secret-keeping; that the girls—in line with social mores—don't *want* anyone knowing about their period, certainly not in the form of a party (an idea elaborated on in chapter 8).

While celebrating menarche may be assumed to be something a mother would do (chapter 1), fathers on screen in fact have also attempted to commemorate their daughter's first period and while perhaps appearing more farcical than heartfelt are nonetheless identifiable.

In an episode of the cartoon sitcom *Family Guy* (1999–), during a flashback, father Peter was shown to shout out to his neighbors during the middle of the night: "Hey everybody! Meg just had her first period . . . I'm just saying I'm proud of her. She's a woman. Yay!" While one interpretation of this scene is it being an endearing demonstration of Peter's genuine pride, it also demonstrates a father's *ignorance* about how a daughter might feel about menarche herself; that while ideally, perhaps, menstruation would be celebrated—if not championed—for a father to do so *today* in a culture where girls still feel anxious and embarrassed about it appears insensitive. Given this scene's presence in a sitcom, it is in fact highly likely that Peter's actions were not about destigmatizing menstruation at all, and instead were designed to cater to the audience's familiarity with cringe-worthy parents. Similar well-intentioned, albeit flawed, menarche commemorations occurred in episodes of sitcoms *Roseanne* and *Something So Right* (1996–1998): Dan (John Goodman) in *Roseanne* said "Good job" to Darlene on her first period, and Jack (Jere Burns) high-fived his stepdaughter Sarah (Emily Ann Lloyd). While both of these fathers acted in ways that they thought were appropriate—and, being sitcoms, did so for comedy effect—in neither case did the father actually imply that menstruation was something positive nor worthy of *actual* celebration; they merely acknowledged that menarche was a big deal *for their daughter*. This idea was particularly well illustrated in the *Californication* (2007–) episode when Becca (Madeleine Martin) got her first period and her father Hank (David Duchovny) took her to buy tampons. As the two entered the gas station, Hank apologized to Becca for his lack of preparation: "I'm so sorry, sweetie, I should have been set up for such a momentous occasion in the life of a young woman." While Hank *said* the right words, as soon as Becca replied, "I'm not going to die or anything, I just got my period," the *very* second she said the word "period" Hank quickly shushed her. Moments later, when trying to secure the last box of tampons, Hank argued with another woman in the store and in the process likened menstruation to incontinence and tampons to diapers (chapter 1). While on one hand Hank *attempted* to say the right things and to acknowledge Becca's first period as momentous, he also shushed her when she dared say it aloud and then proceeded to denigrate menstruation as an entity: the scene was less congratulations and more evidence of Hank's internalized cultural views on menstruation as related to secrecy and sanitation (chapter 1). While thus far I have criticized the responses of fathers in these scenes, it is important to note that, one, the fathers were each shown to actually be trying to do their best, and two, it is important to be mindful—as discussed in chapter 1—that there is no comparable experience for a man and thus it is perhaps expected that fathers find reacting difficult.

While menarche is rarely celebrated on screen with a formal occasion, in scenes from *7th Heaven* (1996–2007) and *According to Jim* (2001–2009), formal festivities were actually organized by fathers. In *7th Heaven*, for example, when Lucy (Beverley Mitchell) finally got her long-awaited period, her father, Eric (Stephen Collins), honored the women of the household by treating them to a special women's dinner; something we sense had also been orchestrated years prior for their oldest daughter. In *According to Jim*, while mom, Cheryl (Courtney Thorne-Smith) was away, Gracie (Billi Bruno) got her first period, thus leaving father Jim (James Belushi) to manage the situation. Jim and family friend Andy (Larry Joe Campbell) used the Internet to educate themselves. During the episode, Andy read from a webpage that "in many cultures you throw a young lady a party to welcome her into womanhood," thus motivating the men to organize a "First Moon Party." While the party was awkward, embarrassing, and poorly attended, the episode presented a very rare example of a formal menstrual celebration—hinting to the menarche celebrations of other cultures—and interestingly, one initiated and organized by men. While it could be argued that the party was in fact *mocking* of new-age rituals,[8] the fact that the men were trying to commemorate the occasion—even if clumsily—certainly makes it an interesting outlier example. Another interesting example of a similar celebration occurs in the sitcom *Community* (2009) when Annie (Alison Brie) mentions the existence of the "period fairy," presumably organized by her parents.

Friends and Menarche Celebrations

Blossom (1990–1995) and *Ready or Not* (1993–1997) were family-oriented television series focused on close relationships between friends, and as relevant to this chapter, both boasted scenes of menarche congratulations. When Busy (Lani Billard) got her first period on the Canadian series *Ready or Not*, her best friend Amanda (Laura Betram) congratulated her by saying, "You're a woman now." When Blossom (Mayim Bialik) got her first period on *Blossom*, her best friend Six (Jenna von Oÿ) similarly said, "Congratulations. Today you are woman." In these examples, congratulations came from *peers*. While able to be construed as perhaps more meaningful—or at least exhibiting more gender-based comprehension—than the fathers' commemorations discussed earlier, these scenes also offer other interpretations, showcasing both naiveté and perhaps also gender-based and experience-based insight. Amanda in *Ready or Not*, for example, had not yet gotten her period: for her, menstruation was something new, adult and exciting. Amanda's excited reaction, in fact, recalls the behavior of Eric on *7th Heaven* who exhibited high-level excitement about his daughter's first period, so much so that his wife Annie (Catherine Hicks) had to temper his enthusiasm (chapter 1). Such scenes present an *outsider's* view of menstruation which evidently involved high-level idealization. On one hand, like the congratulations from mothers noted earlier, Amanda and Eric's behavior can be read as providing a counter-narrative to both the anxious new menstruator and to the audience: in contrast to many on-screen reactions, Amanda and Eric both evidently considered menstruation worth celebrating. Another interpretation of these scenes, however, is that they further remind audiences of just what a closed club menstruation is: that men and children can *never* really understand it and that Amanda and Eric were only excited because they had never menstruated. In her recollections of her first period, for example, writer Erica Jong reflected: "If you were not born knowing about tampons and menstruation, you are considered a retard."[9] While not necessarily *retards*, Amanda and Eric most certainly come across as not being *in the know* in these scenes; Amanda seems hyperactively naïve, and Eric appears foolish. A more cynical interpretation is that Amanda and Eric's reactions deceptively set a young girl up to anticipate that menstruation will be wonderful and transformative only to be dealt a crushing blow to esteem when this does not happen (an idea addressed later in this chapter).

In contrast to Amanda and Eric's behavior, Six in *Blossom* already *had* her period and her congratulations to Blossom was *facetious*: while she was seemingly pleased that "Blossom is blossoming," unlike Amanda and Eric, Six actually knew *intimately* that menstruation isn't effortless, something demonstrated, for example, when she commiserated with Blossom about the feeling of "a kind of overall bloat." Six's congratulations in fact were more akin to the fathers discussed earlier: *saying* what she knew she should—something likely perceived as important in light of the absence of Blossom's mother—but unlike the fathers or Amanda, with knowledge that menstruation was no cakewalk.

While in this section I have discussed narratives associated with menstrual celebrations, menarche is in fact far more likely to be presented on screen with much less fanfare.

MENARCHE AND THE END OF CHILDHOOD

Writer Natalie Angier described menarche as the clearest rite of passage for women: "what a woman really remembers is her first period; now there's a memory seared into the brain with the blowtorch of high emotion."[10] Such sentiments were personalized by Alyssa, quoted in Fingerson's research, who described menarche as: "one of the steps to being a woman, like, a lady" and considered it as a "rite of passage."[11] Nancy Caruso reflected on her first period in the *My Little Red Book* menstruation anthology, describing it as "a coming of age" and a "vajayjay christen[ing]."[12] Similar views were expressed by participants in a study of African American and European American women, many who identified menstruation as the transition point to womanhood.[13]

For menarche to actually serve as a gateway to adulthood, childhood needs to end. On screen this end can spark a spectrum of emotions. In this section I focus on *negative* sentiments, notably anger, feelings of being blindsided, disappointment, and the perception that the whole experience was anticlimactic.

First Period Anger

In *My Little Red Book*, Elizabeth Siciliano recalled her first period, writing: "It was as though our bodies gave us a punishment."[14] In this quote, Siciliano alluded to the routine presentation of menstruation as something awful. The frequently used expression of "the curse"—discussed further in chapter 3—makes explicit that not only are periods routinely construed as bad, but worse, that their recurring nature implies that they are almost like a sentence, a (near) lifelong affliction that any woman would be justified in resenting. Jewel's comments to Tiger Ann in *My Louisiana Sky* discussed earlier certainly demonstrate this idea; for Jewel, menstruation was a curse, an affliction, and only in old age did respite come.

Resentment and anger over menarche have been analyzed in a variety of contexts: academics, for example, have contended that negative reactions from girls are most likely to transpire in cultures which don't celebrate menstruation—and which, frequently in fact, *denigrate* it (chapter 4).[15] A feminist analysis offers another interpretation, basing resentment on the fact that menstruation not only exclusively afflicts women, but is something which delivers girls a bitter taste of biology-based gender inequality: women bleed while men don't; women's lives are restricted, men's are not. This idea is illustrated well in writer Anne Clinard Barnhill's memoir, where she mused about the first time that she heard about menstruation:

> I thought this was the most unfair situation in the world—boys didn't have to curtail their swim schedules; boys didn't have to worry about leaking through their clothes and being embarrassed to death.[16]

As Vada (Anna Chlumsky) in *My Girl* (1994) commented at the arrival of her first period: "It's not fair. Nothing happens to boys." The sharp contrast between the way boys enter adulthood compared to girls on screen is identified in cultural theorist Gregory Woods's discussion of the films *The Blue Lagoon* (1980) and *Return to the Blue Lagoon* (1991), both of which focused on two children—a boy and a girl—entering adulthood on a deserted island:

> Whereas the girls enter womanhood via a moment of implied pain, in the actual bloodshed of menstruation, the boys enter manhood by way of pleasure: masturbation in the first film, a nocturnal erection during evidently pleasant dreams in the second.[17]

This perception of unfairness is identifiable in real-life menarche accounts as well as extensively on screen. In author Patty Marx's recollections of her first period, she described being given a document called *Becoming a Woman*, remembering it as "the booklet we fifth-grade girls received one afternoon when the boys were doing something fun, like pummeling each other."[18] On the episode of *Blossom* discussed earlier, Blossom reflected on being taught about menstruation at school, recalling "the day they sent the boys out of the room and pulled the shades down." Writer Ellen Devine told a similar story: "Nurse Joan had described [it] in detail while the boys in my class got to play an extra game of kickball."[19] In each of these examples, girls were introduced to menstruation in a staid classroom setting while the boys got to have fun outside.

While gender inequality may first be detected during a girl's theoretical introduction to menstruation, for some girls the inequality—real or perceived—will be felt throughout their menstrual lives. Psychoanalyst Clara Thompson, for example, presented a case study of a girl who, upon getting her first period, was no longer permitted to go camping or hiking with her brother: "She was filled with bitterness and envy of her brother and for several reasons centered her whole resentment on the fact of menstruation."[20] Thompson offered a psychoanalytic interpretation suggesting that the girl experienced *penis envy*: that she, much like Marx, Devine, Vada, and Blossom, felt that being a girl meant that her liberation was curtailed; that if she had a penis she would have had freedom.

Discussed in chapter 1 was the shock and horror that Vada experienced in *My Girl* when she first menstruated. Vada, however, also exhibited *anger*. While her anger can be interpreted as rooted in her lack of preparation—a logical reading given that she calmed down considerably after things were explained to her—Vada's reaction can also be read as resentment that her life changed *against her will*: her body decided that her childhood was over and that she had become a woman; something that she might have previously been able to ignore. On getting her first period, Vada keenly felt the restrictions of her gender, typified by her having to refuse Thomas J's (Macaulay Culkin) suggestion that they go swimming; an activity she would have previously agreed to was suddenly perceived as inaccessible.

While Vada was clearly angry, her anger was not as aggressive as the kind presented in the cartoon sitcom *American Dad!* (2005–). In one episode, parents Stan and Francine reflected on their children going through puberty. The parents were shown—via flashback—cowering in a corner; their daughter Haley loomed over them holding a tampon in one hand, a box of tampons in the other, and screamed, "What do you mean every month?!" While it appeared that Haley's rage stemmed from her discovery that the "horror" of her menstruation would be a regular occurrence, the fact that she was holding *tampons* while screaming seemed to indicate that menstrual *products* also fueled her rage; that having to have tampons at the ready, having to change them and to dispose of them all made menstruation hideously unappealing. Feminist philosopher Simone de Beauvoir explained this very burden in her seminal text, *The Second Sex*:

> Day and night she has to think of changing her protection, watching her underwear, her sheets, and solving a thousand little practical and repugnant problems.[21]

Returning to Marx, Devine, and also Blossom's recollections of school sex education, implied in their comments was that not only is bleeding something substantially *less* fun than playing kickball, but that everything associated with it—learning about it right through to disposing of a bloodied tampon—is an ordeal; as social worker Hilary Maddux noted in her research on menstruation, "[m]any girls are also taught that consciously or unconsciously menstruation is a burden."[22] Certainly such early teachings are keenly absorbed: research indicates that the majority of girls *do* in fact perceive their periods as a burden[23]; sentiments readily identifiable in women's accounts of their own menstruation. In chapter 1 I discussed feminist writer Germaine Greer's reflections on her experiences at a time before the widespread availability of disposable products: "I used to creep into the laundry and crouch over a bucket of foul clouts, hoping my brother would not catch me *at my revolting labours*."[24] In feminist writer Jennifer Baumgardner's more recent work, she similarly identified menstruation as "extra work," noting that it mandated: "preparation and sometimes a ruined pair of underpants or sheets. I'm always pretty relieved when it's over."[25] In *The Complete Idiot's Guide to Camping and Hiking*, author Michael Mouland identified the particular burden that periods posed during activities like camping as related to the "special trash" created.[26] Menstruation perceived as a burden is certainly evident on screen. In the *Ready or Not* episode when Busy got her first period, she was shown scrubbing the blood from her underpants. In a scene from *Boys Don't Cry* (1999), transgender Brandon (Hilary Swank) was similarly shown scrubbing blood from his stained jeans. In a scene from the Irish film *The Magdalene Sisters* (2002), the female inmates of the Magdalene

Sisters Asylum were shown hand-laundering blood-stained sheets. The burden of concealment (chapter 1), ruined sheets, the need to have menstrual products available, the associated expense,[27] and the lifestyle restrictions (chapter 3), as well as the necessity to properly dispose of the associated waste are all aspects of menstruation management which, unsurprisingly, frequently ignite negative emotions.

First Period Blindside

While Vada in *My Girl* and Haley in *American Dad!* both exhibited anger, in both cases their reactions stemmed from their first periods having *blindsided* them: they were angry because their period arrived without appropriate warning. Being blindsided—being caught without sufficient education, preparation or supplies—underpins many negative responses to menstruation, both off screen and on.

In Nancy Lee Teaff and Kim Wright Wiley's research on perimenopause, the authors contended that both "[m]enarche and menopause seem to thrust themselves upon us with a timing all of their own, leaving us mumbling, 'Wait, I'm not ready.'"[28] Health researcher Nancy Woods et al. similarly contended that the vast majority of girls are in fact surprised by their first period.[29] Historian Lara Freidenfelds contended that surprise at menstruation is most likely experienced by women insufficiently educated about it beforehand,[30] however, other research argues that prior education doesn't actually always help: that even though the majority of girls *do* actually know about menstruation in advance, surprise is still their typical reaction,[31] if not also repugnance and humiliation.[32] Historian Mary Lynn Stewart, in her discussion of sex education in France, noted that for some girls, even when educated, they actually "repressed" their knowledge at the time of their menarche.[33] One woman quoted in gender researcher Janet Lee's research recalled being told by her mother at menarche that she would need to stop playing with boys. The woman remembered crying and saying, "*I'm not ready to be a lady and I like playing with the boys.*"[34] In pediatricians Kelly Orringer and Sheila Gahagan's research, the authors similarly noted that many of their participants felt as though they *weren't ready* for their first periods. On screen Vada in *My Girl* certainly illustrated these ideas: she clearly *wasn't* ready and was depicted as panicked and scared. In *Ready or Not*, after Busy's suspicion that she was sick was corrected in the school bathroom, she explicitly articulated her lack of readiness, responding: "What? *Already*?" While Busy had learned about menstruation in health class—something we suspect Vada had not—its sudden arrival nonetheless came as a shock. While menopause is addressed in greater detail in chapter 7, it is worthwhile noting that, as Teaff and Wiley contended, *menopause* can also come as an unwelcome surprise. This idea was well illustrated in an episode of the sitcom *All In the*

Family (1968–1979) when daughter Gloria (Sally Struthers) diagnosed her mother Edith (Jean Stapleton) as menopausal and Edith responded: "Oh my! At my age? Oh I ain't supposed to change yet, am I?"

More than just being a nasty surprise, however, first-time bleeders may even completely misinterpret the onset of their bleeding as something more sinister. In artist Suzan Shutan's account of her first period, she recalled "knowing" that she was dying.[35] Writer Michele Jaffe recalled a friend who, "despite having learned all about Getting It at school and from her mom—[knew] she was dying and composed several very moving poem-plus illustration combinations for her tombstone."[36] On screen menarche interpreted as impending death is readily identifiable. In *Ready or Not*, Busy wanted to be taken to the hospital; in *My Louisiana Sky*, Tiger Ann had no idea why she was bleeding from "inside." In *Carrie* (1976), the title character (Sissy Spacek) cried out to the other girls in the school gym showers: "I'm bleeding to death!" In an episode of *Dr. Quinn, Medicine Woman* (1993–1998), Dr Quinn's (Jane Seymour) daughter Colleen (Erika Flores) thought that she was dying because she had "been bleeding for three whole days." Vada in *My Girl* was convinced that she was hemorrhaging. For these characters, their surprise, compounded with their lack of understanding, contributed to them assuming the worst. While expectedly, on-screen menarche overreactions are usually associated with girls, examples do exist of *men* overreacting to menstruation. In the cartoon sitcom *King of the Hill*, for example, Hank's immediate response to Connie's first period was to drive her to the hospital. On the Canadian cartoon sitcom *Braceface* (2001–2003), when Sharon got her first period while on a date with Alden, Alden thought she was having an appendicitis attack and called an ambulance. Whereas girls' overreactions on screen are often used to display naiveté and to acknowledge character (and audience) anxiety, men's overreactions are more in line with their routine portrayal as foolish and as ignorant, as discussed in chapter 1. Such portrayals work to demonstrate that even an adult man like Hank in *King of the Hill* can seemingly travel through life without even the most basic menstrual knowledge, in spite of having a wife.

While a girl's initial response to menstruation will quickly subside[37] — after all, being blindsided by a first period can only be fleeting—the negative emotions that she feels at the time are likely to be, as Angier suggests, "seared into the brain with the blowtorch of high emotion."[38]

First Period Disappointment

While anger and feelings of being blindsided are potent reactions to menarche, another response is disappointment. Orringer and Gahagan identified sadness in the first period reflections of the girls in their study; one eighteen-year-old girl, for example, recalled getting her first period and just "crying and crying":

> I just kinda thought it stunk. . . . That was just kind of like a sad way to like leave, like childhood. . . . I guess you're supposed to feel like you're becoming a woman. . . . I didn't feel any different at all, which I guess was a disappointment to me.[39]

This girl's disappointment exists on at least two levels: one, she was disappointed to leave her childhood, and two, she didn't feel any different: disappointment at childhood lost is addressed in this section; disappointment at the anticlimax of menstruation is addressed in the next.

Patricia Boyd discussed her first period in *My Little Red Book*, noting that along with relief she also experienced sadness: "I also felt sad to realize that someday soon, I would no longer be interested in playing in mud puddles."[40] On screen such a lamentation was identifiable in the episode of *Roseanne* when Darlene got her first period. Roseanne watched her daughter disappointedly pack her sporting goods into garbage bags and the following conversation transpired:

> **Roseanne:** What are you doing?
>
> **Darlene:** Getting rid of all this junk.
>
> **Roseanne:** Oh, I get it. You think you've gotta leave this stuff behind you now. Like women have to give up baseball gloves and start wearing aprons and stuff.
>
> **Darlene:** All I know is I'm not shaving my legs or wearing pantyhose like Becky.

Darlene's reaction to getting her first period was *disappointment*: she was disappointed that her childhood—one that had been defined by sport and her close relationship with her father—was perceived as over, something she made explicit when she sarcastically lamented her father's congratulations: "My life is over and he congratulated me." In *Ready or Not*, at the beginning of the episode Busy picked up a stray basketball, shot it through a hoop and was then invited by the boys playing to join them. This was the tomboy life Busy enjoyed: that is, her *pre*-menstrual life. Later, once she got her first period, Busy had to scrub her stained clothing: her *post*-menstrual life was suddenly on display, one marred by domestic drudgery. Something similar transpired in *My Girl* when Vada—who usually pounced on any opportunity to romp with her best friend Thomas J—declined when she got her first period, telling him, "Get out of here! And don't come back for five to seven days." While each scene portrayed sadness as related to each girl's life changing, of particular interest, each also showcased the new and apparently *unpleasant* role gender now played for them.

Mary McGee Williams and Irene Kane's 1958 book *On Becoming a Woman: A Book for Teenage Girls* attempted to explain some of the potent emotions experienced at menarche:

> One of the reasons that menstruation sets off an explosion of emotions is that for perhaps the first time in your active, tom-boy life, you must accept the fact that you are a girl. For most girls, this acceptance is an exciting, who-wouldn't-want-to-be kind of thing, something you've looked forward to from the first time you saw your mother nursing a baby brother, or dreamed about a kitchen of your own, or imagined yourself a well-loved wife.[41]

In their analysis of this paragraph, Elissa Stein and Susan Kim in their book *Flow* cannily identified what the authors overlooked, in turn working to explain Vada, Darlene, and Busy's disappointment:

> McGee Williams and Kane choose not to mention that fact that for *other girls*, getting one's period is not only confusing and frightening, but often downright depressing. . . . Some of us actually enjoyed being active tomboys and were horrified to learn we would now be expected to give up our swashbuckling ways.[42]

Psychoanalyst Hendrika Freud articulated a similar position:

> Perhaps she previously was a tomboy who had not yet chosen whether she wanted to be a boy or a girl. She thought she still had both options open. Now she has to be a woman, whether she likes it or not.[43]

These ideas highlight two topics worth addressing in the context of screen presentations of menstruation: one, lack of gender choice, and two, the forced acceptance of biological sex. Underpinning the negative feelings associated with menstruation felt by Vada, Darlene, and Busy was their perceived lack of choice: they didn't *choose* to menstruate. Anna, the protagonist in Doris Lessing's novel *The Golden Notebook*, alluded to this lack of choice by describing her menstruation as "the wound inside my body which I didn't choose to have."[44] On *Blossom*, the title character similarly bemoaned: "Why is this happening to me? . . . Why wasn't I consulted?" These characters didn't—and presumably *wouldn't*—have chosen to menstruate—and exhibited menstrual resentment accordingly. Such resentment, of course, is a well-used theme in menstrual product advertising. A series of Kotex print advertisements from the 1940s, for example, used illustrations of teenage girls looking miserable, the copy of one reading, "Why was I born a woman?" and another, "It just isn't fair!" While contemporary advertising tends not to overtly employ this "why me"-victim approach, the idea of periods being thought of as unfair and impinging on women's lifestyles most certainly continues in contemporary advertising whereby the capacity of menstruation to restrict activity is often at the crux (chapter 3).

Something evident in *My Girl*, *Roseanne*, *Ready or Not*, and *Blossom* is resentment that not only is menstruation something foisted upon girls without their consent, but worse, that with it comes the mandate of *femininity*; that regardless of each girl's gender preference, menstruation makes them women in a multitude of ways that they are neither ready for nor interested in. Busy, for example, didn't want her mother's life of domestic drudgery and Darlene didn't want her sister's life of make-up and pantyhose. Such narratives relate to research noting that menstruation forces a girl to actually pay attention to her genitals—something she may not have previously had to do—and thus compels her to accept her sex,[45] if not also her vulnerability as a woman.[46] Vada, Darlene, and Busy were each tomboy characters and each assumed that menstruation would force them to overhaul their identity. A substantially stronger example of this occurred in the film *Boys Don't Cry*. Brandon was born female, identified as male, and dressed accordingly, including padding his trousers. While for most of the time living as a man was possible for him (albeit difficult), his body—his *menstruation*—betrayed his biological sex. One of the most painful scenes in the film showed him using a tampon; the haunting death-wish themed soundtrack of the Charlatans' "Codine Blues" (1966) played in the background as Brandon winced. Despite the fact that Brandon had completely dissociated from his biological gender, menstruation forced him to "reconnect" with his vagina, something he clearly found distressing. In her explanation of electing to have Brandon use tampons in this scene rather than a pad, the film's director, Kimberly Pierce, explained:

> We talked about the pads. But the transsexuals said, "Yeah, but the most important thing is that you pass." If you're passing, and you've got a pad on—and the mess, having the blood be exposed to themselves and then having to throw out the pad, they said that was a bigger reminder of being a woman. Once you put the tampon in, that was it. It was like putting the dick on. And then it could be clean. There was something about blood being a reminder of femininity.[47]

For Vada, Busy, Darlene, and Brandon, prior to menstruation, their biology was insufficient to deter them from shunning a stereotyped feminine identity. At menarche, however, menstrual blood forced them to confront biology and in Brandon's case, actually *exposed* his biological sex. The same kind of exposure narrative transpired in the Afghan film *Osama* (2003), where the female title character (Marina Golbahari) had been dressing up as a boy so that she could work to support her impoverished family. Her first period, running down her bare legs, exposed her biological sex to the men around her. This theme was again apparent in *Pitch Black* (2000): the young "boy" Jack (Rhiana Griffith) was exposed as a girl when it was discovered that the creatures they were running from could follow the group by tracking the scent of Jack's period.

First Period Anticlimax

Earlier in this chapter, I discussed the scene from the *7th Heaven* episode when—in the lead up to Lucy's first period—Lucy's mother Annie had to explain to her husband Eric that menstruation wasn't always as wonderful as he assumed. I also discussed the scene from *Ready or Not* when Busy told her not-yet-menstruating friend Amanda that menstruation was "nothing. It's gross." Eric and Amanda evidently held lofty—and potentially naïve—ideas about menstruation which, while perhaps working to challenge the dominant cultural perception of menstruation as horrible, nonetheless established it as something promising fantastic things for a girl, things which may never eventuate. While anger, disappointment, and feelings of being blindsided may seem like obvious responses to menarche, the idea that the *reality* of menarche is often anticlimactic and *not* life-changing is certainly worth exploring. Sociologist Holly Devor in her discussion of puberty offered a brief explanation of the menarche anticlimax:

> The contours of their bodies have usually already begun to change in obvious ways and thus the more private event of menarche is often somewhat anticlimactic.[48]

De Beauvoir similarly spotlighted this issue, noting that the newly menstruating girl is "soon disappointed because she sees that she has not gained any privilege and that life follows its normal course."[49] The girl from Orringer and Gahagan's study on menstruation quoted earlier expressed discontent when she explained that she "didn't feel any different at all, which I guess was a disappointment to me."[50] A woman, in research on experiences of menstruation in Malaysia, similarly explained: "It didn't change my life. I knew that I was going to get that every month. But I didn't feel like, oh I'm a woman now."[51] In Aliza Shvarts's recollections of her first period, she too expressed the same sentiments:

> I got on the school bus to go home, excited to tell my mother the news. I expected a lot from that talk. I expected secrets to be revealed, meanings to be exposed, and to emerge somehow closer to my mother and her adult world. . . .

But about five or ten minutes into it, her then-boyfriend got home from work and walked into the bedroom. She looked at me, handed me the package, and nothing more was said.[52]

The idea of menarche being anticlimactic is evident throughout popular culture. In Amalie Howard's young adult novel *Bloodspell*, for example, the main character—Victoria—specifically identified her menarche as an anticlimax: "And now that it was here, Victoria felt nothing, just a peculiar sense of anticlimax."[53] In Philip McLaren's novel *Scream Black Murder*, Lisa's menarche was remembered similarly: "[m]any of her friends already had theirs; it was something of an anticlimax when she awoke early to find she was lying on a red, wet spot."[54] The same idea was evident in a menarche vignette quoted in psychoanalyst Joyce McFadden's book on parenting:

> I had my first period on New Year's Day of 1979. I was thirteen. I admit it was anticlimactic. It did not bring with it my long hoped for breasts. It was a bit of a smear on a tissue for a couple of days and that was about it.[55]

Researchers note that at menarche depression in girls becomes twice as prevalent as in boys, whereas *prior* to menarche the rates for both sexes are similar.[56] The *why* of this statistic remains contentious,[57] although psychoanalyst Helene Deutsch offered one explanation: that girls can become significantly perturbed when they are not miraculously changed by their first period.[58] Certainly such a reading is relevant to interpreting Busy and Darlene's reactions: on *Ready or Not*, during Busy's phone conversation with her friend Amanda, Amanda said, "You're a woman now. You can have a baby," and Busy responded, "Yeah right." In *Roseanne* when Darlene moaned, "Oh God, why me?," Roseanne responded, "'Cos you're lucky," and Darlene cynically remarked, "Right." For Busy and Darlene, the benefits of menstruation—like fertility—seemed like distant, abstract concepts; all they knew was an immediate life change, burden, and inconvenience.

Depression and feelings of anticlimax, of course, are amplified by certain triggers. In Shvart's description, her mother's distraction contributed: her mother failed to turn the event into something spectacular. De Beauvoir relayed a case history of a girl who similarly experienced an anticlimax based on her mother's reaction:

> as soon as I was indisposed, I ran joyfully to my mother, who was still sleeping, and I woke her up, shouting, "Mother, I have it!" "And this is why you wake me up?" she managed to say in response.[59]

In circumstances where the mother isn't present at all, these feelings can exacerbate. In author Hope Edelman's work on motherless daughters, for example, she wrote, "[w]ithout a mother in the home, a daughter's first menstruation often represents little more than an anticlimactic and disappointing day."[60] While motherless, the day of Vada's menarche was hardly anticlimactic. A better example is the anti-climax of Blossom's first period on *Blossom*. Her mother was absent throughout the series, and so her solo menarche experience—capped by attempting to purchase menstrual products on her own—jarringly contrasted with the "Women's Day" celebration that she had fondly recalled from *The Cosby Show*. Blossom's idealization, of course, is in line with case studies apparent in academic literature. Edelman discussed Helen, a forty-nine-year-old woman who imagined that had her mother been alive for her first period she "would have turned the event into cause for mutual celebration,"[61] a reaction similar to Blossom's fantasies. Such ideas relate well to gender norms as addressed in the next section; each girl held expectations that her mother would act "perfectly," thus illustrating how a girl's interpretation of her menarche is at least somewhat predicated on the degree to which her mother acted appropriately (read: stereotypically) *maternal.*

MENSTRUATION AND GENDER NORMS

More specific than menstruation being a stepping stone to adulthood is it being a gateway to *womanhood*. Inherent in many of the responses to menarche discussed throughout this chapter are the varying degrees of distress felt by girls regarding the expectations of womanhood. While of course, what it means to be a woman *in practice* is complicated and beyond the scope of this chapter, the onset of menstruation is frequently presented as something that brings about very gendered expectations. In this section I explore the implied or inferred mandate that menstruation necessitates femininity and that at menarche, tomboy behaviors—deemed in contrast to femininity—need to be abandoned in favor of more stereotypically female pursuits.

Older advice on menstruation certainly argued for the cessation of non-feminine activities at menarche. In a 1901 volume on the topic, for example, the authors contended:

> The romping tomboy becomes a shy and self-conscious maiden, with finer tastes and emotional fancies. The subtle forces of sex change the girl's soul into the woman's.[62]

Similar ideas were espoused in psychiatrist Maj-Britt Rosenbaum's more recent work on female adolescence where she contended that "the onset of menstruation frequently brings about a rather rapid swing from the tomboy role. . . . It is as if the experience of menstruation fortifies the feelings of feminine identity."[63] Certainly in qualitative work on menstruation, the assumption that boyish practices should be abandoned at menarche is well documented. In Orringer and Gahagan's research, the authors quoted an eighteen-year-old girl who discussed her first period:

> [My mom] was like, "Now you're like a teenager now that you started your period. Now you gotta act like one, dress like one. Can't go hanging around with the boys no more."[64]

Darlene, quoted in Lee's research, reported receiving similar advice: "I was told by mother that I was a lady now, so that I had to act like one, and not play with the boys anymore."[65] The mothers' advice in these two examples can be interpreted as reflecting a fear that with a daughter's physical maturing may come sexual activity and pregnancy risk: something addressed in the next section. Another reading is that menstruation marks the onset of girls needing to stop *acting* like boys; to stop being tomboys, and to embrace ladylike behavior. In the above examples, it is quite clear that specific gender norms were being imposed *by mothers*. Lee discussed this idea contending that "[m]others often socialize their daughters into the same restrictions associated with femininity that they have endured."[66] Of course, as Lee explained, even in cases where mothers told positive stories to their daughters about menstruation, the consequences were often still the same:

> The values of the culture are strong; children are not raised in a vacuum and quickly internalize the negative messages associated with menstruation.[67]

Such ideas coincide with research discussed earlier where, even in cases where girls received education on menstruation prior to their menarche, they still often exhibited surprise and dismay at their first period; proof that by the time a first period arrives, they have already internalized our culture's persuasive negative messages. Certainly ideas about eschewing sport and tomboy behavior at menarche exist in the literature even without reference to mothers. Barbara, also quoted in Lee's study, had been an athlete in her adolescence and expressed sentiments similar to Vada, Busy, and Darlene at her first period:

> Yeah, I think it was in the sense that it [her menarche] separated me from the boys, and so I felt like I was going to have to dress up and just drop sports by the wayside because now it was like some way of being notified that well, you have had your fun as a tomboy but it is time to really do what you are "supposed" to do.[68]

Barbara didn't mention her mother, and instead referenced the views of culture more broadly. Women's internalization of culture is something that psychologist Dana Crowley Jack describes as the "over-eye," a term explaining the judgmental voice in women's heads that criticizes action:

> The Over-Eye carries a decidedly patriarchal flavor, both in its collective viewpoint about what is "good" and "right" for a woman and in its willingness to condemn her feelings when they depart from expected "shoulds."[69]

The internalization of negative views about menstruation is certainly one way to analyze Vada, Busy, and Darlene's reactions to their menarche: the suggestion of abandoning their tomboy practices was not something imposed by their mothers at all, but rather was something they seemed to intuitively *know*. Where these ideas emanated from for Vada was unclear, but for Busy her understanding of womanhood appeared gleaned from observing her mother who had modeled for her a hard-done-by homemaker. For Darlene, her sister Becky had presented to her a very feminine kind of womanhood. Busy and Darlene each held fixed and undesirable perceptions of what womanhood meant, which for them necessitated abandoning the tomboy behavior they had once enjoyed.

While Vada, Busy, and Darlene clearly exhibited behavior congruent with being influenced by Jack's over-eye, interestingly, such behavior was in fact only fleeting and each girl in fact *returned* to the swashbuckling that she assumed had to be abandoned. This relates to the research discussed earlier regarding the fleeting nature of initial reactions to menarche. It similarly illustrates psychologist Louise Bates Ames's work on human development, where she wrote that while girls initially assume that menstruation will inhibit their activities, that "resentment is usually a passing emotion, and most girls do not curtail their participation in sports."[70] Both off screen and on, while menstruation may initially be shocking and assumed to dramatically—and negatively—affect life, this doesn't necessarily transpire in the long term.

While Vada, Busy, and Darlene were each presented as heterosexual characters, they didn't possess stereotypical feminine identities and each viewed menstruation as something which *imposed* gender on them. Certainly, even if the hard-done-by mother or feminine identities that they had witnessed were eschewed, simply by becoming menstruators, the girls were each delivered a mandate to pay more attention to their bodies and their appearance and participate in the self-surveillance discussed in chapter 1; a reality that may also be considered to contribute to their negative sentiments. Vada, Busy, and Darlene and especially Brandon's reactions in these scenes also relate well to research on lesbians and transsexuals, some who report to have felt extremely disconnected from a feminine identity and who had a particularly traumatic time with menstruation because they associated it with heterosexuality and pregnancy.[71] Sexologist Richard von Krafft-Ebing, for example, presented a case study of transsexual "S" who very much illustrated these ideas: "S. had a horror of speaking of menstruation; that it was a thing repugnant to her masculine consciousness and feeling."[72]

MENSTRUATION AND LOVE GAMES

In an episode of the sitcom *Cheers* (1982–1993), Rebecca (Kirstie Alley) described a "dream date" which involved dinner and a beach walk culminating in sex. When asked when she first started fantasizing about the date, Rebecca admitted that it was on day one of puberty. In this comment, Rebecca references the idea of puberty often instigating feelings of a romantic, if not *sexual* nature. While obviously a gateway to womanhood in the broadest sense, menarche is also sometimes presented on screen as the instigator for adult, romantic feelings: as writer Krista Madsen noted, for her, menarche was "a progression toward romance and motherhood, maturity and death."[73] On screen first periods are frequently presented within narratives that explore other firsts including first kisses and first loves. In *My Girl*, for example, the film explored Vada's first period but also her first crush and first kiss.

On one level menstruation is only one aspect of the broader phenomena of puberty whereby any number of physical, hormonal and psychological changes occur; it seems therefore perfectly logical that menstruating girls become more cognizant of their sexuality at this time:

> The girl who reaches menarche early will find herself losing interest in the types of things her immature peers are interested in and her mind will turn to romantic thoughts more often.[74]

Particularly in popular culture aimed at youth markets, it makes sense that menarche narratives would appear in storylines exploring other adolescent milestones including first forays into love and romance. Karen Houppert in her book *The Curse*, for example, spotlighted this idea in her analysis of the *Diary of Anne Frank* where she identified that Frank's descriptions about sex and sexual feelings only happened *after* she began menstruating.[75] In *Towelhead* (2007), Jasira (Summer Bishil) got her first period and *then* developed an obsession with her older male neighbor. In *Blue Lagoon* and *Return to the Blue Lagoon* the female protagonists got their first period and only *then* developed romantic feelings for their island companion. In *My Girl*, Vada got her first period, and *then* developed an all-encompassing crush on her English teacher. In *I Could Never Be Your Woman*, daughter Izzie divulged her first period to her mother and then said, "Let the games begin." For Izzie, while menstruation indeed marked the beginning of adulthood, of greater importance was its being the catalyst for adult games, including love.

Another explanation for the redirection of attention to romance is the social expectations of heterosexual performance: now that a girl has become a woman in the physical sense, culture insists that she fulfills her obligations as a sexual woman. I have written previously, for example, about the cultural "fixation with heterosexual coupling":

> Advertising, cinema, travel packages, and recipes, for example, are each obsessed with the couple: it often appears mandatory that *everyone* pair off, two by two, all headed for the Ark.[76]

Sociologist Laurel Richardson similarly drew attention to "the old and deep cultural imperative" that insists that a woman should be in a relationship with a man in order to be perceived as regular, normal, and attractive.[77] For a girl to reach sexual maturity, there is an expectation that she quickly direct her attention to the pursuits expected of women, including a preoccupation with the opposite sex. While for some girls like Izzie, the love "games" will be readily embraced, for characters like Busy, Darlene, and Vada these games are interpreted as part of a very gendered identity that they have not yet decided they want to embrace. It should of course be noted that these ideas are indicative of the many confusing—and often contradictory—sexual mores apparent in our culture. Our culture voraciously promotes the idea that girls should like boys and be preoccupied with the idea of coupledom, but simultaneously demonizes girls sexually expressing themselves[78] and views menstruation as the instigator for the most dangerous aspect of female identity: sexuality.

This chapter has highlighted a number of trends in menstrual portrayals which showcase many themes existing in previous research about menstruation, notably the persistence of negative portrayals, the preoccupation with portraying menstruation as something associated with the end of childhood, and as something embarrassing and lifestyle restricting. While of course it is difficult to ascertain the extent to which negative menstruation messages affect women's own perception of their periods—as noted in chapter 1, the attitudes of mothers, friends, older sisters, grandmothers or aunts also likely play a part[79]—the role of screen portrayals can be assumed to have *some* impact. Limiting the impact of negative menstruation messages, however, is not just the real-life and potentially more positive attitudes of friends and family, but *also* media that dare to present a very different message. Also discussed in this chapter—and something infrequently explored in academic literature—are positive portrayals of menstruation whereby it is something *celebrated* by family and friends. Such presentations not only help mitigate the common negative messages, but also create capacity for attitude change and acceptance of this normal bodily function.

In this chapter I have reviewed representations of first periods functioning as a gateway to womanhood in both positive but more commonly *negative* ways. In chapter 3 I continue the exploration of negative representations, focusing on menstruation portrayed as a curse, examining portrayals which not only present it as inconvenient—as introduced in this chapter—but as something that can unleash broader catastrophe.

NOTES

1. See Kathy E. Ferguson, *The Man Question: Visions of Subjectivity in Feminist Theory* (Berkeley: University of California Press, 1993); David Adams Leeming and Jake Page, *The Mythology of Native North America* (Norman: University of Oklahoma Press, 1998); Curtis O. Byer, Louis W. Shainberg, and Grace Galliano, *Dimensions of Human Sexuality* (Boston: McGraw-Hill, 1999); Arnold Van Gennep, *The Rites of Passage* (London: Routledge, 2004).

2. On this issue, gender researcher Chris Bobel wrote: "When it comes to menstruation, the fascination seems to be with faraway people in another time—their bizarre customs, their menstrual huts, their menarche rituals" (Chris Bobel, *New Blood: Third-Wave Feminism and the Politics of Menstruation* (New Brunswick, NJ: Rutgers University Press, 2010), 30).

3. See, for example, a discussion of the menstruation ritual of indigenous Australians in Rita M. Gross, *A Garland of Feminist Reflections: Forty Years of Religious Exploration* (Berkeley: University of California Press, 2009); of Hindus in Vijaya Rettakudi Naharajan, "Threshold designs, forehead dots, and menstruation rituals: Exploring time and space in Tamil Kolams," in *Women's Lives, Women's Rituals in the Hindu Tradition*, ed. Tracy Pintchman (New York: Oxford University Press, 2007); and of Panamanians in James Howe, *The Kuna Gathering: Contemporary Village Politics in Panama* (Tucson: Fenestra Books, 2002).

4. Laura Fingerson, *Girls in Power: Gender, Body and Menstruation in Adolescence* (Albany: State University of New York Press, 2006), 53.

5. Laura Fingerson, *Girls in Power: Gender, Body and Menstruation in Adolescence* (Albany: State University of New York Press, 2006), 96.

6. See, for example Roseanne Barr, "And I Should Know," *New York*, May 15, 2011, nymag.com/arts/tv/upfronts/2011/roseanne-barr-2011-5/ (accessed November 6, 2011).

7. See Will Glennon, *200 Ways to Raise a Girl's Self-Esteem* (Boston: Conari Press, 1999), 41; Shana Nichols, Gina Marie Moravcik, and Samara Pulver Tetenbaum, *Girls Growing Up on the Autism Spectrum* (London: Jessica Kingsley Publishers, 2009), 99–101.

8. A similar mocking of new-age menstruation rituals occurred in an episode of the sitcom *The Office* (2005–). In one episode, Dwight (Rainn Wilson) facetiously commented: "I wish I could menstruate. If I could menstruate, I wouldn't have to deal with idiotic *calendars* anymore. I'd just be able to count down from my previous cycle. Plus I'd be more in tune with the moon and the tides."

9. Erica Jong, "Fear of Fourteen, 1991," in *My Little Red Book,* ed. Rachel Kauder Nalebuff (New York: Twelve, 2009), 17.

10. Natalie Angier, *Woman: An Intimate Geography* (New York: Random House, 1999), 105.

11. In Laura Fingerson, *Girls in Power: Gender, Body and Menstruation in Adolescence* (Albany: State University of New York Press, 2006), 89.

12. Nancy L. Caruso, "A Jealous Vajayjay, 1981," in *My Little Red Book*, ed. Rachel Kauder Nalebuff (New York: Twelve, 2009), 35.

13. Emily Martin, *The Woman in the Body: A Cultural Analysis of Reproduction* (Boston: Beacon, 1987).

14. Elizabeth Siciliano, "Silence, 1930s," in *My Little Red Book*, ed. Rachel Kauder Nalebuff (New York: Twelve, 2009), 34.

15. See, for example, Sharon W. Tiffany and Kathleen J. Adams, *The Wild Woman: An Inquiry into the Anthropology of an Idea* (Cambridge, MA: Schenkman, 1985); Germaine Greer, *The Whole Woman* (New York: Knopf, 1999); SuEllen Hamkins and Renée Schultz, *The Mother-Daughter Project* (New York: Hudson Street Press, 2007).

16. Anne Clinard Barnhill, *At Home in the Land of Oz: My Sister, Autism and Me* (Philadelphia, PA: Jessica Kingsley Publishers, 2007), 48.

17. Gregory Woods, "Fantasy Islands: Popular Topographies of Marooned Masculinity," in *Mapping Desire*, ed. David Bell and Gill Valentine (London: Routledge, 1995), 120.

18. Patty Marx, "Can I Just Skip This Period? 1971," in *My Little Red Book*, ed. Rachel Kauder Nalebuff (New York: Twelve, 2009), 33.

19. Ellen Devine, "Hot Dog on a String, 1993," in *My Little Red Book*, ed. Rachel Kauder Nalebuff (New York: Twelve, 2009), 51.

20. Clara Thompson and Maurice R. Green, *Interpersonal Psychoanalysis: The Selected Papers of Clara M. Thompson* (New York: Basic Books, 1964), 234.

21. Simone de Beauvoir, *The Second Sex* (London: Vintage, 2011), 337.

22. Hilary C. Maddux, *Menstruation* (New Canaan, CT: Tobey, 1975), 12.

23. Janet L. Root, *Women's Perceptions of the Experience of Menstruation*, unpublished PhD Dissertation (Salt Lake City: University of Utah, 1992).

24. Germaine, Greer, *The Female Eunuch* (London: Paladin, 1971), 50. [My emphasis.]

25. Jennifer Baumgardner, "Glamorous, but Not for Long, 1981," in *My Little Red Book*, ed. Rachel Kauder Nalebuff (New York: Twelve, 2009), 65.

26. Michael Mouland, *The Complete Idiot's Guide to Camping and Hiking* (Indianapolis: Alpha Books, 2000), 104.

27. The issue of the expense of menstrual products was humorously referred to in the comedy film *Dirty Love* (2005). Rebecca (Jenny McCarthy) couldn't afford tampons so she had to purchase maxi-pads, something presented as humiliating.

28. Nancy Lee Teaff and Kim Wright Wiley, *Perimenopause: Preparing for the Change* (New York: Random House, 1999), 1.

29. Nancy F. Woods, Gretchen K. Dery, and Ada Most, "Recollections of menarche, current menstrual attitudes, and perimenstrual symptoms," *Psychosomatic Medicine* 44, no. 3 (1982): 285–293.

30. Lara Freidenfelds, *The Modern Period: Menstruation in Twentieth-Century America* (Baltimore: The Johns Hopkins University Press, 2009), 64.

31. A. Schulz, *Das Körperbild weiblicher Jugendlicher und seine Auswirkungen auf. Erleben und Verhalten. [Body Image of Female Adolescents and Its Impact]*. (Bonn: Friedrich-Wilhelms-Universitat, 1991).

32. Feminist philosopher Simone de Beauvoir in her seminal text *The Second Sex* wrote: "whether or not the child has been warned, the event always appears repugnant and humiliating" (Simone de Beauvoir, *The Second Sex* (London: Vintage, 2011), 334.

33. Mary Lynn Stewart, "Sex education and sexual initiation of bourgeois French girls, 1880–1930," in *Secret Gardens, Satanic Mills: Placing Girls in European History, 1750–1960*, ed. Mary Jo Maynes, Birgitte Søland, and Christina Benninghaus (Bloomington: Indiana University Press, 2005). In comedian Tina Fey's memoir *Bossypants*, she reflected on her own menarche, recalling that even though her mother had given her the Modess box with the instructional flyers—and even though she had actually *read* the material—when her period came she was nonetheless thoroughly shocked: nothing she had read actually mentioned that she would *bleed*. (Tina Fey, *Bossypants* (New York: Little, Brown, 2011)). This same idea was referred to in Karen Houppert's book *The Curse*, where she wrote about a 1934 Sears catalog: the catalog boasted "eighteen different kinds of "sanitary" products, yet never once says what they're for" (Karen Houppert, *The Curse: Confronting the Last Unmentionable Taboo: Menstruation* (New York: Farrar, Straus and Giroux, 1999), 15).

34. Janet Lee, "Menarche and the (Hetero)sexualization of the Female Body," in *The Politics of Women's Bodies: Sexuality, Appearance, and Behavior*, ed. Rose Weitz (New York: Oxford University Press, 1998), 91. [My emphasis.]

35. Suzan Shutan, "Burning Secret, 1996," in *My Little Red Book*, ed. Rachel Kauder Nalebuff (New York: Twelve, 2009), 15.

36. Michele Jaffe, "Going to X-tremes, 1982," in *My Little Red Book*, ed. Rachel Kauder Nalebuff (New York: Twelve, 2009), 26.

37. In Fingerson's research, for example, she wrote "By high school, menstruation has moved beyond individual embarrassment" (Laura Fingerson, *Girls in Power: Gender, Body and Menstruation in Adolescence* (Albany: State University of New York Press, 2006), 94). The fleeting nature of first responses to menstruation is also discussed in: Julia A. Graber and Jeanne Brooks-Gunn, "Adolescent girls' sexual development," in *Handbook of Women's Sexual and Reproductive Health*, ed. Gina M. Wingood and Ralph J. DiClemente (New York: Kluwer Academic, 2002).

38. Natalie Angier, *Woman: An Intimate Geography* (New York: Random House, 1999), 105.

39. Kelly Orringer and Sheila Gahagan, "Adolescent girls define menstruation: A multiethnic exploratory study," *Health Care for Women International* 31 (2010): 831–847.

40. Patricia A. Boyd, "Blood on the Tracks, 1972," in *My Little Red Book*, ed. Rachel Kauder Nalebuff (New York: Twelve, 2009), 58.

41. Mary McGee Williams and Irene Kane, *On Becoming a Woman* (New York: Dell, 1959), 20.

42. Elissa Stein and Susan Kim, *Flow: The Cultural Story of Menstruation* (New York: St Martin's Griffin, 2009), 169. [My emphasis.]

43. Hendrika C. Freud, *Electra vs Oedipus: The Drama of the Mother-Daughter Relationship*. [Translated by Marjolijn de Jager.] (New York: Routledge, 2011).

44. Doris Lessing, *The Golden Notebook* (New York: Simon and Schuster, 1962), 290.

45. Lynn Whisnant and Leonard Zegans, "A study of attitudes toward menarche in white middle-class American adolescent girls," *American Journal of Psychiatry* 132 (1975): 809–820.

46. Karen Horney, "Premenstrual tension," in *Feminine Psychology* (New York: W. W. Norton, 1967).

47. In Museum of the Moving Image, "A Pinewood Dialogue With Kimberly Peirce." June 2, 2002, www.movingimagesource.us/files/dialogues/2/54906_programs_transcript_html_246.htm (accessed July 14, 2011).

48. Holly Devor, *FTM: Female-to-Male Transsexuals in Society* (Bloomington, IN: Indiana University Press, 1997, 182).

49. Simone de Beauvoir, *The Second Sex* (London: Vintage, 2011), 337.

50. Kelly Orringer and Sheila Gahagan, "Adolescent girls define menstruation: A multiethnic exploratory study," *Health Care for Women International* 31 (2010): 831–847, 840.

51. Popho E.S. Bark-Yi, *Body That Bleeds: Menstrual Politics in Mala*ysia (Petaling Jaya, Selanor: Strategic Information and Research Development Centre, 2007), 126.

52. Shvarts, Aliza, "The Ming Period, 1999," in *My Little Red Book*, ed. Rachel Kauder Nalebuff (New York: Twelve, 2009), 44.

53. Amalie Howard, *Bloodspell* (Minneapolis, MN: Langdon Street Press, 2011), 8.

54. Philip McLaren, *Scream Black Murder (*Sydney: HarperCollins, 1995), 93.

55. In Joyce T. McFadden, *Your Daughter's Bedroom: Insights for Raising Confident Women* (New York: Palgrave Macmillan, 2011), 67.

56. Raymond J. De Paulo and Leslie Alan Horvitz, *Understanding Depression: What We Know and What You Can Do About It* (New York: Wiley, 2002), 41.

57. One interpretation is that menstruation creates extra work and necessitates that girls pay more attention to their appearance than they had previously had to do; that like the self-surveillance discussed in chapter 1, young girls may feel depressed having these womanly responsibilities when they still viewed themselves as kids. Another reading is the shame which menarche brings; something discussed by feminist philosopher Simone de Beauvoir in her

seminal text *The Second Sex*: "Sometimes, in prepuberty preceding the arrival of her period, the girl does not yet feel disgust for her body... Her first period exposes this meaning and feelings of shame appear" (Simone de Beauvoir, *The Second Sex* (London: Vintage, 2011), 334.

58. Helene Deutsch, *The Psychology of Women: A Psychoanalytic Interpretation*, volume 2 (New York: Grune and Stratton, 1945).

59. In Simone de Beauvoir, *The Second Sex* (London: Vintage, 2011), 338.

60. Hope Edelman, *Motherless Daughters: The Legacy of Loss* (Cambridge, MA: Da Capo Press, 2006), 218.

61. Hope Edelman, *Motherless Daughters: The Legacy of Loss* (Cambridge, MA: Da Capo Press, 2006), 219.

62. Chalmers Watson, *Encyclopaedia Medica*, volume 8 (New York: Longmans, Green & Co, 1901), 2.

63. Maj-Britt Rosenbaum, "The Changing Body Image of the Adolescent Girl," in *Female Adolescent Development*, ed. Max Sugar (New York: Brunner-Mazel, 1993), 71.

64. Kelly Orringer and Sheila Gahagan, "Adolescent girls define menstruation: A multiethnic exploratory study," *Health Care for Women International* 31 (2010): 831–847, 840.

65. In Janet Lee, "Menarche and the (Hetero)sexualization of the Female Body," in *The Politics of Women's Bodies: Sexuality, Appearance, and Behavior*, ed. Rose Weitz (New York: Oxford University Press, 1998), 91.

66. Janet Lee, "Menarche and the (Hetero)sexualization of the Female Body," in *The Politics of Women's Bodies: Sexuality, Appearance, and Behavior*, ed. Rose Weitz (New York: Oxford University Press, 1998), 96.

67. Janet Lee, "Menarche and the (Hetero)sexualization of the Female Body," in *The Politics of Women's Bodies: Sexuality, Appearance, and Behavior*, ed. Rose Weitz (New York: Oxford University Press, 1998), 96. These ideas coincide with other research which indicates that regardless of the amount of information a girl has prior to menstruation, that menarche is still often traumatic (Helene Deutsch, *The Psychology of Women: A Psychoanalytic Interpretation, Volume 1* (New York: Grune and Stratton, 1945)).

68. In Janet Lee, "Menarche and the (Hetero)sexualization of the Female Body," in *The Politics of Women's Bodies: Sexuality, Appearance, and Behavior*, ed. Rose Weitz (New York: Oxford University Press, 1998), 90.

69. Dana Crowley Jack, *Silencing the Self* (Cambridge, MA: Harvard University Press, 1991), 94.

70. Louise Bates Ames, *Your Ten-to-Fourteen-Year-Old* (New York: Dell Publishing, 1989), 118.

71. As a woman in health researcher Shirley Lee's study on menstruation expressed: "I was not put on this earth to reproduce. That annoys me. Associating women with reproduction only" (In Shirley Lee, "Health and sickness: The meaning of menstruation and premenstrual syndrome in women's lives," *Sex Roles* 46, no. 1 (2002): 27–35, 30.

72. Richard von Krafft-Ebing, "Selections from Psychopathia Sexualis with Special Reference to Contrary Sexual Instinct: A Medico-Legal Study," in *The Transgender Studies Reader*, ed. Susan Stryker and Stephen Whittle (New York: Routledge, 2006), 25.

73. Krista Madsen, "Ink blots and milk spots," in *My Little Red Book*, ed. Rachel Kauder Nalebuff (New York: Twelve, 2009), 3.

74. Nan Bahr and Donna Pendergast, *The Millennial Adolescent* (Camberwell, Victoria: ACER Press, 2007), 87.

75. Karen Houppert, *The Curse: Confronting the Last Unmentionable Taboo: Menstruation* (New York: Farrar, Straus and Giroux, 1999).

76. Lauren Rosewarne, *Cheating on the Sisterhood: Infidelity and Feminism* (Santa Barbara, CA: Praeger, 2007), 12.

77. Laurel Richardson, *The New Other Woman* (New York: Free Press, 1985), 4.

78. Lauren Rosewarne, "The wilding of women: Why the media should ease up on girls," *The Conversation*, July 5, 2011, theconversation.edu.au/the-wilding-of-women-why-the-media-should-ease-up-on-girls-2114 (accessed October 26, 2011).

79. Psychotherapist JoAnn Loulan and Bonnie Worthen, for example, argued that "How we feel about it [menstruation] depends on what our mothers, friends, older sisters, grandmothers or aunts have said" (JoAnn Loulan and Bonnie Worthen, *Period: A Girl's Guide* (Minnetonka, MN: Book Peddlers, 2001), 51).

Chapter Three

The Curse of Eve

Cramped Stomachs and Cramped Lifestyles

The supposed curse of menstruation manifests on screen variously from being portrayed as a mere inconvenience that encroaches on sport and sex right through to its materializing as supernatural powers involving prophecy and demonic possession. In this chapter I examine a range of negative presentations of menstruation which depict it as something which makes the lives of women, as well as men, miserable.

THE CURIOSITY OF THE CURSE

In his research on deviance, sociologist John Curra noted that in certain cultures men found something enviable in "[w]omen's ability to produce blood that neither appreciably weakened nor killed them."[1] While envy might exist in some cultures, in others—particularly in the West—this biological "mystery" is generally viewed as less enigmatic and more as suspicious. In social researchers Spring Cooper and Patricia Koch's study on girls' perceptions of menstruation, participants listed words including "fishy" to describe it. While the girls did not explain their use of the word—and while we might speculate that they were referencing the supposed *smell* of vaginas and menstrual blood[2] (chapter 4)—it is worthwhile noting that the word *fishy* is also frequently used to describe something that appears suspicious or untrustworthy: "seeming dishonest or false. *There's something fishy going on.*"[3] The idea of the menstruating woman as fishy and untrustworthy is certainly a common screen presentation.

In the animated film *South Park: Bigger, Longer and Uncut* (1999), the character Mr. Garrison claimed, "I just don't trust anything that bleeds for five days and doesn't die." In *Keys to Tulsa* (1996), Keith (Michael Rooker) argued the same idea: "Never trust anything that bleeds for five days and doesn't die." Chad (Aaron Eckhart) in *In The Company of Men* (1997) suggested: "Never trust anything that can bleed for a week and not die." Marcia, a teenager quoted in sociologist Laura Fingerson's book on menstruation, claimed that her brother "doesn't trust anything that bleeds for seven days and doesn't die."[4] Each variation of the quote boasts the same misogynist undercurrent rendering the menstruator as abject and presenting menstruation as something not only abhorrent but potentially non-human.[5] In the same way that zombies are loathed and feared because they won't die, the (obviously hyperbolic) claim behind these quotes is that a woman's ability to bleed and not die is somehow evil, wrong, or *fishy*. These quotes, while offensive, are comparatively innocuous versions of narratives which present the menstruator as abject, a presentation discussed throughout this chapter. The idea of women portrayed as other and as the embodiment of original sin is an extensively theorized idea. Writer Camille Paglia, for example, described menstrual blood as "the stain, the birthmark of original sin,"[6] and numerous female respondents in pediatricians Kelly Orringer and Sheila Gahagan's research similarly cited the "Curse of Eve" in their explanations of menstruation.[7] Dating back to the biblical story of Eve using her feminine wiles to tempt Adam, the idea of women—of *female sexuality*—as being evil—or at least instigating evil consequences—has a very long history. As criminologist Otto Pollak wrote: "[w]omen disguise sexual response, fake orgasms, conceal their menstruation . . . *women are trained in deception.*"[8] Frequently blamed for men's extramarital affairs, blamed for their own rapes and their own objectification, female sexuality has long been hounded by dark-side concepts associated with temptation and sin; it is therefore unsurprising that on-screen portrayals of periods frequently reference long-standing misogynist ideas about one of the most *female* biological functions.

While the "Curse of Eve" may never have appeared in the bible,[9] references to this idea are well established on screen. In *My Louisiana Sky* (2001), when Tiger Ann (Kelsey Keel) got her first period, her grandmother Jewel (Shirley Knight) lamented, "You got the curse." In an episode of the cartoon sitcom *King of the Hill* (1997–2010), when Bobby's girlfriend Connie got her first period, Bobby's friend Joseph commiserated, "It's all over, Bobby. I heard that when girls get the curse, they only go out with hairy high school guys with cars." In an episode of the sitcom *The Golden Girls* (1985–1992), Blanche (Rue McClanahan) reflected on her menarche, referencing this same curse idea:

> My entire thirteenth year, I slept with the lights on. I knew there was a witch behind every wisteria. I stayed home Halloween. I was a wreck. But the year went by and no curse. Another year went by. No curse.

Blanche, in fact, actually had *already* been having her period for two years by the time her mother took her to the doctor to query the curse's absence; Blanche had simply never made the connection between her periods and the curse that she had been warned about.

Thinking of menstruation as something intrinsically bad and curse-like is certainly well documented in academic literature: researchers have documented elaborate myths, attributing to it all kinds of powers from souring milk, tarnishing mirrors through to destroying crops.[10] While in contemporary Western culture there is an acceptance that menstruation doesn't actually bestow any of these special powers, on screen it is nonetheless routinely portrayed as not only powerful, but able to incite all manner of awful happenings: some relatively innocuous—like inhibiting desired activities—right through to it functioning as a Pandora's box and unleashing turmoil.

NEGATIVE EFFECTS ON LIFE PARTICIPATION

In chapter 2, I discussed menstruation being interpreted by girls as unfair and as something which inhibits freedom. In this section, I expand on this idea, exploring the smaller-scale manifestations of the supposed menstrual curse as evidenced through its on-screen presentation as something negatively impacting on women's participation in sport and sex.

Menstruation and Sports

In an episode of the television drama series *Parenthood* (2010–), during a family football match, Crosby (Dax Shepard) teased his brother-in-law saying, "Are you allowed to play in your cycle?" In another episode, during a basketball match, Crosby asked his brother whether he had menstrual cramps. On an episode of *Californication* (2007–), during an altercation between Charlie (Evan Handler) and Peter Fonda (playing himself), Peter taunted Charlie, "Forget to take your Pamprin this morning?" Crosby and Peter's barbs in these scenes elicit humor from the emasculating idea of a man having a period (further discussed in chapter 4), but most relevant for this section, reference the many traditional restrictions imposed on women during their periods, the prohibition on physical activity being one with a particularly long history. Introduced in chapter 2 was the idea of menstruation being interpreted—notably by first-time menstruators—as something able to curtail participation in sport. In the previous chapter I presented this idea in the context of the ladylike expectations of menstruating women and of sport being construed as masculine and thus needing to be ceased after menarche. In this section I am less concerned with the gendered connotations of sport and more so in the overt physicality of it. Two narrative themes are explored in this section: one, sport's capacity to expose a woman as a bleeder through menstrual leakage, and two, the issue of menstrual cramping and its capacity to inhibit activity; both storylines which are consistently apparent in advertising, the source for most popular allusions to menstruation on screen.

In the 1996 Boston marathon, German runner Uta Pippig was the first woman to cross the finishing line. Crossing the line, Pippig had diarrhea *and* menstrual blood smeared on her thighs. In 2008, paparazzi photographs showed singer Britney Spears wearing fishnet stockings and with what appeared to be a blood-soaked pad at her crotch. In 2010, during a concert in California, teenaged singer Taylor Momsen was photographed wearing blood-stained underwear and with a tampon string visible against her thigh. Pippig, Spears, and Momsen broke social taboos by failing to conceal their menstruation but, most important for this section, became physical incarnations of the fears harbored by women: that a period might leak and that menstruation will be exposed.

Following a scene in *To Sir With Love* (1967) when teacher Mark Thackeray (Sidney Poitier) found a burning sanitary product in his classroom, he reprimanded the girls that he assumed responsible, telling them, "A decent woman keeps certain things private. Only a filthy slut would have done this!" While considerably harsher than we are likely to hear in contemporary narratives, in this scene Mr. Thackeray referred to the very familiar mandate introduced in chapter 1: that menstruation, be it the blood, the smell, and the products associated, *must* be kept private; as psychotherapist Colette Dowling wrote in her book *The Frailty Myth*: "If girls could do nothing else in the world, they were supposed to be able to keep their blood from showing."[11] Just as real blood is always replaced with blue liquid in advertisements, and just as "blood" is rarely spoken aloud in the context of periods and seldom ever seen in public,[12] menstruation continues to be plagued by some notable taboos. While we may no longer insist that menstruating women refrain from baking for fear that they will stop the dough from rising,[13] some myths tarry. While sport may have once been eschewed by menstruating girls because of old-fashioned ideas that doing so was unhealthy[14] or unfeminine, today some girls remain apprehensive about participating—even in the age of widespread tampon usage—because of concerns related to *leakage*.

Communications theorist Elizabeth Kippling noted that approximately one-third of Americans believe that women should restrict physical activity during menstruation, and one-fifth believe that women shouldn't swim or bathe at this time.[15] In a discussion on gender and education, psychologist Margaret Snooks claimed that women are less likely to participate in "vigorous" sports than men.[16] While Snooks didn't identify menstruation as the cause, it is nonetheless worthwhile considering it as a possible explanation.[17] While in this section I focus on activity restriction as specifically identifiable in advertising, allusions to this idea do, of course, also appear in film and television narratives. Upon getting her first period, Vada (Anna Chlumsky) in *My Girl* (1991), for example, vocally declined a suggestion to go swimming. In *Roseanne* (1988–1997), Darlene (Sara Gilbert) tried to discard all of her sporting equipment. In an episode of *The Cosby Show* (1984–1992), mother Clair (Phylicia Rashad) mused about the necessity to properly educate her daughters about menstruation so that they didn't restrict their activity the way that she did: "I will not have my daughter believing that she can't go to the beach, otherwise she'll attract sharks." In an episode of the reality television series *The Real Housewives of Atlanta* (2008–), Kim declined to participate in a scheduled exercise session claiming that she didn't feel like working out because she had her period.

In her book *Fight Like a Girl*, sociologist Megan Seely summarized the pervasive fears surrounding menstruation: "[w]e are bombarded with messages of fear—fear of someone knowing, fear of odor, fear of bloating, fear of leakage, fear of staining, fear of pain, fear, fear, fear."[18] Feminist philosopher Simone de Beauvoir made this same point, noting that young girls' periods are often irregular and thus they are constantly fearful of "dirtying their clothes or their seat; such a possibility makes one live in constant anxiety."[19] Communications theorist Shauna MacDonald illustrated these fears in a discussion about her own participation in martial arts:

> [M]y uniform, by rule of tradition, is blindingly white. And so tournaments, demonstrations, and tests—performances before a predominantly male audience—are filled with a terrorizing fear of the "what if," the "God I hope not," of the period dance I do.[20]

The *My Girl*, *Roseanne, The Cosby Show*, and *The Real Housewives of Atlanta* scenes each made reference to activity restriction. While we may speculate that leakage fears were at the core of these examples, such fears were not explicitly articulated. One place where leakage was indeed named, however, was in the television series *Party of Five* (1994–2000). In the episode when Claudia (Lacey Chabert) got her first period, she didn't want to go to school and the issue of leakage was raised in a conversation with her brothers Charlie (Matthew Fox) and Bailey (Scott Wolf) and her sister Julia (Neve Campbell):

Charlie: Are you afraid of having an accident or something?

Bailey: She's afraid of spilling.

Julia: Staining.

> **Claudia:** Oh God, I'm going to die.

In menstrual product advertising the leakage fear/sport link exists as a permanent and overt narrative theme. In this section I explore allusions to leakage fears and activity restriction as evidenced in menstrual product advertisements: something at the core of a 2012 Kotex advertisement shown in Australia referencing "leakage paranoia," a Libra tampon commercial shown in Australia in the mid-2000s which promised "white skirt confidence," and a 2011 Stayfree "all night white sheet challenge" television campaign used in India, which all explicitly promised to prevent leakage, assumed to be a fear of most women.

In the *Pulling Our Own Strings* anthology of feminist humor, the following joke appeared, providing a 1980s insight into menstrual product advertising, a style which—decades on—seems very familiar:

> A ten-year old boy went to a drugstore with fifty cents to spend. He spent a lot of time looking and finally chose a box of Tampax.
> "Are you *sure* that's what you want?" the druggist asked.
> "You bet!" the boy said. "The box says that with these you can swim, ride, or play tennis, and up to now I haven't been able to do any of those things."[21]

In the episode of the sitcom *King of the Hill* when Connie got her first period, Hank later tried to relay the day's events to his wife, trying hard to avoid saying the word *period*: "You know, that special time in a girl's life . . . with the freshness and all." In *Ten Inch Hero* (2007), when Priestly (Jensen Ackles) walked to the register with a box of tampons for his girlfriend, a teenaged boy heckled him: "Dude, are you having a not so fresh day?" In *Bridesmaids* (2011), Helen's stepson (Matt Bennett) jeered: "I've seen better tennis playing in a tampon commercial." In *Blossom* (1990–1995), when the title character (Mayim Bialik) got her first period, her best friend Six (Jenna von Oÿ) chimed about all the things Blossom could suddenly do: "You can hike, swim, horseback ride. It's better than camp." In an episode of the sitcom *Two and a Half Men* (2003–), father Alan (Jon Cryer) tried to convince his son that even though he shouldn't swim because of an ear infection, there were other things they could do together; the following exchange occurred between Alan and his brother Charlie (Charlie Sheen):

> **Alan:** No, it's OK, pal, we'll have a great weekend. We can go to Disneyland, we can play miniature golf, go bowling, bike riding, whatever you want.
>
> **Charlie:** Alan, relax. You're starting to sound like a tampon commercial.

The Curse of Eve 73

The *Pulling Our Own Strings* joke and the scenes from *King of the Hill*, *Ten Inch Hero*, *Bridesmaids*, *Blossom*, and *Two and a Half Men* are amusing because they rely on our strong familiarity with the clichéd way menstrual products have long been advertised: through innuendo, euphemism and promises of freedom and freshness. Assuaging fears—be they fears of odor, leakage, or staining, as well as those associated with lifestyles being cramped—is at the heart of much menstrual product marketing. These advertisements market a solution to audience fears, and simultaneously tap into a desire for freedom to swim, ride, or play tennis, advertising trends explained well by sociologist Annemarie Jutel:

> In the early twenty-first century, women can purchase menstrual products with names such as Libra, Carefree, and Stayfree—conjuring up images of freedom and the potential for a vast number of experiences, presumably including physical exertion.[22]

One way to interpret the advertisements Jutel described is to view them as countering the idea of activity restriction; in such a reading these commercials can be interpreted as *celebrating* all of the very many things women *can* do—period or no period. Certainly this is the interpretation gleaned by the boy in the joke quoted earlier and facetiously by Six in *Blossom* and the men in *Bridesmaids*, *Ten Inch Hero*, and *Two and a Half Men*. Following such a reading, the famous athletes who have appeared in menstrual product advertising—gymnasts Mary Lou Retton and Cathy Rigby in the 1980s, and tennis player Serena Williams in a 2009 Tampax television commercial, for example—could each be interpreted as *championing* the fusion of menstruation and activity: here are athletes who have reached the pinnacle of their sporting careers and demonstrate triumph *and* menstruation. The Serena Williams commercial in fact quite literally presents this idea through the depiction of Williams's *physical* battle with the Mother Nature character. While advertisers may be hoping that audiences interpret these commercials as being about liberation, other interpretations are indeed possible. The fact that these advertisements were not public service announcements, and rather are part of the lucrative feminine hygiene industry means that there is reason to believe that something more sinister—or at least something *less* concerned with women's liberation—is transpiring: that while the achievements of women might be championed within the storylines, this only occurs because of an overarching desire to peddle remedial products suicide.

Jutel's summary of the trends in menstrual product advertising, she argued that while these advertisements appear to advocate women's ability to engage in a spectrum of activities, they also simultaneously continue to promote archaic ideas about the necessity for concealment, protection, and safety (chapter 1):

> By purporting to solve problems, these marketing strategies recreate and reinforce social beliefs about the female body that often leave women on the sidelines.[23]

By telling a girl that she *can* swim, ride, and play tennis these advertisements also remind her to consider that perhaps she can't, or at the very least, remind her of some of the more embarrassing consequences that ensue if physical activities are participated in. Six's sarcasm in *Blossom* illustrated this idea well: while she *told* Blossom that she can hike, swim, and horseback ride, her comments were facetious and seemingly implied that she knew that while advertising *suggested* that all these activities were possible, the reality is that a woman probably would not choose to do them; or at the very least, is aware that there are consequences. The idea of menstruators being punished for physical activity is a theme depicted in a scene from the Canadian film *Fetching Cody* (2005): Cody (Sarah Lind) got her first period while wearing white shorts and playing badminton at school; she was teased and bullied by her classmates; something that placed her on a trajectory of high school despair. A similar situation took place in *Carrie* (1976): the title character's first period occurred in the school gym showers; like Cody, her high schooling was ruined because of a traumatic leakage event.

While not something discussed by Jutel, her study perfectly encapsulated the media theory of agenda setting, which is one way to think about how contemporary menstrual product advertising reinforces old-fashioned taboos. In their article on advertising and agenda setting, for example, Max Sutherland and John Galloway identified that the goal of advertising is to "focus consumers' attention on what values, products, brands, or attributes to think about rather than to persuade consumers what to think of these."[24] Expanding on Jutel's argument, contemporary menstrual product advertising puts social stigmas about leakage and staining onto the agenda of girls and simultaneously remind them that physical activity can cause awful things to transpire. As is the objective of most marketing, such advertisements subtly remind girls of a problem and then sell a solution, in the process perpetuating cultural myths that the advertiser has a financial interest in upholding. This idea of "modern" advertising purporting to refute popular taboos while actually reinforcing them is evident in a 1987 Midol advertisement. The commercial opened with a voiceover saying that "Today myths about menstrual pain can still affect us." While the voiceover mentioned myths, the video footage—which putatively presented a *modern* portrayal of menstruation—showed a woman dressed in gauzy white fabric, looking thoroughly passive and demure and reinforcing any number of *other* myths about the necessity of purity, cleanliness and femininity. This commercial in fact, provides a useful segue into a discussion of the second activity restriction narrative apparent in advertising: the supposed limits posed on women because of cramps.

Unlike fears associated with odor, leakage, or staining—which have more to do with social stigmas and learned paranoia than reality—cramps are indeed a reality for many women despite suspicion to the contrary, an idea that a 1986 Premesyn print advertisement exploited: "Premenstrual tension is not in your head. It's in your body."[25] The notion, therefore, that pain might restrict lifestyle—in the same ways that women are convinced that odor, leakage, or staining might—is frequently presented in advertising as a way to establish a problem and then market a solution.

While most research on menstruation draws attention to the stereotyped ways menstrual products are advertised—and while the value of the menstrual pain relief industry has been well documented[26]—scarce research has actually examined the styles in which menstrual pain relief drugs are marketed. While academic research has largely not been conducted on this topic, empirical observations certainly indicate that some strong parallels exist between the advertising of pain products and pads and tampons, notably with their respective focus on the agenda setting of social taboos and the retailing of solutions. In his discussion of a Midol print advertisement from the 1930s, historian Roland Marchand quoted the tagline, "Nature won't postpone her process to accommodate social engagements."[27] In research on pain medication advertising from 1936, the stereotypical manner that drugs like Midol were marketed was identified: "one cannot escape the advertising pictures of beautiful women who have been freed of periodic pain by Midol."[28] These early advertisements articulated the capacity for menstrual pain to be restricting and in the process established a standard for how these products would long be marketed. For over half a century the Midol promise of not letting menstrual pain impinge on lifestyle is the standard way it, and drugs like it, are now advertised. In a 1994 Pamprin television advertisement, the drug claimed to help you "get yourself back together again." A 1997 Midol advertisement promised that the product "helps you feel like yourself again." A 1998 Midol advertisement included footage of a girl playing volleyball interspersed with dialogue about how Midol works better than competing brands. A 2003 Pamprin advertisement showed images of a woman running with a dog, girls passing notes in class, and women playing soccer, the voiceover claiming: "this beautiful day without menstrual cramps, bloating . . . [is] brought to you by Pamprin." A 2010 Pamprin advertisement again delivered the same message: "stop your symptoms before they stop you." These pain relief examples each use the very same themes as menstrual product advertisements: they allude to the idea of activity restriction and then sell the promise of remedy.

Menstruation and Sex

It is no surprise that menstruation is widely considered inextricably linked to sex: both happen in the vagina—something perfectly illustrated when, during a sexy phone conversation, Prince Charles and then-mistress Camilla Parker-Bowles considered his reincarnation as her tampon[29]—and the onset of menstruation is frequently viewed as the gateway to sexual adulthood (chapter 2). Another explanation for the inextricable connection is offered by psychologist Deborah Schoolera et al., who contended that girls are "socialized" to connect the two:

> Many girls first learn about menstruation in sex education classes, where both menstruation and sex, are presented as means to the end of procreation.[30]

In the previous section, the presentation of menstruation as something inhibiting participation in sport was discussed as evident in advertising. In this section, the negative and limiting role of menstruation on sex is explored as apparent on screen. Menstruation as a reason *not* to have sex, as well as periods being fabricated to *avoid* sex, are both examined.

In his encyclopedia of sex, Richard Walker summarized the reasons why a couple may choose not to have intercourse during menstruation:

> This may be because the woman is not interested in sex during her period; because her partner is not comfortable about having sex at this time; or because the couple have religious or cultural objections to menstrual sex.[31]

In this section I focus on screen presentations exploring the capacity for periods to prevent sex because of a *woman's* decision not to participate.

As discussed throughout this book—and as is apparent in most discussions of menstruation—there is a very long history of menstruation considered as taboo. While many of the specific taboos such as those related to ruined crops, mirrors, and meals may have waned, the taboo of *menstrual sex* remains intact. This taboo, while perhaps no longer centered on the myths outlined by historian Lara Freidenfelds—who identified fears associated with "open" cervixes prone to infection, blood-borne bacteria infecting men, and children born with leprosy[32]—the idea that menstrual sex is not *normal* remains a standard on-screen presentation. In this section I review the presence of menstrual sex taboos as seemingly internalized by women exhibited both off screen and on.

Despite the fact that contemporary research frequently lauds the *benefits* of sex as a cure for menstrual cramps[33] and identifies it as something that provides self-esteem benefits to the menstruator,[34] some women still choose *not* to have sex when they are bleeding. Psychologist Breanne Fahs identified a number of themes in women's disinclinations: notably, that they don't want the burden of clean-up, that they are concerned about their partner's overt discomfort, and that they harbor negative thoughts about their menstruating bodies.[35] This later point was also identified in research undertaken by psychologist Gordon Forbes et al., which noted that both men *and* women considered women as less sexy while menstruating.[36] fifty-one-year-old Bonnie, quoted in Fahs's study, explained her disinclination, spotlighting a number of anti-menstrual sex rationales:

> I wouldn't have sex on my period because I'd rather not dirty the sheets. I'm sure there are guys that don't mind. Even if they wanted to, I don't think I want to. I think blood is dirty. It just seems like such a hassle. Maybe in the shower, but that's the only place that would make sense to me.[37]

Geena, fifty-one, quoted in the same study, made a similar point:

> It's the pain of cleaning it up and not leaving stains on stuff is why I avoid it, and there's part of me that's always thought that if I'm in the thick of throwing clots, men are not really going to want to do this.[38]

Younger women in the study exhibited similar sentiments: Sonja, twenty-four, for example, remarked:

> It makes me feel a little bit more uncomfortable about my body. It's kind of grosser. I just feel uncomfortable. I have had sex before on my period, but I always feel gross.[39]

Teenager Geri, quoted in human development researchers Katherine Allen and Abbie Goldberg's study on menstrual sex attitudes, articulated her own negative views:

> The thought of having my period blood on some guy's penis makes me want to throw up. People do that? Guys aren't completely grossed out? I still get grossed out when I have to change an overnight pad. Just the thought of it makes me feel uncomfortable. When I am on my period I don't even want to be around a guy. A lot of the reason is because when I am on my period I smell this awful odor that never goes away no matter how many showers you take and bottles of Victoria's Secret body spray you put on. I would hate for a guy to think I smell like that. Is there a pill to get rid of the smell?[40]

While a woman may experience her own period as messy or smelly, these are not perceptions borne in a vacuum. The disgust surrounding menstruation is explored in chapter 4, but for this chapter, it is important to note that while many myths and taboos may have disappeared, some remain—particularly those related to the abject nature of menstrual blood—ideas which continue to inform and impact on a woman's inclination to have sex: while feeling bloated may be physical,[41] a woman thinking of herself as less attractive and as smelly or dirty is a view cultivated by the many negative social messages that men *and* women receive about menstruation; messages consistently delivered through anti-menstrual sex narratives rampant on screen.

While the Fahs and Allen and Goldberg quotes were included in this section as examples of women's strong anti-menstrual sex convictions and to highlight some of the broader social views on menstrual sex, it would be erroneous to infer that menstrual sex remains as taboo as it once was: participation in menstrual sex in fact is likely much more common than these quotes imply. Research from as early as 1978, for example, identified that the menstrual sex taboo was in decline.[42] In Allen and Goldberg's study, nearly half of the women surveyed *did* engage in menstrual sex,[43] and in Fahs's study, just under 30 percent of women had *positive* reactions to menstrual sex.[44] While these studies were each based on small samples, it is nonetheless reasonable to assume that a significant proportion of couples *do* have menstrual sex and presumably don't subscribe to menstrual sex myths, despite broader cultural taboos.[45] This menstrual sex reality, however, contrasts markedly with how the subject matter is presented on screen. While the actual presence of menstrual sex is analyzed in chapter 5, this section focuses on the most common way sex and menstruation are connected in popular culture: menstruation is usually presented as a reason *not* to have sex. A scene from Adam Schwartz's novel *A Stranger on the Planet* introduces this idea well:

> Zelda sat up and removed her top. We embraced each other, her breasts pressing against my partly exposed chest. "Oh, this feels nice," Zelda murmured.
> "Yes," I agreed. My mouth moved to her breasts, kissing and suckling until my lips were numb. Then I remembered that I had another hand, a free hand, and I began to move it down Zelda's belly. She caught it just as I reached the elastic of her bikini bottom.
> "Bummer," she said. "I'm having my period."
> For a moment I was perplexed as to why she was telling me this; then I caught on: Her bottom wasn't coming off.[46]

Menstruation as thwarting sex is the standard presentation on screen. In *Friends (With Benefits)* (2009), Brad (Brendan Bradley) presented a list of 100 life rules; among them was: "78. A period does not equal a week off from sex." In a "Detective Lately" skit from the *Chelsea Lately* (2007–) talk show, host Chelsea Handler played a detective taking a statement from a man who alleged that a woman brazenly had sex with him only to then leave before he woke: Chelsea branded this woman a "serial devirginizer." After ascertaining that this woman had perpetrated this "crime" numerous times, Chelsea shouted, "Dammit! This is the tenth time! This girl doesn't stop. Doesn't this girl get a period?" In *Friends with Benefits* (2011), Dylan (Justin

Timberlake) tried to ascertain whether it was his lover's "special time." He waved his iPhone at her—feigning that he had an app that could determine this—and said, "You're good to go." In *No Strings Attached* (2011), Adam (Ashton Kutcher) visited his lover when she had her period; knowing she was bleeding, he brought her cupcakes, and a "Period Mix" compilation CD, and he spooned her all night on her bed: sex was never an agenda item. In *Sixteen Candles* (1984), Mike (Justin Henry) commented on his sister getting her period on her wedding day: "Should make for an interesting honeymoon, huh?" In *Ron White: You Can't Fix Stupid* (2006)—a televized stand-up routine—the comic said: "When my wife's on her period, she won't have sex with me at all! No way! Which is bullshit, because if the roller coaster's broken, they don't shut down the whole amusement park!" In an episode of television series *Entourage* (2004–2011), Ari (Jeremy Piven) and Vincent (Adrian Grenier) discussed how their mutual friend Eric (Kevin Connolly) hadn't been "getting it":

Ari: I thought the girlfriend was still in play.

Vince: Aww, bad time of the month to come home.

In each of these examples cultural truism is apparent: that if a woman is bleeding, *she* won't want to have sex. Interestingly in these examples, no menstruator gets her own voice on this topic—she has no opportunity to articulate a view on menstrual sex either way—her disinclination is simply *assumed*. There are however, examples when a woman's physical or verbal disinclination is expressed much more overtly. In *Showgirls* (1995), for example, Nomi (Elizabeth Berkley) was shown grinding against the lap of James (Glenn Plummer). As things heated up, Nomi told him that she had her period, he doubted her, she encouraged him to check, which he did, and he said, "It's alright, I got towels." Nomi however, just walked away. In an episode of *Jersey Shore* (2009–), Pauly's plans to have sex were curtailed; as he rationalized, "I couldn't have sex with my girl, she had her period. I go to take her pants off . . . she wouldn't let me . . . no big deal." In another episode, Snooki met a man, Jeff, and decided to take him home. While making out, Snooki suddenly remembered she had her period and said, "I don't think I should," and they stopped. Later she explained: "Jeff is ready to do moves on me . . . but really I had my friggin' period. Story of my life." In another episode, José wanted to have sex with Angelina but she too claimed that she was menstruating. In an episode of the cartoon sitcom *American Dad!* (2005–), wife Francine commented to her husband, Stan, "The cable's out and I just got my period. So there's nothing to do but talk and talk and talk."

Interestingly, for James, Jeff, Pauly, José, and Stan—the menstruator thwarted *their* access to sex; menstruation prevented the *woman* proceeding. In none of these cases did the man actually express sexual disinterest or repulsion toward his bleeding partner: on the contrary, the man actually appeared interested in sex and it was the *woman* who was explicitly disinclined; in these scenes the thwarting of sex during menstruation appeared to be a decision made autonomously by the menstruator. Interestingly, these ideas are identifiable in real-life perceptions of the impact of menstruation on sexual relationships where again, women are assumed to be the sexual gatekeepers. Fingerson, for example, wrote that "[f]or boys, the vagina indicates sexual access."[47] For them, menstruation is construed as something that negatively affects *them* and thwarts *their* opportunity for sex. The same idea was apparent in comments made by men quoted in sociologist Sophie Laws's research:

> I think I thought of it in terms of, as a bloody nuisance, sexually, so it wasn't that it had any sort of, um, sexual significance, it was that it was obviously tied up with sexuality because it happened to women, because it happened to the woman I was sexually involved with.[48]

> I can remember feeling irritated, feeling annoyed, feeling there was nothing . . . that I didn't have any control over the situation and that it was something that women used to exert control.[49]

> [T]hey'll say "well she was fucking on her period, wasn't she?" meaning they didn't have sex. "She wasn't feeling very well," as though she did it on purpose to spite him or something. A lot of men think in those terms.[50]

John, a man interviewed in Freidenfelds's research, recalled "teenage petting" on dates in the early 1950s, noting that girls eschewed sexual contact with the excuse that they were having a period. Freidenfelds narrated, "When asked if he [John] could tell if that was just a convenient excuse, he said he could not be sure."[51] While we can't assume that the women in the no-sex screen examples *fabricated* menstruation as an excuse, the real-life quotes nonetheless allude to men's suspicion of this, something closely related to the ideas discussed at the beginning of this chapter regarding the presentation of women as untrustworthy and the popular perception that women routinely seek ways to avoid sex along the clichéd "headache" route. The idea of menstruation strategically deployed in this manner is certainly detectable in academic literature. In Fingerson's research, for example, she identified that menstruation gives women a "legitimate" reason to say no to sex.[52] In *The Curse*, Janice Delaney et al. similarly claimed that by "[u]sing "the curse" as an excuse, many a woman has enjoyed a dinner date free from the bothersome knowledge that she herself might be the dessert."[53] Psychoanalyst Karen Horney, in her research on women's health, wrote that, "Every practitioner has seen cases in which menstruation is welcomed as an excuse for not having intercourse, even within marriage,"[54] and psychoanalyst Michael Balint presented the same idea, claiming that:

> It is a well-known ruse of women, especially those who are frigid and not in love with their husbands, to simulate menstruation or simply to lie in order to avoid sexual intercourse.[55]

Physician Katharina Dalton even suggested that women sometimes *exaggerated* the duration of their periods to avoid sex.[56] These ideas allude to women's supposed skills at deception but can also be read in other ways. One interpretation of sex avoidance strategies is women feeling a need to provide an excuse—to *lie*—rather than tell their partners that they simply don't want to have sex; presumably they know that their partners won't tolerate simple disinclination and thus they feel an imperative to construct a more "substantial" excuse. Such an issue, of course, raises notable concerns about relationship equality and consent.[57] Another reading, and one related to another popular myth, is that men's sex drives are higher than women's and that men are *always* up for it and that *women* are the stumbling block. This latter point is interesting because operating within a menstruation narrative, men can claim to *want* sex constantly—period or no period—but never actually have to prove their virility because the menstruating woman's appetite is culturally assumed as lower. Another explanation relates to a menstrual disclosure being misconstrued, either deliberately or inadvertently, by men. Thinking back to the examples discussed earlier, while a woman's disclosing her period might *appear* to be an attempt by her to halt proceedings, conversely, she might simply be doing so out of courtesy: that she doesn't actually *want* things to stop, but that she knows that she needs to be upfront; as Laws explained: "The woman may not presume that she will not be found offensive."[58] While some men may attempt to reassure the woman that she is still desirable to him—like James in *Showgirls* or Hank (David Duchovny) in *Californication* when he responded to a menstrual confession by claiming that he cares little for such things—other men who may be squeamish about blood may simply, readily, *assume* that their partner's disclosure means no sex, thus allowing them the opportunity to not have to make a decision, nor risk offending their partner. In the *Jersey Shore* episode discussed earlier, for example, Snooki said, "I don't think I should." While an opportunity existed for Jeff to reassure Snooki that he still found her desirable, this opportunity was not acted on. Another explanation relates to the popular idea of menstrual sex as taboo: a man might decide not to try to coerce a menstruating woman into sex because he does not want to be perceived as a pervert or fetishist.

Despite the popular on-screen idea that women use or fake menstruation to get out of sex, the idea is actually much more likely to be speculated by characters than to actually be apparent in a narrative. Two examples however, where menstruation was actually faked are identifiable in two very different films: *Overboard* (1987) and *Viskningar och rop* (*Cries and Whispers*) (1972). In a scene from the comedy *Overboard*, Grant (Edward Herrmann) tried unsuccessfully to seduce his wife (Goldie Hawn), at one point exasperatedly lamenting, "How can you have your period *every week*?" A darker presentation transpired in the Swedish film *Viskningar och rop* (*Cries and Whispers*), when Karin (Ingrid Thulin) cut her genitals with broken glass to, presumably, avoid sex with her husband. This same idea was also detected in Marge Piercy's novel *Small Changes*, where Beth plotted to avoid sex with her husband: "Dipping a finger in the ketchup, she carefully worked her finger into herself, smearing ketchup on her genitals, on her panties."[59] Emilie Autumn's song "Marry Me" (2006) also alluded to menstruation feigned to avoid sex via a description of inner thighs sliced to produce a blood display.

Given that men are presumably less comfortable with menstruation than women, it might be assumed that on screen *men* will be the ones to articulate an objection to menstrual sex. Contrarily, however, and as demonstrated by the examples discussed above, *women* are much more likely to allow their period to dictate abstinence: men are rarely shown to deem menstrual blood as a barrier; women evidently commonly do. While infrequent, there are indeed a small number of examples where male characters do express antimenstrual sex attitudes. In the *Entourage* episode discussed earlier, for example, Ari expressed his personal aversion, commenting: "I won't even fuck my wife after she plays tennis." Here, Ari implied that sweat is less objectionable to menstrual blood and he won't even go near that, thus implying just how very disgusting he finds menstrual blood. In an episode of *Californication*, when Hank and Mrs. Patterson (Justine Bateman) were about to have menstrual sex, she mentioned her ex's opposition: "God, my ex always cared. He thought it was dirty." A number of interesting explanations exist for the disproportionate presentation of *women's* opposition to menstrual sex rather than men's. One obvious explanation, as noted earlier, is that men are socially expected to want sex anywhere, anytime; as Woody Allen once claimed, "there's no such thing as bad sex." In line with such sentiments, it is presumably more fitting to an appropriately masculine identity for a man to be portrayed as virile rather than reluctant. Another interpretation is that by presenting menstrual sex as something thwarted by women, *women* get blamed; they are the ones presented as difficult, emotional, and irrational, they are the ones ruining things, and they are the ones who get demonized in their gatekeeper role. A further explanation lies in men's resentment toward menstrual blood more broadly. Within such an interpretation, given that menstruation is so widely loathed, menstrual sex won't actually get anywhere *near* the agenda for men to actively oppose it; they would never let things get that close in the first place. Another explanation is that a man's outright opposition to menstrual sex may be construed as sexist, or at the very least politically incorrect. Having a male character articulate an opposition to menstrual sex might result in audiences—particularly *female* audiences—construing him as an awful person, which may prove disruptive to a narrative (chapter 8), therefore the topic will be avoided entirely.

While menstrual blood may not be commonly loathed on screen, the grotesquery of it, of course, frequently gets presented in other ways. Discussed later in this chapter, overt contempt for menstruation is readily identifiable on screen but is commonly portrayed in other more subtle, more coded ways.

As noted, menstrual sex does not have a prominent place in mainstream popular culture. Given that sex-themed narratives more broadly are in fact *staples* in contemporary screen narratives, this absence might seem surprising. One reading could be that menstruation is simply a fact of life and that on screen it is just assumed—without reference to taboo—that sex is not done during this time; that it isn't discussed or negotiated, it just does not happen. When Adam on *No Strings Attached* took cupcakes and a mix-tape to his menstruating lover, for example, the two didn't discuss sex and neither initiated it, both seemingly content with it being *off* the agenda. Another reading could be that perhaps menstrual sex is no longer the taboo it once was and that it actually *does* occur—much like other bodily happenings—in the background of narratives; similar to the fact that we don't often see characters use the toilet or floss their teeth, but of course we assume that they do and that such activities simply happens *off* screen. In such an interpretation, menstruation would be something that couples simply got on with without it existing as a major plot point (chapter 8). While certainly a possible interpretation—and certainly in line with "against the grain" readings of a narrative[60]—the reality is that much taboo still plagues menstrual sex. Given the existence of menstrual-themed porn for example—which presents menstrual sex as a fetish (chapter 5)—compounded with the strong anti-sex reactions of some of the women in the studies referenced earlier—to consider menstrual sex as thoroughly mainstreamed would be premature. Another explanation for the absence could be linked to the infrequent portrayal of menstruation more broadly: given that periods are rarely present, it stands to reason that the appearance of menstrual sex narratives—be they explicit (chapter 5) or of the off-the-agenda kind discussed in this chapter—would be rare.

MENSTRUATION AS A PANDORA'S BOX

One interpretation of the popular curse description of menstruation—and one frequently reinforced by screen narratives—is that it causes all manner of turmoil ranging from mood swings through to destruction. In this section I explore the presentation of menstruation as something bestowed with mystical, often dangerous properties.

In the film *I Could Never Be Your Woman* (2007), upon getting her first period, Izzie (Saoirse Ronan) said to her mother, "Let the games begin." For Izzie menarche marked the start of a new adult life. Menarche in fact is frequently portrayed this way: as a transition point—not just into womanhood (chapter 2)—but more specifically into *trouble*. Discussed earlier in this chapter was the common trope surrounding the evils of female sexuality. Interestingly, these evils are frequently connected to *adult* female sexuality and thus are traits ignited at menarche and are apparently something which permanently taints fertile women. As in *I Could Never Be Your Woman*, menarche serving as the catalyst for the dramas of adult female life is a theme detectable in the films *Prozac Nation* (2001) and *The Runaways* (2010). In *Prozac Nation*, during a reflection on her childhood, Elizabeth (Christina Ricci) discussed her menarche: "One night there was something in my pants, like blood. My mom said, 'oh, hell, your period. This is where all the trouble starts.' She was right." For Elizabeth, the "trouble" was depression and addiction. In *The Runaways*, Cherie (Dakota Fanning) got her first period at the beginning of the film; later the same day she cropped her hair, painted a red streak across her face, and embarked on a journey into glam rock: menarche for Cherie was the catalyst for dramatic behavior change and life as a counter-culture rocker. In these examples, menarche was presented as something that didn't merely end youth and ignite adulthood, but which placed girls on a path to the kind of womanhood associated with a more dangerous female sexuality. These scenes are, of course, quite tame compared to other examples where menstruation instigates much more extreme happenings. On screen the strangeness and danger of menstruation can manifest in all kinds of abject female behavior, from mild psychic premonitions through to demonic possession.

In the pilot of the sitcom *Frasier* (1993–2004), while we don't know precisely *when* her extensively mocked psychic abilities first manifested, Daphne (Jane Leeves) discussed her powers and claimed, "Usually it's strongest around my time of the month." In Doris Lessing's novel *The Golden Notebook*, protagonist Anna selected the first date of her period to document everything she felt, noting particularly strong feelings of intuition at the time. In Erin Healy's novel *The Baker's Wife*, the adult protagonist, Audrey, experienced psychic premonitions which coincided precisely with her period arriving earlier than expected, the implication being that the two happenings were connected. The idea that menstruation is able to connect women to otherworldly powers certainly exists both in anthropological research[61] and in new-age literature. In astrologer Demetra George's book *Mysteries of the Dark Moon*, for example, she wrote:

> Menarche, as a rite of passage, marked her transition from childhood and her initiation into the secrets of womanhood. . . . The flow of her blood also signifies that the currents of her psychic energy are now activated and can be developed.[62]

Other literature has similarly suggested that women—in line with the portrayals discussed above—have heightened creativity,[63] intuition[64], and psychic powers[65] while bleeding. Psychoanalyst Sigmund Freud, for example, noted that in some cultures menarche is often "interpreted as the bite of some spirit-animals,"[66] and certainly on screen in the horror genre, menarche has been repeatedly portrayed as the catalyst for the acquisition of special, if not *malevolent*, powers. In the most famous of all menstrual-themed films—*Carrie* (1976)—the telekinetic powers of the title character (Sissy Spacek) arrived with her first period. In *The Exorcist* (1974), Regan (Linda Blair) similarly obtained her powers as menarche approached; in her case, she became possessed by the devil: her masturbation with the crucifix epitomized her newfound "evil" sexuality. In the Canadian horror comedy film *Ginger Snaps* (2000), Ginger's (Katharine Isabelle) first period triggered her werewolfness: along with the growth of excess hair and a tail, Ginger developed an insatiable appetite for sex and violence. In *The Reaping* (2007), it was assumed that the arrival of Loren's (AnnaSophia Robb) menarche explained why her small town suffered the ten plagues of the bible. The menarche/evil link was also presented in *Pitch Black* (2000): the evil creatures were only able to chase the group because they could smell "Jack's" (Rhiana Griffith) first period. Jack's period, like Loren's and Carrie's, put everyone in danger. While in these examples menarche ignited the evil, menstruation across the course of a woman's life can function similarly. In the comedy *I'm Gonna Git You Sucka* (1998), for example, waitress Cheryl (Dawnn Lewis), complained to a co-worker about her cramps and left work early. She walked home along a dark alley and a man followed. He tapped her shoulder with his cane and said, "Sweet thing, it's time to come home to daddy." Cheryl protested, "Please, please just leave me alone." The man quickly became aggressive and snarled, "Bitch, I said you're coming with me." Cheryl's eyes suddenly glowed white, her hair spontaneously frizzed, and she roared. Cowering, the man said, "You must got the devil in you," and she growled, "No. Cramps," and threw him against a wall.

In these examples, menstruation didn't get loathed through dialogue or overt mockery; instead, the ramifications were left to speak for themselves. In her discussion of *Carrie*, film theorist Barbara Creed explained the role of menstruation in such films, alluding to anthropological and new-age interpretations and writing that "the suggestion is that her blood is both powerful and magical."[67] In social researcher Suzanne Frayser and Thomas Whitby's analysis of *The Exorcist*, they contended that such films "illustrate the depth of fear and potential that menstruation expresses in modern society."[68] In cultural theorist Ken Gelder's discussions of *Carrie* and *The Exorcist*, he similarly identified the repeated presentation of "women's sexuality as the source of all evil and menstruation as the sign of sin."[69] These films can each be read as reiterating the abhorrence of menstruation and of menstruating women: *of course* the bleeding woman is evil *because menstruation is evil*. Another reading, however—and certainly one alluded to by Creed—is that such presentations highlight that menstruation is simply something not understood by men (chapter 1) or even adequately by women,[70] and thus narrative explanations are created to fulfill knowledge gaps. Just as myths and religions are often created to comprehend the incomprehensible, in these scenes the failure to understand menstruation manifests in it being afforded supernatural properties: it does not appear "logical" that a woman can bleed for days and not die, and thus explanations centered on the supernatural are proposed. In chapter 2, I outlined that for many newly menstruating characters, anger was grounded in them being blindsided. This idea of people responding negatively to knowledge gaps may be one explanation for the menstruation/evil connection on screen where something that is not understood is construed as bad if not popularly demonized (addressed further in chapter 4).

Negative portrayals of menstruation have been at the crux of this chapter, illustrating how a normal bodily function gets demonized through its presentation as disruptive, as a passion-killer, and as being connected to evil. Perhaps a useful question to ask as this chapter closes is the motivation behind such demonizing. In chapter 1 I quoted writer John Scalzi, who explained men's lack of understanding about menstruation being grounded in the fact that "there is no parallel in the male experience. . . . We can't even imagine it."[71] This lack of comparable experience is likely central to the loathing of menstruation: it is a *woman's* problem and there is no male equivalent to demonize; menstruation exists as something tangible that can be pointed to as demonstrating what makes women distinctly different from men and the nature of blood exists as a readily loathed substance: factors which, when compounded, justify on screen loathing. Of course, difference on its own presumably isn't enough to justify the contempt extended to menstruation. Instead, it is very likely also the *female* aspect. Rather than simply, arbitrarily, hating women based on different chromosomes, *instead*, menstruation as a messy female bodily function is considered at the root of women's weakness, subordination, and thus, is loathed as a subtler method of misogyny.

This chapter explored the relatively tame downsides of menstruation as examined through restrictions placed on life and sex as well as ones associated with more dire consequences such as unleashed horror and the supernatural. In chapter 4 the more overtly negative portrayals of menstruation are examined, focused on themes of disgust manifested in more overt abhorrence of blood, menstrual products, and femininity.

NOTES

1. John Curra, *The Relativity of Deviance* (Thousand Oaks, CA: Sage Publications, 2000), 55.
2. Spring C. Cooper and Patricia B. Koch, "'Nobody told me nothin': Communication about menstruation among low-income African American women," *Women & Health* 36, no. 1 (2007): 57–78, 69.
3. *Cambridge Academic Content Dictionary* (New York: Cambridge University Press, 2009), 353.
4. In Laura Fingerson, *Girls in Power: Gender, Body and Menstruation in Adolescence* (Albany: State University of New York Press, 2006), 65.
5. Film theorist Barbara Creed discussed the likening of menstruating women to animals—notably, to pigs—in her discussion about *Carrie* (1976): "Carrie/woman is monstrous because she bleeds like 'a stuck pig', as the saying goes" (Barbara Creed, *The Monstrous-Feminine: Film, Feminism, Psychoanalysis* (London: Routledge, 1993), 80).
6. Camille Paglia, *Sexual Personae: Art and Decadence from Nefertiti to Emily Dickinson* (New Haven, CT: Yale University, 1990), 11.
7. Kelly Orringer and Sheila Gahagan, "Adolescent girls define menstruation: A multiethnic exploratory study," *Health Care for Women International* 31 (2010): 831–847.
8. Otto Pollak, *The Criminality of Women* (Philadelphia: University of Pennsylvania Press, 1950). In Ronald B. Flowers, *Female Crime, Criminals, and Cellmates: An Exploration of Female Criminality* (Jefferson, NC: McFarland, 1995), 69. [My emphasis.]
9. As theologian Theresa Sanders noted, "the Bible itself does not mention menstruation as one of Eve's burdens" (Theresa Sanders, *Approaching Eden: Adam and Eve in Popular Culture* (Lanham, MD: Rowman and Littlefield, 2009), 113).
10. Janice Delaney, Mary Jane Lupton, and Emily Toth, *The Curse: A Cultural History of Menstruation* (New York: Dutton, 1976); Thomas C.T. Buckley and Alma Gottlieb, *Blood Magic: The Anthropology of Menstruation* (Berkeley: University of California Press, 1988).
11. Colette Dowling, *The Frailty Myth: Redefining the Physical Potential of Women and Girls* (New York: Random House, 2000), 40.
12. In 2011, feminine hygiene company Always dared to break the decades-old taboo in feminine hygiene advertising and used a red dot on a line drawing of a pad in a print advertisement. While not actually blood, the idea of using red—rather than the standard blue liquid—was considered a "historic moment" (Margaret Hartmann, "In historic moment, feminine hygiene ad shows blood," *Jezebel*, July 6, 2011, jezebel.com/5818826/in-historic-moment-feminine-hygiene-ad-shows-blood (accessed July 21, 2011).
13. Menstruation myths are explored in numerous books, including: Marta Weigle, *Spiders and Spinsters: Women and Mythology* (Santa Fe, NM: Sunstone Press, 2007); Richard Cavendish and Brian Innes, *Encyclopedia of World Mythology* (New York: Marshall Cavendish, 1994).

14. Human kinetics researcher Patricia Vertinsky thoroughly summarized the long history of medical practitioners recommending women avoid participation in sport in her book *The Eternally Wounded Woman*. (Patricia, Vertinsky, *The Eternally Wounded Woman: Doctors, Women and Exercise in the Late Nineteenth Century* (Manchester: Manchester University Press, 1990)).

15. In Elizabeth A. Kissling, "When being female isn't feminine: Uta Pippig and the menstrual communication taboo in sports journalism," *Sociology of Sport Journal* 16 (1999): 79–91, 83.

16. Margaret Konz Snooks, "Expanding the academic knowledge base: Helping students to cross gender's great divide," in *Women in Higher Education: Empowering Change*, ed. JoAnn DiGeorgio-Lutz (Westport, CT: Praeger, 2002).

17. This issue was nonetheless one that feminist philosopher Simone de Beauvoir discussed in *The Second Sex*, where she mentioned sanitary napkins: "This bothersome, annoying object can come loose during violent exercise; it is worse humiliation that losing one's knickers in the middle of the street" (Simone de Beauvoir, *The Second Sex* (London: Vintage, 2011), 338).

18. Megan Seely, *Fight Like a Girl: How to Be a Fearless Feminist* (New York: New York University Press, 2007), 153.

19. Simone de Beauvoir, *The Second Sex* (London: Vintage, 2011), 338.

20. Shauna M. MacDonald, "Leaky performances: the transformative potential of menstrual leaks," *Women's Studies in Communication* 30, no. 3 (2007): 340–357, 341.

21. In *Pulling Our Own Strings: Feminist Humor and Satire*, ed. Gloria J. Kaufman and Mary Kay Blakely (Bloomington: Indiana University Press, 1980), 22.

22. Annemarie Jutel, "Cursed or carefree? Menstrual product advertising and the sportswoman," in *Sport, Culture and Advertising: Identities, Commodities and the Politics of Representation*, ed. Steven J. Jackson and David L. Andrews (New York: Routledge, 2005), 213.

23. Annemarie Jutel, "Cursed or carefree? Menstrual product advertising and the sportswoman," in *Sport, Culture and Advertising: Identities, Commodities and the Politics of Representation*, ed. Steven J. Jackson and David L. Andrews (New York: Routledge, 2005), 225.

24. Max Sutherland and John Galloway, "Role of advertising: Persuasion or agenda-setting?" *Journal of Advertising Research* 21, no. 5 (1981): 25–29, 26.

25. In Daniel Delis Hill, *Advertising to the American Woman, 1990–1999* (Columbus, OH: Ohio State University Press, 2002), 117–118.

26. See Mickey C. Smith, E. M. Kolass, Greg Perkins and Bruce Siecker, *Pharmaceutical Marketing: Principles, Environment, and Practice* (Binghamton, NY: Pharmaceutical Products Press, 2002). The issue was also briefly discussed in Amy Farrell's discussion of advertisements for pain relief medication being printed in the same issue of *Ms.* that included an article about the profiteers were in the PMS industry (Amy Farrell, *Yours in Sisterhood: Ms. Magazine and the Promise of Popular Feminism* (Chapel Hill: University of North Carolina Press, 1998), 130).

27. Roland Marchand, *Advertising the American Dream* (Berkeley: University of California Press, 1986), 228.

28. Rachel Lyn Palmer and Sarah Koslow Greenberg, *Facts and Frauds in Woman's Hygiene: A Medical Guide Against Misleading Claims and Dangerous Products* (New York: Vanguard Press, 1936), 28.

29. In 1993, the "Camillagate" scandal centered on the exposure of some illegally recorded telephone conversations, one which included the couple musing about Prince Charles being reincarnated as a tampon so that he could get even closer to his then mistress, Camilla Parker-Bowles.

30. Deborah L. Schooler, Monique Ward, Ann Merriwether and Allison S. Caruthers, "Cycles of shame: Menstrual shame, body shame, and sexual decision-making," *Journal of Sex Research* 42, no. 4 (2005): 324–334, 324.

31. Richard Walker, *The Macmillan Encyclopedia of Sex and Relationships* (New York: Macmillan, 1996), 95.

32. Lara Freidenfelds, *The Modern Period: Menstruation in Twentieth-Century America* (Baltimore: The Johns Hopkins University Press, 2009), 27–28.

33. See Cindy M. Meston and David M. Buss, *Why Women Have Sex: Understanding Motivations from Adventure to Revenge (and Everything in Between)* (New York: Times Books, 2009).

34. Women in Fahs's study, for example, reported enhanced self-esteem when their partner *wants* to have sex with them while they are menstruating. Janet, for example, was quoted reflecting on menstrual sex with her girlfriend: "In my heart it was like, damn, she doesn't really care, she really loves me, 'cause she doesn't care if I'm bleeding or not, and I don't care if she is." As Fahs concluded: "satisfaction with menstrual sex may reflect feelings of acceptance, validation, warmth and love" (Breanne Fahs, "Sex during menstruation: Race, sexual identity, and women's qualitative accounts of pleasure and disgust," *Feminism & Psychology* 21, no. 2 (2011): 155–178, 166). This same idea was also apparent in an episode of *Californication*. In the episode when Hank (David Duchovny) went home with his daughter's teacher Mrs. Patterson (Justine Bateman), as the two were undressing, Mrs. Patterson divulged that she was having her period; Hank was unperturbed. Mrs Patterson then responded: "I got to tell you, your feelings about periods and pubic hair have just made me a bigger fan."

35. Breanne Fahs, "Sex during menstruation: Race, sexual identity, and women's qualitative accounts of pleasure and disgust," Feminism & Psychology 21, no. 2 (2011): 155–178.

36. Gordon Forbes, Leah E. Adams-Curtis, Kay B. White, and Katie M. Holmgren, "The role of hostile and benevolent sexism in women's and men's perceptions of the menstruating woman," *Psychology of Women Quarterly* 27, no. 1, (2003): 58–63.

37. In Breanne Fahs, "Sex during menstruation: Race, sexual identity, and women's qualitative accounts of pleasure and disgust," Feminism & Psychology 21, no. 2 (2011): 155–178, 163.

38. In Breanne Fahs, "Sex during menstruation: Race, sexual identity, and women's qualitative accounts of pleasure and disgust," Feminism & Psychology 21, no. 2, (2011): 155–178, 163.

39. In Breanne Fahs, "Sex during menstruation: Race, sexual identity, and women's qualitative accounts of pleasure and disgust," *Feminism & Psychology* 21, no. 2, (2011): 155–178, 164.

40. In Katherine R. Allen and Abbie E. Goldberg, "Sexual Activity During Menstruation: A Qualitative Study," *Journal of Sex Research* 46, no. 6 (2009): 535–545, 538. [Emphasis in original.]

41. Feminist philosopher Kate Millet, for example, discussed the idea of a self-fulfilling prophesy in relation to women's bodies: "Patriarchal circumstances and beliefs seem to have the effect of poisoning the female's own sense of physical self until it often truly becomes the burden it is said to be." This argument implies that patriarchal culture encourages women to *think* they are suffering because they have been convinced that menstruation is an ordeal. (Kate Millett, *Sexual Politics* (New York: Doubleday, 1970), 47).

42. Mary Brown Parlee, "The declining taboo against menstrual sex," *Psychology Today* 12 (December 1978): 50–52.

43. Katherine R. Allen and Abbie E. Goldberg, "Sexual Activity During Menstruation: A Qualitative Study," *Journal of Sex Research* 46, no. 6 (2009): 535–545.

44. Breanne Fahs, "Sex during menstruation: Race, sexual identity, and women's qualitative accounts of pleasure and disgust," Feminism & Psychology 21, no. 2, (2011): 155–178.

45. Whether menstrual sex occurs because men and women are more comfortable with it or because women acquiesce to men's desire for sex in spite of the blood are perhaps more complicated issues. In her review of menstrual sex attitudes, Freidenfelds touched on this issue contrasting generational differences in attitudes and highlighting some of the ongoing sexual political issues plaguing menstrual sex: "Unlike the [baby boomer] feminists of the next generation, who would criticize men for regarding women's bodies as disgusting or unfit for contact during menstruation, women of this generation criticized men who pushed them to have sex during menstruation" (Lara Freidenfelds, *The Modern Period: Menstruation in Twentieth-Century America* (Baltimore: The Johns Hopkins University Press, 2009), 29).

46. Adam Schwartz, *A Stranger on the Planet* (New York: Soho Press, 2011), 29.

47. Laura Fingerson, *Girls in Power: Gender, Body and Menstruation in Adolescence* (Albany: State University of New York Press, 2006), 121.

48. In Sophie Laws, *Issues of Blood: The Politics of Menstruation* (Houndmills, Basingstoke, Hampshire: Macmillan, 1990), 40.
49. In Sophie Laws, *Issues of Blood: The Politics of Menstruation* (Houndmills, Basingstoke, Hampshire: Macmillan, 1990), 79.
50. In Sophie Laws, *Issues of Blood: The Politics of Menstruation* (Houndmills, Basingstoke, Hampshire: Macmillan, 1990), 77.
51. Lara Freidenfelds, *The Modern Period: Menstruation in Twentieth-Century America* (Baltimore: The Johns Hopkins University Press, 2009), 29.
52. Laura Fingerson, *Girls in Power: Gender, Body and Menstruation in Adolescence* (Albany: State University of New York Press, 2006), 124.
53. Janice Delaney, Mary Jane Lupton, and Emily Toth, *The Curse: a Cultural History of Menstruation* (New York: Dutton, 1976), 23.
54. Karen Horney, "Psychogenic factors in menstrual disorders," in *The Unknown Karen Horney: Essays on Gender, Culture, and Psychoanalysis*, ed. Bernard J. Paris (New Haven: Yale University Press, 2000), 102.
55. Michael Balint, *Problems of Human Pleasure and Behaviour* (London: Hogarth Press, 1957), 176.
56. Katharina Dalton, *The Menstrual Cycle* (New York: Pantheon, 1971).
57. Menstrual sex and issues of consent are linked in a particularly awful joke quoted in Sophie Laws' research: "A bride refuses to let her husband consummate their marriage the first night because she is menstruating. The second night she has nervous diarrhoea (or a head cold). The third night he appears at her bedside in hip-boots and a raincoat, carrying a storm lantern, and announced, 'Mud or blood, shit or flood, McClanahan rides tonight.'" (Gershon Legman, *The Rationale of the Dirty Joke* (New York: Grove Press, 1968), 278. In Sophie Laws, *Issues of Blood: The Politics of Menstruation* (Houndmills, Basingstoke, Hampshire: Macmillan, 1990), 84).
58. Sophie Laws, *Issues of Blood: The Politics of Menstruation* (Houndmills, Basingstoke, Hampshire: Macmillan, 1990), 53.
59. Marge Piercy, *Small Changes* (New York: Fawcett Crest, 1972), 42.
60. In *Part-Time Perverts: Sex, Pop Culture and Kink Management* I explored this issue, writing: "Not only do individuals interpret media messages differently, but some will in fact *deliberately* read them against the grain and between the lines. Sexual minorities, for example, might deliberately misread a heterosexual text in search of subtext; behavior which is at the cornerstone of queer theory" (Lauren Rosewarne, *Part-Time Perverts: Sex, Pop Culture and Kink Management* (Santa Barbara, CA: Praeger, 2011), 45).
61. In Vern Bullough and Bonnie Bullough's book *Sexual Attitudes: Myths and Realities*, they noted: "Some cultures believe that the young woman has supernatural powers at the onset of menstruation" (Vern L. Bullough and Bonnie Bullough, *Sexual Attitudes: Myths and Realities* (Amherst, NY: Prometheus Books, 1995), 109). Psychiatrists Herant Katchadourian and Donald Lunde similarly discussed the Chiricahua Apaches, for example, who "had elaborate ceremonies at menarche and believed that at this time girls possessed certain supernatural powers, including the power to heal and to bring prosperity" (Herant A. Katchadourian and Donald T. Lunde, *Biological Aspects of Human Sexuality* (New York: Holt, Rinehart and Winston, 1975), 83).
62. Demetra George, *Mysteries of the Dark Moon: The Healing Power of the Dark Goddess* (New York: HarperCollins, 1992), 217.
63. Janet Hopson and Anne Rosenfeld, "PMS: Puzzling monthly symptoms," *Psychology Today* (August, 1984): 30–35.
64. Sara Avant Stover, *The Way of the Happy Woman* (Novato, CA: New World Library, 2011).
65. Kala Trobe, *The Witch's Guide to Life* (St Paul, MN: Llewellyn Publishers, 2003).
66. Sigmund Freud, "The Taboo of Virginity," *The Standard Edition of the Complete Psychological Works of Sigmund Freud*, volume 11 (London: Hogarth, 1953–1966), 197.
67. Barbara Creed, *The Monstrous-Feminine: Film, Feminism, Psychoanalysis* (London: Routledge, 1993), 81.

68. Suzanne G. Frayser and Thomas J. Whitby, *Studies in Human Sexuality: A Selected Guide* (Englewood, CO: Libraries Unlimited, 1995), 208.

69. Ken Gelder, *The Horror Reader* (New York: Routledge, 2002), 69.

70. The idea of women not understanding menstruation was apparent in an episode of the British sitcom *The Vicar of Dibley* (1994–2007). When Geraldine (Dawn French) asked to have a private talk with Alice (Emma Chambers), Alice responded: "Okay, as long as it's not about tampons because I just don't understand them."

71. John Scalzi, "Best personal hygiene products of the millennium," in *Your Hate Mail Will Be Graded: A Decade of Whatever, 1998–2008* (New York: Tom Doherty Associates, 2008), 349.

Chapter Four

The Menstrual Mess

The Disgust, Horror, and Fear of Menstruation

In an episode of the cartoon sitcom *Family Guy* (1999–), Stewie's response to reading a book about menstruation was the exclamation: "that's the most disgusting thing I've seen in my entire life!" The idea that menstruation—that the menstruator, that her blood, that the products used—are abject, are disgusting is the dominant way that periods are presented on screen. In this chapter I examine narratives showing contempt for menstruation ranging from the routine PMS accusations through to narratives exploiting the perceived horror of blood and menstrual products.

THE MENSTRUATION ACCUSATION

The word *synecdoche* describes circumstances when a part of something is used to refer to the whole. Vagina, for example, is frequently used in popular parlance to describe female genitals in their entirety rather just the anatomical vagina. As related to this research, references to *aspects* of menstruation—such as PMS and menstrual products—frequently come to speak for menstruation as a whole. Such shorthand is often used to mock and to solicit laughter without actually showing or describing anything that might be considered offensive; in doing so, menstruation doesn't get overtly loathed, rather just the things associated with it. Given the continuing taboo of menstruation on screen, references to PMS and menstrual products commonly serve as allusions without menstruation being named. In this section I examine occasions when menstruation is accused and presented as responsible for everything from bad moods to perceived irrationality; the inference being that the character is exhibiting symptoms of PMS. Rather than debating the existence of PMS—a diagnosis with much politics and controversy attached[1]—in this section I focus on the accusation being used as a way to minimize, mock, and dismiss women's emotions and to render them as less valid and less rational than men's.

Menstruation as synonymous with bad moods exists as both a perceived truism in real life and certainly as such on screen. In sociologist Laura Fingerson's research, for example, she quoted teenager Matt, who—in answer to the question of why women menstruated—responded "Just to be real bitches I guess, heh heh."[2] On screen this negative view of menstruation—as something defined by bad moods and bitchiness—is effortlessly detected with men, and interestingly also with *women*, frequently hurling this accusation.

Men and the Menstruation Accusation

In a scene from *Juno* (2007), an argument between two lab partners ended with the female (Candice Accola) exclaiming, "I'm going to the infirmary" and the male (Steven Christopher Parker) responding, "Good. Call me when you get off the rag!" In *The Darkness Within* (2009) a similar exchange took place:

> **Dixon Rampart (Sean Pierce):** What's your damage? You on the rag or something? Sure it isn't time to change your tampon?
>
> **Jordan Shelby (Stephanie Maheu):** No actually I like to stew in it, dickhead.

In an episode of *Southland* (2009–), police officer Brown (Arija Bareikis) told her partner Dudek (C. Thomas Howell) that unless he acted with more propriety she would request a new partner. To this, Dudek responded: "Are you on the rag?" The same question was asked by Rizzo (Jay R. Ferguson) to Peggy (Elisabeth Moss) in an episode of *Mad Men* (2007–). In an episode of the cartoon sitcom *South Park* (1997–) one of Stan's birthday gifts was an album that his mother expressly prohibited. Stan's friend Cartman looked on and commented, "Looks like somebody's on the rag." In an episode of *The Killing* (2011–), Detective Holder (Joel Kinnaman) remarked to his partner Detective Linden (Mireille Enos): "Linden, is there one or two days a month you're not PMSing?" In a scene from an episode of *Entourage* (2004–2011), the following dialogue occurred:

> **Lizzy (Autumn Reeser):** You screwed me. And I'm gonna do everything I can to pay you back.

Ari (Jeremy Piven): Is it that time of the month for you Lizzy? Because I think that your hormones are making your brain forget *who you're threatening.*

In the final episode of the sitcom *Everybody Loves Raymond* (1996–2005), the following exchange occurred between Debra (Patricia Heaton) and her husband, Ray (Ray Romano):

Debra: I thought maybe you could meet us at Marco's for dinner tomorrow night. You know, we could just get a pizza, and then come home and . . . [starts crying] put the kids to bed and then, maybe we could watch a movie.

Ray: That time of the month, huh?

In the British series *Jekyll* (2007), Tom (James Nesbitt) asked his assistant, Katherine (Michelle Ryan), what was wrong. "Sorry. Jumpy today. It's nothing," Katherine replied, to which Tom asked, "That time of the month?"

On the surface, something evident in each of these examples is *men* accusing *women* of menstruating or having PMS; both terms are presented as synonymous with irritability. While in the *Juno* scene the girl actually *was* having her period (determined by the menstrual headache she had mentioned earlier), in the other examples, menstruation was not part of the narrative at all: there was no reason to believe that any of the characters were menstruating, thus indicating that the female's behavior—be it surliness, weepiness, bitchiness, and so on—was blamed on a *stereotype*, irrespective of the unsubstantiated nature of the accusation. In many of these examples we actually know that something *other* than menstruation explained the emotion: in *Everybody Loves Raymond*, for example, Ray had just experienced a near-death experience during surgery and his wife was emotionally overjoyed that he had regained consciousness. The motivation behind the menstruation accusation raises some particularly interesting feminist issues, something highlighted in dialogue from the horror film *Jennifer's Body* (2009) between Needy (Amanda Seyfried) and Jennifer (Megan Fox):

Needy: Are you PMSing or something?

Jennifer: PMS isn't real Needy, it was invented by the boy-run media to make us seem like we're crazy.

Jennifer's response, while referencing the controversy surrounding the existence of PMS, also presents a feminist interpretation of the undercurrent of the menstruation accusation. In such a reading, the woman's behavior—be it anything deemed unacceptable to men—is construed as hormonal, as related to menstruation and in turn, as dismissible. In her essay on menstruation, political scientist Iris Young addressed the sexual politics underpinning this issue:

> The stereotypes of the bitch female "on the rag" accompany the construction of women as abject, monstrous, out of control. We are oversensitive, unpredictable, verbally unpleasant because of our womanly natures. . . . [T]hese judgments can be and often are used against us as women whether we are menstruating at a given moment or not. Coworkers may dismiss a woman's anger or impatience as just a symptom of her hormones, and thus not to be taken seriously and addressed.[3]

Feminist writer Jessica Valenti made a similar point in her book on sexual double standards:

> When men get angry, they're taken seriously. It's assumed that they have a reason to be so upset. But it seems that whenever women have the gall to express anything other than effusive chipperness, we're accused of having PMS or being nuts. Or we're laughed at or mocked ("Calm down, little lady!"). Women, it seems, aren't allowed to be just plain pissed off.[4]

From a feminist perspective there is, evidently, a social hierarchy of emotions. Those emotions associated with masculinity—rationality or control, for example—are valued more highly than those associated with women. By attributing women's undesirable emotions to menstruation, the woman gets undermined based on her biology: the inference being that her "bad" behavior is attributable to her biology and thus is feminine, permanent, and enduringly problematic. The biology/menstruation link is well demonstrated—and maligned—in the Australian film *The Adventures of Priscilla, Queen of the Desert* (1994). In one scene, the drag queens at the center of the narrative entered an outback pub. An older woman seated at the bar looked at the group and jeered, "Well, look what the cat dragged in. What have we got here, eh? A couple of showgirls. Where did you ladies come in from? Uranus?" Bernadette's (Terence Stamp) unsubtle response was: "Now listen here, you mullet. Why don't you just light your tampon and blow your box apart? Because it's the only bang you're ever gonna get, sweetheart!" While Bernadette may have been *dressed* as a woman, biologically she is *not* a woman and in this scene she is explicitly insulting a biological woman on the basis of the one thing that makes the two different: the ability to menstruate. In essence, Bernadette is implying that the biological woman is somehow *less than* because she bleeds. Such a presentation relates well to the radical feminist argument that drag parodies, if not *belittles*, biological women by fetishizing the superficial elements of womanhood such as dress and denigrating the less glamorous realities of womanhood like menstruation and menopause.[5] Most interestingly, this scene also references the idea that the "perfect" woman is one who *does not* bleed, something explored more overtly in the film *Annie Hall* (1977) as well as in episodes of *Married with Children* (1987–1997) and *House* (2004–). In a scene from *Annie Hall*, Alvy (Woody Allen) had a dream about being in love with the Wicked Queen from *Snow White and the Seven Dwarfs* (1937):

> **Wicked Queen:** We never have any fun any more.
>
> **Alvy:** How can you say that?
>
> **Wicked Queen:** Why not? You're always leaning on me to improve myself.
>
> **Alvy:** You're just upset. You must be getting your period.
>
> **Wicked Queen:** I don't get a period. I'm a cartoon character.

In an episode of *Married with Children*, Al (Ed O'Neill) remarked, "You know who is a good woman? Veronica. You know, from Archies comics? She never had a period." In an episode of the medical drama *House*, a patient—a professional model (Cameron Richardson)—was assumed by everybody—including herself—to be a woman, only to be discovered by the diagnostic team to be genetically male. The following discussion about her transpired between doctors House (Hugh Laurie) and Cameron (Jennifer Morrison):

> **House:** She's manipulative, yet completely docile. Everybody tells us that outburst on the catwalk was out of character. She's never had a period.
>
> **Cameron:** You're thinking this is hormonal?
>
> **House:** I'm thinking she's the ultimate woman.

In these examples, the implication is that the ultimate woman is one who doesn't inconvenience men by menstruating, notably one who doesn't interrupt sex by bleeding (chapter 3) and whose moods don't make her "unpleasant."

Women and the Menstruation Accusation

While thus far I have discussed men accusing women of having PMS, examples also exist of *women* accusing other women of it, as referenced by Needy's remark in *Jennifer's Body*. In *Center Stage* (2000), for example, ballet dancer Maureen (Susan May Pratt)—who appeared particularly touchy—was asked by her mother, Nancy (Debra Monk): "Did you just start your period?" In the British film *Bad Day* (2008), Jade (Sarah Harding) remarked to Marla (Riana Husselmann), "Christ Marla, who set fire to your tampon?" In *Fab Five: The Texas Cheerleader Scandal* (2008), Lisa (Aimee

Fortier) called out to her coach (Jenna Dewan), "Here!" [took out a tampon] "It's obviously your time of the month." One interpretation of women accusing other women of menstruating is based simply on intimate knowledge, be it intimate knowledge of the other women's menstrual patterns, or more broadly on the stereotyped symptoms of menstruation. A second interpretation is that the accusing women have in fact *internalized* our culture's often negative sentiments about menstruation absorbed through life in a menstrually hostile environment. This latter idea was presented in sociologist Helen Lawson's book *Ladies on the Lot*—which explored women working in car sales. Lawson relayed an anecdote illustrating the socializing aspect of the menstruation accusation:

> Women agents compromise by taking up behaviors that they may not like or have not used before. They adopt a code of anti-ethics. . . . I witnessed a woman agent laugh and agree with a group of men arguing that women who complain are "on the rag" or "not getting enough."[6]

In my book *Cheating on the Sisterhood*, I similarly discussed circumstances whereby feminist-identified women might, for example, engage in behavior—such as infidelity or wearing cosmetics to work—which markedly conflicts with their political values; that such behavior may be participated in for a variety of reasons: "while she may even be politically *opposed* to it, she may do so to assimilate, if not *benefit*"[7]; that such behavior is sometimes necessary for survival in a non-feminist world. In the context of menstrual accusations made by female characters, women can be interpreted as making such claims because they—much better than men—know the sting; women know menstruation and *know* it is an effective slur. These women have allowed the barb into their repertoire, in the process distancing themselves from menstruation[8] (or at least from *that* kind of menstruation) and, ultimately, aligning themselves with men; that is, they have positioned themselves where they deem it most profitable.[9] Another explanation centers on bullying tactics used by women against other women: something well illustrated in the films *Carrie* (1976) and *Fetching Cody* (2005). In both films, a girl gets her first period in public and is bullied by female classmates: while the girls doing the bullying each have, or soon will have, periods *themselves*, evidently they can rationalize their bullying on the grounds of them not being involved in *that* kind of menstruation: that is, in *public* menstruation which fails to conceal something which is supposed to remain private (chapter 1).

Another interpretation for menstrual bullying is one-upmanship on the basis of menstrual knowledge. In chapter 2 I quoted writer Erica Jong who reflected on her own menarche and claimed, "If you were not born knowing about tampons and menstruation, you are considered a retard."[10] In *Carrie,* the title character clearly did not know what was happening to her and thus she was bullied on the basis of her presumed naiveté. In an episode of the Canadian series *Ready or Not* (1993–1997), when Busy (Lani Billard) got her first period, she told the other girls in the school bathroom that she needed to go to the hospital; they laughed at her, presumably trying to convey the impression of their comparative worldliness. In some of the earliest menstrual product advertising the existence of an inner circle of menstrual knowledge was certainly apparent: a series of Kotex print advertisements from the 1940s, for example, used the tagline: "Are you in the know?," implying the necessity to be cognizant of things such as feminine odor, and to be aware of the cultural mandate to purchase remedial products. Contemporary advertising follows a similar idea: a Vagisil feminine wash commercial shown in 2011 included a line: "I found out the hard way," implying that the character's vaginal odors were first detected by *others*; that she *wasn't* in the know regarding appropriate odor control.

Another manifestation of the menstruation accusation is through its use in portraying the woman not only as being bitchy or oversensitive, but rather as *nagging*.

Menstrual Accusations and the Nagging Ragger

In previous research I have noted that, "[t]he hysteric, shrew, nag, fishwife, and harpy are stereotypes . . . that women know well; the necessity to avoid them at all costs has been internalized."[11] Accusing a woman of nagging is a very gendered accusation and, most relevant to this discussion, is one with very specific menstrual links. Since the 1940s, the term "on the rag" has been slang for menstruation and synonymous with irritation. Rag has similarly been used to mean sanitary napkin or pad.[12] In practice, and most relevant to this discussion, the term "ragging" has been defined as "to banter repeatedly or persistently and often annoyingly to the victim."[13] While dictionaries don't generally link ragging to expressions such as on the rag or to menstrual products, of course, in popular parlance, expressions like "I'm ragging"[14] or "I'm ragging it"[15] do describe menstruation, and the expression "ragging"— used to mean nagging, mocking, or even informing on—likely has origins in the menstrual connotations. The use of the term to imply female behavior considered as irritating is apparent in episodes of *Roseanne* (1988–1997) and *The Sopranos* (1999–2007).

In an episode of *Roseanne*, Darlene (Sara Gilbert) explained to her father why she didn't want her mother taking her to college: "Because she's just going to go psychotic when we get up there and she sees I've got my own life now. You know she's going to rag on everything: my school, my apartment, my roommate." In an episode of *The Sopranos*, Janice Soprano (Aida Turturro) described a car trip from years prior: "My father's driving, and she's ragging on his ass. You know how she gets. He's been drinking, I guess. And he takes out his gun!" In both of these examples, the word *ragging* was used to describe the apparently nagging behavior of women. In practice, the word has likely been chosen over other synonyms because it references both gender and a bodily function widely resented.

While there is a strong menstrual link between the word *ragging* and its use to mean nagging, to allege that such connotations are *always* intended by the speaker is hyperbolic. In linguist Sally McConnell-Ginet's research on the sexual connotations of language, for example, she wrote that "[s]ome speakers do not know the history of OTR or of on the rag; for them, it simply means something like 'grouchy.'"[16] This is a point particularly relevant to suspicions of "institutionalized sexism"; what appears as such might simply reflect a lack of understanding about the cultural and sexual significance of a comment or a scene.[17] While in *Roseanne*, Roseanne's PMS *had* in fact been mentioned in numerous episodes, and in *The Sopranos* Janice's mother had always been portrayed as a bitch—thus indicating nagging in these examples likely *was* a menstrual reference—the expression can also be used without the gendered connotations, something illustrated in a scene from *The Simpsons* (1989–):

> **Jimbo:** Hey Simpson, wanna trade belts?
>
> **Bart:** Well, not really, 'cause yours is just a piece of extension cord.
>
> **Kearney:** Hey dude, he's ragging on your cord.
>
> **Jimbo:** Get him!

While in this scene Bart's mocking of Jimbo's belt could be considered akin to stereotypes associated with women's perceived judgment of the appearance of others, it is much more likely that Kearney is using the expression without any thought given to the menstrual connotations whatsoever. Of course, while such lines may not have a menstrual intention, the audience's possible inference of one is another way that menstruation can be considered apparent on screen. As mentioned in chapter 3, reading texts "against the grain" in search of themes traditionally avoided or concealed is frequently done by audiences in the quest to detect taboo subjects.[18] It stands to reason, therefore, that it might be done by some audiences in search of representations of menstruation given the scarcity of such portrayals.

Emasculation and the Menstruation Accusation

While thus far I have discussed menstruation accusations made against women, there are also examples of such slurs directed *at men*, something apparent in scenes from *Chasing Amy* (1997), *Stonewall* (1995), *The Rage: Carrie 2* (1999), and in the television series *Dawson's Creek* (1998–2003), *Scrubs*

(2001–2010), *Californication* (2007–), and *Glee* (2009–). In *Chasing Amy*, Jay (Jason Mewes) remarked to Holden (Ben Affleck), "So why the long face, Horse? Banky on the rag?" In a scene from *Stonewall* (1995), dragqueen Bostonia (Duane Boutte) says to a policeman (Isaiah Washington), "Don't push me, Mary. I am not in the mood," to which the officer responded, "Awww, she ain't in the mood. Ain't we in the mood? Are we on the rag, dearie?" In an episode of *Scrubs*, doctors JD (Zach Braff) and Turk (Donald Faison) shared heart-warming anecdotes with a dying patient. Looking on, another doctor, Denise (Eliza Coupe), cynically commented: "Wow it's like really emotional in here. Any longer and you guys might all start your periods at the same time." In an episode of *Californication*, Hank (David Duchovny) commented to his class about satisfaction being "the death of desire," to which student Jackie (Eva Amurri) remarked, "Do you need a tampon? I think I have an extra in my purse." In *Glee*, Sue (Jane Lynch) offered her archnemesis Will (Matthew Morrison) an iron tablet to keep his strength up while he menstruated. Such sentiments were taken substantially further in a scene from *The Rage: Carrie 2*, when the head football coach (Steven Ford) made one of his players pull down his pants and said, "After that half-assed back block, I just wanted to see if maybe you had a tampon string hanging between your legs." Something similar transpired in *Dawson's Creek* during an argument between Pacey (Joshua Jackson) and his father, John (John Finn):

> **John:** You'll have to excuse my son, boys. His girlfriend moves away and all of a sudden it's his time of the month.
>
> **Pacey:** Screw you, okay? [John grabs his arm and Pacey yanks it back] Get your hands off me! You don't touch me again! Ever!
>
> **John:** Finally, my boy gets a pair and all it took was getting his heart broken by some girl with a few screws loose.

On one level these examples each function in a manner similar to the menstruation accusations directed against women: they are attempts to undermine and belittle emotions considered feminine and thus undervalued. Another interpretation, however, is that when directed at men, the punch of such insults is that men are being likened to women in the worst, most maligned way. Each of these examples uses feminized menstrual imagery to liken men to women and to embarrass, undermine, and notably *emasculate* them.

Similar to the predictable PMS narratives, another way that contempt for menstruation manifests is through fear and loathing centered on menstrual products.

PADS, TAMPONS, AND THE PRODUCTS OF REVULSION

While blood might appear the most obvious example of what is considered disgusting about menstruation,[19] as noted repeatedly throughout this book, menstrual blood seldom actually appears on screen. In lieu of blood, disgust is often directed at *aspects* of menstruation. At the beginning of this chapter I discussed synecdoche; as relevant to this section, on screen menstrual products frequently stand in for everything resented about menstruation. The idea of people being revolted by menstrual products is well established in academic literature. In a study conducted by psychologist Paul Rozin et al., for example, a variety of objects were presented to participants to gauge their levels of disgust. An unused tampon, for example, was considered particularly revolting to both men *and* women, with significant numbers not even daring to touch it.[20] In another study, both male and female college students found a woman who had dropped a packaged tampon to be less competent, less likable, and to be avoided both psychologically and physically compared to a woman who dropped a comparatively less offensive hair clip.[21] Teenager Jim, quoted in Fingerson's study, commented that menstruation and menstrual products are often considered "gross" by men: "even in the wrapper, it's just like 'ughh,' it grosses them out or something."[22] In sociologist Sophie Laws' research, she noted that men find simple references to menstrual products "highly offensive," identifying that:

> Sanitary towels seem to crystallise in one idea everything that men find offensive about menstruation. Since they have nothing to do with men, they seem to symbolise women out of control to men.[23]

Laws relayed a story about a woman who hitched a ride with a lorry driver who was transporting Tampax. The hitchhiker told Laws that the driver "was called 'the daft bleeder' by other drivers . . . you could see he didn't want to drive this lorry, he wanted to drive something respectable and masculine."[24] In this section, revulsion found in both used and unused menstrual products is explored as evidenced through narratives involving menstrual product-themed slurs and the horror of proximity. While disgust and revulsion are reactions *usually* exhibited by men, on occasions, such behavior is, interestingly, also expressed by women.

Being as Awful as a Menstrual Product

Menstrual products existing at the crux of an insult occur on two obvious levels on screen: they can be presented, much like a menstruation accusation, to insult a man by likening him to the most hated aspect of womanhood, and two, they can insult a woman through implying not only that she bleeds, but by making reference to vagina size.

In the film *The Tall Guy* (1989), the clearest example of menstrual product loathing occurred in dialogue between the protagonist Dexter (Jeff Goldblum) and his love interest, Kate (Emma Thompson):

> **Dexter:** All these weeks I've been coming here, I've been wanting to ask you something. What I really want to know is . . . er, what's your name?
>
> **Kate:** Kate . . . Lemmon. Horrid name.
>
> **Dexter:** No, no, not at all. Could have been worse. Could have been called Hitler, Tampon, or something.

In this scene, Dexter implied that the word *tampon* conjures the same kind of negative emotions as Adolf Hitler. As in the menstruation accusation discussed in the previous section, likening a man to a menstrual product is about emasculation, something well illustrated in scenes from the television series *The United States of Tara* (2009–2011) and *House* and from the films *The Sitter* (2011) and *Sexy Beast* (2000). In the pilot of *The United States of Tara*, Tara (Toni Collette)—while in the guise of her teenage alter-ego "T"—says to her husband Max (John Corbett), "Here comes Maxi-pad now, with a bucket of fried dub." In comedy *The Sitter*, babysitter Noah (Jonah Hill) greeted one of his young male charges with the moniker "Tampon." In a scene from *House*, House interrogated his best friend James's (Robert Sean Leonard) ex-wife, Bonnie (Jane Adams), in the process likening his friend to a tampon:

> **Bonnie:** Oh, it was never a date. I was coming off a bad relationship and he said we could go out as friends, you know, go see plays, go to a museum. I didn't think you liked Trenton.
>
> **House:** Love it. So he'd say it's not a date, but then he'd jump you?
>
> **Bonnie:** Oh no, he meant it. James Wilson, carefully calibrating his level of protectiveness for your individual needs.
>
> **House:** Did you just compare Wilson to a tampon?

In one of Don's (Ben Kinglsey) many rants in the British film *Sexy Beast*, he called Aitch (Cavan Kendall) a "Dr. White honkin' jam-rag fucking spunk-bubble." Each of these examples—while presenting a different style of insult—can be interpreted as having menstrual-product loathing at their core. In the *United States of Tara* and *The Sitter*, the accusation may simply be interpreted as immature teenage banter and as emblematic of just how mainstream and normal it is to use menstrual products as slurs. They may, however, also be construed as in line with the menstruation accusation examples discussed earlier where it is implied that the man is *woman-like*; that is, the slur is intended to *emasculate*. This idea is much more obvious in the *House* example where Dr House implied that his friend was *less* of a man because he didn't exploit opportunities to have sex with his vulnerable ex-wife. In the *Sexy Beast* example, Don accused Aitch of being a jam-rag, a slang British expression for a sanitary napkin and which Laws discussed as often used to mean something similar to "you prat."[25] In each of these examples men are insulted through their being likened to something widely loathed; they are being considered as disgusting and as lowly as the products which sop up the resented menstrual mess. Interestingly menstrual products can also be used a way to insult, or at least *embarrass*, women, something evident in *Sex and the City* (1998–2004), *The Aristocrats* (2005), *Ten Inch Hero* (2007), and notably in advertising.

In a scene from *Sex and the City*, Charlotte (Kristin Davis) explained why she couldn't keep tampons in her handbag: "Well, I have them at home but they won't fit in my Kate Spade purse." To this Miranda (Cynthia Nixon) responded, "Wow. Kate must have a tiny vagina." In a scene from *The Artisocrats*, writer Sue Kolinsky recounted: "Once for Hannukah he gave me a box of slim Tampax, and he says, 'Leave them out so men will think you're really tight.'" In *Ten Inch Hero*, while Priestly (Jensen Ackles) was in the supermarket deciding which tampons to buy, he phoned Tish (Danneel Harris) for further instructions:

> **Priestly:** What about the super pluses?
>
> **Tish:** No.
>
> **Priestly:** Why not? They sound, like, better.
>
> **Tish:** Don't, they're huge.
>
> **Priestly:** I thought you liked huge.

A 2006 Australian television commercial for Libra tampons opened with a man doing a tampon run. Inside the supermarket, he examined the range of products, picked up a box that read "mini," and looked down at his crotch and shook his head. He then picked up the box that read "super," looked down at his crotch and nodded smugly. He then asked the woman at the checkout, "Do these come in a larger size?" The woman said, "Nuh. That's it." The man appeared pleased with himself, his theory, presumably, being that if his girlfriend's vagina could accommodate his enormous penis then she would need the biggest tampons available.

In each of these scenes, a reference was made to the size of a woman's vagina through reference to tampons. Interestingly, in each example, while a reference to vagina size may be embarrassing to the woman, the reference achieves a somewhat different objective in each example. The *Sex and the City* scene, for example, appears the most innocuous. While it *could* be interpreted that the designer Kate Spade is being construed as other-worldly and not quite real with her potentially petite vagina, Miranda's comment actually appears more off-the-cuff than truly derogatory. On the contrary, *The Aristocrats* was much more explicitly offensive. In this scene, the implication was that the woman's vagina was assumed *not* to be "tight" and thus would be loathed, so she was advised to convey the *illusion* that she was tighter through a display of small tampons. While vagina size doesn't have the same place in culture as penis size, there are indeed notable examples where women are insulted in this manner. In my book *Part-Time Perverts*, for example, I discussed the "cultural stigma about the huge vagina" as apparent in episodes of *House* and *Curb Your Enthusiasm* (2000–): in both shows, women were accused of having stolen, smuggled, and stored objects in their vaginas.[26] In a sketch from the comedy series *In Living Color* (1990–1994), Jim Carrey played a husband who likened his wife's coldness to a refrigerator, "and with twice the storage space!" In these scenes, the contempt shown for women's bodies was illustrated through reference to the loathed "big vagina." In *Ten Inch Hero* and in the Libra commercial, the inference is similar, if more subtle: in both examples, the man was portraying himself as well endowed; the flipside being that the woman was big enough to accommodate him, thus working as a compliment to him and criticism of her. It should be noted that while these examples do appear to present some contempt for women's bodies, psychoanalysts have a slightly different interpretation. The concept of vagina dentata—the toothed vagina—is perhaps the most well known of men's fears about the vagina: that the vagina is a frightening place ("It's smelly, it's bottomless, it's devouring")[27] where bad things like castration can occur. (The film *Teeth* (2007), for example, was explicitly about this subject.) While culturally the big vagina is maligned—and something that the vaginal cosmetic surgery industry extensively profits from[28]—men's allusions to the big vagina may also be interpreted as reflective of their own lack of knowledge about women's bodies, menstruation, and also their fears of the unknown: as already noted in this chapter, things that are not understood are often mocked and feared.

Continuing the theme of contempt for menstrual products are narratives centered on the physical products themselves rather than the mere idea of them. In the next sections, the horribleness of just being *near* these products is explored.

The Horror of Proximity

Disgust grounded in being in the mere vicinity of menstrual products is well illustrated in scenes from *Ten Inch Hero*, *She's The Man* (2006), *GI Jane* (1997), *To Sir With Love* (1967) and *Carrie*, as well as in the television series *According to Jim* (2001–2009), and *South Park*. In *Ten Inch Hero*, while in the supermarket, Priestly was overwhelmed by the menstrual product choices. At one point he read from a tampon box, "it can handle any amount of"—he paused, alarmed—"Oh my God" and dropped the box. While it appeared that it was likely that the word "flow" troubled him—something implied in his dialogue with Tish afterward—nonetheless, the products in this scene represent what Priestly finds so disturbing about menstruation: the blood. In the sitcom *According to Jim*, when Jim (James Belushi) went to the supermarket with his friend Andy (Larry Joe Campbell) to purchase maxi-pads for his daughter, the men have a physical fight, neither wanting to go down the dreaded "aisle nine." The products become even more frightening to men in *She's The Man*. The premise of the film is that Viola (Amanda Bynes) attended school in place of (and dressed as) her brother, Sebastian (James Kirk), who had gone AWOL. When "Sebastian's" new roommates found unused tampons in her bag, they jumped back from them as though they were somehow filthy, as though menstruation and femininity were contagious. The same idea was exacerbated in *GI Jane*. The film centered on a woman—Jordan O'Neill (Demi Moore)—who had joined the Navy SEALs. In one scene, one of O'Neill's colleagues, Cortez (David Vadim), saw O'Neill's box of tampons and screamed "What about the tampons?!" Seemingly horrified—if not also *terrified*: "Don't you care about the tampons?" he screamed at the other men. In this scene, the tampons represented the abhorrence of menstruation, but more broadly spotlighted the loathing of women: O'Neill's tampons encapsulated everything considered appalling about her involvement with the SEALs. One of the strongest reactions to tampons occurred in a scene from *To Sir with Love* (1967) when the teacher, Mark Thackeray (Sidney Poitier), found a burning sanitary product in his classroom and reprimanded the girls that he assumed were responsible. In this scene, Mr. Thackeray stated, "I'm leaving for five minutes, by which time . . . that disgusting object had better be removed and the windows opened to clear the stench!" The object wasn't simply construed as disgusting because it was burning, but rather because of its connection to menstruation; Mr. Thackeray believed menstruation to be a private thing (chapter 1) and thus the girls' behavior was considered substantially disgusting because it put him in a position of being exposed to their bleeding.

As discussed earlier in relation to *Carrie*, when the title character's (Sissy Spacek) menstruation was discovered, classmates threw tampons at her shouting out slurs such as "plug it up!" While this scene might be interpreted as Carrie being humiliated with the very objects that she seemed to have so little knowledge about, another interpretation is that she was being pummeled with objects widely considered—even by women—as awful, that she was being insulted based on what makes her inferior and weak. In an episode of *South Park*, Mexicans posing as Cherokee Indians were shown selling a product called Cherokee Hair Tampons. While this scene provides scope for analysis in terms of race, heritage, and consumerism,[29] on another level, the hair tampons can't simply be dismissed like the coat-hanger "dreamcatcher" which was also being peddled by the men; tampons carry much more culture baggage. Tampons, already widely considered abhorrent, were made substantially more grotesque in this scene: not only presented as revolting by being made from hair, but their enormous size referenced the huge and loathed big vaginas discussed earlier. Something similar transpired in an episode of the cartoon sitcom *American Dad!* (2005–). The Smith family were discussing all the ways that they had been saving money during the recession and the mother of the household—Fran—volunteered: "Well, I'm doing my part to save this family some money. Look, I'm rolling my own tampons." Francine was then shown rolling large, cigar-like shapes at the dinner table. Again, tampons were made grotesque through their enormous size and lackluster hygiene.

Another way that the horror of proximity is portrayed on screen is by characters having to be involved with menstrual product *purchase*, where characters have to actively *buy* into the horror.

Horror and the Tampon Run

In the film *Just Looking* (1995), Sherrie (Ally Walker) mused, "You see, this is the beauty of short-term relationships. You can have all your whips and chains and never have to deal with the tampon trips to the 7-Eleven." A similar idea transpired in the British sitcom *My Family* (2000–) when Ben (Robert Lindsay) claimed: "Sunny skies and delicate flowers have nothing to do with real love. Flowers don't take the covers from you at night, tell you how to drive or send you for tampons at 2 AM!" As Sherrie and Ben implied, the tampon run is something construed as heinous by men; that in the dream worlds discussed earlier, the ultimate woman would exist *without* a period. On screen the tampon run narrative often manifests in one of several ways: it is refused, or alternatively it is done to demonstrate emasculation or love.

Men's outright refusal to purchase menstrual products is very well illustrated in a 2010 Kotex television commercial, produced in a vox pop style. A woman approached random men on the street asking them to purchase tampons for her (the rationale being that she couldn't leave her bicycle unlocked to go into the store). Each man declined for various reasons, offering to mind her bike instead, or alternatively, simply refusing. In chapter 1 I discussed a scene from the television series *Grey's Anatomy* (2005–) when George (T. R. Knight) refused to buy tampons for his two female housemates: "I am a man! I don't buy girl products." In an episode of *Rescue Me* (2004–), protagonist Tommy (Denis Leary) similarly refused to go near the "vagina aisle." In these scenes, the hostility toward menstrual products is made clear: buying menstrual products is construed as women's work, and ultimately, as emasculating; that by saying no to making such a purchase, a man is protecting—and also asserting—his masculinity.

Examples of men purchasing tampons do, of course, exist on screen; one premise often underlying this storyline is emasculation, to show men under women's thumbs. In *The Proposal* (2009), for example, Margaret (Sandra Bullock) tried to force her assistant Andrew (Ryan Reynolds) into marrying her for the purposes of obtaining a visa. In a speech trying to convince him, Margaret argued:

> Bob is gonna fire you the second I'm gone. Guaranteed. That means you're out on the street looking for a job. That means the time that we spent together, the lattes, the canceled dates, the midnight Tampax runs, were all for nothing and all your dreams of being an editor are gone.

Implied in Margaret's speech is that she *forced* Andrew into doing many degrading things which notably included purchasing tampons for her, that he suffered her abuse and emasculation all for the purposes of advancement. In the comedy *Man of the House* (2005), Roland Sharp (Tommy Lee Jones) was a Texas Ranger charged with the protection of a household of teenage girls who had witnessed a murder. In one scene Roland was sent to buy tampons; comedy ensued predicated on this tough lawman having to do such a *female* task; the scene solicited humor from the fact that only a man as tough as a Texas Ranger could survive such an assault on his masculinity. In the *According to Jim* episode discussed earlier, Jim and Andy went to the supermarket to buy maxi-pads; standing at the end of the aisle looking down, the men exchanged the following dialogue:

> **Andy:** There it is: aisle nine.
>
> **Jim:** No man's land. . . . Alright. Well, [wife] Cheryl's not here so I just have to man up and be a woman. After you, my friend.

Andy: No, whoa, hell no. I'm not going in there. No, there's no telling what darkness lurks at the heart of aisle nine.

Jim: Come on, grow up. Come on, get in touch with your feminine side. Come on.

The men then have a physical fight, each trying to push the other one down the aisle. In these scenes, the tampon run places men uncomfortably in the proximity of menstrual products and it is assumed that in doing so—in making them *touch* (packaged) products –some kind of osmotic feminization will occur.

Another way that the tampon run manifests is as a demonstration of love; that while the run may indeed have all the emasculating connotations discussed above, that more importantly doing so demonstrates *devotion*. This concept is nicely illustrated in actor Jane Lynch's memoir *Happy Accidents*, where she fondly recounted a story of her father purchasing menstrual products for her mother:

> Once, when he had to go buy my mom Kotex at the store, the guy at the counter, embarrassed, slipped them into a paper bag. He started to carry them outside, so my dad could take the bag where no one would see, but my dad just laughed. "It's all right," he said. "I don't need to sneak out the back door."[30]

A 2007 Dr Pepper commercial presented this same idea. Soundtracked by Meat Loaf's "I'd Do Anything for Love (But I Won't Do That)" (1993), the commercial opened with a man purchasing tampons for his girlfriend and closed with him refusing to share his can of Dr Pepper with her: he loved her enough to go on an emasculating tampon run, but not quite enough to share his soda. The central premise of *Fetching Cody* involved Art (Jay Baruchel) traveling back in time to disrupt the events that put Cody (Sarah Lind) on a path of self-destruction. Discussed earlier was Cody's bullying at school when she got her first period, something Art assumed ruined her life. To rectify this, Art time-traveled to equip Cody with menstrual products *before* she first bled: in this film, menstrual products were completely unperturbing to Art; his objective was simply to save Cody. In the *Rescue Me* episode discussed earlier, despite Tommy's initial refusal to go to the "vagina aisle," in the very next scene, he was shown in the supermarket amidst the menstrual products. Despite Jim and Andy's childish fighting on *According to Jim*, they do not return home empty-handed: on the contrary, they bought everything in stock to give Jim's daughter "variety." In an episode of *Party of Five* (1994–2000), Bailey (Scott Wolf) took his newly menstruating sister (Lacey Chabert) to buy menstrual products. Embarrassed, Bailey pulled the first product he saw off the shelf, said, "These look good," and attempted to bundle Claudia and the products out of the store. Presumably, Bailey saw the task as women's work, but he nonetheless went because he loved his sister. In *Ten Inch Hero*, when Priestly walked to the counter with the tampon box, two other boys looked on and laughed. Priestly responded with an interesting monologue:

> Think it's funny that I'm buying tampons? Do you gentlemen—and I use that term loosely—understand what this means? Obviously not. This means that there's a woman with whom I'm so intimate that we're both comfortable with me buying her most personal possessions. This means that our relationship is so solid, so trusting that I'm not embarrassed doing this at all. It means, my friends, that instead of hanging out at a grocery store having a sausage fest with another guy, playing the skin flute or just going a little [mimes head job] all day long, I'm getting laid by a beautiful lady every day and she takes it down town. And everyone here knows it.

Here, Priestly successfully redirected the emasculating connotations of the tampon run onto the boys; he proposed that *they* are less masculine because they don't have a real, bleeding woman who wants to perform fellatio on them.

While, of course, the comic awkwardness of the tampon run is generally premised on the man making the purchase, it is worthwhile noting that *women's* embarrassment in purchasing menstrual products also exists. In Rachel Kauder Nalebuff's discussion of her first period in the *My Little Red Book* anthology, she described being "too ashamed to approach anyone for help."[31] In an essay by John Scalzi, he discussed women in the early 1900s being too embarrassed to ask for menstrual products in drugstores, thus prompting the creation of an "honor box" where women could take the products and leave money without a personal transaction.[32] A girl in psychotherapist JoAnn Loulan and Bonnie Worthen's book on menstruation highlighted her own anxiety over such a purchase:

> I grew up in a small town, so I knew everyone who worked at the drugstore. It was awful for me to have to buy pads from people I knew so I always asked my mother to buy them for me.[33]

While women today are presumably much less concerned with purchasing menstrual products, examples do exist which showcase their continuing embarrassment. On screen this idea was well illustrated in an episode of the sitcom *Blossom* (1990–1995). When the title character (Mayim Bialik) got her first period, she had to go to the store to purchase tampons on her own. At the register she realized that Mitchell (Giovanni Ribisi)—a boy from her school—was the cashier. Panicked, she denied that the tampons were hers, and instead stocked up on dental floss and lighter fluid and left the store without them. These examples, of course, are not necessarily about women's *loathing* of menstrual products—although they may be construed as being about their loathing of menstruation more broadly—but rather relate strongly to the ideas explored in chapter 1 about the mandate of menstrual secrecy; the embarrassment of purchasing menstrual products relates to women wanting to avoid exposing their menstrual secret.

While men's discomfort around menstrual products is, of course, the typical narrative, there are indeed numerous examples where men, like Jane Lynch's father and like Art in *Fetching Cody*, are portrayed as quite relaxed around them.

Menstrual Product Comfort

While thus far I have discussed discomfort and disgust associated with tampons, there are, of course, notable exceptions to this whereby men are shown comparatively *comfortable* around menstrual products. In a 2010 Australian advertisement for Libra, for example, a man who had been left home alone found his girlfriend's wrapped pad. He opened it and proceeded to play with it. The commercial consisted of a number of different scenes with the man using even more pads for different purposes: as arm guards, as a headband, as body armor. His girlfriend eventually returned home with her parents to find him with pads stuck all over his body. In another 2010 Australian Libra advertisement, a woman called out to her boyfriend from the bathroom requesting he retrieve a pad for her. He found two types in the drawer—both unwrapped—and took both to her not sure which one she wanted. While such comfort is rare in the context of screen narratives, some examples exist, notably in *Blossom, She's the Man, Curb Your Enthusiasm, I Love You, Beth Cooper* (2009), *According to Jim*, and *The Unusuals* (2009).

In the *Blossom* episode discussed earlier, Mitchell who worked in the drugstore, didn't seem at all perturbed about the tampons and simply, good-naturedly asked Blossom whether they were hers; working in a drug store, presumably he found tampons much less controversial than she did. In *She's the Man*, upon discovering Viola's tampons, "Sebastian" excused their presence by claiming to use them to fix "really bad nose bleeds." Later we see some of the other male soccer players using tampons in *their* noses. In an episode of *Curb Your Enthusiasm*, Larry (Larry David) similarly deals with a nose bleed through the use of a tampon; in *I Love You, Beth Cooper*, Denis (Paul Rust) does the same thing. The kind of comfort evident in *She's the Man*, *I Love You, Beth Cooper*, and *Curb Your Enthusiasm* notably exemplifies situations whereby menstrual products are destigmatized because of their removal from a menstrual context. Another good example of this is a 2006 Tampax advertisement where a woman and man were in a rowboat. The boat sprang a leak, and the man looked in vain for something to fix it while the woman simply inserted a tampon into the hole. The man appeared impressed and said, "We're good." Something similar transpired in Stephen King's novel *11/22/63* when the ailing Al repeatedly used maxi-pads to cough into to "absorb the expectorants."[34] The men in these scenes appear comfortable with menstrual products because one, they help *them* and two, they are completely disconnected from menstrual usage. In an episode of the television series *The Unusuals*, Detective Walsh (Jeremy Renner) recounted a story of a man who confessed to having stolen a tampon truck; "something about stopping small leaks or something," he surmised. This example contrasts the "daft bleeder" Tampax truck driver discussed earlier; whereas Laws's lorry driver thought the experience of driving tampons was emasculating, the thief in *The Unusuals* was not so perturbed because he—even if misguidedly—saw another application for them, unconnected to bleeding.

A very unique example of men shown comfortable with menstrual products occurred in *Curb Your Enthusiasm*. Girl scout Kyra (Kaitlyn Dever) knocked on Larry's door to sell him cookies. Shortly into the transaction she admitted that she thought she had just gotten her first period. Larry, while initially appearing alarmed, realized his ex-wife left some "stuff that's going to be very valuable to you" and reassured Kyra "you had it in the right place." After Kyra called out to Larry from the bathroom claiming that she didn't know how to use the applicator tampon, Larry retrieved the instructions and read them out to her from the other side of the bathroom door.[35] He opened up one of the tampons and ascertained how to use the applicator in his armpit and then explained it to Kyra. This is a particularly interesting scene because Larry had never previously been portrayed as particularly sensitive toward women: after all, it was *Larry* who made the "big vagina" accusation against his friend's housekeeper in an earlier episode. Interestingly, one of the first things Larry said to Kyra in this scene—something he repeated several times, in fact—was "I got this." One interpretation of this scene is that Larry's enthusiasm for helping is about the rare opportunity for him to take control and be an authority: the humor, in fact, derives from how very amusing such an idea is.

In the aforementioned episode of *According to Jim*, despite Jim and Andy's silly fight at the end of aisle nine, eventually the men do get comfortable enough around menstrual products to the point where Jim claimed "You can't be too safe," and they took *all* the products off the shelves. Similar to the *Curb Your Enthusiasm* episode, Jim and Andy decided to "man up" and construe their task as a mission, something they needed to take charge of. Suddenly it was no longer about the horror of menstruation but rather the necessity to help loved ones. The same mission narrative transpired in *Californication* and *Ten Inch Hero*. During the *Californication* episode when Becca (Madeleine Martin) got her first period, later, her mother, Karen (Natascha McElhone), asked Becca's father, Hank, what happened. Hank nonchalantly responded, "I handled the fuck out of that shit." In *Ten Inch Hero*,

Priestly's time in the supermarket actually began with military music playing in the background and, overwhelmed at the variety of menstrual products, he rang Tish and said, "Code blue. Hostile territory. Aborting mission... I'm at the store, there's too many enemy tampons, I'm bailing." Art's trip back in time on *Fetching* Cody was explicitly a mission of a caliber that neutralized any emasculating effects of contact with menstrual products. In these scenes, menstruation got masculinized through its presentation as something men got to (superficially) manage, in the process sidelining any actual blood.[36]

In *Towelhead* (2007), newly menstruating Jasira (Summer Bishil) was taken to the supermarket by her father, Rifat (Peter Macdissi), to purchase menstrual products. While Rifat seemed comfortable handling the products and talking to his daughter about her "flow," this scene can be analyzed as being less about Rifat's comfort and more about his efforts to control the seemingly uncontrollable: he took Jasira to the supermarket to ensure that she bought *pads* and not tampons; the latter which he claims are only used by "married ladies." In a later scene, Rifat is shown to be holding a used tampon that he has retrieved from the toilet: again, it is seemingly much less about his comfort with tampons and more so an opportunity to control his daughter.

BLOOD AND DISGUST

In chapter 3 I discussed some of the myths of previous generations related to the menstruator's ability to sour milk and stop bread from rising. While these ideas may be considered laughable in contemporary Western culture, the idea of the menstruator as somehow tainted does continue, albeit presented in different guises. In this section I focus on loathing specifically directed at menstrual blood.

The idea of menstrual blood perceived as dirty has global resonance; anthropologists have documented many different cultures expressing similar ideas about the "polluting" elements:[37] historian Edward Shorter noted, for example, that phobias about menstrual blood feature in "virtually every society on record."[38] In contemporary Western society, taboos around blood routinely manifest as stigma and disgust, something identifiable in academic literature and on screen.

In linguists Keith Allan and Kate Burridge's research on repulsion, participants identified feces and vomit as most disgusting, followed by menstrual blood.[39] A man quoted in Laws's research expressed his disgust about menstrual blood similarly:

> I still think of it being sort of dirty or whatever ... more like afterbirth or something like that ... not something I'd like to be touching ... whereas ordinary blood, I wouldn't bother at all.[40]

Another man in Laws's study recalled having had sex and the following morning seeing "a lot of blood on the bed": "and I just puked all over the bed. . . . And she was really freaked out, and I was really freaked out."[41] Of course, it is not only men who feel this way. In Allan and Burridge's study, *women* also included menstruation on their list of most disgusting things immediately after urine, semen, flatulence, pus, and nasal mucus.[42] Likewise, in chapter 3 I quoted Bonnie from gender researcher Breanne Fahs's study who justified her disinclination for menstrual sex based on a belief that "blood is dirty."[43] Seventeen-year-old Ally in Fingerson's research similarly claimed:

> It's messy, and it's gross, and I don't want to have to deal with it. . . . You have to deal with stupid boys and physics class and algebra 2 and I don't want more things to deal with.[44]

In popular culture, while—as noted—rarely is the loathing of menstruation expressed literally, the sentiments are often expressed through narratives whereby loathing is directed at the tangentials like the supposed mess and smell.

The Disgust of Mess

In Binnie Kirshenbaum's book *Pure Poetry: A Novel*, a scene explored Harry's reaction to partner Lila's blood on his sheets:

> "These are Egyptian cotton sheets," he wails. "Do you have any idea how much they cost?"
> "It's not as if you can't still use them," I say. "So there's a stain. It's only menstrual blood."[45]

A similar scene occurred in an episode of *Sex and the City* when Samantha (Kim Cattrall) bled on the sheets of her new lover, Len (Robert LuPone). At the culmination of sex, Len saw the blood and said "Oh Jesus," and then complained, "These sheets are two grand a set." In *Pure Poetry*, Lila actually interpreted Harry's reaction as disgust: "Like his sheets matter to him more than I do, and that he considers menstrual blood as something disgusting. Like pus or vomit."[46] Unlike Lila, Samantha in *Sex and the City* was not in fact offended by Len's reaction—she actually appeared delighted to have an excuse to quickly depart—although *Len* was visibly perturbed.

On one hand, if menstruation is thought of as a "sanitary event"[47] and menstrual blood as similar to excrement or urine, then when taken out of the bathroom and smeared onto sheets, perhaps disgust is a rational response: as a character commented in David Wallace Foster's short story "The Suffering Channel": "Maybe menstrual blood is ultimately more like poo. It's a waste thing, and disgusting."[48] Another explanation is that in the time of AIDS and with blood being considered as a dangerous, if not *deadly*, substance, thinking of menstrual blood as untouchable, as disgusting, and as inappropriate for a public airing may also be a predictable reaction.[49] Another interpretation of the reactions of Harry and Len is male characters portrayed as tolerating menstruation as an abstract concept but viewing it as intolerable when it is actually present and when it negatively affects their lives and when it is spilled across their expensive sheets.[50] Such an idea relates to the loving/loathing relationship our culture has with femininity more broadly: women and femininity are revered until an aspect inconveniences men.

The Grotesquery of Smell

In chapter 3 I quoted Geri from human development researchers Katherine Allen and Abbie Goldberg's study who claimed "when I am on my period I smell this awful odor that never goes away no matter how many showers you take and bottles of Victoria's Secret body spray you put on."[51] In Fingerson's research, Katie similarly commented, "And like, it just—heh heh, my friend and I always talk about this, 'it smells so bad!' you know? Heh heh."[52] Contained within these comments is a preoccupation with menstrual smell. The supposed offensive smell of menstruation is another way contempt for menstruation is depicted on screen.

In the burning menstrual product scene from *To Sir With Love* discussed earlier, Mr. Thackeray announced, "I'm leaving for five minutes, by which time . . . that disgusting object had better be removed. And the windows opened to clear the stench!" The idea of menstruation having a smell is also alluded to in the films *Pitch Black* (2000) and *Anchorman* (2004). In *Pitch Black*, the only reason that the creatures were able to trail the group was because they could smell "Jack's" (Rhiana Griffith) first period. In *Anchorman*, the same idea was presented when Brick (Steve Carell) tried to justify keeping women out of the newsroom: "I read somewhere their periods attract bears. Bears can smell the menstruation." While these examples are from cinema, most references to menstrual smell are actually found in advertising, where such themes are routinely deployed to sell remedial products.

Historian Lara Freidenfelds noted that during the 1930s and 1940s, one of the strongest social offenses referred to in advertising was odor, something illustrated by the extensive advertising of mouthwashes, deodorants, scented shampoos, and douches. The treatment of menstrual odor became part of this social trend, whereby the social horrors of smelly genitals were considered especially heinous: something well illustrated in a 1929 Kotex advertisement for deodorized pads which warned, "whenever women meet the world, they are in danger of offending others at certain times."[53] In a series of print advertisements from the 1920s, Mum brand deodorant cream espoused the all-importance of "personal daintiness," recommending the product be used under the arms as well as on menstrual products. A 1948 advertisement for Lysol douches showed a husband sneaking out the front door while his wife looked distressed in a chair: "Why does she spend her evenings alone? Because she keeps her home immaculate, looks as pretty as she can and really loves her husband, BUT she neglects that one essential . . . . personal feminine hygiene." In a 1969 print advertisement for Pristeen feminine spray, the text read: "Unfortunately the trickiest deodorant problem a girl has isn't under her pretty little arms"; the product existed to help a woman be "an attractive, nice-to-be-with girl." Modern advertising exploits this same idea: in a 2011 television commercial for Vagisil intimate deodorant, the tagline was "100% woman, 100% of the time." Here the implication is that without deodorising one's genitals, a woman is less feminine and thus in our culture *less desirable*.

In sex writer Violet Blue's book on cunnilingus, she wrote, "It's hard not to worry about odor with all those annoying, virginal Summer's Eve and Massengill commercials coded into our brains."[54] Sexologist Yvonne Fulbright made the same point in her book on cunnilingus: "Thanks to commercials, like those by Massengill and Summer's Eve, females in particular are brainwashed into thinking that they need to smell like morning dew or blossoms 24–7, lest they stink."[55] Certainly, decades of advertising about the horrors of menstrual odor have influenced women in real life; as Fingerson contended:

> Many girls and women are concerned about odors. There are constant admonishments in the historical advice literature about the odor of menstruation and tips on how to contain this undesirable smell.[56]

One of the participants in Freidenfelds's research noted: "I thought that everybody would be able to smell it, if I had an odor. And then everybody would know, right?"[57] In Ani DiFranco's song "Blood in the Boardroom" (1993) the same smell concerns were articulated when she pondered whether her male colleagues could smell her menstrual blood through her clothing.

While the smell of menstrual blood is often thought to contribute to widespread disgust, there are indeed rare exceptions whereby the smell is actually considered pleasant, if not *arousing*. Sex researcher Shere Hite, for example, quoted a man who claimed: "I love the smell of my lover's vagina while she is menstruating. I want her to menstruate in my mouth and on my face—it tastes so sexy and smells so good."[58] Laws similarly discussed a man who liked the smell of dried blood on his hands, which existed to remind him of an earlier sexual encounter.[59] In *Part-Time Perverts* I discussed a range of perfumes launched in 2007 by the French fragrance house Etat Libre d'Orange:

One scent, Sécrétions Magnifiques (Magnificent Secretions), was marketed to smell like milk, blood, sweat, sperm, and saliva; the image on the front of the bottle shows a cartoon of an ejaculating penis.[60]

As related to this fragrance, to have blood mixed in with other sexual scents conveys the impression that the smell references menstruation, which evidently is a scent with arousing connotations.

This chapter advanced the theme of menstruation being presented on screen as something negative. While, as discussed in chapter 3, multiple reasons exist for men's inclination to denigrate menstruation and in turn women, in this chapter, examples of *women* participating in this behavior were discussed. Despite menstruation being a *female* bodily function, women are also shown on screen bullying other women and likening men and women to menstrual products. Proposed already in this chapter was the notion of some women deeming it profitable to align themselves with men and in turn distance themselves from the maligned and subordinated menstrual status. This idea taps into the popular argument of women being their "own worst enemy" and being responsible for the failures of feminism due to their inability to prioritize women as a collective above individual wants.[61] While women being cruel to one another is perhaps unsurprising, that such behavior transpires in the context of *menstruation*—something so intimate, personal, and near universal—appears particularly surprising.

In this chapter I examined depictions of menstrual disgust and the ways that such portrayals connect to broader views about menstruation, many centered on myth, taboo, and misogyny. In chapter 5, I examine representations significantly distanced from the negative portrayals discussed thus far and explore those associated with sexuality and titillation.

NOTES

1. Stein and Kim, for example, discussed the preoccupation with "pathologizing" premenstrual symptoms in the West (Elissa Stein and Susan Kim, *Flow: The Cultural Story of Menstruation* (New York: St. Martin's Griffin, 2009), 28).
2. In Laura Fingerson, *Girls in Power: Gender, Body and Menstruation in Adolescence* (Albany: State University of New York Press, 2006), 116.
3. Iris Marion Young, "Menstrual meditations," in *On Female Body Experience* (New York: Oxford University Press, 2005), 118.
4. Jessica Valenti, *He's a Stud, She's a Slut, and 49 Other Double Standards Every Woman Should Know* (Berkeley: Seal Press, 2008), 66–67.
5. Sexuality theorist Steven Cohan discussed this issue in his research on masculinity: "camp—in large part when it is solely equated with drag queens and their adoration of female stars—has a history of being read for its hostility to feminism. Camp was repudiated for its apparent misogyny in parodying 'women's oppression,' reflecting the tension between the feminist gay rights movements of the 1970s." (Steven Cohan, "Queer Eye for Straight Guise:

Camp, Postfeminism, and the Fab Five's Makeovers of Masculinity," in *Interrogating Postfeminism: Gender and the Politics of Popular Culture*, ed. Yvonne Tasker and Diane Negra (Durham, NC: Duke University Press, 2007), 200, n. 24).

6. Helen M. Lawson, *Ladies on the Lot* (Lanham, MD: Rowman and Littlefield, 2000), 3.

7. Lauren Rosewarne, *Cheating on the Sisterhood: Infidelity and Feminism* (Santa Barbara, CA: Praeger, 2009), 104.

8. This same idea appeared in research on women's health: "women who deny the effects of menstruation may be motivated to hold such beliefs because of the similar need for self-esteem maintenance" (Pamela Kato and Diane N. Ruble, "Toward an Understanding of Women's Experience of Menstrual Cycle Symptoms," in *Psychological Perspectives of Women's Health*, ed. Vincent J. Adesso, Diane M. Reddy, and Raymond Fleming (Washington, DC: Taylor and Francis, 1994), 212). On screen this idea was illustrated well in an episode of the supernatural-themed television show *Charmed* (1998–2006) when Paige (Rose McGowan) said to her sister, "You get so emotional when you're PMS-ed," and Phoebe (Alyssa Milano) responded, "And you get mean." Paige retorted, "I do not get mean. I'm above it all. Nothing happens to me."

9. Cultural theorist Tony Magistrale discussed the menarche bullying scene in *Carrie* (1976), and analyzed it similarly: "The locker room scene in which Carrie's menstruation is realized and abjectified is so unsettling in part because it is orchestrated by women who also menstruate but have been so molded by patriarchal norms that they will forcibly reject that which threatens their social standing, even if it is an essential facet of being a woman" (Tony Magistrale, *Hollywood's Stephen King* (New York: Palgrave Macmillan, 2003), 29).

10. Erica Jong, "Fear of Fourteen, 1991," in *My Little Red Book*, ed. Rachel Kauder Nalebuff (New York: Twelve, 2009), 17.

11. Lauren Rosewarne, *Cheating on the Sisterhood: Infidelity and Feminism* (Santa Barbara, CA: Praeger, 2009), 45.

12. Barbara Ann Kipfer and Robert L. Chapman, *American Slang* (New York: HarperCollins, 2008), 399.

13. *Merriam-Webster's Dictionary of Synonyms* (Springfield, MA: Merriam-Webster Incorporated, 1984), 85.

14. For example, a girl in Karin Martin's research used this expression to describe her own menstruation (in Karin A. Martin, *Puberty, Sexuality, and the Self: Boys and Girls at Adolescence* (New York: Routledge, 1996), 30).

15. In Kim Price-Glynn, *Strip Club: Gender, Power, and Sex Work* (New York: New York University Press, 2000), 116.

16. Sally McConnell-Ginet, *Gender, Sexuality, and Meaning: Linguistic Practice and Politics* (New York: Oxford University Press, 2011), 71.

17. In Tina Fey's memoir, *Bossypants*, she discussed pitching a Kotex-themed sketch in a comedy show. Her male colleagues kept making excuses not to run with it and Fey surmised, "They didn't know what a maxi pad belt was. It was the moment I realized that there was no 'institutionalized sexism' at that place. Sometimes they just literally didn't know what we were talking about. . . . [F]or all those years that I was *sure* that boys could tell when I had a loaf-of-bread-size maxi pad going up the back of my pants, they actually had no idea." (Tina Fey, *Bossypants* (New York: Little, Brown, 2011), 141).

18. In *Part-Time Perverts: Sex, Pop Culture and Kink Management* I explored this issue, writing: "Not only do individuals interpret media messages differently, but some will in fact *deliberately* read them against the grain and between the lines. Sexual minorities, for example, might deliberately misread a heterosexual text in search of subtext; behavior which is at the cornerstone of queer theory" (Lauren Rosewarne, *Part-Time Perverts: Sex, Pop Culture and Kink Management* (Santa Barbara, CA: Praeger, 2011), 45).

19. In cultural theorist William Miller's work on disgust, he draws attention to the disgust of menstrual blood, writing: "for all the delight which travel literature, anthropology, history, and archaeology have taken in showing that the substance of the disgusting varies cross-culturally and trans-temporally, there is a noteworthy convergence in just what things and kinds

of actions will prompt disgust. Some claim feces, others menstrual blood, as universal disgust substances" (William Ian Miller, *The Anatomy of Disgust* (Cambridge, MA: Harvard University Press, 1997), 15.

20. Paul Rozin, Jonathan Haidt, Clark McCauley, Lance Dunlop, and Michelle Ashmore, "Individual differences in disgust sensitivity: Comparisons and evaluations of paper-and-pencil versus behavioral measures," *Journal of Research in Personality* 33 (1999): 330–351.

21. Tomi-Ann Roberts, Jamie L. Goldenberg, Cathleen Power, and Tom Pyszczynski, ""Feminine Protection": The Effects of Menstruation on Attitudes Towards Women," *Psychology of Women Quarterly* 26, no. 2 (2002): 131–139.

22. In Laura Fingerson, *Girls in Power: Gender, Body and Menstruation in Adolescence* (Albany: State University of New York Press, 2006), 104.

23. Sophie Laws, *Issues of Blood: The Politics of Menstruation* (Houndmills, Basingstoke, Hampshire: Macmillan, 1990), 87.

24. Sophie Laws, *Issues of Blood: The Politics of Menstruation* (Houndmills, Basingstoke, Hampshire: Macmillan, 1990), 50.

25. In Sophie Laws, *Issues of Blood: The Politics of Menstruation* (Houndmills, Basingstoke, Hampshire: Macmillan, 1990), 71.

26. Lauren Rosewarne, *Part-Time Perverts: Sex, Pop Culture and Kink Management* (Santa Barbara, CA: Praeger, 2011), 134.

27. John Weir cited in Sheena J. Vachhani, "Vagina dentata and the demonological body," in *Bits of Organization*, ed. Alison Linstead and Malmo Rhodes (Sweden: Liber, 2009), 163.

28. For a discussion of this, see Lauren Rosewarne, *Part-Time Perverts: Sex, Pop Culture and Kink Management* (Santa Barbara, CA: Praeger, 2011).

29. See for example Jolene Armstrong, "Miss Information: Consumer Excess, Health Care and Historical Guilt in 'Cherokee Hair Tampons,'" in *The Deep End of South Park: Critical Essays on Television's Shocking Cartoon,* ed. Leslie Stratyner and James R. Keller (Jefferson, NC: McFarland and Company, 2009).

30. Jane Lynch, *Happy Accidents* (New York: Hyperion, 2011, 8–9).

31. Rachel Kauder Nalebuff, "Introduction," in *My Little Red Book*, ed. Rachel Kauder Nalebuff (New York: Twelve, 2009), 3.

32. John Scalzi, "Best personal hygiene products of the millennium," in *Your Hate Mail Will Be Graded: A Decade of Whatever, 1998–2008* (New York: Tom Doherty Associates, 2008), 350.

33. In JoAnn Loulan and Bonnie Worthen, *Period: A Girl's Guide* (Minnetonka, MN: Book Peddlers, 2001), 51.

34. Stephen King, *11/22/63* (New York: Simon and Schuster, 2011), 54.

35. Interestingly, a near identical situation is recounted in sociologist Jean Elson's book on hysterectomies, where she wrote, "When Allison complained to her father about the mess her period made, he not only convinced her mother to let her wear tampons, but he also stood outside the bathroom door reading the manual while she practiced inserting the first one" (Jean Elson, *Am I Still a Woman? Hysterectomy and Gender Identity* (Philadelphia: Temple University Press, 2004), 70).

36. Worth noting is that this mission theme was also used in an episode of the sitcom *Roseanne* (1988–1997) centered on Roseanne's period. The episode spoofed *Apocalypse Now* (1979) with husband Dan (John Goodman) lying in bed, saying, "Today's the day. Twenty-four hours of hell. I must get out of the house. Far from ground zero."

37. For example, this is discussed in the context of Iran in Bryan J. Good, "The heart of what's the matter: The semantics of illness in Iran," in *The Art of Medical Anthropology: Readings*, ed. Sjaak van der Geest and Adri Rienks (Amsterdam: Het Spinhuis, 1998); Malaysia in Popho E. S. Bark-Yi, *Body That Bleeds: Menstrual Politics in Malaysia* (Petaling Jaya, Selanor: Strategic Information and Research Development Centre, 2007); China in Emily A. Ahern, "The power and pollution of Chinese women," in *Studies in Chinese Society*, ed. Arthur P. Wolf (Stanford, CA: Stanford University Press, 1978); Botswana in Frederick Klaits, *Death in a Church of Life: Moral Passion During Botswana's Time of AIDS* (Berkeley: University of California Press, 2010); and India in Sarah Pinto, *Where There Is No Midwife: Birth and Loss in Rural India* (New York: Berghahn Books, 2008).

38. Edward Shorter, *A History of Women's Bodies* (Plymouth: Basic Books, 1982), 287.

39. Keith Allan and Kate Burridge, *Euphemism and Dysphemism: Language Use as Shield and Weapon* (New York: Oxford University Press, 1991).

40. In Sophie Laws, *Issues of Blood: The Politics of Menstruation* (Houndmills, Basingstoke, Hampshire: Macmillan, 1990), 33.

41. In Sophie Laws, *Issues of Blood: The Politics of Menstruation* (Houndmills, Basingstoke, Hampshire: Macmillan, 1990), 34.

42. Keith Allan and Kate Burridge, *Euphemism and Dysphemism: Language Use as Shield and Weapon* (New York: Oxford University Press, 1991).

43. In Breanne Fahs, "Sex during menstruation: Race, sexual identity, and women's qualitative accounts of pleasure and disgust," *Feminism & Psychology* 21, no. 2 (2011): 155–178, 163.

44. In Laura Fingerson, *Girls in Power: Gender, Body and Menstruation in Adolescence* (Albany: State University of New York Press, 2006), 1.

45. Binnie Kirshenbaum, *Pure Poetry: A Novel* (New York: Simon and Schuster, 2000), 172.

46. Binnie Kirshenbaum, *Pure Poetry: A Novel* (New York: Simon and Schuster, 2000), 172.

47. In Hope Edelman's book *Motherless Daughters: The Legacy of Loss*, she quoted psychologist Naomi Lowinsky who commented, "Without a mother, a first menstruation is just a big sanitary event" (Hope Edelman, *Motherless Daughters: The Legacy of Loss* (Cambridge, MA: Da Capo Press, 2006), 218).

48. David Foster Wallace, "The Suffering Channel," in *Oblivion* (New York: Little Brown and Company, 2008), 308.

49. In *Part-Time Perverts* I discussed the issue of the fetishization of blood on screen: "blood is nonetheless afforded a specific taboo factor—particularly in the time of AIDS—offering a unique life/death blur thrill (chapter 7); the emergence of menstrual porn is likely partly explained by this" (Lauren Rosewarne, *Part-Time Perverts: Sex, Pop Culture and Kink Management* (Santa Barbara, CA: Praeger, 2011), 66).

50. The ruined sheet idea was also mentioned in an episode of *Californication* when Hank discarded a sheet set when a woman that he had met at Starbucks got her period on them.

51. In Katherine R. Allen and Abbie E. Goldberg, "Sexual Activity During Menstruation: A Qualitative Study," *Journal of Sex Research* 46, no. 6 (2009): 535–545, 538. [Emphasis in original.]

52. In Laura Fingerson, *Girls in Power: Gender, Body and Menstruation in Adolescence* (Albany: State University of New York Press, 2006), 100.

53. Lara Freidenfelds, *The Modern Period: Menstruation in Twentieth-Century America* (Baltimore: Johns Hopkins University Press, 2009), 128.

54. Violet Blue, *The Ultimate Guide to Cunnilingus* (Berkeley: Cleis Press, 2002), 15.

55. Yvonne Fulbright, *His Guide to Going Down* (Avon, MA: Adams Media, 2011), 118.

56. Laura Fingerson, *Girls in Power: Gender, Body and Menstruation in Adolescence* (Albany: State University of New York Press, 2006), 41.

57. Lara Freidenfelds, *The Modern Period: Menstruation in Twentieth-Century America* (Baltimore: The Johns Hopkins University Press, 2009), 154.

58. In Shere Hite, *The Shere Hite Reader: New and Selected Writings on Sex, Globalization, and Private Life* (New York: Seven Stories Press, 2006), 193.

59. Sophie Laws, *Issues of Blood: The Politics of Menstruation* (Houndmills, Basingstoke, Hampshire: Macmillan, 1990), 61.

60. Lauren Rosewarne, *Part-Time Perverts: Sex, Pop Culture and Kink Management* (Santa Barbara, CA: Praeger, 2011), 94.

61. See Lauren Rosewarne, *Cheating on the Sisterhood: Infidelity and Feminism* (Santa Barbara, CA: Praeger, 2009).

Chapter Five

I Want to Suck Your Blood

Sex, Sexiness, and Menstruation

In entertainer Carnie Wilson's biography, *I'm Still Hungry*, she reflected on her experience posing for *Playboy*: "I suddenly realized that my tampon string was tickling my thigh. . . . On the rag at *Playboy*—can you believe it?"[1] Implied in Wilson's comment was an irony she found in having her period at the same time as posing sexily: she was evidently all too aware of the distinct line our culture draws between sex and menstruation. As explored in chapter 3, mainstream popular culture invariably *avoids* sex during periods: menstruation is frequently shown to give women an excuse to decline sex, to provide men something to blame women's sexual disinclination on, and to allow men a respite from expectations to perform. While not common, there are actually examples of menstrual sex taking place in mainstream screen narratives and extensively in porn. This chapter focuses on the different ways menstrual sex is portrayed with specific focus on the menstruating woman as sexy, menstrual sex as natural, as kinky, and as the ultimate expression of intimacy. Also explored is the eroticization and fetishization of menstrual blood.

THE HORNY MENSTRUATOR

In feminist writer Jessica Valenti's book on virginity, *The Purity Myth*, she quoted from a news report about girls getting their periods earlier than in previous generations: "Earlier onset of puberty is associated with health concerns beyond the loss of youthful innocence." Commenting on the report,

Valenti asked, "If being premenstrual is "innocence," does that make those of us with periods *guilty*?"[2] Valenti's question is a pertinent one, linking menarche to womanhood and womanhood to sin. Throughout this book I have discussed menarche being frequently portrayed as the transition point from girlhood to womanhood. A key aspect of this transition is a move toward a sexual identity: a move, that—as the report Valenti cited implied—results in the loss of innocence. While female sexuality is indeed often portrayed as dangerous (chapter 3), even more frequently it is portrayed as *alluring*; as something attractive, appealing and seductive, and certainly not always coupled with punishing consequences. In their discussion of adolescence, psychologists Susan Moore and Doreen Rosenthal wrote that at menarche "[a]ll the social meanings of being a woman are activated, such as ideas about sexiness, reproductive capacity, 'availability' and pressures towards stereotyping."[3] In this section I am particularly interested in the connection of menarche—and of menstruation more broadly—to sexiness; of menstruation motivating a desire for sex.

In chapter 3 I referred to research claiming that both men and women generally thought of menstruating women as *less* sexy.[4] In chapter 4 I quoted girls who described feeling "gross" when they had their periods, sentiments which reflect the dominant cultural perception of the menstruator as being unattractive and also *feeling* unattractive. A dominant portrayal perhaps, but certainly not the only experience on or off screen. The manner in which women experience their menstruation varies markedly, and while there are indeed women who consider their periods horrible and disgusting, there are others for whom menstruation is a less arduous and potentially even *sexy* experience. In his encyclopedia of sex, Stefan Bechtel identified that "[s]ome women *do* feel randiest during their periods."[5] Marlene Wasserman in her sex manual similarly acknowledged, "You may even find that you are horniest when you are menstruating."[6] Anthropologist Emily Martin reported on women's views of menstruation, some which clearly illustrated Bechtel and Wasserman's ideas:

> I feel sexy when I'm menstruating. I realized at some point in college that that was when I was most likely to get dolled up and go to parties. I think I met several boyfriends while menstruating. From ovulating through menstruation I am most interested in sex. [7]

Other women quoted in sex research have expressed similar sentiments:

> I often find that I feel sexiest when I'm having my period, so making love is particularly enjoyable then. [8]

> I'm definitely at my horniest during my period. [9]

The same allegations also appear extensively in sex discussions online:

> Yes, yes, yes. Thought I was the only one! Mainly before, as well as during. But during for some reason it's like that song. . . . I can't get no satisfaction! Just keep wanting to have sex. It's odd. Haha that is a qualification for a potential boyfriend—he has to be able to have sex with me during that time of the month :)[10]

> The strange thing is though I do however get really horny during my period so quite often I will play with myself but only in private in bed when my boyfriend isn't there or in the toilet or bath.[11]

Much menstrual-themed porn—discussed later in the chapter—is in fact predicated on the idea that women do feel horny during their periods; an idea which is sometimes presented as a female-driven fantasy as in alternative porn, and at other times as a male fantasy in menstrual fetish porn. In mainstream screen narratives, the idea of horniness connected to the menstrual cycle is most commonly referenced through the "on heat" expression. In an episode of *Glee* (2009–), for example, Santana (Naya Rivera) jeered, "She's like a cat in heat." In an episode of *House* (2004–), Dr. Cuddy (Lisa Edelstein) had to tell Dr. House (Hugh Laurie) that she was "not in heat." In *Law Abiding Citizen* (2009), Clyde (Gerard Butler) remarked, "there you go—you jump on it like a bitch in heat." The same idea is apparent in music: Missy Elliott has a song titled "Dog in Heat" (2001), Rod Stewart mentioned a tiger in heat in his song "Red Hot in Black" (1986) and 2 Live Crew sang of a freak in heat in "Baby Baby Please (Just a Little More Head)" (1991). While in popular parlance the expression doesn't refer to actual menstruation, it nonetheless references the menstrual cycle, implying that there is a connection between menstruation and sexual desire. Of course, there are some screen examples where the menstruator is actually portrayed as sexy *while bleeding*.

THE AUDIENCE'S SEXY MENSTRUATOR

In film theorist Laura Mulvey's seminal research on spectatorship, she contended that women's roles on screen are frequently defined by their "to-be-looked-at-ness": that they are routinely used as a decorative device and the object of the audience's gaze.[12] In this section I explore the audience gaze being deliberately directed to the body of the young menstruating woman, thus establishing her as sexy.

In chapter 2 I explored a number of narratives centered on the menarche experiences of girls in films including *Carrie* (1976), *The Blue Lagoon* (1980), and *Return to the Blue Lagoon* (1991). As exemplified by these examples—as well as in many others discussed in this book—first periods get a starring role in narratives far more frequently than any other period. One explanation for this is that menstruation is only interesting the first time it happens. Horror, surprise, elation, confusion are emotions that can only be felt the first time a girl bleeds, thus for narrative purposes, only a *first* period can exploit these ideas. Another explanation is the *voyeuristic* connotations related to the sexual development of young girls: that is, the provision of a sexy menstruator for the *audience*. *Carrie*, *The Blue Lagoon*, and *Return to the Blue Lagoon* were each controversial for a variety of reasons, but something apparent in each film was young female nudity. *Carrie*, for example, opened with the title character (Sissy Spacek) in the shower; the camera lingered on her naked body; the audience watched her soap herself, including her breasts. Even when the broader locker room came into view, the audience's gaze was simply redirected to the bodies of *other* young women, each in various stages of undress. In cultural theorist Shelley Stamp Lindsey's discussion of films including *Carrie*, she wrote that "[v]oyeurism is crucial."[13] Such voyeurism was similarly essential in *The Blue Lagoon* films: at the most cursory level, both centered on pairs of young, attractive youths alone without clothes on an island; something that was a clear selling point. Michael Ferguson in his book *Idol Worship* in fact referenced this idea in his discussion of the marketing of *The Blue Lagoon*, noting how the female lead, Brooke Shields, was "shamelessly sold as a teen (and pre-teen) sex pot" and noted that "prurience played a major role in the film's marketing and box office."[14]

While there are many examples of the sexuality of young people used to sell cinema tickets, this issue is particularly relevant to a menstruation discussion because it is not just arbitrary young bodies used in *Carrie* and the *Blue Lagoon* films, but young *female* bodies which were explicitly presented as newly menstruating; that their sexiness, at least in part, was connected to their bleeding. Sociologist Laura Fingerson noted that "few experiences . . . [are] subjected to as much secrecy" as menstruation.[15] The idea that an audience has been allowed such intimate access to a young woman is unique, particularly in a culture so seemingly perturbed about the sexualization of girls. In my book *Sex in Public*, I examined a 1980 Calvin Klein advertisement which featured a fifteen-year-old Brooke Shields saying, "Nothing comes between me and my Calvins." In that book I discussed the manner in which Shields' dialogue was telling audiences that she was pantiless; her posturing—her hips thrust upwards—drew attention to her pelvis and invited the audience to consider what was, or wasn't, between Shields's genitals and her jeans.[16] *Carrie*, *Blue Lagoon*, and *Return to the Blue Lagoon* are actually much less subtle than the Calvin Klein advertisement: through the mentioning of menstruation, the audience was prompted not to simply think about the girls' genitals in an abstract sense, but about their bleeding vaginas and emerging sexuality more broadly.

Just as on-screen narratives can gift audiences a sexy menstruator, such a presentation is also identifiable *within* storylines.

THE NARRATIVE'S SEXY MENSTRUATOR

The presentation of menstrual sexiness in mainstream popular culture is rare, but certainly not undetectable. One such example is the presentation of the feeling of sexiness that emerges at menarche. Discussed in previous chapters was the scene from *I Could Never Be Your Woman* (2007), when, on getting her first period, Izzie (Saoirse Ronan) said to her mother, "Let the games begin." While her remark likely alluded to the love games that Izzie planned on embarking on (chapter 2), another interpretation is that Izzie suddenly saw *herself* as sexual; her menstruation brought with it a sexual consciousness. In music, the idea of a woman seeing herself as sexy during menstruation is well illustrated in Laurie Anderson's song "Beautiful Red Dress" (1989). The song alludes to menstruation through references to things such as a full moon, a woman being at "high tide," and the concept of women occasionally going "crazy," and is based around the premise of bleeding *and* dressing up and going out; a woman who—like the women quoted earlier—feels sexual. Throughout the song, the woman not only feels sexy in her "red dress" but readily assumes that others would find her as such.

As noted in chapter 3, advertising is where most mainstream menstruation references are made. It therefore is unsurprising that it is in advertising where the sexy menstruator is most easily detected: a place where menstrual products are routinely marketed through images of attractive women promising to make the consumer feel similarly. A 1999 Australian advertisement showcased this particularly well. A woman, running late, raced through a university building. She reached a classroom (a classroom which she, incorrectly, assumed was "life drawing"), moved to the front of the room, and hurriedly started removing her clothing. She took off her bra; the class of *architecture* students looked on, captivated. She then moved to remove her underpants and then the scene cut to a flashback memory of the woman in a bathroom reaching for a pad: the voiceover said, "Stayfree ultra thins: protection so good you can forget it." The central message of the commercial was that the woman's menstruation was so very well "controlled" that she could forget about it enough to disrobe in front of a classroom of strangers: she was able to maintain a sexy identity during an *unsexy* time. The feeling-sexy-enough-to-forget-menstruation narrative in fact is very well established in advertising. Carefree tampons ran a print campaign in the 1970s using the tagline "Carefree tampons are so different . . . you forget what day it is," complete with photographs of women riding bicycles, the implication being that tampons enable women to forget all about activity restriction (chapter 3).

A notable way that the sexy menstruator is apparent in advertising is via the use of celebrity endorsements. In chapter 3 I discussed celebrity athletes in such advertisements, but in fact there are many examples of celebrity actors and models—known and revered primarily because they are considered attractive—who have also appeared in such commercials: Ali MacGraw, Carol Lynley, Courteney Cox, Susan Dey, Brenda Vaccaro, Christina Chambers, Cybill Shepherd, Alessandra de Rossi, Suzy Parker, and Cheryl Tiegs. These women—celebrated for their sexy appearances—were used as spokeswomen for a product routinely considered *unsexy*; a product in fact, which has perpetual difficulty attracting celebrity endorsements (chapter 8).[17] A central premise behind the use of celebrities in any advertisement is so that the qualities associated with the celebrity—be it glamour, athletic prowess, or sexiness—come to be associated with the advertised product. The message in menstrual product advertising is that through the purchase of the advertised product, the woman in the audience can also be a sexy menstruator. This has long been the standard way menstrual products are advertised, and is something apparent even in those rare circumstances when attempts are made to modernize—if not mock—the style through self-reflection and humor. A 2010 Kotex commercial, for example, attempted such postmodern comedy, showing an attractive girl dressed in white telling the camera:

> I'm a believably attractive eighteen- to twenty-four-year-old female. You can relate to me because I'm racially ambiguous, and I'm in this tampon commercial because market research shows girls like you love girls like me.

While this advertisement was set up to poke fun at the way that menstrual products have long been advertised (discussed further in chapter 3), the Kotex advertisement uses exactly the same tropes that such advertising always has: an attractive woman successfully combining menstruation *and* sexiness. Social theorist Natasha Campo alleged that the underlying message of much menstrual product advertising is that "[m]enstruation need not impair their sexual attractiveness; women could remain empowered, sexy and vital all year round."[18] This perpetual-sexiness-even-during-menstruation idea was similarly alluded to in a blog written by the company SexyPeriod.com, purveyors of stain-proof underwear:

> One thing we didn't expect was hearing people say: "I don't WANT to be sexy when I have my period, so don't tell me to be."[19]

Both Campo and the SexyPeriod.com blog highlight women's *resistance* to a perceived mandate that menstruators *be* sexy during their periods; that they in fact considered menstruation as an opportunity for *respite* from this (chapter 6). In a stand-up routine, comedian Roseanne Barr once claimed, "Women complain about PMS, but I think of it as the only time of the month when I can be myself." In a similar vein, critics of the sexy menstruator idea evidently endorsed an opportunity *not* to have the burden of sexiness for at least a couple of days per month. While of course these advertisements—like all media—are apt targets for analysis relating to their role in impacting body image and potentially making real women feel less attractive in comparison to models (chapter 4), they also present scope for an alternate analysis. Another interpretation of the stereotypical sexy menstruator is that she in fact helps *counter*—or at least mitigate—the crazed menstrual monster images dominant in popular culture (chapters 3 and 4); that such images *challenge* the dominant presentation by creating the possibility of viewing the menstruator as attractive, perhaps even sexy. Whether or not this alternate, sexualized version of menstruation has traction with audiences is difficult to ascertain, but certainly many people find the menstrual monster image unrelatable,[20] suggesting that perhaps lived reality, along with advertising images, help diffuse the screen's more extreme presentations.

In Anderson's song discussed earlier she alluded to the possibility that the menstruating woman might be found attractive. While popular culture more frequently presents images to the contrary—with presentations often focusing on negative aspects of menstruation such as PMS—real-life and popular culture sometimes do entertain the possibility of men finding the menstruator sexy, or at the very least suitable to be had sex with. In chapter 3 I discussed menstruation frequently presented as something that inhibits sex. For some men, menstruation is perceived as a barrier erected *by women* and which prohibits them accessing the sex they desire. Other men, however, will not be perturbed, something evident in the opinion of a man cited in an article on menstrual sex:

> If the guy is really attracted to the girl, it really doesn't matter. Heavy flow or not, you're a guy and there's a naked girl in front of you—very little will stop you from sleeping with her.[21]

Similar sentiments were expressed in *Jackass* star Stephen Glover's memoir *Professional Idiot*, when he identified that for him sex is much more important than menstruation:

> In Boston, I met a girl at a party who came back to my hotel. When we got to fooling around, she told me it was a "bad time of the month." I didn't believe there were any bad times of the month, so we yanked out her tampon and started having sex.[22]

One reading of these comments is the simple idea that men want sex and thus will brave potentially bloody consequences in pursuit of it. Such an interpretation certainly has visibility in popular culture. In Hunter S. Thompson's book *Hell's Angels: A Strange and Terrible Saga*, for example, he wrote about the attainment of a "red wings" badge which connoted that "the wearer has committed cunnilingus on a menstruating woman."[23] While wearing such a badge can be interpreted as representing pride, it can also be viewed as testimony to an *accomplishment*—war-medal style—of bravery in the face of adversity.[24] Such an idea relates well to menstrual sex euphemisms like "parting the red sea" and "riding the crimson wave," each of which has overt connotations of challenge and accomplishment. On screen this theme was detectable in the episode of *Californication* (2007–) when Hank (David Duchovny) went home with his daughter's teacher Mrs. Patterson (Justine Bateman). When the two were about to have sex, Mrs. Patterson divulged that she was having her period. Hank responded that it didn't matter because he was in 'Nam. While Hank *wasn't* actually ever in Vietnam, one reading of his joke was that he thought of himself as too brave to be perturbed by a little blood. In such a reading, sex with a menstruating woman is construed as a feat, a sign of manhood, and similar to the way tampon runs can be, as discussed in chapter 4. The manhood connotations of overcoming squeamishness is certainly recurrent in online discussions about menstrual sex:

> Man up son and stick it in there. A little blood won't hurt you. . . . Just get piss ass drunk to the point where u dont care and go for the kill. girls are more horny on their period anyways.[25]

> When the river runs red, take the dirt path instead. Or just man up and do it anyway. A bit of blood doesn't bother me the slightest bit.[26]

In such examples, blood is portrayed as something needing to be tolerated for the broader objective of sex: that sex is sexy and menstruation is accepted; that the truly masculine man does not let anything interrupt his sexual pursuits. While scant published research exists on men's attitudes to menstruation[27]—and thus, research on their attitudes to *menstrual sex* is even rarer—some references do exist of men claiming not merely to tolerate menstruation but actually find it *sexy*. In sociologist Sophie Laws's book *Issues of Blood*—which exists as some of the only research exploring men's views on menstruation—one man mentioned liking the smell of dried blood on his hands which existed to remind him of an earlier sexual encounter.[28] Similar comments were quoted in sex researcher Shere Hite's research:

> I love the smell of my lover's vagina while she is menstruating. I want her to menstruate in my mouth and on my face—it tastes so sexy and smells so good.[29]

The same sentiments are also easily sourced in online discussions:

> For my part, most of the time I enjoy making love with my GF while she's menstruating. But occasionally the idea gives me the squicks for no apparent reason. When that happens we just go with the flow, as it were. [30]

> I love it. Some of the girls I've dated say no and some want it during their period. It is just another fluid. Get over it. It's more lubrication and it feels better for guys, plus many women are actually hornier during their period. I...LOVE...IT!![31]

Two memorable mainstream examples of the sexy menstruator appear in episodes of the television series *King of the Hill* (1997–2010) and *Degrassi: The Next Generation* (2001–). In the cartoon sitcom *King of the Hill*, when Connie got her first period, Bobby—who considered himself her boyfriend—had difficulty identifying where he would fit in light of her new sexual maturity. Joseph, a friend of Bobby's, made this worse by commiserating, "It's all over, Bobby. I heard that when girls get the curse, they only go out with hairy high school guys with cars," to which Bobby lamented, "I've got peach fuzz and a bike!" In this scene, Connie's menstruation was portrayed as positioning her as suddenly sexually mature and out of Bobby's league. A similar idea was presented in the Canadian series *Degrassi: The Next Generation*. In one episode, Emma (Miriam McDonald) got her first period at school on her new white skirt. After she changed into some oversized gym shorts, she delivered a scheduled book report. At the conclusion of her presentation, classmate JT (Ryan Cooley) teased her about her shorts and asked whether she had wet herself. Emma corrected him by nonchalantly stating that she was having a period. JT raised his eyebrows. At least two possible interpretations exist for JT's expression: one is that he was impressed with Emma's matter-of-fact response and forthrightness; two is that he found her declaration sexy. While we can't go so far as to infer that he found *menstrual blood* sexy, it certainly seems reasonable that he found sexual maturity sexy, found confidence regarding sexuality to be sexy, and that he suddenly saw *Emma* as sexual.

A simple interpretation of the "manning up" idea is that menstrual blood is a reality: that it is not wicked or grotesque or other worldly or even specifically arousing, rather, that it is just life. Menstruation as a bloody reality is the first in a series of ways menstrual sex is explored in this chapter as identifiable on screen: as a natural occurrence that is just part of real life and real sex.

THE BLOODY REALITY

In Giuliana DePandi's self-help book, *Think Like a Guy*, she advised women to keep their periods thoroughly concealed from men: "don't reveal it. Instead, use Mother Nature's intrusion as an opportunity to blow him off for the night."[32] In her justification for this advice, DePandi wrote:

> In no way do you benefit by sharing this tidbit of information. He'll just think "ew" or "gross." . . . He certainly won't think, "Damn that's hot!" or "Geez, she's so real, I love it."[33]

DePandi's assumption is that men find reality—in all its guises—unappealing. In an episode of the television series *Ugly Betty* (2006–2010), Christina (Ashley Jensen) countered this idea, declaring that "real women snort when they laugh, they have fat arses, wobbly upper arms, fart and get PMS." *Real women get periods*. This reality means that if a woman is in a sexual relationship menstruation will exist and will play a major or minor role, be it simply disruptive to sex or something that stains sheets. While DePandi explicitly contended that men *won't* find the reality of menstruation sexy, screen presentations do exist which show male and female characters accepting menstruation as part of a normal, healthy sex life. Such presentations demonstrate that menstruation is not necessarily the passion killer DePandi implied nor is it something particularly erotic as certain porn would purport (addressed later in this chapter) but rather is just a normal, natural bodily function.

Menstruation existing as a sexual reality is portrayed in two dominant ways on screen: one is the method discussed in chapter 3 where it is a reality that is both lived and sexually disruptive, and two, as I discuss in this section, it is lived but proves trivial: that sex occurs and that sometimes bleeding occurs. This matter-of-fact presentation style was very well illustrated in British artist Tracey Emin's 1999 installation "My Bed," which involved a reproduction of Emin's bedroom. Amongst the debris littering the installation, the work included blood-stained sheets and condoms, the suggestion being menstrual sex had been had. The piece wasn't *about* menstrual sex, it was about a lived-in bedroom more broadly; menstrual sex simply took place there along with other activities. A similar portrayal was evident in Ruthann Robson's short story "Women's Music," where the protagonist reflected on her sexual encounters:

> Occasionally, one will apologize that she is menstruating, attempting to deflect my hand from her tampon. But I pull the string, toss the cotton cylinder, and then kiss her stomach, very gently, without any teeth at all. She will be a bit nervous when my tongue reaches her blood, but I never, never bite and soon she relaxes, letting me taste and taste.[34]

In this scene, the protagonist mused on consuming the menstrual blood of her lovers in exactly the same way she would consume other sexual secretions;[35] such sex was not *about* menstruation, but menstruation was part of it.

On screen such presentations are much rarer, although examples exist. In an episode of *Law and Order: Special Victims Unit* (1999–), the following dialogue transpired between a detective and a suspect:

> **Odafin "Fin" Tutuola (Ice T):** CSU just called from his crib. . . . We found blood on your sheets—same type as Kelly's. Explain that, playa.
>
> **Eric Lutz (Michael Trucco):** Guys, come on. It was her time of the month. It's not exactly a deal breaker for me.

While the presence of blood on sheets can, of course, mean numerous things—Detective Tutuola, for example, assumed foul play—the suspect claimed that the blood was from menstrual sex; he was making the seldom publicly articulated claim that for him, menstruation was *not* a reason to avoid sex. Mentioned earlier in this chapter was the episode of *Californication*, when Hank went home with his daughter's teacher Mrs. Patterson. As the two were undressing, they had the following conversation:

> **Mrs. Patterson:** Just so you know, I'm on my period.
>
> **Hank:** Not sure I needed a verbal on that, but I care very little about such things. I was in 'Nam.
>
> **Mrs. Patterson:** God, my ex always cared. He thought it was dirty.
>
> **Hank:** Oh, it is dirty. But in a good way.

In this scene, Hank and Mrs. Patterson wanted to have sex. She was on her period but evidently it was not a big deal to Hank, it was just a fact of sex. In another episode of the series, after Marcy's (Pamela Adlon) tampon blocked the toilet, her husband, Charlie (Evan Handler), cleared the mess. Later the two kissed passionately. While the scene ended soon into the kiss, it is not unreasonable to assume that the kiss progressed to sex: for them, menstruation was presumably *not* enough to deter normal marital sexual activity.

While for some women periods arrive like clockwork, for others, a period may be a surprise. This is another way that menstruation can enter a narrative: that it becomes part of sex *accidentally*. This storyline transpired in Tom Perrotta's novel *Little Children* after Larry and Joanie had sex:

> They made love with unusual tenderness, in honor of the vast mystery of life, only to find blood on the sheets and themselves when they were finished.[36]

While this is a sad scene because it connoted that Joanie was not actually pregnant as she had assumed, the blood was neither horrifying nor eroticized; it was simply part of life. A similar portrayal occurred in Abby Lee's memoir *Diary of a Sex Fiend*:

> This has happened to every woman, I am sure. There's always that final dreg of blood to our period. . . . I've even had that final spurt when Karl was eating my pussy some years ago:
>
> 'I thought you tasted metallic,' he said to me later.[37]

Lee's lover seemingly wasn't horrified, he wasn't disgusted, he just mused on the taste of metal. In a different episode of *Californication*, Hank mentioned once discarding a set of sheets stained by a lover who had her period. Hank told the story matter-of-factly, evidently for him menstruation—and ruined sheets—was simply a sexual reality. The same idea was also apparent in a scene from *Sex and the City* (1998–2004). In one episode, Samantha (Kim Cattrall)—whose period was late and she feared menopause—agreed to date an older neighbor, Len (Robert LuPone). At the culmination of unexciting sex with him, Len said "Oh Jesus" and "Baby, either you're a virgin or Flo just came to town." While Len was clearly irritated at the staining of his expensive sheets, this scene nonetheless highlights the unpredictability of menstruation and the reality of menstrual sex, even if unplanned.

In the aforementioned *Sex and the City* scene, Samantha's spontaneous menstruation also functioned as a way to demonstrate the distance between the two characters; Samantha was young enough to still be menstruating while Len was an old man with a fake hip; Len complained of stained sheets, Samantha got the opportunity to abscond as a seemingly younger woman. In stark contrast to this portrayal, menstrual sex can be used as a way to show true intimacy and to demonstrate just how close two people can be, as addressed in the next section.

BLOOD AND INTIMACY

In the British film *Submarine* (2010), Oliver (Craig Roberts) wrote a love letter to his girlfriend Jordana (Yasmin Paige) which included the line "I could drink your blood." The line was funny within the narrative because it perfectly illustrated Oliver's propensity toward histrionics. The line, however, also presented the idea of some love being so deep, of wanting so much closeness with one's lover that the consumption of bodily fluids is deemed a spiritual act; as an act of *true devotion*. Certainly in the age of AIDS—where blood consumption raises particular issues related to disease and death—blood consumption can also be thought to convey true trust and potentially also true recklessness.[38]

In a scene from Philip Roth's novel *The Dying Animal*, literature professor David had an affair with a much younger student, Consuela. David's relationship was portrayed throughout the novel as consuming and obsessive, his high emotions reaching a crescendo when he watched Consuela remove a tampon:

> Then came the night that Consuela pulled out her tampon and stood there in my bathroom, with one knee dipping toward the other and, like Mantegna's Saint Sebastian, bleeding in a trickle down her thighs while I watched. Was it thrilling? Was I delighted? Was I mesmerized? Sure, but again I felt like a boy. . . . I was at her feet. I was on the floor. My own face was pressed to her flesh like a feeding infant's, so I could see nothing of hers.[39]

This scene, like all of Roth's work, offers wide scope for the analysis of masculinity, religion, sexual anxiety and guilt, but the idea of David being *mesmerized* by menstrual blood is particularly fascinating. His rapture is not about blood in the generic sense—David is not a man with a blood fetish—rather, it is about *Consuela*'s blood; he is mesmerized by her; her blood is yet another thing to connect him to her and his consumption of it is portrayed as the one thing he can do to get closest. In Scott Spencer's novel *Endless Love*, the same obsessive, all-encompassing love was again illustrated through a menstrual sex scene when protagonist David pondered girlfriend Jade's blood:

> I thought of *her* blood and in a dizzy leap of hunger and exhaustion I longed to *be* her blood, to be the stuff that made the constant circuit through every inch of her. Her menstrual blood.[40]

For David in *Endless Love*, he wanted to be as physically close as possible to Jade, potentially being *in her* in a manner perceived as even more intimate than penetration. In Erica Jong's novel *Parachutes and Kisses*, the same ideas were apparent in a scene between Isadora and her lover Bean. In one scene, Bean's penis was "covered with her blood" and very shortly after

> He lowered himself between her legs and started to eat her again, revolving his tongue on her clit, filling both cunt and ass with fingers.[41]

Moments later, Bean "picked up the discarded bloody Tampax from the floor and began to suck on it."[42] In Binnie Kirshenbaum's book *Pure Poetry: A Novel*, Lila, the protagonist, remembered her ex-husband, Max:

> The very first time I had occasion to say, "I've got my period," and Max dipped his finger inside me. With my blood, Max drew a heart on the sheet.... As if he'd made a meal of me and used the sheet for a napkin, and blood was on Max's hands and wrists and mouth and groin and thighs and chin and between his toes.[43]

While these scenes are each open to a potential feminist reading—as examples of men being truly comfortable with women's bodies and of men being *avant garde lovers* (an idea returned to later in this chapter)—such scenes are particularly good illustrations of menstrual sex being a demonstration of true devotion. Such a reading does not necessarily eliminate the horror of menstrual blood—although this could be contended—but presents love, passion, and obsession as far stronger emotions than squeamishness.[44] Also worth referencing is research on women construing menstrual sex as something that enhances their self-esteem; just as the man may engage in menstrual sex as a sign of true devotion, the woman may psychologically benefit from interpreting it similarly.

In this section I explored menstrual sex as connoting closeness and potential obsession. In the next, I discuss the fetishization of menstrual blood, notably as manifested in the broader arousal found in blood.

BLOOD AND KINK

As the continuing success of vampire-themed narratives implies, many people find something thoroughly beseeching about those who survive through the consumption of the blood of live humans. Despite the fact that it seems quite obvious to audiences that menstruation might be a ready source of nutrients for vampires—something particularly obvious in light of the menstrual cunnilingus scenes discussed in the previous section—exploring such a taboo within mainstream vampire narratives seldom occurs on screen: as noted in cultural theorist Natalie Wilson's book on the *Twilight* saga: "As many fans have noted, the text fails to address what happens when Bella menstruates given that Edward is inexorably drawn to her blood."[45] The same point was made in gender researcher Anne Daugherty's analysis of the television series *Buffy the Vampire Slayer* (1997–2003): "Even *Buffy*, which obviously promotes female strength and power, still avoids open mention of menstruation."[46] While the slew of mainstream vampire films and television examples avoid depicting menstrual sex, such an absence does not mean menstrual sex is completely invisible. In *Part-Time Perverts*, for example, I discussed the concept of subtlety and allusion in cinema with particular reference to the work of Alfred Hitchcock and his theory that showing everything is unnecessary for audiences to infer true horror: "Suspense is like a woman. The more left to the imagination, the more the excitement."[47] The question of Bella and Buffy's menstruation likely exists in the minds of fans even without it being shown because the issue seems so obvious. By presenting a "sexy" relationship, by fetishizing blood and by referring to issues of adolescence—of which menstruation is key—audiences may simply join the dots and speculate themselves. While certainly not an explicit kind of portrayal, such presentations nonetheless put the possibility of menstrual sex on the agenda of the audience. Certainly, as apparent in a "nasty sex" manual where menstrual sex was even described as "a little Edward-on-Bella role play,"[48] evidently the audience can infer a reference even if the narrative doesn't present it explicitly.

Another way menstruation can exist in a mainstream screen narrative is through substitution; that while actual menstruation might be avoided to evade the rancor of censors, menstrual sex can appear in different and coded forms. In *The Curse*, for example, Janice Delaney et al. discussed a real life, if rare condition called "vicarious menstruation": "a monthly bleeding from a mucous membrane other than the uterus."[49] The authors used this idea to discuss *metaphoric* menstrual bleeding on screen, where another kind of bleeding substitutes for menstruation. One example they provided was from the film *Body Double* (1984):

> The hero, an unsuccessful actor, has a job playing a vampire in a porn movie. Before the final scene is to be shot, the actress cautions, "My breasts are very tender and I've got my period." Then follows a potent visualization of vicarious menstruation: the vampire buries his face in the actress-victim's bleeding breasts. Blood, biting, pain, periodicity—all of these horror motifs have menstrual implications.[50]

While blood on screen can mean many different things—in other research, for example, I have discussed the role of blood substituting for semen[51]— certainly in scenes of intimacy and in scenes whereby—as in *Body Double*—

sex is a narrative theme, blood has two other likely interpretations: virginity loss and, as relevant to this discussion, *menstruation*. Such a reading, of course, is very reliant on the assumption of a subtext. In sex scenes where violence and blood are present, one could interpret such scenes as exploiting the audience's knowledge of the menstruation/sex link and potentially reading a narrative against the grain. This is something possible in the violent film *The Killer Inside Me* (2010). In one scene, Lou (Casey Affleck) had sex with Joyce (Jessica Alba) and then beat her to death. Because this gory murder occurred in a bed—and in the context of a sex scene—interpreting such a scene as a reference to menstruation is certainly possible given the audience's intellectual knowledge of menstrual sex and our familiarity with the possible connotations of stained sheets.

While the explicit eroticization of menstrual blood in porn is explored in the next section, it is worthwhile identifying the occurrence of menstrual sex on screen as a manifestation of non-vanilla[52] sexual practices, as sex that is left-of-center and engaged in by people who are socially non-conforming; as Hank said in the episode of *Californication* discussed earlier, menstrual sex is "dirty. But in a good way." This idea was discussed in gender researchers John Rempel and Barbara Baumgartner's work on menstruation:

> Thus is seems that women who have engaged in menstrual sex not only experience greater sexual desire but they are also uniquely aroused by sexual acts that push the boundaries of social convention. By implication, sexual activity during menses may carry with it an element of being unconventional or avant-garde.[53]

In Rempel and Baumgartner's argument, menstrual sex is an outlier and associated with fringe and taboo practices. For the characters in *The Dying Animal, Endless Love, Parachutes and Kisses,* and *Californication,* each character was indeed presented as largely sexually uninhibited and thus their participation in menstrual sex fit with their character's sexually adventurous, anything goes identity. Certainly the perception of menstrual sex as abnormal and possessing specific taboo appeal is apparent in real-life menstrual reflections. In Laws's research, for example, men commented:

> I actually seemed to enjoy sex more these days when my partner was actually menstruating. . . . I find it has an extra thrill about it, which is presumably something to do with breaking the taboo.[54]

> The first time I had sex with a woman when she was menstruating I definitely remember feeling. . . . It was almost as if I'd knocked down one more taboo. I felt a bit cocksure of myself.[55]

While menstrual sex portrayals are uncommon in the mainstream, one place to look for Rempel and Baumgartner's "avant-garde" presentations is advertising. While, of course, advertising doesn't include menstrual sex, it does occasionally depict men who are comfortable with menstruation to the extent that it is feasible to consider *them* as avant-garde. Such advertisements contrast the stereotype of the male grossed out by menstruation (chapter 4) and instead show men at ease with it. In chapter 4 I discussed the 2010 Libra advertisement shown in Australia where a man retrieved pads from a drawer for his girlfriend. The advertisement opened with his girlfriend in a bra struggling to pull on ultra skinny jeans—at one point writhing on the bed and tugging at the pants. Her boyfriend was seated on the end of the bed watching and waiting. When she stood, she attempted to squeeze into a tight-fitting singlet; the boyfriend reached out to touch her affectionately but she didn't notice, moving on to squeeze into tight boots. The woman then entered the bathroom and called out, "Hey Nick, can you get a pad out of the drawer for me?" While we can't assume that this couple necessarily *has* menstrual sex, nonetheless, the boyfriend certainly appeared comfortable around his menstruating partner and around her menstrual products and even attempted affection with her; it therefore does not seem too big a leap to consider this man as an avant garde character and to speculate that the two may have an avant-garde relationship which includes menstrual sex.

While the dearth of menstrual sex portrayals in mainstream popular culture often necessitates reading against the grain and analyzing subtext to find allusions, in menstrual-themed porn such sex doesn't need to be uncovered: it is explicitly ever present.

MENSTRUAL PORN

In this section I examine menstrual porn, exploring the category as an entity and then analyzing two very different manifestations of it in the alternative porn (alt-porn) and fetish porn categories.

Amongst the many feminist criticisms of porn are those which condemn the medium as being filled with idealized, unrealistic, and unattainable representations of women:

> Like the prostitute, the pornographic film actress is another representation of ideal female sexuality. She is compliant and perpetually available for use.[56]

> [T]he difficulty with pornography is that the created image is unattainable. The women who pose in pornographic magazines are not the average women in life. Additionally, their photos have been touched up and their poses are not the natural ones you will experience in healthy marital sex.[57]

> [W]hereas in early pornography models often seem to be left "as they are," in *GQ* models are obviously retouched, improved on, or aesthetised, reminding the viewer that the female has been "made," constructed and authored by the male.[58]

The presumption of an idealized beauty aesthetic in porn is particularly interesting and relevant to this discussion because presumably the appearance of menstruation would sharply contradict this idea: menstruation is, by its nature, messy. On the most basic level this idea would suggest that the menstruating woman has no place in the idealized world of porn; that her blood would dirty a scene. In making his distinction between the work of the Marquis de Sade and porn, biographer Neil Schaeffer noted that unlike de Sade's work, "the characters in pornography are idealized, fictionalized, sanitized."[59] While Schaeffer doesn't expand on his idea of "sanitized," we might assume that the word references the assumption of cleanliness in porn: psychological *and* emotional; something inferred given that porn is frequently devoid of a storyline. Another interpretation, however, relates to hygiene. In her discussion of what she terms "clean porn," writer Susann Cokal contended that "the ideal of female sexual attractiveness is a firm body with large breasts, flat stomach, and—surprise—a hairless vulva."[60] Certainly much research on porn documents a move toward hairlessness, but of particular interest in Cokal's chapter is her discussion that hairlessness is part of contemporary understandings of *cleanliness*. While she doesn't discuss menstruation, it is certainly feasible to assume that like pubic hair, menstruation would be construed as part of unappealing female messiness: as Fingerson contended, the idea of menstruation as *dirty* is certainly popular: "[m]enstruation, as shown by boys' gross joking, contaminates and pollutes sex; it does not enhance it and thus should be concealed and hidden."[61] In such a reading, porn would eschew pubic hair and menstruation in an effort to remove the "unclean" and less appealing aspects of womanhood, in the process presenting audiences with a sanitized, idealized version of female sexuality. Porn which conflicts with these ideas—which dares to show hair and blood—is therefore considered outlier, fringe, and thus relegated to one of the two subsets of the medium: alt-porn or fetish porn.

In *Part-Time Perverts* I discussed alt-porn with reference to the FurryGirl.com website which boasts an "all natural" unshaven woman; porn which explicitly contrasts the dominant air-brushed aesthetic of mainstream porn. Perhaps one of the most famous of such sites is SuicideGirls.com:

> With a vibrant, sex positive community of women (and men), SuicideGirls was founded on the belief that creativity, personality and intelligence are not incompatible with sexy, compelling entertainment. . . . The site mixes the smarts, enthusiasm and DIY attitude of the best music and alternative culture sites with an unapologetic, grassroots approach to sexuality.[62]

In her discussion about the site, sex columnist Emma Taylor described the contents: "The chicks are actually alternative-looking, too—most of them aren't traditionally pretty or playboy hot."[63] Sites like SuicideGirls.com boast hairy women, tattooed girls, and pierced girls: that is, women whose looks deviate from the standard conventions of beauty usually proffered by porn. Given that menstruating women are frequently considered unattractive and are excluded from standard porn, the fringe sexualities and appearances found in alt-porn serve as a home for such material. SuicideGirls.com does not actually include menstruation representations; there are, however, a number of other alt-porn sites that do. BloodyTrixie.com, for example, is explicitly menstrual-themed and purported to be run by an "all-natural college educated" woman in her thirties who claims:

> It's very rewarding to prove that a woman doesn't have to fake orgasm, wax her asscrack, or buy thousands of dollars of cosmetic surgery to inspire other people to get off.[64]

The focus of BloodyTrixie.com, as the title indicates, is Trixie's menstruation: the site is full of images of Trixie posing naked, her menstruation running freely. EroticRed.com, another alt-porn site, similarly depicts alternative-looking hairy, tattooed, and pierced girls who are each photographed bleeding:

> Erotic Red stands as a proud outpost of sense and sensuality in a world of internet porn gone terribly boring. We're not here to sell menstruation as a gross-out fetish, but to show that it is a healthy, interesting, and fun part of the lives of all female-bodied folk. We're happy to shake up silly old taboos and encourage every woman to love her body and sexuality—every day of the month.[65]

BloodyTrixie.com and EroticRed.com—while both unashamedly pornographic—show non-*Playboy* women posing, masturbating and very seldom with partners, thus distinguishing the category markedly from other kinds of contemporary porn. To contend that BloodyTrixie.com and EroticRed.com show women *celebrating* their bodies and their menstruation is perhaps too lofty an assumption—after all, like standard porn, BloodyTrixie.com and EroticRed.com are still commercial enterprises—but these sites nonetheless do present a focus on *natural* menstruation, purporting to use *real* menstrual blood, something that the menstrual fetish porn discussed later in this section does not. The use of real blood is in fact particularly important and can be read as evidence of acceptance and possible reverence of *actual* menstruation as opposed to the gore and shock/horror of blood as exploited in menstrual fetish porn. Rather than large quantities of blood, menstrual-themed alt-porn focuses on women playing with the blood that they have seemingly bled themselves, presenting them as comfortable with their own menstruation and experiencing their bleeding as sexy. Such sites also try to convey the idea that real women in their natural state are beautiful. That unlike standard porn which sanitizes female sexuality, alt-porn attempts to arouse through a presentation of unadulterated female sexuality in all its messy guises.

Another, vastly different kind of menstrual porn is fetish porn, more akin to "gross-out" urine and scat-themed material, something Trixie from BloodyTrixie.com attempted to distance her alt-porn genre from:

> Leaving menstruation out of porn and lumping graphic sexual depictions of menstruation together with shit and piss reflect and reinforce a primitive backwater ignorance about women and the human body, reinforcing centuries-old myths, suspicions, and fears about blood and the function of women's cycles. This type of ignorance is the TRUE obscenity.[66]

Menstrual fetish sites such as MenstruationSluts.com and MenstrualPorn.com differ dramatically from alt-porn sites like BloodyTrixie.com and EroticRed.com. The women in MenstrualSluts.com and MenstrualPorn.com, for example, are far closer in appearance to "playboy hot." The biggest difference between the two genres, however, is the role of blood: whereas in alt-porn the blood is part of a broader presentation of alternative sexuality, in fetish porn, the blood is *the* central focus: vast quantities of it are splattered, smeared, and spread and while clearly distancing itself from "clean porn," appears less celebration of menstruation and more so as fetishization of it.

In menstrual-themed porn—notably in fetish material, although not exclusively—there are a number of distinct elements which get fetishized, as are discussed in the next sections: the blood, the smell, the humiliation and the products.

Eroticizing the Blood

Blood is obviously the central drawcard in menstrual fetish porn, the more in quantity, the redder, the better. The website MenstrualPorn.com, for example, markets itself with the following text:

> Our hot babes get extremely horny when they are on their period. Some guys don't like fucking girls when they are on their period, but our studs love nothing more than to feel the sticky red stuff on their swollen cocks, some even go for a little taste![67]

The website offers photos and videos where bright red blood is smeared on thighs, penises, and mouths and where blood-soaked tampons are frequent props. Blood is everywhere, raising numerous issues for discussion. As noted repeatedly throughout this book, every woman's menstrual experience is different. While some women may bleed heavily—like comedian Margaret

Cho, who described her menstruation as "heavy, long, arduous" and her mattress as a crime scene[68] —the reality is that the amount of blood present in menstrual porn differs markedly from the amount of blood likely present during an actual period. Alt-porn site EroticRed.com in fact provides an interesting page comparing the look and feel of *real* blood-soaked tampons to the fake ones common in porn. Aside from the sheer unrealistic *quantity* of blood portrayed in menstrual fetish porn, there is the color and texture: the blood in menstrual fetish porn is always bright red and fluid; real blood in comparison dries on skin and doesn't *stay* bright red. Of course, bright red smears *look* how audiences might imagine it, thus helping to present a seemingly convincing menstrual blood portrayal and also helping to cater to an audience of voyeurs.[69]

In chapter 1 I explored the lack of understanding of menstruation on the part of men. One aspect of this knowledge gap is epitomized in comments regarding assumptions about the *quantity* of blood during menstruation. In Fingerson's research, for example, she quoted fourteen-year-old Brian who understood menstruation as: "[w]hen girls get really mean and they bleed everywhere."[70] The same idea was evident when Tom Tucker on the cartoon sitcom *Family Guy* (1999–) asked, "Can a woman really become mayor, or will she just bleed all over the city?" In an episode of the sitcom *The New Adventures of Old Christine* (2006–2010), Barb (Wanda Sykes) similarly described the gym restroom—where they had run out of maxi-pads—as being "like a CSI crime scene." A far more extreme presentation of this occurred in the comedy *Dirty Love* (2005). Rebecca (Jenny McCarthy) went on a tampon run but arrived at the supermarket too late and flooded the floor with her menstrual blood. These scenes reflect and exploit misconceptions about menstruation, in turn exaggerating the quantity of blood as well as the "gushing." Certainly a central component of menstrual fetish porn centers on providing images that exploit the interest in the supposed grotesque nature of menstruation and, of course, in othering. Rather than presenting menstrual blood loss as something subtle and manageable or natural and sexy, instead, menstrual fetish porn portrays it as a bloodbath: it is shown as disgusting, abhorrent, and proof of a widespread reluctance to allow such a substance in one's bed.[71]

Eroticizing the Smell

As discussed in chapters 3 and 5, part of both men and women's disgust in menstruation is centered on smell. Whether considered fishy, earthy, or metallic, the smell of menstruation—be it the *actual* smell or merely the assumed one—gets extensive attention in popular culture. In *The Silence of the Lambs* (1991), one of the inmates says to Clarice (Jodie Foster), "I can smell your cunt." While we don't know whether the sinister remark was centered on menstruation, this is certainly a possibility. In chapter 4 I discussed examples from *Pitch Black* (2000) and *Anchorman* (2004) where the smell of menstruation was also referenced. In porn, the smell is often presented as a way to convey and embellish the fetishistic qualities of periods. In stills from the "Nika & Amalia" video on the MenstruationSluts.com website, for example, one woman held up a blood-stained pad to the nose of another woman. While we might interpret this as a cheeky presentation predicated simply on taboo, it can otherwise be interpreted as reflecting disgust in line with a humiliation narrative (addressed later in this chapter). In the online erotic story repository Literotica.com, menstrual porn stories spotlighting the smell of menstrual blood are relatively common:

> I licked all around her two holes noticing a slightly different flavour than her sister. A little more feminine and pungent as if she was coming close to menstruation.[72]

> That afternoon my suspicions were confirmed, when I got a strong whiff of her menstrual cycle aroma. What a turn-on! I had always had fantasies about girls and their time of the month. And I had always been fascinated and aroused by feminine hygiene products.[73]

> Carol now started licking and sucking Brenda's cunt as if she were starving. Immediately, I settled in behind Carol's massive ass and yanked off her hot red panties. The room reeked the smells of menstrual flow.[74]

Certainly it is feasible to consider the smell of menstruation to be a turn-on for some people; that the smell—like others associated with certain sexual practices and fetishes—helps to create a scene, something particularly relevant in *written* porn where sensual details are needed in lieu of images. Another interpretation, however, is its connection to humiliation: being *forced* to smell menstrual blood—much like being forced to *taste* it (as discussed in the next section)—is portrayed as erotic. On the SaraDomina.com website, for example, a film described as "Degradation with champagne, smelly underwear and dirty kotex pads" involved the mistress *forcing* her slave to sniff her blood-stained pad. This notion of the *forced* smell of menstrual blood provides a useful segue to a discussion of another way menstruation frequently appears in porn: as part of a humiliation narrative.

Eroticizing the Humiliation

In *Part-Time Perverts*, I discussed fat-themed porn, identifying a specific kind of arousal stemming from the humiliating connotations of body shapes that aren't normally considered attractive:

> [T]heir attraction is borne from the freak-show factor found in fucking someone "disgusting." ... [L]ike many humiliation-related fantasies, the popularity of fat porn is about attraction to that which we should not find arousing; an attraction to porn that is humiliating to masturbate to.[75]

Such an analysis is equally applicable to interpreting the appeal of menstrual fetish porn. As discussed in chapter 4, men frequently find menstruation disgusting. While in some menstrual-themed porn the blood is found erotic, in others, the man's *forced* interaction with it is part of the fantasy; he is participating in behavior he finds disgusting and degrading; he is aroused by being "forced" to do sexual things that he finds despicable. This idea is particularly well demonstrated in Richard Dee's erotic novel *The Pampered Black Queen*:

> She lay back on the pillow he provided and basked in the total feeling of power and relaxation she felt with her slave's face still buried in her blood stained pussy. She smiled to herself as she remembered the night in her apartment when she had called him into her bathroom. She had told him to kneel in front of her while she pulled her tampon out. "Now tilt your head back and open your mouth," she had told him. She had then proceeded to squeeze blood from the tampon into his open mouth.[76]

Unlike the tampon-sucking scene in Jong's novel discussed earlier—which was instigated by the man seemingly for his own pleasure—here, the act occurred as part of a power play scene; it was a way for the female master to exert dominance over her slave. Similar scenes exist on the Menstruation Sluts.com website which advertises "60 menstruation lezdom photos" and which exploits this same idea, that the forced smelling and tasting of menstrual blood is something particularly abhorrent and is grotesquely suitable for use in humiliation and punishment-themed fantasies.

Interpreting menstruation in fetish porn as a humiliating experience for the bleeding woman is also a possibility. While some anti-porn commentators would consider *any* woman's appearance in porn to be humiliating and degrading, for this section the humiliation I discuss occurs on a narrative rather than a political level. Amidst the many vaginal penetration photos and videos on sites such as MenstrualPorn.com, many depict bleeding women who are shown either anally penetrated or performing fellatio on a man. While anal sex is a staple in contemporary porn—as American pornographer John Stagliano once proclaimed, "pussies are bullshit"[77]—and while fellatio is also a porn standard, scenes of "menstruating" women participating in such acts may be interpreted as establishing a narrative focused on the tasks that the menstruating woman *has* to do; that this is how she services a man while her vagina is "out of action." In the mainstream comedy *50/50* (2011), for example, in a discussion with his friend Kyle (Seth Rogen), Adam (Joseph Gordon-Levitt), mentioned that his girlfriend doesn't like fellatio. Kyle responded that *of course* she doesn't—that no one "likes to have a dick in their mouth"—and that "that's why it's called a blow *job*." The phrase "blow job week"—appearing extensively online—is used to describe the ways that a man can benefit from his menstruating partner being "out of action." Interpreted this way, the anal and fellatio scenes in menstrual porn can be construed as a humiliating duty for the menstruating woman: in such a reading, menstruation is less fetishized than the ways a man can exploit it and the ways a woman can be punished for it. Another way a woman can get humiliated by her menstruation in porn is through its control by a partner. In academic research, the use of periods as a way to exert control over subordinates has been examined in the context of prisons.[78] On screen porn scenarios alluding to menstrually themed sadomasochism are certainly identifiable. In a Literotica.com story titled "Curing Cynthia's Monthly Misbehavior," for example, a submissive woman was humiliated and controlled through menstrual products: her female master prohibited her from wearing tampons:

> I stared at her and she slowly lowered her panties and tugged on the string. The tampax that emerged was somewhat more soiled than the one she had left behind. I took a tissue and allowed her to drop it in the tissue as she handed it to me. I took a maxipad out of the box and told her to put it in her panties and pull them back up.

> She grimaced but did what she was told, for fear of worse to come. I watched as she pulled the paper strip off and stuck the pad onto the crotch of her undies. Indeed, I was intent on making it worse right away. "You're restricted to maxipads for the rest of this period," I told her. "Until you show me that you've started to behave like a grown-up and clean both the room and yourself, you are off tampons."[79]

The same idea occurred in the mainstream film *Towelhead* (2007), where Jasira's (Summer Bishil) father (Peter Macdissi) controlled her menstruation by prohibiting tampons. As discussed in chapter 2, the consequences of being without product is something well known (and feared) by women. In this Literotica scene, the general embarrassment of menstruation was turned into a humiliating experience through the withholding of menstrual products.[80]

The final fetishistic aspect of menstrual porn explored in this chapter is the products associated with it, notably the pads, tampons, and menstrual cups.

Eroticizing the Products

In chapter 3 I discussed the infamous 1993 "Camillagate" phone tap scandal where, during a telephone recording, Prince Charles and then-mistress Camilla Parker-Bowles pondered his reincarnation as her tampon.[81] While this conversation can be interpreted variously, it does allude to the products associated with menstruation being potentially construed as erotic. In the Camillagate scandal, the tampon was sexualized as an imagined way for a lover to reside *inside* his partner, thus can be construed as a manifestation of intimacy akin to the examples discussed earlier. Of course, in porn it is even more likely that menstrual products are presented as taboo, private objects which get fetishized because of their rarely seen—if not "gross out"—qualities.

In the aforementioned MenstrualPorn.com website, included are scenes showing tampon removal. MenstruationSluts.com shows both men and women licking used tampons. Even on the alt-porn sites of BloodyTrixie.com and EroticRed.com, used menstrual cups, tampons, and napkins feature prominently. One interpretation of this is the appeal of the blood, particularly relevant for the alt-porn—given that the amount of blood shown is not as gratuitous as in fetish porn—the display of blood-stained tampons, napkins, and emptied menstrual cups facilitates a more bountiful blood display. Another interpretation is the shock value of menstrual products: the products associated with menstruation are generally considered taboo—rarely seen anywhere publicly—so the opportunity to see them in their blood-stained state may provide an illicit thrill. Discussed in the previous section was the humiliation theme inherent in menstrual porn. Aside from smelling them and tasting them, men's own *use* of menstrual products is also detectable. A man forced to wear a menstrual product was, for example, an inclusion in *Letters to Penthouse IV*:

> My penis, which Mistress insists I refer to as my "pussy," is encased in an openended length of plastic hose and tucked back between my legs. . . . I am required to wear a sanitary napkin to absorb any discharge of semen.[82]

In a blog titled "The Submissive Husband" a similar scenario unfolded:

> What a night! Mistress kept me in vet wrap cock bondage and forced me to wear a sanitary napkin and when i needed to piss she tightened it even further and added a twist by making me bend over and grab my ankles while she stuck a tampon up my ass. To keep me from sucking it in she tied the string around the applicator tube so i ended up with the tube in my crack.[83]

While again, such scenes can be interpreted as reflective of the curiosity and taboo aspects of the usually hidden products of menstruation, another reading is their transgender connotations, akin to drag. In such a reading, the man wearing menstrual products is being humiliated, forced to wear something as disgusting as a pad or tampon. Another reading is his forced feminization, of him being made to be *like a woman* in all of the worst and widely resented ways.

This chapter has explored the idea of sex and sexiness as being presented as something congruent with menstruation on screen. While of course not a common presentation, the idea of menstruation being conceived of as sexy evokes numerous ideas about the complex nature of both desire and desirability. As discussed at various junctures in this book, women often make assumptions about men finding menstrual blood offensive and men often make assumptions about women's disinclination for sex during a period. The examples discussed in this chapter, however, present menstruation and sex as perfectly congruent, working to highlight that sexuality is complicated and that in practice it can transcend stereotypes and prejudices and result in attraction and arousal from scenarios which outside of sex and intimacy may be interpreted completely differently.

In this chapter I explored the ways menstruation is presented as connected to sex and sexuality. In chapter 6, I continue with the idea of comparatively more positive presentations, exploring its on-screen associations with empowerment.

NOTES

1. Carnie Wilson, *I'm Still Hungry: Finding Myself Through Thick and Thin* (Carlsbad, CA: Hay House, 2003), 127.
2. Jessica Valenti, *The Purity Myth: How America's Obsession with Virginity Is Hurting Young Women* (Berkeley: Seal Press, 2009), 72.
3. Susan Moore and Doreen Rosenthal, *Sexuality in Adolescence: Current Trends* (New York: Routledge, 2006), 65.
4. Gordon Forbes, Leah E. Adams-Curtis, Kay B. White, and Katie M. Holmgren, "The role of hostile and benevolent sexism in women's and men's perceptions of the menstruating woman," *Psychology of Women Quarterly* 27, no. 1, (2003): 58–63.
5. Stefan Bechtel, *Sex Encyclopedia: A to Z Guide to Latest Info on Sexual Health Safety* (New York: Fireside, 1993), 208.
6. Marlene Wasserman, *Pillowbook: Creating a Sensual Lifestyle* (Cape Town: Oshun Books, 2007), 144.
7. In Emily Martin, *The Woman in the Body: A Cultural Analysis of Reproduction* (Boston: Beacon Press, 2001), xiv.
8. William H. Masters, Virginia E. Johnson, and Robert C. Kolodny, *Human Sexuality* (New York: HarperCollins, 1995), 95.
9. In Kerry Rogers, *Women's Bodies: A User's Manual* (Cape Town: SchreiberFord Publications, 2006), 154.
10. Christyd87, "Girls: Do you get hornier during your period?" Message posted to GirlsAskGuys, www.girlsaskguys.com/Sexuality-Questions/72517-girls-do-you-get-hornier-during-your-period.html (accessed August 3, 2011).
11. Pippa, Message posted in Maya Horowitz, "Behind Closed Doors: Take a ride on the red tide," February 17, 2009, flathatnews.com/content/70008/behind-closed-doors-take-ride-red-tide (accessed August 3, 2011).
12. Laura Mulvey, "Visual Pleasure and Narrative Cinema," in *Movies and Methods*, ed. Bill Nichols (Berkeley: University of California, 1985).

13. Shelley Stamp Lindsey, "Horror, femininity and Carrie's monstrous puberty," in *The Dread of Difference: Gender and the Horror Film*, ed. Barry Keith Grant (Austin, TX: University of Texas Press, 1996), 282.
14. Michael Ferguson, *Idol Worship: A Shameless Celebration of Male Beauty in the Movies* (Sarasota, FL: StarBooks, 2004), 207.
15. Laura Fingerson, *Girls in Power: Gender, Body and Menstruation in Adolescence* (Albany: State University of New York Press, 2006), 94.
16. Lauren Rosewarne, *Sex in Public: Women, Outdoor Advertising and Public Policy* (Newcastle: Cambridge Scholars Publishing, 2007), 41.
17. Karen Houppert, for example, noted that the British pop band the Spice Girls declined participating in a menstrual product advertisement: "even this group, all about girl power, wanted nothing to do with pads." (Karen Houppert, *The Curse: Confronting the Last Unmentionable Taboo: Menstruation* (New York: Farrar, Straus and Giroux, 1999), 17).
18. Natasha Campo, *From Superwoman to Domestic Goddesses: The Rise and Fall of Feminism* (New York: Peter Lang, 2009), 18.
19. "Guest Blog Post: The Defense of Sexy," July 6, 2011, sexyperiod.com/store/blog/category/sexy---period-/ (accessed August 3, 2011).
20. In psychologist Joan Chrisler et al.'s research, they noted that most people didn't have experience with the kind of extreme PMS stereotype dominant in popular culture (Joan C. Chrisler, Jennifer Gorman Rose, Susan E. Dutch, Katherine G. Sklarsky, and Marie C. Grant, "The PMS illusion: Social cognition maintains social construction," *Sex Roles* 54 (2006): 371–376, 371).
21. In Libby Rumelt, "Men See Red - 3 Men's Opinions on Period Sex," April 29, 2011, evolvedworld.com/sex/item/297?layout=item (accessed August 2, 2011).
22. Stephen Glover, *Professional Idiot: A Memoir* (New York: Hyperion, 2002), 154.
23. Hunter S. Thompson, *Hell's Angels: A Strange and Terrible Saga* (New York: Modern Library, 1999), 109.
24. Yet another reading—presented in Dave Nichols's book on outlaw bikers—is that the badge was reflective of a "macabre sense of humor" (Dave Nichols, *One Percenter: The Legend of the Outlaw Biker* (St. Paul, MN: Motorbooks, 2007), 152).
25. MacDaddy0924, "It's gonna be that time of the month," Message posted to Relationship Help, February 28, 2008, forum.bodybuilding.com/archive/index.php/t-7581271.html (accessed August 3, 2011).
26. tis_me_lord, "Does your bf mind sex when you're on your period?" Message posted to Health and Relationships, October 12, 2008, www.thestudentroom.co.uk/showthread.php?t=748871 (accessed August 3, 2011).
27. Political scientist Iris Young noted this lack of research on male attitudes to menstruation in her essay on menstruation (Iris Marion Young, "Menstrual meditations," in *On Female Body Experience* (New York: Oxford University Press, 2005), 116). An obvious exception, and one that Young refers to, is: Sophie Laws, *Issues of Blood: The Politics of Menstruation* (Houndmills, Basingstoke, Hampshire: Macmillan, 1990).
28. Sophie Laws, *Issues of Blood: The Politics of Menstruation* (Houndmills, Basingstoke, Hampshire: Macmillan, 1990), 61.
29. In Shere Hite, *The Shere Hite Reader: New and Selected Writings on Sex, Globalization, and Private Life* (New York: Seven Stories Press, 2006), 193.
30. Chazz, "Guys: Is period sex a turn off? What's normal?" Message posted to "Sexual Health - Men Message Board," June 8, 2004, June 8, www.healthboards.com/boards/showthread.php?t=180458&page=2 (accessed August 2, 2011).
31. DraigStudio, "Sex during a woman's period: Yay or nay?" Message posted to Scandalish, July 8, 2010, www.datingish.com/729633329/scandalish-period-sex----yay-or-nay/?page=4#viewcomments (accessed August 2, 2011).
32. Giuliana DePandi, *Think Like a Guy: How to Get a Guy by Thinking Like One* (New York: St. Martin's Press, 2006), 62.
33. Giuliana DePandi, *Think Like a Guy: How to Get a Guy by Thinking Like One* (New York: St. Martin's Press, 2006), 63.

34. Ruthann Robson, "Women's Music," in *The Struggle for Happiness: Stories* (New York: St. Martin's Press, 2000), 106.

35. A man quoted in Sophie Laws's research in fact makes this link, identifying that he associated menstrual blood with "sexual secretions" (In Sophie Laws, *Issues of Blood: The Politics of Menstruation* (Houndmills, Basingstoke, Hampshire: Macmillan, 1990), 33).

36. Tom Perrotta, *Little Children* (New York: St. Martin's Press, 2004), 208.

37. Abby Lee, *Diary of a Sex Fiend: Girl with a One Track Mind* (New York: Ebury Press, 2007), 228.

38. In *Part-Time Perverts* I discuss this very issue: "in the time of AIDS — [blood play] offering a unique life/death blur thrill" (Lauren Rosewarne, *Part-Time Perverts: Sex, Pop Culture and Kink Management* (Santa Barbara, CA: Praeger, 2011), 66).

39. Philip Roth, *The Dying Animal* (New York: Houghton Mifflin, 2001), 71–72.

40. Scott Spencer, *Endless Love* (New York: Knopf, 1979), 244.

41. Erica Jong, *Parachutes and Kisses* (New York: Penguin, 1984), 283.

42. Erica Jong, *Parachutes and Kisses* (New York: Penguin, 1984), 283.

43. Binnie Kirshenbaum, *Pure Poetry: A Novel* (New York: Simon and Schuster, 2000), 172-173.

44. Such an idea is referenced in Stephen King's novel *11/22/63* when George recalls a Japanese proverb: "If there is love, smallpox scars are as pretty as dimples." (Stephen King. *11/22/63* (New York: Simon and Schuster, 2011), 580).

45. Natalie Wilson, *Seduced by Twilight: The Allure and Contradictory Messages of the Popular Saga* (Jefferson, NC: McFarland and Company, 2011), 111.

46. Anne Millard Daugherty, "Just a girl: Buffy as icon," in *Reading the Vampire Slayer: The Unofficial Critical Companion to Buffy and Angel*, ed. Roz Kaveney (New York: I. B. Tauris, 2001), 159.

47. In Donald Spoto, *Dark Side of Genius: The Life of Alfred Hitchcock* (New York: De Capo Press, 1999), 431.

48. *Dirty Sanchez's Guide to Buck Nasty Sex* (Berkeley: Amorata Press, 2010), 116.

49. Janice Delaney, Mary Jane Lupton, and Emily Toth, *The Curse: A Cultural History of Menstruation* (New York: Dutton, 1988), 249.

50. Janice Delaney, Mary Jane Lupton and Emily Toth, *The Curse: A Cultural History of Menstruation* (New York: Dutton, 1988), 157.

51. See Lauren Rosewarne, *Part-Time Perverts: Sex, Pop Culture and Kink Management* (Santa Barbara, CA: Praeger, 2011), 67.

52. Queer theorist Gayle Rubin provided a very useful definition for vanilla sex: "[H]eterosexual, married, monogamous, procreative, noncommercial, paired, relationship-oriented, between persons of the same generation, private, pornography free, uses only bodies (no toys), and is vanilla" (Gayle Rubin, "Thinking Sex: Notes for a Radical Theory of the Politics of Sexuality," in *The Lesbian and Gay Studies Reader*, ed. Henry Abelove (New York: Routledge, 1993), 13.

53. John K. Rempel and Barbara Baumgartner, "The relationship between attitudes towards menstruation and sexual attitudes, desires, and behavior in women," *Archives of Sexual Behavior* 32, no. 2 (2003): 155–163, 162.

54. In Sophie Laws, *Issues of Blood: The Politics of Menstruation* (Houndmills, Basingstoke, Hampshire: Macmillan, 1990), 114– 115.

55. In Sophie Laws, *Issues of Blood: The Politics of Menstruation* (Houndmills, Basingstoke, Hampshire: Macmillan, 1990), 74.

56. Anthony Ferguson, *The Sex Doll: A History* (Jefferson, NC: McFarland and Company, 2010), 97.

57. Alfred Ells, *Restoring Innocence* (Nashville, TN: Nelson Publishers, 1990), 87.

58. Stella Viljoen, "The aspirational aesthetics of 'Gentlemen's pornography,'" in *Sex, Gender, Becoming: Post-apartheid Reflections*, ed. Karin van Marle (Pretoria: Pretoria University Law Press, 2006), 53.

59. Neil Schaeffer, *The Marquis de Sade: A Life* (Cambridge, MA: Harvard University Press, 2000), 352.

60. Susan Cokal, "Clean porn: The visual aesthetics of hygiene, hot sex, and hair removal," in *Pop-Porn: Pornography in American Culture*, ed. Ann C. Hall and Mardia J. Bishop (Westport, CT: Praeger, 2007), 137.
61. Laura Fingerson, *Girls in Power: Gender, Body and Menstruation in Adolescence* (Albany: State University of New York Press, 2006), 128.
62. "About Suicide Girls," suicidegirls.com/about/ (accessed August 4, 2011).
63. In Kate Sullivan, "The Punk Pornographers," *Spin* 19, n. 2 (February 2003), 78.
64. "About Me (Profile of a Menstruating WebWhore!)," www.bloodytrixie.com/about-me.html (accessed August 4, 2011).
65. "Home," www.eroticred.com/home.html (accessed August 4,2011).
66. "Menstruation: the Last Taboo," www.bloodytrixie.com/blood-shit-piss.html (accessed August 4, 2011).
67. MenstrualPorn.com (accessed August 4, 2011).
68. Margaret Cho, "Let She Who Is Without Period Stains Throw The First Tampon," *Huffington Post* (January 22, 2008), www.huffingtonpost.com/margaret-cho/let-she-who-is-without-pe_b_82713.html (accessed August 4, 2011).
69. In *Part-Time Perverts*, I discussed, for example, the idea that some people choose to become *audiences* to porn depicting certain fetishes because "obtaining the children, or animals, or props required to [physically] fulfill a fantasy might be difficult, expensive, dangerous, messy or even completely impossible" (Lauren Rosewarne, *Part-Time Perverts: Sex, Pop Culture and Kink Management* (Santa Barbara, CA: Praeger, 2011), 44).
70. In Laura Fingerson, *Girls in Power: Gender, Body and Menstruation in Adolescence* (Albany: State University of New York Press, 2006), 1.
71. In *Part-Time Perverts* I discussed that one of the central appeals of fetish porn is to allow audiences vicarious access to a perversion without them having to endure the mess and smell in their own bedrooms (Lauren Rosewarne, *Part-Time Perverts: Sex, Pop Culture and Kink Management* (Santa Barbara, CA: Praeger, 2011)).
72. NorthwestRain, "Sweet Gushing Pussies," January 15, 2002, www.literotica.com/s/sweet-gushing-pussies (accessed August 2, 2011).
73. jimmy22990, "Breeding Lynn Ch. 01," March 23, 2008, www.literotica.com/s/breeding-lynn-ch-01 (accessed August 2, 2011).
74. hotpup, "Menstrual Love Doubled," June 26, 2004, www.literotica.com/s/menstrual-love-doubled (accessed August 4, 2011).
75. Lauren Rosewarne, *Part-Time Perverts: Sex, Pop Culture and Kink Management* (Santa Barbara, CA: Praeger, 2011), 119.
76. Richard Dee, *The Pampered Black Queen*, 2007, books.google.com (accessed August 2, 2011), 20.
77. In David Aaronovitch, "Come on Baby, Let Me Know," *Independent*, March 10, 2001, www.independent.co.uk/news/uk/this-britain/come-on-baby-let-me-know-695464.html (accessed September 29, 2009).
78. Sophie Laws discussed this issue, writing, "Women in prison often complain that menstruation is used to punish or humiliate them, for example by the prison authority's withholding adequate sanitary wear" (Sophie Laws, *Issues of Blood: The Politics of Menstruation* (Houndmills, Basingstoke, Hampshire: Macmillan, 1990), 65).
79. lesliejones, "Curing Cynthia's Monthly Misbehavior," www.literotica.com/s/curing-cynthia-s-monthly-misbehavior (accessed August 5, 2011).
80. A similar idea is also evident in mainstream cinema. In a scene from *Dirty Love* (2005), for example, Rebecca (Jenny McCarthy) couldn't afford tampons so she had to purchase maxi-pads, something which worked to further her humiliation.
81. In 1993, the infamous "Camillagate" scandal was exposed, centering on the release of some illegal recorded telephone conversations, one which included the couple musing about Prince Charles being reincarnated as a tampon so that he could get even closer to his then mistress, Camilla Parker-Bowles.
82. In *Letters to Penthouse IV: Erotica Unleashed and Uncensored* (New York: Warner Books, 1994), books.google.com. (accessed August 5, 2011).

83. "Bondage and Release," March 12, 2010, cmccrkn.thumblogger.com/home/ (accessed August 4, 2011).

Chapter Six

Bleeding Out Proud

Menstruation and Empowerment

While much of this book has explored screen examples which present menstruation as something negative, this chapter redirects attention, exploring comparatively positive portrayals. From the freedom to be feminine as depicted in advertising through to narratives presenting the strategic deployment of menstruation as an excuse and its embrace as something worth championing, this chapter explores periods portrayed as something *beneficial* to women.

THE FREEDOM TO BE FEMININE

In chapter 3, I discussed the trend in feminine hygiene advertising whereby products are marketed through promises of unrestricted lifestyles. Such a strategy is in sync with personal products being marketed through promises of liberation and empowerment. In chapter 3 I discussed liberation and empowerment in the context of facilitating leakage-free activity participation, but advertising also offers empowerment through *self-actualization*. In her work on menstrual product advertising, gender researcher Kate Kane discussed a 1980s Carefree tagline: "Carefree's something I do for me." In her commentary, Kane noted that this advertisement "asserts a pseudo-feminist stance, in which standing up for one's rights is conflated with spending money on feeling good, which is defined as feeling good about oneself."[1] Feminist theorist Susan Bordo similarly addressed the "my choice" and "for me"–type platitudes, contending that "it would be reasonable if 'for me' was meant as 'for me, in order to feel better about myself in this culture that has made me feel in adequate as I am,'" but as she argues, people rarely mean this.[2] While Kane and Bordo are critical of the kind of faux-empowerment offered in advertising, such representations are not unimportant and as relevant to this chapter, can in fact be construed as offering a sharp contrast to the routine negative portrayals of menstruators found in other media. For this chapter, I propose that such advertising presents menstruation as empowering through its ability to be controlled. Menstruation is a reality for the vast majority of women: loved or loathed, it is something that needs to be dealt with on an ongoing basis. Since the 1980s, advertising has dramatically distanced itself from the "why me"–victim approach discussed in chapter 2, and instead, presents periods as something intrinsically feminine and something that when appropriately controlled, concealed, and deodorized, can actually be *beneficial* for women. Throughout this book I have contended that mess, smell and leakage are *real* concerns for women regardless of how socially constructed they might be construed. Contemporary advertising's presentation of menstruation as manageable and something congruent with femininity and sexiness can be viewed as an empowering portrayal: the simple message conveyed is that periods don't have to be a miserable experience if appropriately tended to. While radical feminists have long criticized women's interest in beauty pursuits, and women's preoccupation with controlling and restricting their bodies is frequently considered oppressive (addressed later in this chapter), the reality is that many women are interested in pursuing femininity; in fact, the *cessation* of menstruation at menopause is frequently construed as catastrophic to the self-esteem of some women because with it comes a femininity crisis (chapter 7). While the artifice aspects of femininity are addressed in the next section, it would be erroneous to ignore the contrast that the images presented in modern advertising provide compared to menstruators portrayed in other media. Advertising suggests that a woman can be feminine, sexy, *and* bleeding all at once, thus offering an opportunity for menstruation to be reconceptualized.

ARTIFICES RELAXED

In Karen Houppert's book *The Curse*, she described the bathroom as "one of the few places where girls and women can relax their artifices for a while."[3] Houppert's idea introduces two key points relevant to this section: one, that women frequently operate with an artifice, and two, as relevant to a discussion on *positive* menstrual portrayals, that opportunities exist where this artifice can be relaxed.

Dictionary definitions of artifice describe it as a cunning and clever ruse. In practice, and as specifically relevant to women, it can be defined as the performance of gender. In Kane's discussion she alluded to the issue of artifice through a discussion of a 1980s Carefree campaign which used the slogan "Carefree every day because you're a woman every day." The advertisement showed a woman in a range of different outfits, at work, at play, to which Kane surmised: "no matter whether she is professional or playful, her essential being is female/raw-rotten; in order to be feminine/fresh, she must perform the daily Carefree ritual."[4] The idea of gender being a *performance* and existing as something separate from sex—which is distinguished as biological—is a topic extensively discussed in queer theory where the categories of male and female are viewed as fluid and malleable.[5] While, as Houppert argues, menstruation provides "irrefutable proof that you're a woman"[6] and is one of the *most* biologically female things a woman can do, culturally, many of the typical associations—moodiness, mess, smell (chapter 4)—are things considered *unfeminine* and incongruent with femininity. In *No Strings Attached* (2011), for example, when Adam (Ashton Kutcher) visited his lover Emma's (Natalie Portman) home, he found that her period was synced with her housemates. During this scene, Adam commented to the women: "You're women and I think that's a beautiful thing." In response to this lofty remark, housemate Patrice (Greta Gerwig) replied—while lying on her back eating a cupcake—"It's like a crime scene in my pants." While Adam may have wanted to believe that menstruation is part of the beauty of womanhood—or at least felt an imperative to say so—Patrice highlighted the darker, messier, and less "feminine" reality.

As Patrice aptly demonstrated, it is generally difficult for women to present menstruation as something pretty or feminine; as noted in chapter 5, the presentation of the sexy menstruator occurs infrequently. This situation creates two response possibilities for a woman: one, she can attempt to *disprove* cultural stereotypes and do her best to portray menstruation as the epitome of embodied femininity (as is the style of most contemporary menstrual product advertising, discussed above), or two, she can instead choose to *corroborate* negative perceptions and embrace menstruation as an opportunity to *stop* performing femininity. Here lies an obvious on-screen opportunity for menstruation to be portrayed comparatively positively. Quoted in chapter 5 was comedian Roseanne Barr: "Women complain about PMS, but I think of it as the only time of the month when I can be myself."[7] Roseanne alluded to both a cultural expectation that women act appropriately feminine,[8] but identified that for her menstruation provided an opportunity *not* to and to instead be her authentic self.

Feminist writers have discussed the sexual corveé which is the "unpaid, beauty-related chores that women participate in patriarchal society to be attractive to men."[9] Such chores involve make-up and high heels, if not also diet and exercise, and are considered as emblematic of women's self-surveillance and acceptance that their appearance is always under scrutiny (chapter 1). The possibility of relaxing feminine artifices during menstruation is a topic alluded to in writings on menstruation as well as on screen. In Alexandra Pope's self-help book *The Wild Genie: The Healing Power of Menstruation*, she described menstruation as a time for relaxation and rejuvenation.[10] Cardiologist Stephen Sinatra similarly suggested that menstruation is "a time to go inward, quiet the mind, and create a sacred space for yourself," advising that women should "give yourself permission to call 'time out.'"[11] In family therapist Claudia Bepko's book *The Responsibility Trap*, she presented a case of a woman who used menstruation as an excuse to take a "day off" from having to maintain her perfectionist standards.[12] These ideas are very much in line with spiritual feminist responses to menstruation and the proposition that women should appropriately "honor" their bleeding.

In practice, relaxing artifices and taking "time out" to bleed can be interpreted as taking time out from expectations to perform sexually and femininely. In *No Strings Attached*, the menstruating housemates were shown lying around the loungeroom wearing pajamas, eating cupcakes, and eschewing gender expectations as related to grooming, sexiness, and menstrual secrecy (chapter 1); *instead*, the women were shown to *submit* to their menstruation.

While on screen it is actually rare that women are given the opportunity to relax their artifices enough to appear *un*feminine, relaxed artifices are nonetheless identifiable. In the next section I explore screen examples of menstruation providing women an excuse to shirk mandates of good behavior.

THE OPPORTUNE EXCUSE

In comedian Aaron Karo's book *I'm Having More Fun Than You*, he wrote, "To me, a woman's true power lies in her ability to fake a period. . . . [C]hicks can use the same excuse over and over again because we're never going to call them out on it."[13] While Karo's point was made in the context of sex avoidance (something addressed in chapter 4), the idea that women can use menstruation as an excuse because it rarely gets contested has much traction, both off screen and on. In this section, I am less interested in the veracity of menstruation claims—knowing a "truth" is usually difficult in narratives anyway, given that menstruation is seldom discussed and virtually never shown (chapter 8)—and instead focus on its existence on screen as something able to be strategically deployed to excuse bad behavior.

Women Behaving Badly

In their 1936 book *Facts and Frauds in Woman's Hygiene*, Rachel Palmer and Sarah Greenberg discussed strategic use of menstruation, identifying that menstruating women can:

> [E]xercise a bit of subtle tyranny over their husbands, and sometimes children as well, by making the most of the traditional belief that at a particular time of the month women must be treated with special solicitude and tenderness and that any emotional or temperamental vagaries on their part should be met with special forbearance.[14]

While the tyrannical menstruator was discussed in chapter 4 and is frequently a stereotype used *against* women both in real life and on screen, as Palmer and Greenberg note, the stereotype can also be utilized by women *themselves*. Menstruation providing women an excuse to justify bad behavior exists both on screen and off.

In 1893, Lizzie Borden was tried in the U.S. for the ax murder of her father and stepmother. During the trial, Borden's lawyer attributed her behavior to her "monthly indisposition."[15] While Borden's case exists as perhaps the most famous and extreme use of the menstrual excuse, it is by no means the only time periods have been connected to crime. Criminologist Ronald Flowers reviewed numerous studies linking the two and summarized that "female deviant behavior occurs most often during certain phases of the menstrual cycle—the 4 premenstrual days and the first 4 days of menstruation."[16] The menstruation/crime connection was similarly acknowledged in Germaine Greer's seminal text *The Female Eunuch*.[17] Even without actually breaking the law, however, extremes in women's behavior are routinely connected to menstruation. In an episode of the British series *Rumpole of the Bailey* (1978–1992), Horace (Leo McKern) made an offhanded remark about a judge: "There he is. Giving me a look of vague disgust. Like Queen Victoria with a bad period." In this remark, Horace referred to the extensively documented PMS of Queen Victoria,[18] the reigning English monarch from 1837 to 1901. Queen Victoria's notorious PMS has been extensively discussed; endocrinologist Geoffrey Redmond, for example, contended that the queen's PMS "could reduce her ministers, among whom were the most powerful men in the world, to abject terror."[19]

While high-profile cases like Borden and Queen Victoria are rare, the idea of menstruation existing as an explanation for women's behavior—notably, as an explanation used by women *themselves*—is well documented. In psychologist Jane Ussher's research on PMS, she quoted women who linked their moods to their menstrual cycles:

> [It] makes me feel as if I'm not in control . . . it's not being in control of my own body and the way I behave.[20]

> It might build up throughout a day and my, um, something might annoy me . . . I'll feel like reacting aggressively.[21]

A similar description appeared in nurse practitioner Mia Lundin's self-help book:

> I get agitated, have no tolerance, and yell like a crazy woman. I truly feel like I am insane and begin to feel like I had better not be alone with the children or else.[22]

Even in Laurie Anderson's song "Beautiful Red Dress" (1989) discussed in chapter 5, Anderson mentions—in the context of menstruation—women sometimes going "crazy" at certain times of the month.

In Houppert's book, she discussed women's use of the PMS excuse and described it as "an acceptable excuse for women who are reluctant to claim their anger: 'I was not myself.'"[23] Ussher discussed the same idea, contending that women frequently "split" their identities between their PMS selves and their normal selves.[24] Such an idea relates well to research on compartmentalization and to both men and women rationalizing "out of character" behavior by psychologically segregating it to a minor part of identity.[25] In these cases, women attribute bad behavior to a non-dominant self and simultaneously hint at diminished responsibility. On screen this can be witnessed in the television series *Buffy the Vampire Slayer* (1997–2003). In one episode, Cordelia (Charisma Carpenter) pleaded, "And if you get me out of this, I swear I'll never be mean to anyone ever again. Unless they really deserve it or if it's that time of the month, in which case I don't think you or anyone else can hold me responsible." In another episode a similar point was made by Willow (Alyson Hannigan), "Yeah, okay, werewolf. But three days out of the month I'm not much fun to be around either." Here, both characters implied that PMS exists as a caveat: that no woman can *really* be expected to behave during this time because moods are essentially *out* of a woman's control, that menstruation provides an excuse for bad behavior.

Teenager Derek, quoted in sociologist Laura Fingerson's research, alleged that girls use menstruation as "an excuse to get pissed."[26] In chapter 4, I discussed numerous on-screen examples of men making the same claim. Of particular relevance to this chapter are those menstrual moodiness accusations which allude to the possibility of women not simply being in a bad mood, but rather, women *using* menstruation—consciously and strategically—as a reason, if not *motivation*, to lash out. In an episode of *Married with Children* (1987–1997), for example, Al Bundy (Ed O'Neill) remarked, "I don't know—I'm not a doctor—but I think that PMS stands for Pummels

Men's Scrotums." Here, Al alluded to the menstrual monster stereotype but *also* presented PMS as both a diagnosis and cause of bad behavior. In an episode of *Everybody Loves Raymond* (1996–2005) this idea was made even clearer when Ray (Ray Romano) made a similar accusation during an argument with his wife, Debra (Patricia Heaton): "You know what I think? I think that you enjoy your ladies' days 'cause you think I deserve to be treated like that. Oh look what day it is, come here Ray, pow pow [mimes punching and yelling]." In this scene, Ray contended that Debra exploited menstruation as an opportunity to lash out at him. While both Al in *Married with Children* and Ray in *Everybody Loves Raymond* had reputations for being insensitive to the needs of their wives—and were frequently shown to exhibit sexist behavior—in these scenes they also implied that PMS made their wives act *uncharacteristically*; that the women were *less nice* at this time of the month and failed to exhibit the "effusive chipperness"[27] more commonly associated with their character and their gender. While neither Debra nor Peggy Bundy (Katey Sagal) in *Married with Children* were pushovers, both women did fulfill mother and homemaker roles and in both cases normally exhibited stereotypical feminine attributes expected of wives and mothers. For Debra and Peggy, their menstrual symptoms can be viewed as having provided them an opportunity to relax their own feminine, maternal artifices and act in ways more extreme than audiences are used to seeing them: that instead of bottling anger or neediness, they unleashed it. Certainly on *Roseanne* (1988–1997), the title character actually confessed to the *deliberate* deployment of PMS during an episode where she feared that she was pregnant. In the episode, Roseanne explained to her sister how she had hidden her absent period from her husband: "I faked PMS. I even added an extra day for the heck of it." In that episode—with thorough smugness—Roseanne illustrated strategic use of well-known menstrual symptoms and also highlighted how easily men can be manipulated by menstruation (addressed later in this chapter).

As in her stand-up routine discussed earlier, Roseanne embraced PMS as an opportunity to be her authentic self. In her sitcom, *Roseanne*, the comedian was never portrayed as the typical female sitcom character; as communications researcher Jib Fowles wrote, "Corpulent and brash, Roseanne is anything but the usual prime-time homemaker."[28] Gender researcher Jennifer Reed described the character similarly:

> Roseanne has made her reputation in mass culture as a loud, aggressive, overweight, working-class woman who always says what is on her mind, who will not be pushed around, who tells her own uncomfortable truths.[29]

Unlike Debra or Peggy, Roseanne never had a stereotypical feminine homemaker identity to take respite from: she was never effusively chipper; she didn't look the part and certainly didn't act the part. Nevertheless, even for Roseanne, PMS provided an excuse to *amplify* her already forthright personality. In an episode titled "PMS I Love You," Roseanne's PMS was presented as—what her husband, Dan (John Goodman), described as—"a twenty-four-hour roller-coaster ride with Sybil at the switch." The episode began as a spoof on *Apocalypse Now* (1979) with Dan lying in bed, saying, "Today's the day. Twenty-four hours of hell. I must get out of the house. Far from ground zero," and progressed to presenting Roseanne's behavioral extremes from hostility, insecurity regarding her appearance, unnecessary housework, extreme randiness, and irrationality. While Roseanne on a good day might actually appear to exhibit the PMS attributes of a more docile character, nevertheless PMS gave Roseanne—like Peggy and Debra—an opportunity to portray a self without artifice. In an episode of *The Closer* (2005–), Brenda (Kyra Sedgwick) discovered that she was going through early menopause. In the same vein as Roseanne feigning symptoms, Brenda acted similarly, lashing out at her parents and insisting on privacy. Like the PMSing woman, Brenda *knew* that no one would challenge her, and thus her bad behavior went uncriticized.

More tangible than the excuse to be moody, menstruation is exploited as an opportunity to avoid undesirable activity. In chapter 4 I discussed menstruation used to avoid sex and research has similarly documented its use in avoiding rape.[30] In this section I examine its use as an excuse to avoid work and school.

Menstruation and Absenteeism

Menstrual leave is a policy idea that has existed for many decades and, like any other kind of sick leave, is predicated on the idea that for some women menstruation is painful—a condition medically known as dysmenorrhea—and thus makes working difficult. Union demands for menstrual leave began in the 1940s in Japan, and today some workplaces do indeed offer menstrual leave to employees. For this section, I am less concerned with the politics of the leave—something notoriously controversial[31]—and instead am interested in the premise behind it: that menstruation can make certain activities difficult and that women sometimes need to be excused because of it (an idea which is often the justification for such leave being considered sexist). While research indicates that in practice, women are often reluctant to actually *utilize* such leave,[32] its existence nevertheless creates a "free rider" opportunity for it to be used by women whose menstruation is *not* painful but theoretically *might* be. Whether use of the leave by women without dysmenorrhea is exploitative or simply rationalized as compensation for the general gender burden of menstruation, the idea that it can be strategically deployed to evade employment responsibilities exists both in real life and on screen.

As noted, for reasons including embarrassment and privacy, women with menstrual leave available to them often won't take it.[33] Making a connected point, sociologist Sophie Laws in her work on menstruation noted that "women very rarely mention menstruation in the workplace even to excuse themselves because of menstrual pain."[34] For other women, however, no choice exists: dysmenorrhea *demands* absence from their workplace. In organizational theorist Joanna Brewis's research on gender in the workplace, for example, she quoted women who took time off because of their periods and who identified that PMS *did* affect their performance.[35] Physician Katharina Dalton made similar claims, estimating that menstruation-based absenteeism ranged from 3 percent to 8 percent of a company's personnel costs, with some companies noting sharp declines in productivity as a result.[36] In connected research, nearly half of the housewives surveyed in a study on menstruation in India claimed to be pleased to menstruate every month because it brought them relief from domestic labor.[37]

On screen absenteeism linked to menstruation is a rare portrayal. In *I'm Gonna Git You Sucka* (1998) Cheryl (Dawnn Lewis), a diner waitress, leaves work early to tend to her period. *No Strings Attached*, discussed earlier, is another outlier example where the female housemates were all presented at home tending to their synced periods. While it is unclear whether the women had actually taken the day off, this can be assumed because they all worked in the same hospital and the film devoted much time to documenting their busy schedules, thus implying that it would otherwise be strange that they had synced leisure time. This example is particularly interesting because it presents menstruation as something that genuinely warrants time off, even by female doctors who aren't assumed to be squeamish or weak-willed. In music, an example of a woman using menstruation as an excuse to leave work exists in Ani DiFranco's song "Blood in the Boardroom" (1993). In the song, a woman, bored during a meeting, used her period as justification to exit prematurely. Such portrayals, of course, are unusual; instead, on screen absenteeism is much more likely to be associated with school, highlighting again that most menstruation narratives focus on school-aged girls for whom menstruation is a "newer" and seemingly more interesting, if not also more worrisome, experience.

Dalton discussed girls missing school because of menstruation,[38] and menstrual excuses have been identified as one of the leading causes of school absenteeism.[39] In an episode of the cartoon *The Simpsons* (1989–), when teacher Mrs. Krabappel suggested Bart take a make-up test, he groaned, clutched his stomach, and moaned, "Ohh, my ovaries!" While, of course, Bart was not menstruating, he was nevertheless evidently aware that "women's problems" can get girls out of class. Such an idea was also referenced in an episode of *Party of Five* (1994–2000). When Claudia (Lacey Chabert) got her first period, she wanted to be excused from school. While Claudia didn't actually exhibit any symptoms of dysmenorrhea, she was nonetheless worried about leakage and exposing her menstruation to others (chapter 3) and wanted time off accordingly. The excuse was used much more explicitly by Cher (Alicia Silverstone) in *Clueless* (1995), when she explained to her teacher that her tardiness was attributable to the fact that she was "surfing the crimson wave."

By far the most common way menstruation functions as a school-based excuse is when it is deployed to avoid physical education and gym classes. In journalist Rowenna Davis's *Guardian* article, for example, she reflected on her own menarche:

> As far as I could see, the only advantage this monthly deluge could possibly serve was getting me out of my school's spider-ridden swimming pool every four weeks.[40]

In historian Bonnie Morris's research on teenagers in the 1950s, she quoted Helen, who reflected: "And we tried to get out of gym; my sister had ingenious ways. She had her period every day, for instance."[41] Contemporary education research also documents use of the same excuse.[42] Certainly in popular culture, the excuse almost appears to be a cliché: in Kimberly Derting's young adult novel *Desires of the Dead*, for example, Violet was running late for school because she had slept in. Her friend Chelsea commented, "You should have said diarrhea. Or at least menstrual cramps, then you could get out of PE. It's like a twofer."[43] Certainly on screen the excuse is frequently used for comic effect in sitcoms.

In an episode of *The Office* (2005–), when Pam (Jenna Fischer) visited her old school gym she reminisced: "Pretending I have PMS so I didn't have to play volleyball. Pretending I have PMS so I didn't have to play basketball. Those were the days." The same excuse was recalled in an episode of *Designing Women* (1986–1993): Mary Jo (Annie Potts) asked if anyone wanted to go jogging with her to which Suzanne (Delta Burke) responded: "Mary Jo, I had my period five years straight in high school to avoid P.E. Okay?" An episode of *The Nanny* (1993–1999), opened with the title character Fran (Fran Drescher) arriving home to find teenager Maggie (Nicholle Tom) lying on the couch. Fran asked, "Oh Maggie, what are you doing home so early. Are you sick?" to which Maggie responded, "my monthly friend." Fran, however, didn't believe her, and said:

> You've had your period four times this month. . . . Women don't get their period every week. If they did, all the men in the world would be institutionalized. . . . Now what gives? You're not having problems with your boyfriend, you're not failing any classes, you're trying to get out of gym!

In the pilot of *George Lopez* (2002–2007), the same scenario unfolded: it was discovered that daughter Carmen (Masiela Lusha), had been forging notes to get out of swim class on the basis of a period that she hadn't actually started. After discovering a pile of forged notes, her mother, Angie (Constance Marie), asked, "How many weeks have you been having this period?"

These scenes are humorous because male *and* female audiences are aware of the excuse. Actual use of the excuse is also funny because of the predictable effect its deployment has: given that so much taboo surrounds menstruation, teachers—particularly *male* teachers—are unlikely to challenge a girl who makes such a claim.[44] In his discussion about menstrual leave in workplaces in Japan, historian Edward Beauchamp drew attention to the awkward conversations that would transpire when women requested such leave:

> Their requests, by their accounts, was met by a strangled silence and then a confused but generally positive response from the official responsible for sick leave and other related matters, who was apparently struck dumb with embarrassment.[45]

Fingerson highlighted similar themes, noting that "some girls use their symptoms to manipulate and intimidate boys and male teachers who are not going to question the girls' menstrual status."[46] Writer Nancy Friday in her book on women's sexuality, *My Mother/My Self*, quoted author Paula Weideger who made the same claim, contending that the young girls in her research were less embarrassed about menstruation than women of her generation: "they would gleefully tell me how they could get a male teacher to let them off homework by hinting they had cramps. They *use* menstruation."[47] On screen menstruation *used* to exploit men's awkwardness is identifiable in a scene from the film *Mean Girls* (2004). During an assembly, school principal Mr. Duvall (Tim Meadows) talked to the female students about their awful behavior; a conversation student Bethany (Stefania Drummond) participated in:

> **Mr. Duvall:** Now, what we're gonna try to do is fix the way you young ladies relate to each other. OK? Lady to lady. So who has a lady problem that they'd like to talk about? Yes?
>
> **Bethany:** Somebody wrote in that book that I'm lying about being a virgin because I use super-jumbo tampons. But I can't help it if I've got a heavy flow and a wide-set vagina.
>
> **Mr. Duvall:** Yeah, I can't do this.

Despite his lofty intentions, evidently menstruation was enough to distract Mr. Duvall from addressing his students' behavior. In *Clueless*, Cher's tardiness was similarly quickly excused by her male teacher (Wallace Shawn). The idea of women using menstruation to unsettle men and to allow their behavior to remain unquestioned is also evident in a sketch from the British comedy *The Meaning of Life* (1983). In a restaurant scene, a morbidly obese American man, Mr. Creosote (Terry Jones), who had ordered—and eaten— everything on the menu, requested a bucket. He vomited into it repeatedly, proceeding to then vomit all over everything else. At the next table, a table of four obviously very polite—but nevertheless disgusted—British people wanted to leave. Being too polite to explain to the waiter that they were revolted, one of the women excused the four, saying, "I'm having rather a heavy period." While the humor of this scene can be interpreted variously, one reading is that the woman gave the ultimate conversation stopper; no one would dare question the veracity of her claim, thus allowing the four to politely exit without incident.

A third excuse that menstruation provides women is for overindulgence; that it enables a menstruator to attribute her cravings for salty, sweet, and fattening food to her period.

The Pig Out Excuse

In an episode of *House* (2004–), Dr. House (Hugh Laurie) had been told that he would have to wait until a patient's menstruation stopped before he could perform a procedure. To this, House commented: "Well, let's hope she can hold out 'til then. In the meantime, get her a pint of cookie dough ice cream and a DVD of *Beaches*." In a *Saturday Night Live* (1975–) skit parodying an advertisement for a one-menstrual-cycle-per-year contraceptive pill, a scene showed the catastrophe unleashed when one woman eventually got her period: she ate someone else's entire birthday cake. Both of these scenes solicited humor from the stereotype of women using menstruation as an excuse to overindulge. Certainly women's menstrual cravings are identified in academic research on menstruation. In chapter 1, I quoted teenager Kasey from Fingerson's study, who claimed that she and her mother craved chocolate during their periods: "[I]t's this mother-daughter thing . . . we always have chocolate in our house for a least two weeks a month."[48] While the idea of menstruation being associated with various food cravings is indeed well documented,[49] notable is women reporting *giving in* to such cravings; something highlighted well by women who discussed menstrual cravings in Anne Fletcher's book on weight loss: "I give in, in moderation. It makes me feel better—the acceptance of 'okay, I need salt and sugar,'" and "I want to binge before my period. It is usually only one day, and I do give in."[50]

On screen women submitting to menstrual cravings is evidenced in *No Strings Attached*, *House*, *The Cosby Show* (1984–1992), *The Golden Girls* (1985–1992), and *Community* (2009–). In chapter 1 I discussed the *House* episode where Dr. House admitted to having monitored the periods of his boss, Dr. Cuddy (Lisa Edelstein). In the episode he observed:

> Once a month, when you leave the kids' cancer ward, your eyes glisten. About three days later, you break your ban on sugar and chow down a bucket of frozen yogurt in the cafeteria, sprinkles included. Based on the last yogurt sighting, you've got another week before you ovulate.

In *No Strings Attached*, Adam brought cupcakes for Emma and her housemates; the cupcakes were rapidly devoured by the menstrually synced women. In an episode of *The Cosby Show*, Clair (Phylicia Rashad) celebrated daughter Rudy's (Keshia Knight Pulliam) first period by eating ice cream with her while watching *Gone With the Wind* (1939). In an episode of *Community*, when Annie (Alison Brie) was menstrually moody, Abed (Danny Pudi) gave her chocolate to placate her which she enthusiastically took. In the sitcom *The Golden Girls*, the menstrual overindulgence idea was referenced when Dorothy (Bea Arthur) mused about the positives of menopause: "Look at it this way: you don't get cramps once a month. You don't go on eating binges once a month. You don't get crazy once a month." As apparent in much research about women's body image, a central theme is discipline and self-control, something explained well in psychologist Helen Malson's book on eating disorders:

> The thin body is so frequently presented to us as the desired end-product of dietary restraint. And dietary restraint, so we are told, is a form of virtuous self-control. To eat less than we want to, to go hungry is, apparently, to exert control. And to be thin is both the proof of that virtuous exertion and the reward for it.[51]

In light of the preoccupation many women have—or at least, are *expected* to have—with controlling their bodies, menstruation exists as a possible excuse, if not *reason*, to have respite. That just as with the sexual corvée/beauty labor discussed earlier, menstruation provides an opportunity for eschewing the artifice and expectations of femininity and indulging; it can provide women an excuse to give in to menstruation, cravings and all.

Menstruation used opportunistically as an excuse for bad behavior and absenteeism is a popular idea on screen. A more positive presentation—in line with considering menstruation as something *empowering* rather than something that makes women vulnerable—is menstruation presented as the catalyst for political activism: as Fingerson contended, "I believe that because menstruation is now more in the open, there are opportunities for girls to use menstruation as a source of power and agency."[52] Such ideas are addressed in the next section.

MENSTRUAL ACTIVISM

Gender researcher Chris Bobel, in her book *New Blood: Third-Wave Feminism and the Politics of Menstruation*, charted the roots of menstrual activism and the work of activists:

> Beginning in the 1970s, increasing numbers of women began to question the safety of menstrual products and, more fundamentally, the social construction of menstruation as little more than a shameful process. They cultivated a critical menstrual consciousness.[53]

One of the participants in Bobel's study discussed the rationale for the activism, describing a realization that "it was feminist for us not to hide our blood in shame."[54] Certainly a central triumph of such activism is the many post-1970s references to menstruation detected on screen and discussed throughout this book. While many representations do continue to portray menstruation as something shameful and embarrassing, examples also exist where it is portrayed in more positive ways. In this section, I focus on three types of menstrual activism: subtle activism associated with women taking vocal ownership of their menstruation and shunning secrecy mandates; moderate activism showing women not only admitting to their menstruation but advocating for a broader menstrual consciousness; and extreme activism which explores menstrual artworks as a way to bring menstruation out from the so-called "great medicine cabinet of American culture."[55]

Subtle Menstrual Activism

In Elissa Stein and Susan Kim's book *Flow*, the authors made an interesting point about the continuing taboo of menstruation in an otherwise increasingly open, if not *confessionary*,[56] environment:

> While it's apparently okay to share your political beliefs with a total stranger or post naked pictures of yourself on the Internet, divulging straight-faced details of your last period is still considered the ultimate faux pas.[57]

A similar idea was proposed in communications scholar Elizabeth Kissling's research when she discussed girls frequently using circumlocutions and omission to avoid *naming* their menstruation in conversation,[58] as well as in Fingerson's research where she identified girls using "code words" for theirs.[59] Interestingly, while in many contexts the silence imperative may be intact, some girls—particularly for those identifying as third-wave feminists—actually feel comfortable naming their menstruation and discussing it proudly. Fingerson articulated this idea in her research:

> [T]he girls in our interviews expressed feelings and attitudes in line with third wave feminist thinking. They are not ashamed of their bodies, use terms like "ragging" to describe menstruation, find it funny to confront boys and men openly about menstruation, and work to define their own bodies in their own terms.[60]

Normalization, if not also comfort and pride in menstruation, is considered a success of the second- and third-wave feminist movements and advocating for such normalization is one, almost innocuous, way that girls can be menstrual activists. On screen such activism is detected in episodes of *Degrassi: The Next Generation* (2001–) and in the sitcoms *Cybill* (1995–1998) and *According to Jim*. In an episode of the Canadian series *Degrassi: The Next Generation*, Emma (Miriam McDonald) got her first period at school on her new white skirt and had to change into a pair of oversized gym shorts. Classmate JT (Ryan Cooley) teased Emma and asked whether she had wet herself. Emma corrected him by nonchalantly stating that she was having a period. In this example, Emma—who was initially anxious about her period—hastened her time of menstrual acclimatization and quickly took ownership of it, turning a potentially humiliating moment into one of pride, if not also sexual confidence (chapter 5). In an episode of the sitcom *According to Jim*, when Gracie (Billi Bruno) got her first period, her father Jim (James Belushi) tried to converse with her about it by referring to it as "the thing." Each time her father said "the thing," Gracie promptly corrected him by saying "period." Throughout the episode, Gracie was presented as confident about her menstruation: she evidently saw no need for euphemism or circumlocution; instead, while not necessarily wanting to embarrass her father, she nonetheless appeared keen to repel his attempts at imposing the secrecy imperative on her. In an episode of *Cybill*, the title character (Cybill Shepherd) and friend Maryann (Christine Baranski) were seated in a restaurant discussing Cybill's perimenopause symptoms. Maryann asked Cybill whether she still had her "friend" and whether "Aunt Flo" was still arriving; like Jim, Maryann was deliberately avoiding saying "period." Cybill, of course, was offended by this behavior: "Just say it!" she reprimanded. "Period period period." While, of course, Gracie and Cybill were at vastly different life stages—Gracie just beginning her menstruation and Cybill soon to end hers—neither character was at all interested in social niceties or in corroborating with the menstrual taboo, and instead chose to speak frankly about it, even if embarrassing the characters around them. These episodes show subtle menstrual activism by presenting women not just comfortable discussing their menstruation, but correcting others, normalizing the conversation topic, and articulating a lack of shame.

Subtle activism is also achieved through the championing of menstruation, of menstruation presented as something that provides women tangible benefits. In feminist Gloria Steinem's famous *Ms* magazine essay titled "If Men Could Menstruate" she wrote, "The answer is clear—menstruation would become an enviable, boast-worthy, masculine event."[61] While Steinem's essay was intended to be humorous, it can also be read as a counternarrative to the way menstruation is more frequently presented in the media: instead of being something that *weakens* women, it can be viewed as something that *strengthens* them. In psychotherapist JoAnn Loulan and Bonnie Worthen's book on menstruation, the idea of periods delivering physical empowerment was highlighted by one girl who claimed, "If anything, I guess I have a little more energy during my period than at other times."[62] In Sara Shepard's young adult novel *Flawless* the same idea was briefly referenced: "when Emily's butterfly times were three-tenths of a second faster, it means she had her period."[63] While not common, similar subtle activism as related to the powers of menstruation can also be detected on screen. In an episode of *Sex and the City* (1998–2004), for example, Charlotte (Kristin Davis) briefly mentioned winning a junior gymnastics competition while having her period. When Darlene (Sara Gilbert) got her first period on *Roseanne*, she lamented, "I'm probably going to start throwing like a girl now anyway." Her mother, Roseanne, championed, "Definitely. And since you've got your period you're gonna be throwing a lot farther." In this episode, Roseanne—who, as already discussed in this chapter, experienced her own difficulties with menstruation—helped her daughter see a more positive side. While normally on screen the positives associated with menstruation are those connected to fertility (chapter 1), in this episode, Roseanne contended that menstruation bestowed physical strengths unavailable to girls prior to menstruation. More broadly, Roseanne welcomed Darlene to a sisterhood of bleeders, saying, "Now you get to be a part of the whole cycle of things. You know, the moon and the water and the seasons. It's almost magical, Darlene." Roseanne presented menstruation as something positive by alluding to two potent ideas: one, that Darlene's period made her part of something bigger than herself—that is, a sisterhood; and two, the "I bleed therefore I am" brand of cultural feminism discussed by Bobel[64] and the "Celebrate-Your-Cycle feminists" described by Houppert.[65] While indeed a feminist, Roseanne generally did not exhibit earth mother or spiritualist tendencies during the series. By doing so in this episode, she alluded to an idea that can be interpreted as broader than simply an earth mother or bohemian narrative: a belief that menstruation connects women to nature. While this idea is more frequently presented in the form of supernatural happenings as outlined in chapter 3, it is nevertheless very much the way menstruation is handled in self-help texts like Pope's book discussed earlier. Just as Roseanne referred to the moon, water and seasons, cultural feminist work on menstruation similarly presents menstruation as something divine and spiritual.[66]

Taking political activism slightly further is moderate activism manifested as public consciousness-raising.

Moderate Activism

In the *Degrassi: The Next Generation* episode discussed earlier, initially Emma was anxious about her period, but quickly adjusted and nonchalantly admitted having it to a male classmate. By the end of the episode Emma's menstrual consciousness had progressed to her collecting signatures on a petition to get a tampon dispenser installed in the girls' bathroom: in just one episode Emma had gotten her first period and became a full-fledged menstrual activist; she didn't just quietly accept her own menstruation but advocated for the acceptance of it by others. In the *Californication* (2007–) episode when Becca (Madeleine Martin) got her first period, while she initially allowed her father to hush her when she dared name it out loud in the gas station, later in the episode—at her mother's wedding—she fronted her band and performed a cover of Alice Cooper's "Only Women Bleed" (1975): while not necessarily publicly *outing* her menstruation, she nonetheless certainly presented a public version of acceptance of it, if not embrace of it. Something similar transpired in *The Runaways* (2010) when Cherie (Dakota Fanning) got her first period and on the same day painted a *red* streak on her face. Wendy Wasserstein's play *Uncommon Women and Others* (1977)—and the film of the same name (1978)—centered on a group of women reminiscing about their university days. During a conversation about sexual politics, Rita (played by Swoosie Kurtz in the original staging of the play and in the film) confessed, "I've tasted my menstrual blood." Referencing the suggestion made in Greer's book *The Female Eunuch*,[67] Rita too had become a menstrual activist. She didn't just privately taste her own blood, rather, she admitted doing so to her friends, challenging both their revulsion and attitudes to their own bodies and attempting to demystify and destigmatize menstrual blood.

While menstrual activists are rarely portrayed on screen, they are indeed detected elsewhere in popular culture, notably online. In gender researcher Michele Polak's discussion, she noted that while for several decades Judy Blume's *Are You There God? It's Me, Margaret* served as the source for most girls' information about menstruation, the Internet dramatically changed this:

Many contemporary discussions about menstruation have moved to the information sharing medium of the Internet. . . . Forums such as message boards, chat rooms, and online social networking communities are where most discussions of relevance concerning menstruation take place. . . . The information-sharing activities of contemporary teen girls indicated that they will no longer settle for silence around issues of menstruation.[68]

Such ideas relate to Fingerson's research where she identified girls using menstruation as "a resource in social interaction: for telling stories and for making connections with others through shared experience."[69] Polak surmised that the contemporary adolescent girl has become increasingly vocal about her menstruation, contending that "not only has she found her voice; she knows how to use it."[70] The manner in which girls use their voices highlights one of the important ways that moderate menstrual activism occurs in popular culture. Polak contended that as a result of girls rewriting the menstruation narrative, they have in turn "ripped apart" the familiar narrative of secrecy.[71] While I would contend that the fact that the Internet offers *anonymity* means that there are distinct limitations to how menstrually "out and proud" we might presume these girls to be, nonetheless, the fact that they are actually participating in these discussions and telling their stories does indeed function on a conscience-raising level, working to disseminate information and to provide an opportunity for exchanging anxieties, demystifying periods, and changing attitudes more broadly. In chapter 2 I discussed the anxiety that female characters felt at menarche: education and the existence of a forum where menstruation can be frankly discussed undoubtedly help girls transition to womanhood.

Extreme Activism

In chapter 1, I discussed Judy Chicago's installation "Menstruation Bathroom" (1972) which depicted a bin overflowing with bloodied menstrual products. Another of her famous works was "Red Flag" (1971), a photolithographic showing a close-up of the artist removing a bloodied tampon from her vagina. When this image was first exhibited, apparently many in the audience were confused as to what it depicted, some thinking it was a bloodied penis. In response, Chicago commented that such confusion was "a testament to the damage done to our perceptual powers by the absence of female reality."[72] This absence of female reality is one central motivation behind art we might consider as extreme menstrual activism work. Chicago's comments—made at the beginning of the second-wave feminist movement—highlighted a central goal of feminist artists at the time; to rectify some of the glaring omissions in art. In Michael Hatt and Charlotte Klonk's work on post-1970s women's art, menstruation was similarly listed amongst topics including childbirth and oppression as popular subjects for feminist artists because such themes had not previously been "represented in canonical art."[73]

While each artist's efforts manifest differently, most menstrual-themed work can be situated in one of three categories: public menstruation, menstrual blood as a medium, and menstrual-themed. In their book *The Curse*, for example, authors Janice Delaney et al. wrote about organizing a small, private "bleed-in" to celebrate menstruation as well as to stimulate their writing.[74] While—according to their accounts—the bleed-in was more menstrual celebration that *public bleeding*, their idea nonetheless referenced the possibility of something more literal transpiring. Barrie Jean Borich in her novel *My Lesbian Husband*, for example, alluded to the idea of a bleed-in in a brief reference to menstrual art: "Exhibitions of menstrual art—a sort of organic action painting created when the artist stood over a blank canvas at a time of heavy flow."[75] In 2004 in the UK, artist Carlota Bérard actually did publicly bleed for her art in a performance titled "Aqua Permanens" where she danced over a white cloth, letting her menstrual blood drip freely onto the fabric. Bérard's performance exemplifies work that emerges from the feminist performance art movement of the 1970s whereby the female artist's own body is used to challenge traditional notions of female objectification:

> Performance art as an expression of feminist ideology often fought the standardized, contained female body as part of the rebellion against prescribed gender roles.[76]

While not deliberate, actor Essie Davis ended up similarly performing her menstruation during a naked scene on Broadway where she unexpectedly got her period and had to decide whether to stop or continue through it.[77] More common than public menstruation, however, is art which uses menstrual blood as a medium. Artist Vanessa Tiegs, who uses menstrual blood mixed with acrylic in her work, claimed that rather than her work being "offensive shock art," her objective is to "present images about menstruation in a thoughtful way."[78] Jennifer Weigel, who also paints with her menstrual blood, similarly alleged:

> By making art about menstruation and even using the by-products of this natural occurrence, I hope that I might encourage more women to find ways to celebrate their own cycles through art. Meanwhile, I seek to redefine the idea of art and artmaking while further demystifying this process of the female body.[79]

The Internet has similarly created a means by which multimedia artists can create a space for their menstrual-themed work. On the user-generated video site YouTube, for example, many girls have uploaded their own menstruation-themed videos, highlighting another contemporary form of menstrual art. Such videos—which can be distinguished from Polak's online discussions referred to earlier (because these women frequently identify themselves)—range from spoofs on menstrual product commercials, animations explaining menstruation, how-tos related to tampon and menstrual cup usage, and recorded menstrual-themed conversations between friends are each concerned with education, activism, demystification, and oftentimes also aesthetics. Even in the more established medium of documentaries activism related to menstruation can also be detected: Diana Fabianova's documentary *The Moon Inside You* (2009), for example, is a very good example of menstrually themed visual art which used Fabianova's own painful periods as its starting point.

While menstrual art can be analyzed variously, for the purposes of my discussion, it can be discussed together in its efforts at consciousness raising: as cultural theorist Kim Hewitt wrote in her discussion of works such as Chicago's, "[t]he graphic depiction of menstruation speaks, and makes visual, the previously unspeakable and unshowable."[80] Menstrual art challenges the secrecy imperative and moves the taboo subject of menstruation out of the private realm of underpants and bathrooms and repositions it in the public domain. Such art challenges the routine relegation of menstruation to the bathroom (chapter 1) and spotlights the possibility of celebration; as Hewitt wrote, "Because of the potency of menstrual blood as an inner fluid that enables life, the image is a powerful claim for women's importance to the human race."[81]

SWEET SECRETS AND GIRLS OWN EXCITEMENT

As evident in the screen examples discussed throughout this book, most menstruation narratives involve young girls for whom menstruation is still interesting and novel. Menarche narratives exist as another means by which menstruation can be portrayed as something positive: when a girl is presented as *pleased* with the arrival of her first period. In her famous diary, Anne Frank wrote about her menstruation, describing: "in spite of all the pain, unpleasantness, and nastiness, I have a sweet secret."[82] While one analysis of this remark reflects the secrecy mandate discussed in chapter 1, Anne's description of it as "sweet" alludes to the possibility of young girls excitedly *embracing* their menstruation. When Margaret got her period in *Are You There God? It's Me, Margaret*, she thanked God, evidently interpreting its arrival as a good thing.[83] In Shalom Victor's account of her first period in the *My Little Red Book* anthology, she described feeling "inexpressible joy."[84] While on screen first period excitement is seldom shown, two scenes where it is evident occur in *The Legend of Billie Jean* (1985) and *Puberty Blues* (1981). In *The Legend of Billie Jean*, Putter (Yeardley Smith) got her first period during a car chase. She reacted with a broad smile and chimed, "It's about time!" In the Australian film *Puberty Blues* (1981), Debbie (Nell Schofield), while seated on the toilet, looked down at her underpants, smiled and threw her head back in delight. She then said to her best friend, "Guess what?" and happily revealed her discovery. In contrast to the negative emotions associated with menarche discussed in chapter 2, these scenes showed girls displaying genuine delight.

The focus on positive portrayals of menstruation in this chapter highlights a central achievement of feminism. The successes of feminism have facilitated female and especially *feminist* filmmakers to make their own films and utilize an opportunity to tell their own stories, menstruation being one example. While I discuss in greater detail in chapter 8 why menstruation *isn't* a story told with as much frequency as one might expect given how common it is in real life, the very existence of menstrual portrayals on screen—especially positive ones—highlights one impact that feminism has had: taking traditionally private matters and moving them into the public sphere. This book has focused nearly entirely on film and television made after the 1970s and this situation is likely informed—in varying degrees—by women's changing roles in society over the past four decades and greater comfort in presenting previously taboo female experiences.

While audiences are more familiar with negative menstruation examples, as discussed in this chapter, there are outlier examples where menstruation is presented as something positive. In chapter 7 I focus on screen representations of absent periods, examining their presentation in the context of pregnancy, infertility, and menopause narratives.

NOTES

1. Kate Kane, "The Ideology of Freshness in Feminine Hygiene Commercials," *Feminist Television Criticism*, eds. Charlotte Brunsdon, Julie D'Acci, and Lynn Spigel (New York: Oxford University Press, 1997), 297.
2. Susan Bordo, *Twilight Zones: The Hidden Life of Cultural Images from Plato to OJ* (Los Angeles: University of California Press, 1997), 32.
3. Karen Houppert, *The Curse: Confronting the Last Unmentionable Taboo: Menstruation* (New York: Farrar, Straus and Giroux, 1999), 93.
4. Kate Kane, "The Ideology of Freshness in Feminine Hygiene Commercials," *Feminist Television Criticism*, eds. Charlotte Brunsdon, Julie D'Acci and Lynn Spigel (New York: Oxford University Press, 1997), 296.
5. See, for example, Judith Butler, *Gender Trouble: Feminism and the Subversion of Identity* (New York: Routledge, 1990); Judith Butler, *Bodies That Matter: On the Discursive Limits of "Sex"* (New York: Routledge, 1993).

6. Karen Houppert, *The Curse: Confronting the Last Unmentionable Taboo: Menstruation* (New York: Farrar, Straus and Giroux, 1999), 110.

7. In Elissa Stein and Susan Kim, *Flow: The Cultural Story of Menstruation* (New York: St. Martin's Griffin, 2009), 75.

8. The "good woman" is expected to be stable, emotionally secure, kind, forbearing, supportive, contented, giving, feminine, beautiful, pure, chaste, noble, self-sacrificing, self-abnegating, self-restraining, and self-denying. This list comes from my book *Cheating on the Sisterhood: Infidelity and Feminism* where I summarized much literature on the construction of femininity (Lauren Rosewarne, *Cheating on the Sisterhood: Infidelity and Feminism* (Santa Barbara, CA: Praeger, 2009), 43).

9. Lauren Rosewarne, *Sex in Public: Women, Outdoor Advertising and Public Policy* (Newcastle: Cambridge Scholars Publishing, 2007), 153. See also Sheila Jeffreys, *Beauty and Misogyny* (East Sussex: Routledge, 2005).

10. Alexandra Pope, *The Wild Genie: The Healing Power of Menstruation* (Bowral, New South Wales: Sally Milner, 2001).

11. Stephen T. Sinatra, *Heartsense for Women: Your Plan for Natural Prevention and Treatment* (Washington, DC: LifeLine Press, 2000), 323.

12. Claudia Bepko, *The Responsibility Trap* (New York: Free Press, 1985), 67.

13. Aaron Karo, *I'm Having More Fun Than You* (New York: HarperCollins, 2009), 73.

14. Rachel Lynn Palmer and Sarah Koslow Greenberg, *Facts and Frauds in Woman's Hygiene: A Medical Guide Against Misleading Claims and Dangerous Products* (New York: Vanguard Press, 1936), 54.

15. Discussed in Ronald B. Flowers, *Female Crime, Criminals, and Cellmates: An Exploration of Female Criminality* (Jefferson, NC: McFarland & Co, 1995), 89.

16. Ronald B. Flowers, *Female Crime, Criminals, and Cellmates: An Exploration of Female Criminality* (Jefferson, NC: McFarland & Co, 1995), 89.

17. In *The Female Eunuch*, Greer wrote: "It may be that women commit crimes during the premenstrual and menstrual period, but it is still true that women commit far fewer crimes than men" (Germaine Greer, *The Female Eunuch* (New York: Farrar, Straus, and Giroux, 1970), 59).

18. See Geoffrey Redmond, *The Hormonally Vulnerable Woman* (New York: HarperCollins, 2005), 84; Katharina Dalton and Wendy Holton, *Once a Month: Understanding and Treating PMS* (Salt Lake City, UT: Publishers Press, 1999), 138.

19. Geoffrey Redmond, *The Hormonally Vulnerable Woman* (New York: HarperCollins, 2005), 84.

20. In Jane M. Ussher, Myra Hunter, and Susannah J. Browne, "Good, bad or dangerous to know: Representations of femininity in narrative accounts of PMS," in *Culture in Psychology*, ed. Corinne Squire (Philadelphia: Taylor and Francis, 2000), 88.

21. In Jane M. Ussher, Myra Hunter, and Susannah J. Browne, "Good, bad or dangerous to know: Representations of femininity in narrative accounts of PMS," in *Culture in Psychology*, ed. Corinne Squire (Philadelphia: Taylor and Francis, 2000), 88.

22. In Mia Lundin, *Female Brain Gone Insane: An Emergency Guide for Women Who Feel Like They Are Falling Apart* (Deerfield Beach, FL: Health Communications, 2009), 73.

23. Karen Houppert, *The Curse: Confronting the Last Unmentionable Taboo: Menstruation* (New York: Farrar, Straus and Giroux, 1999), 141.

24. Jane M. Ussher, *Managing the Monstrous Feminine: Regulating the Reproductive Body* (New York: Routledge, 2006).

25. In *Cheating on the Sisterhood: Infidelity and Feminism*, I discussed compartmentalization in the context of people rationalizing participation in infidelity. In *Part-Time Perverts: Sex, Pop Culture and Kink Management*, I similarly discussed this idea in the context of participation in non-vanilla, non-mainstream sexual practices (Lauren Rosewarne, *Cheating on the Sisterhood: Infidelity and Feminism* (Santa Barbara, CA: Praeger, 2009); Lauren Rosewarne, *Part-Time Perverts: Sex, Pop Culture and Kink Management* (Santa Barbara, CA: Praeger), 2011)).

26. Laura Fingerson, *Girls in Power: Gender, Body and Menstruation in Adolescence* (Albany: State University of New York Press, 2006), 135.

27. In chapter 4 I quoted from Jessica Valenti's book on double standards where she wrote: "it seems that whenever women have the gall to express anything other than effusive chipperness, we're accused of having PMS or being nuts" (Jessica Valenti, *He's a Stud, She's a Slut, and 49 Other Double Standards Every Woman Should Know* (Berkeley, CA: Seal Press, 2008), 66–67).

28. Jib Fowles, *Advertising and Popular Culture* (Thousand Oaks, CA: Sage, 1996), 186.

29. Jennifer Reed, "Roseanne: A "Killer Bitch" for Generation X," in *Third Wave Agenda: Being Feminist, Doing Feminism*, ed. Leslie Heywood and Jennifer Drake (Minneapolis: University of Minnesota Press, 1997), 123.

30. See Kathy McCoy, *The Teenage Survival Guide* (New York: Simon and Schuster, 1981); John M. MacDonald and David L. Michaud, *Rape: Controversial Issues: Criminal Profiles, Date Rape, False Reports and False Memories* (Springfield, IL: Charles C. Thomas, 1995); Alexandra Bandon, *Date Rape* (New York: Crestwood House, 1994); Ingrid Foeken, "Confusing realities and lessons learned in wartime: Supporting women's projects in the former Yugoslavia," in *Assault on the Soul: Women in the Former Yugoslavia*, ed. Sara Sharratt and Ellyn Kaschak (Binghamton, NY: Haworth Press, 1999).

31. See Germaine Greer, *The Female Eunuch* (New York: Farrar, Straus, Giroux, 1970); Patricia Morley, *The Mountain in Moving: Japanese Women's Lives* (Vancouver: University of British Columbia Press, 1999).

32. Because they don't want to identify themselves as menstruating to their (male) superiors (something in line with the secrecy mandates discussed in chapter 1) (Susan J. Pharr, "Status Conflict: The Rebellion of the Tea Pourers," in *Women and Women's Issues in Post World War II Japan*, ed. Edward R. Beauchamp (New York: Taylor and Francis, 1998), 231. Another reason for women not to claim such leave is that in practice they know they won't actually get it (Nisha Agrawal, *Indonesia: Labor Market Policies and International Competitiveness* (Policy Research Working Paper, Washington, DC: World Bank, 1995)).

33. Susan J. Pharr, "Status Conflict: The Rebellion of the Tea Pourers," in *Women and Women's Issues in Post World War II Japan*, ed. Edward R. Beauchamp (New York: Taylor and Francis, 1998), 231.

34. Sophie Laws, *Issues of Blood: The Politics of Menstruation* (Houndmills, Basingstoke, Hampshire: Macmillan, 1990), 30.

35. Joanna Brewis, "How does it feel? Women managers, embodiments and changing public sector cultures," in *Transforming Managers: Gendering Change in the Public Sector*, ed. Stephen M. Whitehead and Roy Moodley (New York: Routledge, 1999).

36. Dalton, Katharina, *Once a Month: The Original Premenstrual Syndrome Handbook* (Claremont, CA: Hunter House, 1990).

37. R.Bhatt and M. Bhatt, "Perceptions of Indian women regarding menstruation," *International Journal of Gynecology and Obstetrics* 88, no. 2, (2005): 164–167.

38. Dalton, Katharina, *Once a Month: The Original Premenstrual Syndrome Handbook* (Claremont, CA: Hunter House, 1990).

39. Ian Milsom, "Dysmenorrhea," in *Urogenital Pain in Clinical Practice*, ed. Andrew Paul Baranowski, Paul Abrams, and Magnus Fall (New York: Informa Healthcare USA, 2008).

40. Rowenna Davis, "What my period means to me," *Guardian*, October 2, 2009, www.guardian.co.uk/lifeandstyle/2009/oct/02/period-menstruation (accessed September 26, 2011).

41. Bonnie J. Morris, *The High School Scene in the Fifties: Voices from West LA* (Westport, CT: Bergin and Garvey, 1997), 78.

42. Cathrine Himberg, Gayle E. Hutchinson, and John M. Roussell, *Teaching Secondary Physical Education: Preparing Adolescents to Be Active for Life* (Champaign, IL: Human Kinetics, 2003), 82; Popho E. S. Bark-Yi, *Body That Bleeds: Menstrual Politics in Malaysia* (Petaling Jaya, Selanor: Strategic Information and Research Development Centre, 2007).

43. Kimberly Derting, *Desires of the Dead* (New York: HarperCollins, 2011), 167.

44. Such discomfort for male teachers is likely amplified in our culture of heightened concern about sexual predators and possible misinterpretations about a man asking questions about girls' menstrual cycles.

45. Susan J. Pharr, "Status Conflict: The Rebellion of the Tea Pourers," in *Women and Women's Issues in Post World War II Japan*, ed. Edward R. Beauchamp (New York: Taylor and Francis, 1998), 231.

46. Laura Fingerson, *Girls in Power: Gender, Body and Menstruation in Adolescence* (Albany: State University of New York Press, 2006), 137.

47. In Nancy Friday, *My Mother My Self: The Daughter's Search for Identity* (New York: Dell Publishing, 1977), 127.

48. In Laura Fingerson, *Girls in Power: Gender, Body and Menstruation in Adolescence* (Albany: State University of New York Press, 2006), 53.

49. Katharina Dalton, *Once A Month: The Original Premenstrual Syndrome Handbook* (Claremont, CA: Hunter House, 1990); Mary Turck, *Food and Emotions* (Mankato, MN: Capstone Press, 2001); Alexandra W. Logue, *The Psychology of Eating and Drinking* (New York: Brunner-Routledge, 2004).

50. In Anne M. Fletcher, *Eating Thin for Life: Food Secrets and Recipes from People Who Have Lost Weight and Kept it Off* (New York: Houghton Mifflin, 1997), 86.

51. Helen Malson, *The Thin Woman: Feminism, Post-Structuralism and the Social Psychology of Anorexia Nervosa* (New York: Routledge, 1998), 120.

52. Laura Fingerson, *Girls in Power: Gender, Body and Menstruation in Adolescence* (Albany: State University of New York Press, 2006), 104.

53. Chris Bobel, *New Blood: Third-Wave Feminism and the Politics of Menstruation* (New Brunswick, NJ: Rutgers University Press, 2010), 42.

54. In Chris Bobel, *New Blood: Third-Wave Feminism and the Politics of Menstruation* (New Brunswick, NJ: Rutgers University Press, 2010), 42.

55. In Kim and Stein's book *Flow*, the authors wrote that menstruation "remains hidden in a figurative box (scented, of course), stuffed deep inside the great medicine cabinet of American culture: out of sight and unmentioned" (Elissa Stein and Susan Kim, *Flow: The Cultural Story of Menstruation* (New York: St. Martin's Griffin, 2009), ix).

56. This issue of society's preoccupation with confession is addressed extensively in: Lauren Rosewarne, *Part-Time Perverts: Sex, Pop Culture and Kink Management* (Santa Barbara, CA: Praeger, 2011).

57. Elissa Stein and Susan Kim, *Flow: The Cultural Story of Menstruation* (New York: St. Martin's Griffin, 2009), xii.

58. Elizabeth A. Kissling, "Bleeding out loud: Communication about menstruation," *Feminism and Psychology* 6 (1996): 481–504.

59. Laura Fingerson, *Girls in Power: Gender, Body and Menstruation in Adolescence* (Albany: State University of New York Press, 2006).

60. Laura Fingerson, *Girls in Power: Gender, Body and Menstruation in Adolescence* (Albany: State University of New York Press, 2006), 135.

61. Gloria Steinem, "If Men Could Menstruate," *Ms Magazine* (October 1978).

62. In JoAnn Loulan and Bonnie Worthen, *Period: A Girl's Guide* (Minnetonka, MN: Book Peddlers, 2001), 51.

63. Sara Shepard, *Flawless: A Pretty Little Liars Book* (New York: HarperTeen, 2007), 69.

64. Chris Bobel, *New Blood: Third-Wave Feminism and the Politics of Menstruation* (New Brunswick, NJ: Rutgers University Press, 2010), 95.

65. Karen Houppert, *The Curse: Confronting the Last Unmentionable Taboo: Menstruation* (New York: Farrar, Straus and Giroux, 1999), 214.

66. It should also be noted that the spiritual feminist interpretation of menstruation is also mocked in popular culture. In an episode of the sitcom *The Office* (2005–), for example, Dwight (Rainn Wilson) commented: "I wish I could menstruate. If I could menstruate, I wouldn't have to deal with idiotic *calendars* anymore. I'd just be able to count down from my previous cycle. Plus I'd be more in tune with the moon and the tides."

67. In *The Female Eunuch*, Germaine Greer wrote: "If you think you are emancipated, you might consider the idea of tasting your menstrual blood—if it makes you sick, you've a long way to go, baby" (Germaine Greer, *The Female Eunuch* (New York: Farrar, Straus, Giroux, 1970), 57).

68. Michele Polak, "Menstruation," in *Girl Culture: Studying Girl Culture: A Readers' Guide*, ed. Claudia Mitchell and Jacqueline Reid-Walsh (Westport, CT: Greenwood Press, 2008), 433.

69. Laura Fingerson, *Girls in Power: Gender, Body and Menstruation in Adolescence* (Albany: State University of New York Press, 2006), 94.

70. Michele Polak, "Menstruation," in *Girl Culture: Studying Girl Culture: A Readers' Guide*, ed., Claudia Mitchell and Jacqueline Reid-Walsh (Westport, CT: Greenwood Press, 2008), 433.

71. Michele Polak, "From the Curse to the Rag: Online gURLs Rewrite the Menstruation Narrative," in *Girlhood: Redefining the Limits*, ed. Yasmin Jiwani, Candis Steenbergen, and Claudia Mitchell (New York: Black Rose Books, 2006), 192.

72. In Chris Bobel, *New Blood: Third-Wave Feminism and the Politics of Menstruation* (New Brunswick, NJ: Rutgers University Press, 2010), 47.

73. Michael Hatt and Charlotte Klonk, *Art History: A Critical Introduction to Its Methods* (New York: Manchester University Press, 2006), 147.

74. Janice Delaney, Mary Jane Lupton, and Emily Toth, *The Curse: A Cultural History of Menstruation* (New York: Dutton, 1976).

75. Barrie Jean Borich, *My Lesbian Husband: Landscapes of a Marriage* (Saint Paul, MN: Graywolf Press, 1999), 72.

76. Kim Hewitt, *Mutilating the Body: Identity in Blood and Ink* (Bowling Green, OH: Bowling Green State University Popular Press, 1997), 96.

77. Essie Davis told this story during a 2012 appearance on the Australian talk show *Adam Hills in Gordon St Tonight* (2011–).

78. In Spiraling Moon blog, spiralingmoon.livejournal.com/2003/02/12/ (accessed September 24, 2011).

79. Jennifer Weigel Art, jenniferweigelart.com/Awareness/Identity/Menstruation.html (accessed September 24, 2011).

80. Kim Hewitt, *Mutilating the Body: Identity in Blood and Ink* (Bowling Green, OH: Bowling Green State University Popular Press, 1997), 96.

81. Kim Hewitt, *Mutilating the Body: Identity in Blood and Ink* (Bowling Green, OH: Bowling Green State University Popular Press, 1997), 96.

82. Frances Goodrich and Albert Hackett, *The Diary of Anne Frank* (New York: Dramatists Guild Fund, 2000), 46.

83. Judy Blume, *Are You There God? It's Me, Margaret* (New York: Random House, 1970).

84. Shalom Victor, "The Lie, 1948," in *My Little Red Book*, ed. Rachel Kauder Nalebuff (New York: Twelve, 2009), 21.

Chapter Seven

You Don't Know What You've Got 'Til It's Gone

Absent Menstruation

On those rare occasions when menstruation is included in a screen narrative, the storyline most often concerns a young girl's menarche, or alternatively focuses on the negative elements of the adult woman's menstruation. Another distinct way it is depicted on screen is when it is *absent*: notably in storylines centered on pregnancy and menopause. This chapter focuses on late periods, absent periods and ceased periods, exploring those rare times when periods are bestowed with extensive significance: when they don't arrive, when they arrive unexpectedly, or when they stop entirely.

MENSTRUATION AND THE PREGNANCY POSSIBILITY

Menarche may mark the beginning of a girl's fertility, but the connection between periods and reproduction is generally much more complicated. With intercourse most likely pursued for recreation rather than reproduction, periods exist as an important signifier that a woman remains *un*pregnant. In this section I examine three manifestations of the menstruation/fertility link: screen narratives which celebrate menstruation's role in pregnancy; absent period narratives alluding to possible pregnancy; and narratives centered on periods arriving late and thus *avoiding* pregnancy.

The Celebration of Fertility

Off screen the significance of menstruation is often explained to girls as "you can get pregnant and have babies now."[1] When surveyed, women frequently identify menstruation as important primarily because it enables them to become mothers.[2] Despite the burden that women routinely consider menstruation to be (chapter 2), interestingly, at menopause it is the loss of reproductive capacity that women frequently mourn (an idea returned to later in this chapter). On screen menstruation portrayed as significant because of its link to reproduction is certainly detectable. In *My Louisiana Sky* (2001), for example, when Tiger Ann (Kelsey Keel) got her first period, her mother, Corrina (Amelia Campbell), reassured her:

> It's not a curse! It's beautiful! Oh, it's a little messy and sometimes your tummy hurts, but I couldn't have you til I was bleedin' every month, and havin' a baby, havin' you, was the best thing that ever happened to me.

In an episode of the sitcom *The Cosby Show* (1984–1992), when Rudy (Keshia Knight Pulliam) got her first period, her mother Clair (Phylicia Rashad) said, "See, some day you'll be able to have children of your own." In an episode of the the sitcom *Roseanne* (1988–1997), upon getting her first period, Darlene (Sara Gilbert) asked her mother to "Name one good thing that could come out of this whole mess," to which Roseanne responded: "Okay I'll name three. Becky, DJ, and . . . what's that other kid's name?" In these examples, menarche was presented as something with an inextricable link to fertility: menstruation is *the* signal that the girl is a woman and, at least theoretically, can bear children.[3] One explanation for mothers lauding the fertility opportunities of menstruation likely reflects the target audiences of these narratives: spotlighting fertility places a positive spin on periods for the newly menstruating characters, but also for the girls in the audience who are likely experiencing their own anxieties. The fertility reminder can also be interpreted as a subtle reminder to girls—again within the narrative but also in the audience—of their new responsibilities: that menstruation delivers new concerns, including the "threat" of conception that comes with their burgeoning sexuality.[4]

While for young girls menstruation marks the beginning of womanhood, for sexually active women, the possibility of pregnancy means that an *absent* period can be a serious concern.

Possibly Pregnant

One interesting way that menstruation is alluded to in narratives is when an expected period fails to arrive, thus instigating a pregnancy scare narrative. In chapter 4 I discussed the notable absence of references to menstruation in

Stephenie Meyer's popular—and explicitly blood-themed—*Twilight* saga. Notably, the scantest of menstrual references occurred in an exploration of an *absent* period: in the final book, while on her honeymoon, Bella noticed a box of tampons while searching in the bathroom for something to quell her nausea; it was at that moment that she suspected pregnancy.[5] While for Bella unused tampons provided a hint to a missed period, on screen such a suspicion is usually expressed through the use of the popular "I'm late" circumlocution, emblematic of the kind communications researcher Elizabeth Kissling discussed: Kissling noted that girls frequently avoid describing their menstruation in explicit terms and instead favor euphemisms and circumlocutions.[6] In an episode of *Californication* (2007–), sixteen-year-old Mia (Madeline Zima) said "I'm late," and middle-aged Hank (David Duchovny)—who Mia had had sex with in an earlier episode—immediately protested: "What? That's not possible. I—I—I—I—I wore a condom." While in this scene Mia eased Hank's panic by saying, "I'm late for school," Hank immediately feared pregnancy because "I'm late" is an expression that sexually active people are familiar with; it functions as a safer, less offensive, less clinical, and less descriptive alternative to naming one's absent period. In an episode of *Beverly Hills 90210* (1990–2000), teenager Brenda (Shannen Doherty) told her boyfriend Dylan (Luke Perry): "Dylan, I'm late." Dylan, with a blank expression, responded, "What are you late for?" to which Brenda restated, "No, you know, I'm *late*." In an episode of *Dawson's Creek* (1998–2003), teenage Joey (Katie Holmes) similarly revealed her pregnancy fears to her friend Gretchen (Sasha Alexander) by saying "I'm late." In an episode of *Mad Men* (2007–), Joan (Christina Hendricks) divulged her pregnancy to her affair partner, Roger (John Slattery), by saying, "I'm late. I'm very late."

While use of the "I'm late" expression in these examples highlighted continuing discomfort with frank discussions of menstruation—even by adults—it can also be an expression deployed for comic effect. In chapter 1, I discussed the presentation of menstrual dolts. Amongst the examples detailed was the confusion exhibited by Kryten (Robert Llewellyn) in the British comedy *Red Dwarf* (1988–). In one scene, a female colleague's use of the "wrong time of the month" expression humorously befuddled Kryten, to the extent that he purchased her a new calendar. In the aforementioned *Beverly Hills 90210* episode, the "I'm late" expression worked similarly to—at least initially—confuse Dylan and, perhaps most importantly, to remind audiences that menstruation will always be a female thing which men will never truly comprehend (and thus will be permanently excluded from). The *Californication* episode worked similarly to highlight how men can be at the mercy of women's menstrual cycles.

While an absent period can create a pregnancy fear, a period that arrives late can also *assuage* such a concern.

Happily Not-Pregnant

In feminist writer Jennifer Baumgardner's description of her menarche, she reflected on her initial reaction which, predictably, quickly waned:

> The second day of my period was exciting, too, as I told all of my friends. But after that, I can't say I loved getting it anymore, unless I was worried I was pregnant.[7]

While fading first reactions to menstruation relate well to ideas explored in chapter 2, of relevance to this chapter is Baumgardner's comment that menstruation is only exciting and memorable for adults when it quashes fears of unwanted pregnancy. In chapter 1, I referenced a study of women, many who identified periods as signaling failed reproduction and serving as a reminder that pregnancy had not occurred.[8] Gynecologist Sir Norman Jeffcoate once vividly—and histrionically—presented this same idea, describing menstruation as "the weeping of a disappointed uterus."[9] Whereas a pregnancy test can give a false positive,[10] the appearance of menstruation is generally construed as an irrefutable sign that conception has not occurred, a sign that can be interpreted variously given the circumstances.

Given the long-standing avoidance of showing or discussing menstruation on screen, pregnancy suspicions are generally settled through the use of an at-home pregnancy test. While audiences may assume that a missed period may have initially motivated a woman to take a test, rarely is menstruation actually mentioned: the audience is left to draw this conclusion themselves. There are, however, some rare examples when a period actually does answer the pregnancy question, notably when a character divulges a period to end a pregnancy scare storyline. In this section I discuss two common reactions to the arrival of a late period: relief and ambiguity.

In the *Beverly Hills 90210* episode discussed earlier, Brenda kept on "checking and waiting" for her period and finally got it at the gynecologist's office: "What a relief!" she exulted. In an episode of British sitcom *Two Pints of Lager and a Packet of Crisps* (2001–), Donna (Natalie Casey) feared she was pregnant. After two episodes centered on her anxiety, she walked into a room where her friends and boyfriend were seated and said: "Well, I started my period," and smiled broadly. In *Where the Heart Is* (2000), Novalee's (Natalie Portman) pregnancy fears were settled in a gas station restroom: she entered the stall and shouted "Yes!" and "Thank you Lord! Thank you so much." For each character, the arrival of their late period was construed as something positive; these characters did not desire pregnancy and thus the arrival of their period provided uncomplicated relief.

While in these three examples the late period was heartily embraced, there are circumstances when it is met with more ambiguity. An episode of *Sex and the City* (1998–2004), for example, centered on a baby shower and had a parallel storyline of Carrie's (Sarah Jessica Parker) late period and pregnancy scare. Only at the very end of the episode—as she walked alone through the streets of Manhattan—did Carrie reveal (via voice over): "On the way home I got my period." Carrie avoided a life-transforming pregnancy but her level of comfort was unclear; while a pregnancy wasn't something that she had planned, evidently she had let herself consider life with a child, even if only briefly. In an episode of the sitcom *Ellen* (1994–1998), Paige's (Joely Fisher) period was late and she suspected she was pregnant. In solidarity, Paige's friends Ellen (Ellen DeGeneres) and Audrey (Clea Lewis) each took pregnancy tests with her. One of the pregnancy tests showed a positive so the assumption was that Paige was indeed pregnant. Later in the episode, Paige visited Ellen at work and the following scene transpired:

> **Paige:** There's no baby.
>
> **Ellen:** What?
>
> **Paige:** I'm—I'm not pregnant. I got my period.
>
> **Ellen:** Is that a good thing? Or is that a bad thing?
>
> **Paige:** I don't know. It's weird. I mean, first I was scared. Then I was, then I was upset. Then I was resigned. And then I was kinda happy. And then, I don't know. Listen to me! I can't even blame it on hormones anymore.

As in the *Sex and the City* episode, while a pregnancy would have been accidental for Paige, she clearly viewed getting her period as bittersweet; Paige—like Carrie—had allowed the pregnancy possibility to enter her consciousness. A very similar reaction occurred in a scene from Emily Giffin's novel *Baby Proof*: Jess entered the bedroom of her best friend and said, "Claudia. I'm bleeding . . . I got my period . . . I'm not pregnant anymore."[11] Like Carrie and Paige, Jess's reaction was ambiguous. Even more so than Carrie or Paige, Jess had actually considered herself *as* pregnant. While she hadn't necessarily embraced the idea, her pregnancy had nonetheless settled into her consciousness and its ending delivered multifaceted feelings.

One reading of the ambiguity in these scenes relates to cultural expectations of femininity and the assumption that *of course* a woman would want children; even if unplanned. In these examples, while each pregnancy would have been accidental, relief was coupled with slight sadness over the "what if" possibility in line with an essentialist view of femininity mandating motherhood. Another interpretation is that the ambiguous reactions were simply the safest way to handle a narrative where an actual child would have been inconvenient: presenting joy at the arrival of a period may have seemed crass, so a modicum of loss or sadness was presented. A similar idea was elaborated on in media theorist Lynne Joyrich's book *Re-viewing Reception*. Joyrich discussed the miscarriage storyline in the television series *Moon-

lighting (1985–1989) and noted that given that the series was very much defined by sexual tension, having the sexy female central character—Maddie (Cybill Shepherd)—become a mother would have completely changed the show. To circumvent this, a miscarriage storyline was deployed:

> In an attempt to extricate themselves from this dilemma, the producers of *Moonlighting* ended Maddie's troublesome pregnancy in an astonishing way.[12]

The convenient miscarriage is certainly an interpretation for the events transpiring in an episode of *Party of Five* (1994–2000). Julia (Neve Campbell) was pregnant and decided to abort. At the abortion clinic the character discovered that she had actually miscarried; an abortion was no longer necessary. In *Party of Five*, the pregnancy was unwanted; in *Moonlighting* it was inconvenient: actual abortions in both narratives would have been controversial—likely too much so given the youth audience of *Party of Five* and the political climate in the era of *Moonlighting*—so *instead* both pregnancies were handled in a socially acceptable way. Rather than Julia or Maddie becoming "baby killers," they were "gifted" miscarriages which cast them as figures of sympathy; the ending of their pregnancies was taken out of their hands and thus the women were (albeit temporarily) transformed into tragic figures.

While late-arriving periods can bring both joy and ambiguity, a period also exists as a very obvious sign of failed conception for women who have miscarried or who were trying to conceive, an idea identifiable both off screen and on.

Failed Conception

In women's accounts of miscarriage, periods are routinely identified as something that compounds pain:

> We aren't supposed to be getting our periods. We're supposed to be pregnant. It is another physical and painful reminder that we aren't pregnant anymore. That first period (and many subsequently thereafter) will hit you harder than you wish they would. It's not just a cycle anymore. It's a non-pregnancy.[13]

> Each time my period starts I get very depressed and talk about pregnancy and motherhood, and how I feel I'm running out of time. My husband must be fed up with it, although he's very patient. With each period I feel I'm reliving the loss of my baby.[14]

This idea of menstrual blood functioning as a non-pregnancy is identifiable in Adam Schwartz's novel *A Stranger on the Planet*: in one scene Molly started crying and said, "I'm sorry . . . but every time my period comes I feel the loss of our baby all over again."[15] While the miscarriage narrative is easily detectable on screen,[16] a storyline much more relevant to a menstruation discussion is one concerned with characters trying to conceive but where menstrual blood denotes failure. Many television shows, including—but certainly not limited to—*Gavin and Stacey* (2007–2010), *How I Met Your Mother* (2005–), *Offspring* (2010–), *Friends* (1994–2004), *Parenthood* (2010–), *Coupling* (2000–2004) have had major plotlines involving couples' quests to conceive. Interestingly, in most of these narratives, menstruation was never actually discussed; instead, audiences have to assume that the arrival of a period was the unspoken reason why the couple knew that conception had failed; that menstruation was why they needed to "keep trying": as Will (Eric McCormack) said to Grace (Debra Messing) in an episode of the sitcom *Will and Grace* (1998–2006): "we'll try again in two weeks. You know, when you're ovulating again." This same "we'll try again" narrative transpired in an episode of *Grey's Anatomy* (2005–): staring at the negative pregnancy test stick, Derek (Patrick Dempsey) said to wife Meredith (Ellen Pompeo), "We just have to keep doing it until we get it right." While on screen characters deciding to "keep trying" subtly implies that menstruation had thwarted previous attempts, there are some examples where menstruation's role in dashing pregnancy hopes is made much more explicit. In chapter 5, for example, I quoted a scene from Tom Perrotta's novel *Little Children* when Larry and Joanie have sex:

> They made love with unusual tenderness, in honor of the vast mystery of life, only to find blood on the sheets and themselves when they were finished.[17]

In this scene, the couple had been trying for a baby—*thought* they were pregnant—only to have their hopes dashed by Joanie's period. In an episode of the sitcom *Scrubs* (2001–2010), nurse Carla (Judy Reyes), commented "I got my period. . . . This really sucks. I've been trying to get pregnant for two months now." The same idea was presented much more explicitly—and repeatedly—in Matthew Miller's memoir *Maybe Baby: An Infertile Love Story*, where he explored his and his wife's long struggle to conceive:

> Wednesday's second pee, arriving courtesy of a twenty-four ounce strawberry smoothie only thirty minutes after the first, yielded the first spots of blood from the ten-days-late period. "I'm not pregnant," Constance said. She sat on the toilet crying into my shoulder for five minutes.[18]

> Confidence or ignorance fueled me as I opened the door to the bathroom . . . I saw a red-soaked wad of white cotton being held aloft like a gruesome exhibit on some tacky cop show.
> "It's didn't work," she said. "I got my period. The insemination didn't work."[19]

"I'm pretty sure it's my period," Constance said, once again lifting a piece of toilet paper for me to inspect. "It's been light all day, but definitely feels like there's a lot more coming right now."[20]

The *Grey's Anatomy* scene provided a good clue as to why a negative pregnancy test is far more likely to demonstrate unsuccessful pregnancy on screen than a vivid menstrual display as in *Maybe Baby*. In *Grey's Anatomy*, it was stated early into the episode that Meredith took her pregnancy test on "day ten"; that is, *very* soon after attempting conception. While we know that she and Derek were keen to conceive—and were probably very eager to find out whether their efforts were successful—their use of the pregnancy test provided the opportunity for the episode to follow the "show, don't tell" narrative mantra: it is more dramatic television to have the characters stare at the words "not pregnant" on a pregnancy test stick rather than to have the woman simply *say* she had gotten her period; *showing* her period would, of course, be virtually impossible (chapter 8).

One particularly interesting pregnancy scare narrative is when a missed period is construed as pregnancy but in fact proves to be an early sign of menopause.

THE MISINTERPRETED PREGNANCY SCARE

In a season two episode of *The Closer* (2005–), a pregnancy test kit was visible in Brenda's (Kyra Sedgwick) handbag. Later in the episode—and without taking the test—Brenda confided to her boss, "I think I'm pregnant." By the end of the episode, Brenda finally took the test and it was negative. In the follow season, after many episodes portraying her hot flashes and irritability, it was discovered that Brenda was going through early menopause. While her season two pregnancy scare and season three discovery were not explicitly linked in the narrative, it may be suspected that the initial scare was an early sign of menopause as manifested in a disrupted menstrual cycle. Other narratives present this idea much more explicitly, as evidenced in *The Golden Girls* (1985–1992), *7th Heaven* (1996–2007), and *That '70s Show* (1998–2006).

In an episode of *The Golden Girls*, Blanche (Rue McClanahan) missed a period. Blanche was presented as thoroughly oblivious to the idea that this was potentially a sign of menopause and instead assumed pregnancy, going so far as to take a test. Her doctor in fact informed her that she was menopausal. In an episode of *7th Heaven*, Annie (Catherine Hicks)—who was exhibiting symptoms associated with her previous pregnancies like napping, crying and strange cravings—was assumed to be pregnant by her husband, Eric (Stephen Collins), and seven children; instead, she was at the earliest stages of menopause. In an episode of *That '70s Show*, Kitty (Debra Jo Rupp) believed she was pregnant. Like Blanche, she went to a doctor to confirm; she too discovered that she was going through menopause.

While the episode of *The Golden Girls* prompted the four central characters to reflect on their individual experiences with menstruation, in *7th Heaven* and *That '70s Show*, menstruation wasn't discussed at all: the audience simply had to assume that an absent period set in motion the pregnancy possibility narrative. Such scenes weren't really about menstruation of course, but rather, like the "I'm late" circumlocution discussed earlier, focused on the events that the *absence* of menstruation created. Such scenes also functioned to befuddle certain characters and in turn solicit humor. In *That '70s Show*, for example, Kitty's husband, Red (Kurtwood Smith), and son, Eric (Topher Grace), evidently had no idea about menopause—Eric, for example, asked his mother, "are you going to lose your hair?"—and thus the men had to consult the *World Book*. In *7th Heaven*, the entire family appeared to readily assume pregnancy; no thought at all was given to menopause. While Blanche and Kitty saw themselves as young and fertile, the audience found this entertaining based on the characters each having fully grown children and being assumed to be *beyond* fertility. In each example, menopause functioned as something dividing those in the know from those who don't, a standard source of humor and similar in tone to narratives whereby menstruation is something portrayed as separating men and women and dividing those who *understand* from the "retards" (chapters 2 and 4).

Interestingly, sometimes the pregnancy/menopause mix-up is subverted. In the British sitcom *Absolutely Fabulous* (1992–2004), for example, this was done for comic effect when Patsy (Joanna Lumley) facetiously discussed her mother: "She didn't want a child. She would've got rid of me, but she mistook being pregnant for the menopause. When she found out it was too late"; Patsy thought of herself as a "change of life baby." The "change of life" baby storyline similarly transpired in the Australian family drama *Packed to the Rafters* (2008–): Julie (Rebecca Gibney) actually assumed that she was going through menopause, presumably—although not discussed— by a missed period. The character was in fact pregnant with a baby nearly two decades younger than her youngest son. In an episode of the sitcom *Maude* (1972–1978), the title character (Bea Arthur), like Julie, found herself pregnant in her late forties. In a surprising move for the genre and era— notably pre-dating the *Roe v. Wade* decision—Maude and her husband, Walter (Bill Macy), decided to abort, agreeing that having a child so late in life would be a bad decision. In *Sex and the City*, while her friends assumed that Samantha's (Kim Cattrall) late period denoted pregnancy, Samantha in fact *assumed* menopause; claiming to be "drying up" and describing herself as "day-old bread." Samantha's focus on her appearance and identity in this episode provides a nice segue to the presentation of ceased periods as something which negatively impacts identity.

Just as menstruation can prove relevant to a narrative when its absence indicates pregnancy, for many women, the integral role of menstruation in identity and femininity is only fully realized when a woman's menstruation ends. The end of periods at menopause can generate a variety of different feelings; on screen most are presented as negative.

THE MENOPAUSAL IDENTITY

Throughout this book I have contended that the cultural preoccupation with relegating menstruation to the private sphere largely explains the dearth of menstruation presentations on screen. While not a common narrative, the *cessation* of menstruation is the most common way that menstruation appears on screen; more precisely, its conclusion. While indeed shown more frequently than menstruation, menopause in fact shares much of menstruation's taboo because it is still about women, about women's bodies and notably about women's "plumbing." This idea of continuing taboo is well illustrated in scenes from sitcoms *Pushing Daisies* (2007–2009), *Cybill* (1995–1998), and *That '70s Show*. In a scene from *Pushing Daisies*, Lily (Swoosie Kurtz) claimed that it was "[i]mpolite to discuss a person's menopause in mixed company." In an episode of *Cybill*, the title character, Cybill (Cybill Shepherd), was accused of ruining Christmas by openly discussing her menopause. In the *That '70s Show* episode, when Kitty tried to discuss menopause with her elderly mother (Betty White), her mother claimed not to have ever gone through it, clearly not wanting to discuss it. These three examples highlight that while menopause may be more common than menstruation on screen, portrayals still carry complex social messages and taboos.

Teenager Nancy quoted in sociologist Laura Fingerson's study on menstruation commented that while she "hates" menstruating, she considered it "part of me" and "who I am."[21] In the next section I examine the central role of menstruation in body image and fertility as illustrated by menopause narratives on screen.

Menstruation and Body Image

In *Gynaecology Illustrated*, gynecologists Matthew Garrey et al. discussed menopause, writing that for some women, "it appears to present a threat to their body image, menstrual bleeding being a visible red badge of femininity."[22] A gynecologist, quoted in sociologist Jean Elson's book on hysterectomies, similarly described menstruation as a "badge of femininity."[23] While on one hand the menstruation/femininity link makes sense—nearly every woman menstruates[24] and perhaps more than any other body function it works to link women *and* exclude men—conversely the link to femininity can also be construed as peculiar; so many things associated with menstruation (i.e., mess, moodiness, and smell) are often considered *incongruent* with femininity (chapter 4). This paradox, of course, reflects the volatile relationship society has with femininity more broadly: it is simultaneously loved *and* loathed. Another apparent dichotomy—and one particularly relevant to a discussion of menopause—is that while women routinely consider their menstruation as a burden (chapter 2), when their periods stop, they "deplore the loss of this valued activity."[25] Evidently, even when loathed, menstruation is perceived as central to identity. It, therefore, likely comes as no surprise that while the cessation of it can bring relief,[26] it can also create a gender crisis. In feminist theorist Joan Callahan's book on menopause, she discussed—and critiqued—the popular perception that menopause is "an estrogen-deficiency disease, a deviation from the norms of true femininity."[27] Callahan's discussion spotlights the menstruation/femininity link, but most relevantly presents the idea of "normal" femininity involving menstruation: that the normal, healthy woman bleeds, that the abnormal woman doesn't. Certainly much of the justification for hormone therapies—both academic and in advertising—touts the benefits of helping women feel more "normal," a state which presumably is synonymous with femininity.

In gynecologist Robert Wilson's seminal work on menopause, he dubbed menopause "nature's defeminization."[28] Underpinning this moniker is the idea that not only is menopause considered *abnormal*, but more so, that menopause is abnormal because it distances women from their "natural" femininity. This idea of femininity lost is, of course, incredibly complicated. *Losing* one's femininity, for example, assumes that femininity is not only desirable but *biological*—that "the essence of femininity is tied to a woman's ovaries"[29]; a contestable assertion given that much of what classifies as "feminine" is artifice and performance (chapter 6). Assuming that femininity is *able* to be lost is also peculiar: as feminist Françoise Grioud commented, "As though femininity is something you can lose the way you lose your pocketbook: hmm, where in the world did I put my femininity?"[30] Assuming that femininity *can* be lost disregards feminist criticisms of femininity as being something subordinating[31] and instead presents its loss as naturally negative and worth mourning. Regardless of whether femininity is innate and whether it can be lost, lost femininity is nevertheless the common way menstruation and menopause are explored in academic literature and notably on screen.

A menopausal woman quoted in social scientist Karen Ballard's book *Understanding Menopause* claimed that she doesn't "feel as feminine . . . I miss feeling feminine."[32] In gynecologist Heather Currie's book on the same topic, one woman claimed, "My pubic hair has become so thin since the menopause. I feel old and less feminine."[33] Strongly linked to the femininity lost narrative are waning feelings of attractiveness, something perhaps unsurprising given that in contemporary culture, female attractiveness is predicated on a youthful and notably *feminine* appearance.[34] Writer Kathryn Petras, for example, recounted her menopause, claiming that it "made me feel distinctly undesirable. I felt old, fat, and generally unsexy."[35] A woman in journalist Dianne Hales's book on menopause similarly claimed, "It's hard to feel sexy when you're drenched in sweat and can't stand anyone touching you."[36]

Earlier in this chapter I discussed episodes of *That '70s Show* and *The Golden Girls* where older female characters misconstrued their menopausal symptoms for pregnancy: both characters clearly—in contrast to the laughing audience—thought of themselves as too young for menopause; for them, menopause was something reserved for old, unattractive women. While assuming pregnancy can be one way for a character to dissociate from menopause, the same sentiments can manifest in a variety of other ways. While audiences watched Brenda endure hot flashes through several episodes of *The Closer*, the character adamantly asserted that she was simply suffering from stress. In *Cybill*, when the protagonist was on a film set and was suffering from a hot flash, a young co-star said, "You're like acting all weird. You're way hot and cranky. Like when my mom went through the change." Cybill, appearing thoroughly shocked at the suggestion, responded, "Menopause. Are you like mental?" In an episode from the sitcom *All in the Family* (1968–1979) centered on Edith's (Jean Stapleton) menopause, daughter Gloria (Sally Struthers) tried to explain menopause to her seemingly oblivious mother. Edith, astonished, responded, "Oh my! At my age? Oh I ain't supposed to change yet, am I?" In *The Golden Girls*, when Blanche began menopause, she expressed similar bemusement to her doctor: "I can't believe we're having this conversation about me." While each woman's denials were designed to be humorous—when Edith said, "At my age," for example, the live studio audience roared with laughter—most interesting is that each woman's surprise was predicated on the assumption that she saw *herself* as too young to be menopausal; more so, that she deemed menopause as the ultimate sign of old age and with age, lack of desirability (if not also death). Fears of fading attractiveness are certainly prominent themes in menopausal narratives on screen.

In *The Closer*, Brenda eventually articulated her menopausal fears: "I'm going to be old and wrinkled and retain water." In *The Golden Girls*, Blanche similarly lamented: "I'm not a real woman anymore. . . . Only yesterday, I was magnolia queen." As noted earlier, when Samantha feared she was going through menopause on *Sex and the City*, she described herself as "drying up" and as "day-old bread." On *All in the Family*, when Gloria told her mother that menopause can start any time after forty, Edith responded: "And when it does it can turn you into an old woman." When Gloria dared suggest that menopause was "a natural, beautiful time of life," Edith angrily responded, "Beautiful? Well I don't feel very beautiful," and later lamented, "When Archie hears about this he ain't gonna love me no more."

On one hand these examples can be read as women's hyperbolic reactions to menopause presented for comic effect. Particularly as related to Blanche on *The Golden Girls*, only *Blanche* actually considered herself as vibrant and sexy; her vanity, in fact, was a recurring joke in the series. Edith's fears about her husband no longer desiring her were also likely construed as farcical: not only was Edith *never* presented as a sexually appealing character, her highly volatile relationship with her husband led audiences to assume that Archie (Carroll O'Connor) likely *already* found her somewhat unappealing. Perhaps most interesting, these scenes tap into a much more complicated social phenomenon: the widespread social contempt for older women. Research I conducted for my book *Sex in Public: Women, Outdoor Advertising and Public Policy* demonstrated that older women are much less likely to be portrayed in advertising than younger women.[37] One explanation for the sidelining of older women relates to Western society's preoccupation—if not fetishization—of youth:

> Once a woman starts to age, once she loses her ability to reproduce, once the grey hair and wrinkles begin, suddenly she is rendered unattractive, and in a society so preoccupied with beauty, unattractiveness is synonymous with uselessness.[38]

In *The Closer*, *The Golden Girls*, *All in the Family*, and *Sex and the City*, faced with menopause, the female characters each articulated fears that are actually very well grounded if predicated on the scarce older female figures of popular reference on screen.

In the quote above, I mentioned both loss of the ability to reproduce and uselessness: to be attractive is to be fertile which, presumably, is to be useful. The idea of lost fertility, of women's lost *meaningfulness*, is addressed in the next section.

Menstruation and Fertility

In Elson's book *Am I Still a Woman?*, one explanation offered for the femininity crisis experienced by some women at menopause centered on the fact that "menstruation and childbirth are strongly associated with female gender identity."[39] Sociologist Sophie Laws made a very similar point:

[A]s long as the ability to bear children is held to be the "purpose" of womankind, women who do not menstruate can be regarded by some as not fully female.[40]

In Gabriele Kushi's anthology about menopause, women repeatedly detailed their own experiences which highlighted a distinct identity/fertility/femininity link:

Men are inherently attracted to someone who can fulfill their need to procreate. I can't provide that anymore. Does it mean I'm losing my femininity and charms as a woman?[41]

My identity as a woman was found within rhythms of fertility. It was all I knew of life, and I did not want to imagine life without it.[42]

While Blanche in *The Golden Girls* and Kitty in *That '70s Show*—each with adult children—were assumed by audiences to have *had* all the children they were ever going to, the arrival of their menopause distinctly upset them. In an episode of *The Cosby Show* centered on Clair's menopause, daughter Vanessa (Tempestt Bledsoe), and son, Theo (Malcolm-Jamal Warner), discussed their mother's "condition":

Vanessa: Well I think I know what mom is going to miss most. You know she can't have any more children.

Theo: I don't think Mom wanted more children.

Vanessa: Yeah, Theo, but still . . .

Highlighted in this scene is the central idea underpinning the reactions of Blanche, Kitty, and also Clair herself toward the end of that episode: even if no further children were desired, that they no longer existed as an *option* was considered perturbing. Interestingly, Blanche's depression on *The Golden Girls* was particularly pronounced: as a single woman, her identity was very much pinned to men finding her sexy; she assumed that with the loss of fertility, so too would her sexiness be. A similar theme was detected in *Sex and the City*: when Samantha's period was late and she assumed that she was going through menopause, her response was to consider herself as no longer attractive thus prompting her to (temporarily) lower her standards and date an elderly neighbor who she was not attracted to.

Like menstruation, menopause is frequently portrayed on screen through references to things associated with it—hot flashes and mood swings, for example—rather than simply by name.

MENOPAUSE, SYNECDOCHE, AND STEREOTYPES

In chapter 4 I discussed the concept of synecdoche as related to menstruation: that frequently things associated with menstruation are used *in place* of menstruation on screen. The same thing occurs as related to menopause portrayals whereby references to it are frequently made via allusions to aspects. In this section four elements—hot flashes, mood swings, excess hair, and forgetfulness—are discussed as four ways where menopause is alluded to even if not necessarily mentioned by name. It is also worth highlighting that unsurprisingly—and as occurs with menstruation—portrayals of menopause frequently focus on *negative* aspects of the experience, working to reiterate that menopause, like menstruation, is something that *afflicts* women and *inconveniences* men.

Menopause and Hot Flashes

In the episode of *The Cosby Show* centered on Clair's menopause, her children—exhibiting thorough internalization of negative stereotypes about menopause—exchanged horrible menopause anecdotes. Clair's cousin Pam (Erika Alexander), for example, volunteered her own story about the hot flashes of a neighbor:

> The lady that owned the tropical fish store in my neighborhood got them. Yeah, she used to leave the air-conditioner on high all winter. Kept all the doors open. The fish froze.

Clair, annoyed that her cousin and children were "pulling out all the clichés," decided—with her husband Cliff's (Bill Cosby) help—acted out some of their children's stereotypes to exploit and mock their prejudices. One performance involved Clair faking a hot flash and demanding water, ice, and wet towels before abruptly thrusting her head into the freezer. While mocked and fabricated in *The Cosby Show*, hot flashes are, of course, synonymous with the menopausal experience in academic literature and also on screen: sociologist Heather Dillaway, for example, described hot flashes as "one of the most commonly cited signs of menopause,"[43] and psychologist Pamela Kalbfleisch et al. noted that according to her review of popular media "[h]ot flashes and vaginal dryness may be the two most feared symptoms of menopause."[44] While vaginal dryness would obviously be far too difficult a problem to tackle on screen[45] (chapter 8), hot flashes do indeed play an identifiable role.

Watching Brenda on *The Closer* repeatedly fan herself and remove items of clothing, audiences likely presumed—long before the character did—that she was going through menopause; audiences know about hot flashes even if

Brenda didn't want to. In the *All in the Family* episode discussed earlier, Edith and husband Archie argued about whether or not the window should be opened. Later, Edith described her own symptoms: "I feel like I'm jumping in and out of a hot bath and somebody is twisting a rubber band around my head." In an episode of the sitcom *Cybill*, Cybill remarked how hot the set she was working on was. Her co-star, dressed warmly, described the same set as "Arctic." Later in the episode, while in a restaurant, Cybill began removing articles of clothing and poured cold water down her blouse. "One minute I'm freezing, the next I'm burning up," she explained. As noted, hot flashes are frequently used as a way to solicit laughter from the audience. Like menstruation, they can't be comprehended by those who have never experienced them; thus the display appears foreign, farcical, if not also hyperbolic. Like many menstruation references, hot flashes are also a way to portray women as so *very different* to men, and notably as comparatively unpredictable. This idea of unpredictability in fact is exaggerated further by the use of the popular menopausal mood swing narrative.

Menopause and Mood Swings

In *All in the Family*, Edith returned home from the market, snapped angrily at her husband and daughter, smashed pots and pans in the kitchen, and then vacillated between niceness, crying, and singing: as Archie diagnosed, "After twenty years of stifles the dingbat turns on me." Later Archie described Edith's behavior as her "mentalpause." In *Manhattan Murder Mystery* (1993), Larry (Woody Allen) remarked to wife Carol (Diane Keaton), "What has gotten into you lately? For crying out loud, save a little craziness for menopause." The same idea was apparent in *The Misadventures of Margaret* (1998): exasperated husband Edward (Jeremy Northam) said to his wife Margaret (Parker Posey): "Save some insanity for menopause!" In an episode of the reality television show *Roseanne's Nuts* (2011–), Jake—Roseanne Barr's son—reflected on Roseanne's upcoming appointment to have her hormones tested: "after eight years of being bat-fucking-crazy I think she's finally ready." In an episode of *The Sopranos* (1999–2007), when Carmela (Edie Falco) finally ordered her mobster husband Tony (James Gandolfini) out of the family home, Tony rationalized Carmela's behavior as irrational and presumed that Carmela was "having a hard time because of the change." Very similar in style and function to the countless PMS scenes, these examples reflect a preoccupation with showing women as emotionally unstable. More complicated than the PMS portrayals, however—which are largely just sexist stereotypes—the menopausal craziness storyline places much of the responsibility on age: that a woman *getting old* is what truly sparks the insanity.

In their book on menopause, psychologists Carol Landau and Michele Cyr addressed the long-standing menopausal craziness idea, identifying that it is part of a myth instigated and perpetuated by media stereotypes of older women:

> [O]ur society is particularly harsh on midlife and older women. Images and stereotypes of evil and crazy older women are pervasive, from the old witches in fairy tales to the Wicked Witch of the West in *The Wizard of Oz* and Cruella DeVil in the Disney film *101 Dalmatians*.[46]

I opened this section with a variety of menopausal representations where women were construed as acting crazy; such examples certainly comply with Landau and Cyr's idea that negative stereotypes fuel the popular stereotype. While such narratives may contribute to stereotypes, this is not the only way they can be interpreted. Women in real life in fact frequently report their *own* feelings of craziness at menopause:

> I felt like I was going insane. I had hundreds of hot flashes each day, so bad that my clothes would be drenched. I would cry for no reason at all. Sometimes I'd be furious for no reason—I'd find myself yelling at my daughter and then I'd feel so bad for yelling. It was a nightmare. I didn't feel like myself. And I didn't like the person I had become.[47]

> I'd fly off the hand, which wasn't really like me . . . and I was really trying and I couldn't, couldn't just be nice. And I was lashing out, that's what I do. I lashed out . . . but when you're there, there is nothing you can do.[48]

These real-life anecdotes reflect the possibility that the menopause representations on screen actually reflect a real-life version of the menopausal experience for some women. As with menstruation, women's experiences of menopause are individual and vary markedly, and while perhaps the screen examples are somewhat exaggerated, nonetheless they may be considered as part of a caricature which is grounded in some experiences that audiences are familiar with, thus explaining their humor.

While these scenes may have some basis in reality, they also exemplify the media's preoccupation with focusing almost exclusively on *negative* aspects of womanhood: while menstruation is commonly presented as horrific, its ending is routinely presented in exactly the same fashion. This encapsulates society's loving/loathing relationship with femininity and the damned if you do/damned if you don't reality of womanhood which results in women portrayed negatively *irrespective* of the reason. In terms of these menopausal craziness examples, one rationale—like the PMS narratives—is to portray women as fickle. At various junctures in this book I have contended that attributing women's behavior to their hormones is done to dismiss their actions as unreasonable and less valid than men's; such arguments are similarly relevant to a discussion of menopause. The *Sopranos* example discussed earlier illustrated this particularly well. Tony was a criminal and was compulsively unfaithful and yet he rationalized that *if only* his wife Carmela was in her normal—rather than *menopausal*—state of mind, she never would have asked him to move out; for him, her actions were exclusively attributable to her hormones. In such an interpretation Tony didn't have to take responsibility for his actions and in turn projected his problems back onto his wife. In these narratives, menopause, like PMS, works to dismiss and devalue women on the basis of biology.

Menopause and Memory Loss

In an episode of the soap opera *Passions* (1999–2008), rivals Ivy (Kim Johnston Ulrich) and Grace (Dana Sparks) were engaged in their standard sparring. At one point, Grace snarled: "I wouldn't worry about it. Because I hear that memory loss is common in menopausal women." In an episode of *Cybill*, the title character's menopausal forgetfulness was a plotline when she forgot what time she needed to pick up her mother from the airport. In an episode of the drama series *In Treatment* (2008–), therapist Dr. Weston (Gabriel Byrne) treated a patient, Frances (Debra Winger), who was a middle-aged actor struggling to remember her lines; the question of whether menopause might be responsible was moot. In *The Cosby Show* episode centered on Clair's menopause, part of her performance of menopause involved pretending to forget her children's names and that "the red stuff" was called ketchup. As with the menopausal craziness discussed in the previous section, one interpretation of menopausal forgetfulness relates to women's lived experiences of forgetfulness *off* screen:

> I couldn't think, I was so forgetful that I couldn't remember who I was calling on the telephone.[49]

> My memory, for instance, was worse . . . and it just seems to be getting worse every day. . . . I have to set reminders on my phone for everything.[50]

> [T]hat memory thing is ridiculous. . . . I waste more time walking from one room to another, in and out. . . . And even reading a book, if I leave it down, and I might only leave it down for two hours, or the next night . . . and I'll open it where I have the book mark and I'll read the page and I'm going "What's this about?"[51]

Like hot flashes and mood swings, for some women forgetfulness is actually a real part of the menopause experience. Of course, like hot flashes and mood swings, forgetfulness is one of the negative aspects of menopause that gets disproportionate attention for comic effect. Much like forgetfulness blamed on pregnancy—often called "baby brain" or "mommy brain"—these narratives work to constantly reinforce the idea that women are ruled by their hormones, by their emotions, unlike men, and thus are *biologically* less rational and less trustworthy and less able to make sound decisions.

Menopause and Excess Hair

In Colette Bouchéz's book on menopause, she discussed the "classic menopause mustache."[52] While Bouchéz and writers on menopause more broadly frequently draw attention to the issue of excess hair, it is also something distinctly apparent on screen. In *That '70s Show*, when Eric and his father looked up menopause in the *World Book*, Eric said, "Oh no, look at the symptoms. Temperamental behavior, mood swings, facial hair." In *All in the Family*, daughter Gloria tried to reassure her mother that menopause was manageable; in this scene her mother mentioned facial hair:

> **Gloria:** Oh ma, there's nothing to worry about. Look, it says right here, "nowadays, with simple hormone treatment, there are no unpleasant manifestations."
>
> **Edith:** Well, my Aunt Elizabeth went through this and she didn't get manifestations, she got a mustache.

In *The Golden Girls*, facial hair was discussed by friends Dorothy (Bea Arthur), Sophia (Estelle Getty), and Rose (Betty White) in the episode centered on Blanche's menopause:

> **Dorothy:** What is the big deal, Blanche? It's nothing. Look at it this way: you don't get cramps once a month. You don't go on eating binges once a month. You don't get crazy once a month.
>
> **Sophia:** You just grow a beard.
>
> **Dorothy:** Don't listen to her.
>
> **Sophia:** I woke up one morning, I looked like Arafat.
>
> **Blanche:** Oh my God!
>
> **Rose:** I never grew a beard.
>
> **Sophia:** You never grew brains either.

References to old women with facial hair frequently exist as an off the cuff quip used for comic effect. In an episode of *Californication*, Hank joked that a benefit of dating older women was nipple hair. In the British film *Weekend* (2011), Russell (Tom Cullen) similarly mused about the origins of a tea cup, guessing that an old woman with a mustache was the previous owner. In an episode of *Married with Children* (1987–1997), during a conversation between Al (Ed O'Neill) and Roger (Chris Latta) the same idea was apparent:

> **Roger:** Al, this legend of Ironhead Haynes could be as phony as your wife's hair color.
>
> **Al:** Or it could be real like your wife's hair color, Roger. I know it's real, because it matches her mustache!

On an episode of the sitcom *3rd Rock from the Sun* (1996–2001), Tommy (Joseph Gordon-Levitt) lamented to the elderly Mrs. Dubcek (Elmarie Wendel), "You know, it's really not fair. I can grow a pimple, but not a mustache. What's your secret?" Interestingly, the facial hair of younger women is also used as a source of comedy on screen: in the sitcom *Whitney* (2011–), for example, the title character (Whitney Cummings) was caught by her partner while removing hair from her upper lip; in *Everybody Loves Raymond* (1996–2005) Debra (Patricia Heaton) was similarly sprung by her husband bleaching her upper lip. While these two examples involved women who were not yet menopausal, the effect was similar: to solicit humor based on women's biology and their breaches of femininity mandates. For older women to have facial hair, however, other aspects exacerbate the humor and also the horror. In an episode of *Sex and the City*, Charlotte (Kristin Davis) commented, "In some cultures, heavy women with mustaches are considered beautiful." This is, of course, *not* the case in Western culture; perhaps more so than any other characteristic, facial hair is considered *unfeminine*: to be unfeminine is to be unattractive and whereas younger female characters like Whitney or Debra might get away with having facial hair—or at least be tolerated for having it and *removing it* because they have youth and beauty on their side—this is not the case for older women who are viewed as being *without* redeeming features. Just as older women can be quickly dismissed for being crazy and forgetful, they are also readily dismissed based on being considered unattractive. This issue was highlighted well by author Erica Jong:

> [I]t's hard enough to be a good girl and a pretty woman—but try being old and female in a culture that hates the latter even more than the former.[53]

Our society places a premium on beauty, particularly as related to women: figures of popular reverence tend to be widely considered beautiful; women who do not comply with the conventional idea of beauty—who do not groom and style themselves to fit the ideal—are considered unattractive: "in a society so preoccupied with beauty, unattractiveness is synonymous with uselessness."[54] Older women who are considered unattractive get dismissed based on their concerns, opinions, and emotions being deemed less valid.

Thus far I have explored absent periods taking the form of menopause, but before concluding, it should be noted that amenorrhea can occur for other health-related reasons, something identifiable both on screen and off.

MENSTRUATION AND GOOD HEALTH

In psychologist Rochelle Semmell Albin's work on women's health, she wrote that women can feel more comfortable with menstruation "by seeing it as a sign that our bodies are working well."[55] In pediatrician Chrysta De Freitas's book on childhood sexuality, she wrote, "Remember, having your period means your body is working well and is doing what it's supposed to."[56] In gynecologists Derek Llewellyn-Jones and Suzanne Abraham's book *Everygirl*, the authors referred to studies indicating that many women believed that "having regular periods indicated that their body was working properly."[57] Given that medical advice and popular perception is that menstruation is a sign of good health, questions are then raised about the health—and also the *femininity*—of women who do not menstruate, that is, who experience amenorrhea.

While pregnancy and menopause are standard explanations for missed periods, amenorrhea can also be a sign that something is medically wrong. Amenorrhea can be caused by a variety of reasons—drug addiction, morbid obesity, extreme exercise, chemotherapy, or high stress, for example—but the most common is dramatic weight loss: as psychiatrist Dasha Nicholls et al wrote in their research on eating disorders: "Amenorrhea or failure of onset of menarche are integral to the diagnosis of anorexia nervosa."[58] Given that menstruation is uncommon on screen, medically diagnosed amenorrhoea is scarcely portrayed. One allusion, however, occurred in an episode of the television drama house *House* (2004–): a six-year-old patient had menstrual bleeding and the diagnostic team considered that she might have cancer, prompting the following exchange between doctors Cameron (Jennifer Morrison) and House (Hugh Laurie):

> **Cameron:** If menstruating is a symptom of cancer, I should be getting chemotherapy right now.
>
> **House:** Now that's ridiculous. You're way too skinny to be menstruating.

While House was attempting to be humorous, he also alluded to the idea that women with a low body weight may not have periods, and in the process insulted a colleague based on her slender appearance. Another way amenorrhea is portrayed is when it functions to imply that a woman is insufficiently feminine. This is another interpretation of the *House* scene: Cameron was considered insufficiently *womanly* to menstruate. The same idea was made much more obvious in an episode of *Glee* (2009–) and also in the film *GI Jane* (1997). In *Glee*, the following exchange took place between Sue (Jane Lynch) and her archnemesis Will (Matthew Morrison):

Sue: [Getting off an exercise machine]. Just blasting my hammies.

Will: Oh.

Sue: Iron tablet? [Throws him a pill bottle.] Keeps your strength up while you're menstruating.

Will: I don't menstruate.

Sue: Yeah? Neither do I.

In another episode, Sue remarked that she never wanted kids: "don't have the time, don't have the uterus." Sue's character is portrayed as a humorously cruel, brutish cheerleading coach; while Sue *appears* to be a woman, she is portrayed as one who has done away with the less convenient, less *strong* aspects of womanhood, her uterus being a classic example. This idea conveys the impression that Sue only dons the *artifice* of femininity, but inwardly is masculine, something exemplified by her lack of periods. In *GI Jane*, Jordan (Demi Moore) was a woman in training with the Navy SEALs. While the film included a scene—discussed in chapter 4—where her tampons were discovered by a fellow officer, Jordan's periods in fact ceased during her service. While there are physical explanations for her amenorrhea—she has been training extensively and had very low body fat—another interpretation was that of the many aspects of her womanhood that Jordan relinquished as a SEAL, the loss of her periods was a physical one, much like the loss of her hair was an aesthetic one.

Perhaps predictably, absent period storylines are easily detectable on screen. Most obviously this is attributable to the media's default position of *not* presenting menstruation and instead allowing it to remain a taboo. While the many explanations for menstruation's absence on screen are the focus of chapter 8, as noted in this chapter, the absent or late period narrative—by virtue of being missing—still puts menstruation on the agenda. For minority groups it is often argued that *any* presentation is better than *no* presentation and that some visibility is always better than the alternative. In the examples discussed in this chapter, quite clearly menstruation gets some attention; therefore some visibility for a traditional maligned subject matter may be considered positive.

Thus far in this book I have contended that the scarce number of menstruation portrayals on screen is largely attributable to cultural mandates pertaining to secrecy and the taboo nature of menstruation. In chapter 8 I propose alternative ways of reading the absence, including the idea that menstruation is not that big a deal in the scheme of things and explanations related to the visual nature of film and television.

NOTES

1. Mariamne H. Whatley and Elissa R. Henken, *Did You Hear About the Girl Who? Contemporary Legends, Folklore, and Human Sexuality* (New York: New York University Press, 2000), 33.

2. Emily Martin, *The Woman in the Body: A Cultural Analysis of Reproduction* (Boston: Beacon, 1987).

3. It should be noted that while generally menstruation does connote the beginning of a woman's fertile years, it should not be assumed that its presence guarantees that conception will be possible (Kutluk H. Oktay, Lindsay Nohr Beck, and Joyce Dillon Reinecke, *100 Questions and Answers About Cancer and Fertility* (Sudbury, MA: Jones and Bartlett Publishers, 2008).

4. The connection between menstruation and growing responsibility for girls was alluded to in Zanette Lewis' reflections of her menarche: "In this summer of my twelfth year, I was experiencing that same feeling of being exposed and having more responsibility for myself" (Zannette Lewis, "Loss and Gain of Responsibility, 1969," in *My Little Red Book*, ed. Rachel Kauder Nalebuff (New York: Twelve, 2009), 40).

5. Stephenie Meyer, *Breaking Dawn* (New York: Little, Brown, 2008).

6. Elizabeth A. Kissling, "Bleeding out loud: Communication about menstruation," *Feminism and Psychology* 6 (1996): 481–504.

7. Jennifer Baumgardner, "Glamorous, but Not for Long, 1981," in *My Little Red Book*, ed. Rachel Kauder Nalebuff (New York: Twelve, 2009), 65.

8. Emily Martin, *The Woman in the Body: A Cultural Analysis of Reproduction* (Boston: Beacon, 1987).

9. In Sophie Laws, *Issues of Blood: The Politics of Menstruation* (Houndmills, Basingstoke, Hampshire: Macmillan, 1990), 93.

10. This idea in fact occurs in an episode of sitcom *Ellen* (1994–1998). Three friends take pregnancy tests, one stick shows a positive. No woman actually ended up pregnant.

11. Emily Giffin, *Baby Proof* (London: Orion Books, 2006), 209.

12. Lynne Joyrich, *Re-viewing Reception: Television, Gender, and Postmodern Culture* (Bloomington: Indiana University Press, 1996), 108.

13. Samantha Evans, *Love Letters to Miscarried Moms* (Bloomington: WestBow Press, 2011), 34–35.

14. In Christine Moulder, *Miscarriage: Women's Experiences and Needs* (New York: Routledge, 1990), 99.

15. Adam Schwartz, *A Stranger on the Planet* (New York: Soho Press, 2011), 194.

16. Media theorist Lynne Joyrich discussed miscarriage narratives in *Moonlighting* (1985–1989), *thirtysomething* (1987–1991), and *Hooperman* (1987–1989). More recently the storyline can be detected in episodes of *King of Queens* (1998–2007), *Desperate Housewives* (2004–), *Grey's Anatomy* (2005–), *Without a Trace* (2002–2009), *Brothers and Sisters* (2006–2011), *Rescue Me* (2004–), and *Big Love* (2006–2011).

17. Tom Perrotta, *Little Children* (New York: St. Martin's Press, 2004), 208.

18. Matthew Miller, *Maybe Baby: An Infertile Love Story* (Deerfield Beach, FL: Health Communications, 2008), 77–78.

19. Matthew Miller, *Maybe Baby: An Infertile Love Story* (Deerfield Beach, FL: Health Communications Inc, 2008), 230.

20. Matthew Miller, *Maybe Baby: An Infertile Love Story* (Deerfield Beach, FL: Health Communications Inc, 2008), 259.

21. Laura Fingerson, *Girls in Power: Gender, Body and Menstruation in Adolescence* (Albany: State University of New York Press, 2006), 71.

22. Matthew M. Garrey, *Gynaecology Illustrated* (Edinburgh: Churchill Livingstone, 1972), 70.

23. In Jean Elson, *Am I Still a Woman? Hysterectomy and Gender Identity* (Philadelphia: Temple University Press, 2004), 77.

24. As writer Natalie Angier contended: "Not all women breed, but nearly all women bleed, or have bled." (Natalie Angier, *Woman: An Intimate Geography* (New York: Random House, 1999), 104). Of course, it is also worthwhile noting the disclaimer Chris Bobel puts forth in her book on menstruation: "not all women menstruate, and not only women menstruate. Postmenopausal women, women posthysterectomy, and some athletes, for example, do not menstruate, and some preoperative transmen do menstruate (as do many intersexuals)." (Chris Bobel, *New Blood: Third-Wave Feminism and the Politics of Menstruation* (New Brunswick, NJ: Rutgers University Press, 2010), 11–12).

25. Marvin G. Drelich and Irving Bieber, "The psychologic importance of the uterus and its functions," *Journal of Nervous and Mental Diseases* 126, no. 1 (1958): 322–336, 330.

26. Research on women's attitudes toward menopause across a wide range of populations found that women consistently felt relief over the cessation of their periods (Nancy E. Avis, "Women's perceptions of the menopause," *European Menopause Journal* 3 (1996): 80–84.

27. Joan C. Callahan, *Menopause: A Midlife Passage* (Bloomington: Indiana University Press, 1993), 62.

28. In Tara Parker-Pope, *The Hormone Decision* (New York: Pocket Books, 2007), 40.

29. Linda Ojeda, *Menopause Without Medicine* (Alameda, CA: Hunter House, 2003), 11.

30. In Stephanie Marston, *If Not Now, When? Reclaiming Ourselves at Midlife* (New York: Warner Books, 2001), 57.

31. Feminist psychologist Dee Graham, for example, wrote, "Femininity describes a set of behaviours that please men because they communicate a woman's acceptance of her subordinate status. Thus, feminine behaviours are survival strategies. Like hostages who bond to their captors, women bond to men in an attempt to survive, and this is the source of women's strong need for connection with men and of women's love of men" (Dee Graham, *Loving to Survive: Sexual Terror, Men's Violence, and Women's Lives* (New York: New York University Press, 1994), xv).

32. In Karen Ballard, *Understanding Menopause* (Hoboken, NJ: John Wiley and Sons, 2003), 26.

33. In Heather Currie, *Menopause* (London: Class Publishing, 2006), 28.

34. See, for example, Joann Ellison Rodgers, *Sex: A Natural History* (New York: Henry Holt, 2001); Randy Thornhill and Steve W. Gangestad, *The Evolutionary Biology of Human Female Sexuality* (New York: Oxford University Press, 2008).

35. Kathryn Petras, *The Premature Menopause Book: When the "Change of Life" Comes too Early* (New York: HarperCollins, 1999), 138.

36. In Dianne Hales, *Just Like a Woman: How Gender Science Is Redefining What Makes Us Female* (New York: Bantam Books, 1999), 228.

37. Lauren Rosewarne, *Sex in Public: Women, Outdoor Advertising and Public Policy* (Newcastle: Cambridge Scholars Publishing, 2007).

38. Lauren Rosewarne, *Sex in Public: Women, Outdoor Advertising and Public Policy* (Newcastle: Cambridge Scholars Publishing, 2007), 167.
39. Jean Elson, *Am I Still a Woman? Hysterectomy and Gender Identity* (Philadelphia: Temple University Press, 2004), 70.
40. Sophie Laws, *Issues of Blood: The Politics of Menstruation* (Houndmills, Basingstoke, Hampshire: Macmillan, 1990), 4–5.
41. In Gabriele Kushi, *Embracing Menopause Naturally: Stories, Portraits, and Recipes* (New York: Square One Publishers, 2006), 61.
42. In Gabriele Kushi, *Embracing Menopause Naturally: Stories, Portraits, and Recipes* (New York: Square One Publishers, 2006), 55.
43. Heather E. Dillaway, "Menopause and misbehaving," in *Embodied Resistance: Challenging the Norms, Breaking the Rules*, ed. Chris Bobel and Samantha Kwan (Nashville, TN: Vanderbilt University Press, 2011), 197.
44. Pamela J. Kalbfleisch, Karen H. Bonnell, and Tina M. Harris, "Media portrayals of women's menstrual health issues," in *Evaluating Women's Health Messages: A Resource Book*, ed. Roxane L. Parrott and Celeste M. Condit (Thousand Oaks, CA: Sage, 1996), 85.
45. A rare example of this topic addressed on screen occurs in *Sex and the City 2* (2010) when Samantha (Kim Cattrall) attempts to control some of the symptoms of menopause—including vaginal dryness—through a variety of hormone therapies.
46. Carol Landau and Michele G. Cyr, *The New Truth About Menopause* (New York: St. Martin's Press, 2003), 14.
47. In Kathryn Petras, *The Premature Menopause Book: When the "Change of Life" Comes Too Early* (New York: HarperCollins, 1999), 127.
48. In *Women's Experiences and Understandings of Menopause* (Dublin: Women's Health Council, 2008), 129.
49. In Suzanne Somers, *Ageless: The Naked Truth About Bioidentical Hormones* (New York: Three Rivers Press, 2006), 227.
50. In *Women's Experiences and Understandings of Menopause* (Dublin: Women's Health Council, 2008), 127.
51. In *Women's Experiences and Understandings of Menopause* (Dublin: Women's Health Council, 2008), 127.
52. Colette, Bouchéz, *Your Perfectly Pampered Menopause* (New York: Random House, 2005), 164.
53. Erica Jong, *Fear of Fifty, A Midlife Memoir* (London: Chatto and Windus, 1994), 236.
54. Lauren Rosewarne, *Sex in Public: Women, Outdoor Advertising and Public Policy* (Newcastle: Cambridge Scholars Publishing, 2007), 167.
55. Rochelle Semmell Albin, *Health and Beauty* (Philadelphia: Westminster Press, 1984), 81.
56. Chrysta De Freitas, *Keys to Your Child's Healthy Sexuality* (Hauppauge, NY: Barron's Educational Series, 1998), 67.
57. Derek Llewellyn-Jones and Suzanne Abraham, *Everygirl* (Oxford: Oxford University Press, 1999), 47.
58. Dasha Nicholls, Rose de Bruyn, and Gordon Isky, "Physical assessment and complications," in *Anorexia Nervosa and Related Eating Disorders in Childhood and Adolescence*, ed. Bryan Lask and Rachel Bryant-Waugh (New York: Brunner-Routledge, 2002), 133.

Chapter Eight

Where Have All the Menstruators Gone?

Rereading Missing Menstruation

Throughout this book I have suggested that the dearth of menstrual portrayals on screen can be considered symptomatic of long-standing taboos. While I suspect that such taboos *are* indeed the most likely culprit, other explanations are worth considering. In this chapter I propose a range of alternate explanations for scarce portrayals, from the personal—with menstruation construed as actually not all that important—through to those related to censorship and to the visual nature of film and television.

MENSTRUATION: THE NON-EVENT

In author Michele Jaffe's recollections of her first period, she wrote, "By the time My First Period came, it was a nonevent, so much less exciting than the purchasing [of menstrual products] that led up to it."[1] Similar sentiments were expressed by girls in sociologist Laura Fingerson's book on menstruation, *Girls in Power*: Ally, for example, described menstruation as "like breathing. You know, it's like second nature. 'Oh look,' blood, pad, done."[2] In pediatricians Kelly Orringer and Sheila Gahagan's research, one girl lamented the lack of momentousness, claiming that when she got her first period she "didn't feel any different at all, which I guess was a disappointment to me."[3] A girl in psychotherapist JoAnn Loulan and Bonnie Worthen's book *Period* aptly noted, "For me, having my period was never any big deal."[4]

While women claiming that menstruation is no big deal can be interpreted as wanting to distance themselves from the stereotypical image of a woman who complains about menstruation (chapter 4), a less cynical reading is simply that for many women menstruation actually *isn't* all that important; that for most of the time they don't see any overwhelming need to talk about it or complain about it or even to *honor* it, that it is simply something that needs to be gotten on with. This attitude was well illustrated in an episode of the sitcom *The Golden Girls* (1985–1992): Sophia (Estelle Getty) reflected on getting her first period: "I got it, no one told me. I didn't get it, no one told me. I figured, this is life, and went back to my meatballs." When viewed as a non-event and as not very exciting, menstruation becomes like other aspects of the human experience—toenail clipping or ear wax removal, for example—as an activity which is just part of life and something that needs to, as Sophia suggested, be dealt with. Of all the possible explanations for the lack of menstrual portrayals on screen, I suspect that the ordinariness of it is likely a central explanation. Aside from those times when pregnancy is feared or desired (chapter 7), there are few times when menstruation is experienced as particularly memorable or gets bestowed with any great significance.

Noted earlier was cultural pressure for women not to complain about menstruation. On one hand, menstruation may indeed be dismissed as just another sanitary event (discussed in the next section); another interpretation, however, is that women have been *conditioned* to downplay it; to not complain, to not catastrophize. As discussed in chapter 1, women are taught from a very early age to keep their menstruation concealed, to not discuss it, and not to let anyone know about it, see or smell it. Women in the workforce, for example, have long been encouraged to *downplay* any negative symptoms so as to not appear weaker or less capable than their male counterparts.[5] Women who experience severe cramps, for example, reportedly often resist divulging them to doctors for fear of "overstating" them and being thought of as a complainer.[6] Such behavior works to reinforce the idea that menstruation is unimportant. As a result, the supposed unimportance of menstruation may become internalized: that women *learn* to believe that it doesn't matter. Women, therefore, don't necessarily consider their periods trivial, but they come to believe that doing so is socially expected. The absence of menstruation from screen narratives contributes to the cyclical nature of this idea.

Connected to the secrecy mandate is that for menstruation to actually be present on screen, someone evidently let the menstruation secret slip. In chapter 1, I discussed the scene from *To Sir With Love* (1967) where a menstrual product is burned and I quoted Mark Thackeray (Sidney Poitier) who reprimanded the girls he believed responsible: "A decent woman keeps things private. Only a filthy slut would have done this!" As noted in chapter 1, Mr. Thackeray spotlighted the derogatory perceptions of women who ignore cultural dictums and allow men to discover their bleeding. If the characters are talking about their periods, worse, if blood is visible on clothing or if a period is in any way made public, then the woman has failed in her duty to hide her period. As discussed in chapter 1, the most important rule of menstruation is appreciating the all-importance of concealment; if audiences see it, she has neglected her most important feminine obligation. By infrequently portraying menstruation, the secrecy imperative is upheld.

A QUESTION OF TASTE

In research conducted by *Advertising Age*, it was contended that feminine hygiene advertisements topped both men *and* women's most hated advertisements lists.[7] While I have alluded to contempt for menstruation throughout this book, the *Advertising Age* research spotlights some important issues. While we may suspect that the loathing of menstrual product advertising is simply about the loathing of menstruation, another explanation is that such advertising poses some very specific problems related to taste and forced exposure. In her discussion of such advertising, gender studies researcher Kate Kane alluded to the issue of "bad taste," noting that audiences might loathe, such advertisements simply because they are considered inappropriate for the public sphere.[8] While Kane doesn't address this issue in great detail, it is an interesting way to think about the absence of menstrual portrayals from the screen: that audiences—both male and female—may be uncomfortable with being exposed to such content and thus it is avoided.

The topic of taste has been extensively theorized by academics; philosopher Pierre Bourdieu, for example, argued that one of the most significant influences on taste is "a taste for what [we] are anyway condemned to."[9] Applied to a menstruation discussion, it could be argued that audiences are uncomfortable with menstruation portrayals because they are unusual; that such presentations are considered in bad taste because they are seldom seen and have not yet been mainstreamed or normalized.

Regardless of where our particular tastes stem, the idea that the absence of menstrual portrayals is attributable to people finding them in bad taste is certainly worth considering. Throughout this book I have discussed the secrecy imperative with girls and women both perceiving a mandate to keep their periods private. When menstruation leaves the private sphere and enters public space through advertising and screen narratives, suddenly, something that is "supposed" to be private is made public. In making menstruation public, opportunities are created for uncomfortable audience moments. Certainly public menstruation being considered in bad taste is very well established. In chapter 3 I discussed the cases of Uta Pippig, Britney Spears, and Taylor Momsen who, in varying degrees, exposed their menstruation and each became connected to controversies related to taste and decency. Other similar menstrual-themed taste scandals have also been discussed. In Shirley Eskapa's book *Woman Versus Woman*, for example, she wrote of infidelities sometimes being exposed through the discovery of another woman's menstrual blood on sheets[10]: most certainly perceived as poor taste. In 1992, Donita Sparks from the American band L7 apparently was being heckled by a rowdy audience; her response was to pull out her tampon, hurl it at the crowd, and shout, "Eat my used tampon, fuckers!"—again, an act considered distasteful.[11] The taboos attached to menstruation, the public loathing and the well established disgust surrounding it routinely renders menstrual acts as far more grotesque that any other bodily fluids.

Also worth noting is that the bad taste reminder may also function as a way to remind audiences about women's pollution: that both men and women would prefer not to be reminded about something that makes women unsexy, again, highlighting that the "ideal" woman is one who doesn't menstruate (a topic returned to later in this chapter).

RESISTING TELLING THE FEMALE STORY

In Fingerson's research, she contrasted the intimate knowledge that teenagers have about each other's menstruation with her own experiences as an adult:

> I generally have no idea when my friends and co-workers are menstruating, what their symptoms are, and we generally do not share our everyday menstrual status. Yet these girls are highly in tune with not only their friends' cycle timing, but also their friends' symptoms and management strategies.[12]

Fingerson's comments highlight that while menstruation is new and interesting for young girls, it quickly ceases to be important for older women. This idea might therefore suggest that by the time an adult woman is telling stories in a professional capacity through art and screen narratives, the significance of menstruation for her may have faded; that *adult* women's stories get told instead. I have referenced the *My Little Red Book* anthology of first period stories at various junctures in this book. The editor, Rachel Kauder Nalebuff, was a high school student when she compiled the volume. Whereas an adult woman might be more distanced from her period and potentially less interested, Nalebuff exists as an outlier example of a young woman who had the opportunity to explore a routinely neglected topic in a culture generally more interested in adult stories.

Another explanation for the menstruation story rarely being told is that focusing too keenly on such a topic may be viewed as limiting one's opportunities as a producer or filmmaker. Research on academia, for example, identifies fears amongst young female academics that aligning oneself too closely with feminist or women's studies research will limit opportunities for career advancement. Labor researcher Kaye Broadbent, for example, drew on her own experiences to illustrate this idea:

> As a beginning PhD candidate, I was discouraged from conducting research on women and work because I might be pigeon-holed as a women's studies person.[13]

This same idea was articulated in anthropologist Heather Howard-Bobiwash's work:

> I hesitate to identify myself as "a feminist." This hesitancy may have been spurred by the "kind" advice given to me as a new graduate student by a senior male faculty member not to align or identify myself too closely with "Feminism" lest I find myself pigeon-holed and thus, I gathered, my professional opportunities constrained.[14]

In these examples, Broadbent and Howard-Bobiwash identified concerns related to pigeon-holing; that being involved with topics perceived as feminist may result in their work being interpreted as narrow and thus potentially limiting their audience. In the creative world, these concerns certainly appeared to plague singer Joni Mitchell, who expressed strong objections to being considered a "women's artist":

> For a while it was assumed that I was writing women's songs. Then men began to notice that they saw themselves in the songs too. A good piece of art should be androgynous. I'm not a feminist. That's too divisional for me.[15]

As related to screen narratives, the consequence of an artist being pigeonholed links to fears of reducing an audience and also dramatically reducing prestige; that women's stories are not viewed as serious enough or *canonical* enough to be held in high esteem and thus other stories get told instead. This latter idea was alluded to in cultural theorist Christina Lane's book *Feminist Hollywood*:

> Historically, women directors have been less likely to direct "universal" genres such as the Western, the musical, or the buddy film, as they find themselves pigeon-holed into women's films. Not only is their exclusion a problem in the realm of production, but . . . so called women's pictures are rarely canonized due to an evaluative bias toward male genres and auteurs.[16]

Here, Lane spotlighted the problem that if women become too closely identified with issues deemed niche and exclusively of interest to women—menstruation being an obvious example—a filmmaker may be considered as less serious, less of an artist, and her works as less worthy for accolade. As related to menstruation, the widespread absence of menstruation stories can be considered as attributable to female filmmakers' fears that telling such a story might be professionally problematic, that doing so would render their work only of interest to newly menstrual girls to whom menstruation remains novel.

THE FEMINIST DEFENSE

Throughout this book I have contended that of all the many women's stories, menstruation is one of few associated with virtually *all* women. On one level, given that menstruation is so common to the female experience and that so many taboos exist surrounding it, it might be assumed that *including* it in narratives might be considered a feminist act: that—as one menstruation activist quoted in chapter 6 claimed—"it [is] feminist for us *not* to hide our blood in shame."[17] Such an idea would suggest that liberation for women might only be achieved through the recognition and acceptance of *all* aspects of womanhood, particularly those traditionally excluded and maligned like menstruation. Certainly the telling of the tales of minorities—gay and lesbian stories being a good example[18]—have been considered fundamental to pursuits of equality. An alternate reading is that too strong a focus on menstruation might be construed as doing gender equality a *disservice*. That like the feminists referred to in chapter 6 who opposed menstrual leave on the grounds that it inhibited women's equality in the workplace, as related to screen narratives, it could be suggested that focusing on menstruation might achieve similar and negative effects: that women become viewed as fundamentally different from men, weaker than men, *less than men*. Under such an interpretation, a feminist filmmaker may eschew a menstruation narrative in favor of more universal storylines in line with the liberal feminist objective of presenting women as more *similar* rather than more *different* to men. Earlier in this chapter I discussed some of the reasons women might wish to downplay their menstruation. In chapter 4 I similarly discussed that women might unleash menstrual accusations against *other* women to align themselves more closely with men. In both circumstances, women are presented as distancing themselves from their periods. While this may be seen as distancing themselves from *womanhood* and thus eschewing feminist dictums entirely, another reading is simply a disinclination to focus on *differences* between the sexes in favor of telling a more broadly *human* story.

For menstruation to take a central role in a narrative, it will exist—deliberately or not—as a reminder of a fundamental physical difference between men and women. In sociologist Sophie Laws's book on men's attitudes to menstruation, for example, she discussed menstrual sex and the etiquette involved, noting "The woman may not presume that she will not be found offensive."[19] Thinking about the scene from the episode of *Californication* (2007–) when Hank (David Duchovny) had sex with his daughter's teacher Mrs. Patterson (Justine Bateman), as they were undressing, Mrs. Patterson said, "Just so you know, I'm on my period." Mrs. Patterson, in line with Laws's comments, didn't automatically *assume* that Hank would be fine with it—in fact, she stated that her ex *wasn't* fine with it—and thus gave Hank the opportunity to exit. By mentioning menstruation in a sex scene, it exists as a glaring biological power imbalance: while the woman can indeed use it to thwart sex (chapter 3), more troubling from a feminist perspective is that men can use it to *reject* the woman based on her biology. One interpretation of the absence of menstruation narratives is that by excluding the topic, a female character is given the opportunity to go toe-to-toe with her male counterparts; that she can be as sexually aggressive as she likes and not have to query—as Mrs. Patterson did on *Californication*—whether her partner is bothered by her menstruation and thus not be limited by her biology; that she can act with more autonomy and fuck more like a man.[20] While there is likely some merit to this idea, the reality is that on screen women's biology is *ever present*. Eliminating reference to menstruation certainly doesn't make female characters any less female; in fact, disproportionate inclusion of, and focus on, women who are stereotypically *femininely* attractive demonstrates that the biological differences between men are women continue to be crucially important on screen.

Connected to the idea of sexual politics being eschewed by avoiding menstruation is the similar avoidance of racial politics, something alluded to in chapter 1. As is obvious across the spectrum of Western world narratives, white women are more commonly portrayed on screen than women of ethnic minorities. As evident in this book, the vast majority of examples of menstrual scenes involve *white* women. On one hand this situation reflects the media landscape more broadly, however, there is another possibility to consider as related to racial politics. Historian Lara Freidenfelds explored the class-based acts of washing and deodorizing during menstruation[21] and in philosopher Jami Anderson's work on prisons she discussed the connotations of female prisoners requesting menstrual products:

> Just what are we to make of that woman who unashamedly asks [a] male guard for a sanitary pad or tells all and sundry about her menstrual cycle? She's a vulgar hussy—no wonder she's in prison.[22]

One explanation for *not* portraying ethnic minority menstruators on screen may be to avoid further complicating the minority representation: that is, avoiding a black woman being portrayed as someone classless enough to forget her tampon or a Hispanic woman as loathsome enough to keep talking about her periods. It might be contended that through eschewing images of ethnic minorities—or, for that matter, *any* minority—in a menstrual narrative, the minority character gets judged on her own merits and not with the added burden of a social taboo.

AVOIDING THE DISTRACTION

Alluded to in the previous section was the capacity for menstruation to deliver a narrative with more sexual politics than might be desirable. This alludes to another potential explanation for the avoidance of menstruation on screen: that it is simply a distraction. While showing a character eating or drinking or doing any other mundane activity might be irrelevant to a script, such a scene is unlikely to be *distracting*; eating or drinking can simply, innocuously, decorate a scene because they are activities which normally don't have extensive cultural taboo attached. Having a character participate in something widely considered taboo, however, can distract an audience (and also commentators) and thus potentially derail a narrative. In chapter 7 I discussed storylines from *Party of Five* (1994–2000) and *Moonlighting* (1985–1989) where characters were spared abortions through timely miscarriages: *had* those characters actually aborted, those narratives would have come to be *defined* by that one intensely political act. Cigarette smoking is a good contemporary example of this. When a character smokes on screen today, because the act is often considered controversial—and given the ever increasing restrictions on the activity—smoking is no longer always excused as merely incidental; today the act is frequently construed as a controversial if not also a *political* screen inclusion. Following the release of the cartoon film *Rango* (2011), for example, a media firestorm was created with anti-smoking campaigners claiming that the film normalized cigarette smoking. While there are of course, a spectrum of differences between menstruation and smoking, one thing that they have in common is the potential to focus an audience's attention on something tangential to the storyline. Whether or not the producers of *Rango* wanted the controversy as related to the smoking, they certainly got it; smoking is what many people will remember the film for. In chapter 4 I discussed a study that contended that both male and female college students found a woman who had dropped a packaged tampon to be less competent and less likable compared to a woman who dropped a hair clip.[23] In that chapter I proposed that the study was an example of the continued loathing of menstrual products and the proliferation of negative stereotypes about menstruating women. For the purposes of this chapter, the study *also* highlights the potentially character-transforming nature of menstruation:

a woman being in the mere vicinity of tampons was, for whatever reasons, thought of *differently* compared to the woman in the proximity of the hair clip. To include menstruation in a narrative, producers need to be mindful that for some audiences assumptions will be made about the bleeding female character and that these assumptions may be completely irrelevant to the storyline: actions, moods, comments, or expressions may be inadvertently attributed to menstruation instead of to other events in the narrative. Menstruation therefore may be sidelined to circumvent the unavoidably distracting connotations drawn from its mention.

THE TABOO OF THE TOILET

In chapter 1 I introduced the idea of thinking about menstruation as a "sanitary event"; this term is derived from a psychologist quoted in Hope Edelman's book *Motherless Daughters* who commented, "Without a mother, a first menstruation is just a big sanitary event."[24] Historian Joan Brumberg made a similar point in her book *The Body Project*, noting that in the Victorian age, menstruation was primarily a *hygiene* event.[25] In chapter 1 I discussed some of the feminist criticisms of these ideas interpreting it as objectionable to liken menstruation to urination or defecation. A second reading proposed was that the "sanitary event" interpretation was less about considering menstruation as akin to a waste product and more that it was simply considered a *private* bodily function. In this section I expand on the idea of menstruation as a private bathroom event and propose that it is absent from screen narratives for the same reasons that urination and defecation generally are: because the act is considered personal, and thus is inappropriate for the screen. In this section I attribute the absence of menstruation to long-standing taboos related to bathrooms and toilets as apparent in American popular culture.

In his discussion about the early censorship of television, communications researcher Robert Pondillo discussed Stockton Helffrich, who was the National Broadcasting Company's (NBC) first manager of censorship in the earliest years of television. Among Helffrich's famous dictums were some very strict guidelines as related to bathrooms on screen: for example, "a pajamaed man in front of a bathroom medicine chest" was permitted but that it was important to keep "out of camera range [the] shot of popular plumbing."[26] Under Helffrich's guidelines, advertising toilet *paper*, for example, was considered completely inappropriate. The taboo of bathrooms was similarly discussed in Patrick McGilligan's book on Alfred Hitchcock where he chronicled the director's battles to get certain controversial scenes passed by censors. One tussle discussed was Hitchcock's fight—and victory—over a scene of a flushing toilet in *Psycho* (1960): an unprecedented inclusion for cinema at the time.[27] Many academics have also documented a long-standing reluctance in American popular culture for censors to permit toilet humor in the ways that other cultures, such as the English, have.[28]

Today, bathrooms are much more commonplace and certainly the taboo of showing interiors has waned. The television series *Ally McBeal* (1997–2002), for example, is particularly memorable because many of the scenes actually took place *inside* the unisex bathrooms.[29] While taboos related to showing the physical spaces of the bathroom may have faded, bodily fluids—with the exception of non-menstrual blood which of course, is plentiful—are still infrequent inclusions, particularly when simply portrayed as natural, everyday happenings. While, of course, there are scenes when "disgusting" bodily fluids appear in narratives, such fluids are presented through scenes of exaggeration and stupidity: that by presenting ridiculous quantities of a substance or by placing the substance in a bizarre location, a scene becomes more stupid than offensive. The explosive diarrhea scenes in *Dumb and Dumber* (1994) and *Along Came Polly* (2004), for example, or semen used as hair gel in *There's Something About Mary* (1998) are examples of this: they are humorous because they depict *unusual* events, bodily fluids taken out of a normal context. A rare example of a madcap menstruation portrayal occurred in the comedy *Dirty Love* (2005). Bucking the taboo of showing menstrual blood on screen, in one scene, Rebecca (Jenny McCarthy)—who had gone on a tampon run—was shown in the supermarket, blood pouring out between her legs and flooding the floor. Much like the semen and diarrhea scenes discussed earlier, such a scene was so ridiculous and exaggerated that offense likely gets mitigated. A similar scene occurred in the supernatural-themed British series *Misfits* (2009–). In the episode when Curtis (Nathan Stewart-Jarrett) first changed sex and became "Melissa" (Kehinde Fadipe), one of his first experiences as a woman was to get a period: Melissa's clothes spontaneously got soaked with blood. The blood in this scene was amusing by virtue of the supposed hilariousness of a man battling the tribulations of womanhood.

While indeed examples exist where characters *simply* go to the toilet in a matter-of-fact manner—*Eyes Wide Shut* (1999), for example, opened with Alice (Nicole Kidman) wiping herself after using the toilet, in *Notes on a Scandal* (2006) a scene showed Sheba (Cate Blanchett) using the toilet, in *Melancholia* (2011) the sound of Justine (Kirsten Dunst) urinating on a golf course was distinct, and in *Shame* (2011) we saw Brandon (Michael Fassbender) urinate—such scenes are certainly not common and most definitely don't reflect the regularity in which real people go to the toilet. One interpretation of this is that generally speaking, urination and defecation are still considered private activities; that while a given character may experience all kinds of private ablutions *off screen*, showing such events is unnecessary for most plots and can simply be inferred to happen in the background, if at all. A shortcoming of this idea is that it relies on an assumption that menstruation has been mainstreamed and accepted to the extent that explicitly mentioning it is no longer necessary. Feminists are, of course, often critical of postfeminist arguments because they rely on the assumption that feminism has achieved its objectives and now it is no longer necessary. As related to a menstruation discussion, we actually haven't yet had a time where menstruation was mainstreamed for its normalization to no longer be necessary.

Of course, a character simply going to the toilet would not be enough to actually show the audience menstruation anyhow: while Alice in *Eyes Wide Shut* and Sheba in *Notes on a Scandal* were shown using toilets, in neither scene do we see the inside of their toilet bowl or their used toilet paper. While censorship and cultural taboos may have shifted substantially from Helffrich's prohibition on toilets and toilet paper, it still remains thoroughly unusual to see the contents of a toilet bowl. Rare examples, of course, can be detected. In *Spun* (2002), a constipated Cookie (Mena Suvari) strained on the toilet; the camera then showed the result of her exhausting labors. As specifically relevant to the themes of this book, in a very unusual scene from *Californication*, Marcy's (Pamela Adlon) used tampon was seen floating in the bloodied water of a toilet bowl. Such a scene is, of course, very rare. This idea of menstruation necessitating very intimate, graphic scenes to actually be *shown* is another explanation for its absence.

THE VISUAL NATURE OF THE SCREEN

Most books on filmmaking will repeatedly state the "show don't tell" mantra: that it is far better to *show* an idea rather than have characters talk about it or to utilize a voiceover; that *showing* distinguishes screen narratives from other media. In chapter 7, for example, I discussed a scene from the television series *Grey's Anatomy* (2005–) where Derek (Patrick Dempsey) and wife Meredith's (Ellen Pompeo) attempts at conception had failed yet again. *Showing* a failed pregnancy is difficult: menstrual blood would be one way to do so; an alternative—and the method deployed in *Grey's Anatomy* and in most other screen examples—was to show the characters stare at the words "not pregnant" on a pregnancy test stick. An explanation therefore for the infrequent inclusion of menstruation on screen is that film and television are *visual* mediums and having characters *discuss* their periods is far less interesting than a visual display. *Showing* them, however, remains inappropriate for most narratives so instead the topic is largely shelved.

A connected interpretation is that screen narratives are rarely concerned with the minutiae of an individual's life in the way that a medium like literature is. This relates to menstruation portrayals because it, much like other bodily functions, is generally experienced privately. While it may become a public event by happening in a social or sexual setting or because it gets exposed in some unexpected way, most often the sight of menstrual blood is experienced only by the menstruator herself. Therefore, in most narratives, the audience *seeing* menstrual blood would seem exceedingly invasive: while we may see Alice in *Eyes Wide Shut* or Sheba in *Notes on a Scandal* use the toilet, taking the scene any further and showing them—showing the audience—what is on their toilet paper would seem thoroughly inappropriate and invasive. Take, for example, three scenes from literature where blood was sighted on toilet paper. In a scene from Laila Halaby's novel *Once in a Promised Land*, for example, Salwa "wiped herself and looked at the toilet paper. More blood, though this was pinker, fainter."[30] In Susan Isaacs's book *Close Relations*, the narrative was told from the point of view of Marcia: "I looked at the toilet paper in my hand, soaked with blood."[31] In Anica Vesel Mander's memoir *Blood Ties: A Woman's History* the same thing transpired:

> After peeing I looked at the toilet paper that I had used to wipe myself with. I don't know exactly why I looked, perhaps I always did, without thinking. I wondered about that afterward. There was some red on it. [32]

In chapter 7, I similarly discussed a number of scenes from Matthew Miller's memoir *Maybe Baby: An Infertile Love Story* where the same blood-on-toilet paper idea was repeatedly presented. Each of these scenes works in the context of literature because written works allow for greater intimacy with characters; a greater focus is given to the protagonist's point of view and the medium is able to eschew the constraints of having to avoid visually controversial displays. On screen, however, a live version of these scenes would be excessively controversial so the storyline is avoided in its entirety; alternatively, the same idea is conveyed in another way.

Given the constraints on showing menstrual blood, for menstruation to enter a screen narrative it needs to be done through a shared experience; most commonly dialogue. Rare examples do, however, exist where a *show* of menstruation occurs because numerous characters witness the event. The public menstruation of the title characters in *Carrie* (1976) and *Fetching Cody* (2005), for example, was able to show menstrual blood because it was blood that was made visible to a cast of characters within a scene. Even in the unusual scene of Marcy's floating tampon on *Californication*, the only reason the audience saw it was because it blocked the toilet on the very day that her home was open for inspection; a number of other characters saw it too. In a scene from *The Whistleblower* (2010), in one scene some bloodied tampons were visible amongst debris. This unusual sight was only visible to the audience because the protagonist, Kathryn (Rachel Weisz), saw them; the tampons were out of context and in the narrative worked to illustrate the squalid living conditions of trafficked women; they were as shocking a sight for Kathryn as for the audience. Because menstrual blood would be construed as too graphic for most screen narratives, it is most likely to enter a narrative through characters talking about it than its physical presence, an idea illustrated by the majority of scenes discussed in this book.

GENITAL TABOOS

The visual nature of the screen means that unless menstruation is spoken about by characters, it has to be shown—something done very rarely. Discussed earlier were taboos on showing used toilet paper. Taboos related to genitals are another obvious explanation for infrequent menstruation portrayals on screen. While there are indeed scenes of full-frontal male nudity in a small number of mainstream films such as *Borat* (2006), *Forgetting Sarah Marshall* (2008), and *The Hangover Part II* (2011), and full-frontal female nudity in the television series *Boardwalk Empire* (2010–) and films *A History of Violence* (2005) and *Broken Flowers* (2005), such scenes are rare in American film and television. Menstrual blood comes from female genitals and thus with genitals rarely shown, it is predictable that menstruation would not be present either. Of course, as noted in the earlier section, simply going to the toilet isn't enough to depict menstruation and neither is *simple nudity*. Unless blood is flowing freely—as it might be in menstrual-themed porn (chapter 5)—it is unlikely for *any* bodily fluids to ever be shown actually excreting from genitals in mainstream cinema because genitals themselves are rarely shown. In the context of menstruation, one subtle way it could be conveyed is through the use of a tampon string: by showing a tampon string, a woman's genitals could be concealed by underwear but a period still conveyed without a blood display. Such a scene, of course, is an exceptionally rare sight. As discussed in chapter 4, tampons are still highly controversial both on screen and off. Similarly, a visible tampon string would indicate that the tampon has actually been *inserted* and thus would reference both a penetrated vagina and *menstrual* flow, likely a compounding of far too many taboos. Controversy related to such an image in fact transpired following a 1995 issue of the *Village Voice*: the cover showed a side view of a naked woman, genitals concealed, one leg raised and a tampon string visible against one inner thigh. In *The Curse*, Karen Houppert discussed this image and the offense it apparently caused.[33] In 2010, the then sixteen-year-old singer Taylor Momsen was photographed performing in California; photographs were taken that showed her tampon string: controversy similar to the *Village Voice* cover ensued both related to the upskirt photographs but notably to the fact that Momsen had failed to conceal her string.

Given the taboo nature of genitals, tampon strings potentially can exist as a comparatively safe way to show menstruation without actually showing vaginas or menstrual blood. Of course, because tampons have to be inserted *internally*, there is a perception of them being far too personal for the screen. The fact that tampons continue to remain so controversial provides yet another justification for menstruation avoidance.

THE REAL VERSUS THE IDEAL

Former British prime minister Winston Churchill once claimed that:

> Advertising nourishes the consuming power of men. It sets up before a man the goal of a better home, better clothing, better food for himself and his family. It spurs individual exertion and greater production.[34]

Churchill's comments were a defense of advertising and of commerce more broadly, but for the purposes of this discussion usefully allude to the hallmark of advertising: the marketing of a *better* life. Advertising has a vested interest in portraying an *idealized* version of reality to encourage consumption: that such a lifestyle can be acquired through purchases. When thinking about menstruation, while advertising is indeed the place where many menstruation allusions are found, menstruation can only become part of a *better* life when it is adequately concealed (chapter 1), when lifestyle isn't encroached upon (chapter 3), and when the menstruator is able to remain sexy (chapters 5 and 6); each is aided through the use of marketed products. Such scenes avoid focusing on the darker, negative aspects of menstruation because advertisers have a vested interest in marketing products that distance the consumer from them.

While some media—like advertising—frequently present an idealized life that audiences are encouraged to desire, in film and television a stronger intent than an *ideal* world is simply the presentation of a *different* one. German playwright Bertolt Brecht once wrote that "art is not a mirror held up to reality, but a hammer with which to shape it." Sociologist George Gerbner similarly commented that television is "not a window on or reflection of the world, but a world in itself."[35] These ideas are useful in thinking about screen narratives and our, perhaps naïve, expectations of *seeing* menstruation on screen. That while menstruation might have *real-life* significance, it has no place in the fictitious worlds of film and television. In chapter 4 I examined scenes from *Married with Children* (1987–1997), *House* (2004–), and *Annie Hall* (1977), where male characters each implied that the perfect woman was one who did not menstruate. While in chapter 4 I interpreted those comments as a critique on menstruation and on the bleeding woman, another analysis is to read them as reflecting elements of a fictitious world: that fiction enables things like menstruation to be rendered unnecessary. In communications researcher Nancy Signorielli's work on television, she noted that television characters are rarely depicted *actually* working.[36] In psychologist Margaret Matlin's research, she similarly contended that "women on television programs may mention their professions, but they are seldom shown actually *working* on the job."[37] These ideas are very relevant to a discussion of the real world versus the fictitious worlds portrayed on screen. Innumerable screen narratives are set in workplaces, but very rarely are they actually *about* the work; instead, they focus on the relationships within and the dramas that ensue. Such an idea applied to menstruation suggests that while innumerable screen narratives may focus on women's lives and women's sexuality, the actual nitty-gritty of life and things like menstruation are sidelined. In a scene from *Annie Hall*, for example, as part of Alvy's (Woody Allen) dream, the Wicked Witch says, "I don't get a period. I'm a cartoon character." In the *Married with Children* scene, Al's (Ed O'Neill) thoughts on menstruation were similarly grounded in fiction, as evidenced when he remarked, "You know who is a good woman? Veronica. You know, from Archies comics? She never had a period." In both scenes, ideal women are fictitious; they are ideal because they are unreal. While certainly these examples are open to interpretation as establishing unattainable standards for real women, another way to think about them is simply that they reflect the opportunities that film and television offer: escapism to a world where the less than desirable aspects of reality are unnecessary to a plot.

Thus far I have presented the unreal worlds of screen and television as an explanation for the sidelining of menstruation. A connected explanation—referenced by Churchill's comments earlier—is that the screen commonly presents an ideal world where no one *has* to actually work very hard and where no woman *has* to menstruate. Thinking about an ideal world as one without menstruation is not completely farcical: in Fingerson's research, for example, the majority of girls said that they would act on an opportunity not to menstruate again if they could still have children.[38] In an Australian study on female clerical workers, 50 percent of women surveyed stated that they would prefer not to menstruate.[39] Anthropologist Tine Gammeltoft's research with rural Vietnamese women indicated that most would prefer not to menstruate and to be "as clean as men."[40] In recent years a market has been created for pills which abolish, or at least dramatically reduce, the number of periods a woman has in a year. Gynecologist Elsimar Coutinho's book *Is Menstruation Obsolete?* was enormously popular primarily *because* it tapped into a market of women who find menstruation undesirable. For many women and men, the ideal world is one without periods. One explanation for the existence of film and television is to provide audiences an escape. Gifting audiences a world without too much work and without menstruation potentially fulfills this brief.

DISINCLINED ACTORS

In chapter 5 I listed some of the small number of famous women who have appeared in advertisements for menstrual products, and also noted the difficulty menstrual product companies have long had in recruiting celebrity spokespeople. Houppert, for example, spotlighted that the British pop band the Spice Girls declined participating in a menstrual product advertisement: "even this group, all about girl power, wanted nothing to do with pads."[41] Such ideas highlight that celebrities and actors are evidently disinclined to be too closely associated with menstruation.

Sex in the vast majority of mainstream films is simulated. While many things explain this—most notably censorship restrictions—another reason is that actors are disinclined to participate in work that they feel might cheapen their brand. This same idea was once thought to explain film actors being disinclined to act in television narratives for fear of devaluing their star power. Much like the academics and artists discussed earlier in this chapter who were reluctant to pigeonhole themselves as feminist or women's studies researchers, actors may similarly not want to restrict their career prospects by being portrayed in a menstrual narrative. In chapter 5, I discussed that a central premise behind the use of celebrity endorsers is for the qualities associated with the celebrity—be it glamour, athletic prowess, or sexiness—to come to be associated with the advertised product. Considered in reverse is the fear that the qualities associated with *the product* may come to be associated with the celebrity and in turn damage a celebrity's career. Celebrities are scarcely seen selling items such as toilet paper or kitty litter because there is no glamour or prestige associated. Given the widespread loathing of menstrual products (chapter 4), such products—and menstrual narratives on screen more broadly—may be viewed by many actors as something that would attach negative connotations to their identity and thus would negatively impact on their brand. Menstrual portrayals, therefore, get sidelined because actors simply don't want to be associated with them.

Just as I have deemed analyzing menstrual portrayals as important enough to justify seven chapters of attention, of equal importance is understanding why menstruation is not more frequently portrayed. Discussed throughout this book have been overtly feminist-themed explanations, however, there is evidently also a range of other, less political, more industry-related and medium-specific explanations too. Such explanations highlight that the frequent exclusion of menstruation from popular culture is indicative of the multifaceted problem of social contempt for menstruation, misunderstandings of menstruation, the devaluing of it, and also women's own internalized contempt. While persistent cultural taboos likely explain the absence of menstruation from the screen, it would be amiss to neglect the other factors that also work to shape and sway cultural narratives, as discussed in this chapter.

NOTES

1. Michele Jaffe, "Going to X-tremes, 1982," in *My Little Red Book*, ed. Rachel Kauder Nalebuff (New York: Twelve, 2009), 27.
2. In Laura Fingerson, *Girls in Power: Gender, Body and Menstruation in Adolescence* (Albany: State University of New York Press, 2006), 37
3. Kelly Orringer and Sheila Gahagan, "Adolescent girls define menstruation: A multiethnic exploratory study," *Health Care for Women International* 31 (2010): 831–847, 840.
4. In JoAnn Loulan and Bonnie Worthen, *Period: A Girl's Guide* (Minnetonka, MN: Book Peddlers, 2001), 51.
5. Anthropologist Barbara Tedlock, for example, discussed that "in the early days of the industrial revolution, men doubted that women in the workforce were actually able to carry out their tasks day in and day out. Social reformers hired researchers to prove that women could perform their work when they were menstruating as easily as when they were not." (Barbara Tedlock, *The Woman in the Shaman's Body: Reclaiming the Feminine in Religion and Medicine* (New York: Random House, 2005), 197).
6. This issue is elaborated on further in Robert R. Franklin and Dorothy Kay Brockman, *In Pursuit of Fertility: A Fertility Expert Tells You How to Get Pregnant* (New York: Henry Holt and Company, 1990), 31.
7. Scott Hume, "'Most hated' ads: Feminine hygiene." *Advertising Age* (1988: 18 July).
8. Kate Kane, "The Ideology of Freshness in Feminine Hygiene Commercials," *Feminist Television Criticism*, eds. Charlotte Brunsdon, Julie D'Acci, and Lynn Spigel (New York: Oxford University Press, 1997).
9. Pierre Bourdieu, *Distinction: A Social Critique of the Judgment of Taste* (Cambridge: Harvard University Press, 1984), 199.
10. Shirley Eskapa, *Woman Versus Woman* (London: Heinemann, 1984), 43
11. Discussed in Germaine Greer, *The Whole Woman* (New York: A.A. Knopf, 1999).
12. Laura Fingerson, *Girls in Power: Gender, Body and Menstruation in Adolescence* (Albany: State University of New York Press, 2006), 88.
13. Kaye Broadbent, *Women's Employment in Japan: The Experience of Part-Time Workers* (New York: RoutledgeCurzon, 2003), acknowledgments.
14. Heather Howard-Bobiwash, "Feminist fields: Conversations to be continued," in *Feminist Fields: Ethnographic Insights*, ed. Rae Bridgman, Sally Cole, and Heather Howard-Bobiwash (Orchard Park, NY: Broadview Press, 1999), 298.
15. In John M. Murrin, Paul E. Johnson, James M. McPherson, Gary Gerstle, Emily S. Rosenberg, and Norman L. Rosenberg, *Liberty, Equality, Power* (Belmont, CA: Thomson Higher Education, 2009), 799.
16. Christina Lane, *Feminist Hollywood: From Born in Flames to Point Break* (Detroit, MI: Wayne State University Press, 2000), 66.
17. In Chris Bobel, *New Blood: Third-Wave Feminism and the Politics of Menstruation* (New Brunswick, NJ: Rutgers University Press, 2010), 42. [My emphasis.]

18. See, for example, John Preston, "The importance of telling our stories," in *Positively Gay: New Approaches to Gay and Lesbian Life*, ed. Betty Bergon (Berkeley, CA: Celestial Arts, 1992).

19. Sophie Laws, *Issues of Blood: The Politics of Menstruation* (Houndmills, Basingstoke, Hampshire: Macmillan, 1990), 53.

20. In *Cheating on the Sisterhood*, I had a section titled "Gendered Agency and Fucking Like a Man" where I contended that for a "woman to shirk these *good woman* obligations and instead act independently—in pursuit of her own interests and happiness—allows for her actions to be construed as liberating." (Lauren Rosewarne, *Cheating on the Sisterhood: Infidelity and Feminism* (Santa Barbara, CA: ABC-CLIO, 2009), 76–77).

21. Lara Freidenfelds, *The Modern Period: Menstruation in Twentieth-Century America* (Baltimore: Johns Hopkins University Press, 2009).

22. Jami Anderson, "Bodily privacy, toilets and sex discrimination: the problem of 'manhood' in a woman's prison," in *Ladies and Gents: Public Toilets and Gender*, ed. Olga Gershenson and Barbara Penner (Philadelphia: Temple University Press, 2009), 99.

23. Tomi-Ann Roberts, Jamie L. Goldenberg, Cathleen Power, and Tom Pyszczynski, "'Feminine Protection': The Effects of Menstruation on Attitudes Towards Women," *Psychology of Women Quarterly* 26, no. 2 (2002): 131–139.

24. Hope Edelman, *Motherless Daughters: The Legacy of Loss* (Cambridge, MA: Da Capo Press, 2006), 218.

25. Joan Jacobs Brumberg, *The Body Project: An Intimate History of American Girls* (New York: Random House, 1997).

26. In Robert Pondillo, *America's First Network TV Censor: The Work of NBC's Stockton Helffrich* (Carbondale: Southern Illinois University Press, 2010), 171.

27. Patrick McGilligan, *Alfred Hitchcock: A Life in Darkness and Light* (New York: HarperCollins, 2003), 596.

28. Joseph W. Slade, *Pornography and Sexual Representation: A Reference Guide*, Volume 3 (Westport, CT: Greenwood Press, 2001); Frank Walsh, *Sin and Censorship: The Catholic Church and the Motion Picture Industry* (New Haven, CT: Yale University Press, 1996); Gerald Gardner, *The Censorship Papers: Movie Censorship Letters from the Hays Office, 1934–1968* (New York: Dodd, Mead, 1987).

29. In his book on *Ally McBeal*, communications theorist Greg Smith contended that, "The unisex bathroom was one of the most frequently remarked features of the show in its first season" (Greg M. Smith, *Beautiful TV: The Art and Argument of Ally McBeal* (Austin, TX: University of Texas Press, 2007), 234, n. 155).

30. Laila Halaby, *Once in a Promised Land* (Boston: Beacon Press, 2007), 80.

31. Susan Isaacs, *Close Relations* (New York: HarperCollins, 2009), 132.

32. Anica Vesel Mander, *Blood Ties: A Woman's History* (Berkeley, CA: Moon Books, 1976), 140.

33. Karen Houppert, *The Curse: Confronting the Last Unmentionable Taboo: Menstruation* (New York: Farrar, Straus and Giroux, 1999).

34. In David Ogilvy, *Confessions of an Advertising Man* (London: Longmans, Green, 1963), 147.

35. Dennis McQuail and Sven Windahl, *Communication Models for the Study of Mass Communication* (London: Longman, 1993), 100.

36. Nancy Signorielli, "Television and adolescents' perceptions about work," *Youth and Society* 24, no. 3 (1993): 314–241.

37. Margaret Matlin, *The Psychology of Women* (Belmont, CA: Thomson Higher Education, 2008), 45.

38. Laura Fingerson, *Girls in Power: Gender, Body and Menstruation in Adolescence* (Albany: State University of New York Press, 2006), 71.

39. In Suzanne F. Abraham, "The challenges of adolescence," in *Handbook of Psychosomatic Obstetrics and Gynaecology*, ed. Lorraine Dennerstein and Graham D. Burrows (New York: Elsevier Biomedical Press, 1983).

40. Tine Gammeltoft, *Women's Bodies, Women's Worries: Health and Family Planning in a Vietnamese Rural Community* (Richmond, Surrey: Curzon, 1999), 112.

41. Karen Houppert, *The Curse: Confronting the Last Unmentionable Taboo: Menstruation* (New York: Farrar, Straus and Giroux, 1999), 17.

Conclusion

A Strange Phenomenon[1]

Each month, for a good few days at a stretch, across the course of some *thirty years*, virtually all women will menstruate. Of all the experiences exclusive to women, menstruation is the most common, the most regular, and the most enduring. Off screen it is *the* archetypal women's story. A first period exists near the top of women's seldom-forgotten milestones list and each month recurs as a reminder of the gender/biology/sexuality convergence that is menstruation.

In real life, while the psychological and physical importance of menstruation may differ between women and vary across the lifespan, its regular appearance in the lives of most women makes it something that, whether loved or loathed, needs to be tended to. Women may have become more equal in the West, but it is still only those born biologically female who are adhering pads to their underwear, inserting tampons, rinsing out menstrual cups and going to bed with hot water bottles. Off screen menstruation remains one of the most important issues exclusively impacting women.

On screen, however, the situation is much more complicated. In real life, while approximately one in seven women will be menstruating at any one time,[2] on screen the statistics are nowhere near this high. Menstruation does, however, have a presence on screen and I consider the analysis of this presence an important act of feminist media studies.

In preparation for this book I was able to compile a surprisingly large sample of menstrual references from film, television, and advertising. Scenes showing first period narratives, tampon runs, menstrual sex scene,s and menstrual activism were detected across a wide variety of sitcoms, television dramas and films of all genres. Menstruation *does* have a role on screen. This role, however, is not a simple one. On screen the regularity, normalcy and uneventfulness of real-life menstruation is rarely portrayed. The mundane and regular tampon purchases, pad changes, and product disposals that punctuate real life are overwhelmingly *absent*.

Instead, when menstruation does appear, it is treated as a drama. It is traumatic, embarrassing, distressing, offensive, comedic, or thoroughly catastrophic: that is, it is portrayed in a high-drama fashion that *justifies* its inclusion in a screen narrative. More than just being dramatic however, the presentation of menstruation on screen is an overwhelmingly *negative* one. For those rare examples of girls shown gleeful at menarche or those scarce scenes of menstruating women presented as sexy, there is a veritable deluge of portrayals where menstruation is considered evil, disgusting and the root of all female evil. This is a dark picture that remains of concern to feminists.

While audiences are gifted a multiplicity of media messages and thus speculating that any one message is more influential than another is fraught, it is nonetheless reasonable to suspect that the deluge of negative portrayals does more harm than good. With girls in real life viewing menstruation as a hassle and women happily filling prescriptions to make it go away, with men mocking it, loathing it, and rarely understanding it, on-screen presentations likely have some complicity. It is here that another problem is highlighted. On one hand, it could be contended that as with the representation of any taboo or marginalized topic, *any* visibility is better than no visibility. Given that once upon a time menstruation was *never* discussed on screen, the fact that I was able to compile a list of hundreds of screen examples might be considered a monumental triumph for feminism. With so many negative portrayals, however, the question is raised whether no portrayals would actually be preferable. A tangential issue is how much of a social engineering role we want our media to have in regard to manipulating public views and whether anyone—men or women—actually has an appetite for positive period portrayals purely out of a perceived social good.

The depiction of menstruation on screen is complicated, but it is this complexity perhaps that most of all mirrors the real-life menstrual experience. It is an individual one which impacts on women's lives in a variety of different ways. For some women, menstruation is an ongoing horror movie and for others it just blends seamlessly in with the ablutions and toilet trips of real life. There is no one type of real-life menstruator and there is similarly no typical menstruator on screen. The experience is infinitely more complicated. Period portrayals provide a fascinating glimpse into the representation of a real-life women's story that more than any other continues to have much controversy, mythology, and misunderstanding attached.

NOTES

1. The title of this conclusion references Kate Bush's song "Strange Phenomena" (1979) which was described in the *Guardian* as "a frank paean to menstruation" (Tom Doyle, "I'm not some weirdo recluse," *Guardian*, October 27, 2005, www.guardian.co.uk/music/2005/oct/28/popandrock [accessed November 3, 2011]).

2. Karen Messing, "One-Eyed Science: Scientists, Workplace Reproductive Hazards, and the Right to Work," *International Journal of Health Services* 29, 1 (1999): 147–165.

Media References

Television

30 Rock (2006–)
3rd Rock from the Sun (1996–2001)
7th Heaven (1996–2007)
Absolutely Fabulous (1992–2004)
According to Jim (2001–2009)
Adam Hills in Gordon St Tonight (2011–)
All in the Family (1968–1979)
Ally McBeal (1997–2002)
American Dad! (2005–)
Beverly Hills 90210 (1990–2000)
Big Love (2006–2011)
Blossom (1990–1995)
Boardwalk Empire (2010–)
Braceface (2001–2003)
Brothers and Sisters (2006–2011)
Buffy the Vampire Slayer (1997–2003)
Californication (2007–)
Charmed (1998–2006)
Cheers (1982–1993)
Chelsea Lately (2007–)
Community (2009–)
Coupling (2000–2004)
Curb Your Enthusiasm (2000–)
Cybill (1995–1998)
Dawson's Creek (1998–2003)
Degrassi: The Next Generation (2001–)
Designing Women (1986–1993)
Desperate Housewives (2004–)
Dr. Quinn, Medicine Woman (1993–1998)
Ellen (1994–1998)
Entourage (2004–2011)
Everybody Loves Raymond (1996–2005)
Family Guy (1999–)
Frasier (1993–2004)

Friends (1994–2004)
Gavin and Stacey (2007–2010)
George Lopez (2002–2007)
Glee (2009–)
Grey's Anatomy (2005–)
Hooperman (1987–1989)
House (2004–)
How I Met Your Mother (2005–)
In Living Color (1990–1994)
In Treatment (2008–)
Jekyll (2007)
Jersey Shore (2009–)
King of Queens (1998–2007)
King of the Hill (1997–2010)
Law and Order: Special Victims Unit (1999–)
Life Goes On (1989–1993)
Mad Men (2007–)
Married with Children (1987–1997)
Maude (1972–1978)
Misfits (2009–)
Moonlighting (1985–1989)
Murphy Brown (1988–1998)
My Family (2000–)
My Wife and Kids (2001–2005)
Offspring (2010–)
Packed to the Rafters (2008–)
Parenthood (2010–)
Party of Five (1994–2000)
Passions (1999–2008)
Pushing Daisies (2007–2009)
Ready or Not (1993–1997)
Red Dwarf (1988–)
Rescue Me (2004–)
Ron White: You Can't Fix Stupid (2006)
Roseanne (1988–1997)
Roseanne's Nuts (2011–)
Rumpole of the Bailey (1978–1992)
Saturday Night Live (1975–)
Scrubs (2001–2010)
Sex and the City (1998–2004)
Something So Right (1996–1998)
South Park (1997–)
Southland (2009–)
That '70s Show (1998–2006)
The Big Bang Theory (2007–)
The Closer (2005–)
The Cosby Show (1984–1992)
The Golden Girls (1985–1992)
The Killing (2011–)
The Nanny (1993–1999)
The New Adventures of Old Christine (2006–2010)
The Office (2005–)
The Real Housewives of Atlanta (2008–)
The Simpsons (1989–)
The Sopranos (1999–2007)
The United States of Tara (2009–2011)

The Unusuals (2009)
The Young Ones (1982–1984)
thirtysomething (1987–1991)
Two and a Half Men (2003–)
Two Pints of Lager and a Packet of Crisps (2001–)
Ugly Betty (2006–2010)
Vicar of Dibley (1994–2007)
Whitney (2011–)
Will and Grace (1998–2006)
Without a Trace (2002–2009)

Film

101 Dalmatians (1996)
50/50 (2011)
A History of Violence (2005)
A Walk on the Moon (1999)
Along Came Polly (2004)
Anchorman (2004)
Annie Hall (1977)
Apocalypse Now (1979)
Bad Day (2008)
Beaches (1988)
Body Double (1984)
Borat (2006)
Boys Don't Cry (1999)
Bridesmaids (2011)
Broken Flowers (2005)
Carnage (2011)
Carrie (1976)
Center Stage (2000)
Chasing Amy (1997)
Clueless (1995)
Cocoon (1985)
Dirty Dancing (1987)
Dirty Love (2005)
Dumb and Dumber (1994)
Eyes Wide Shut (1999)
Fab Five: The Texas Cheerleader Scandal (2008)
Feng kuan de dai jia (The Price of Frenzy) (1989)
Fetching Cody (2005)
First Blood (1982)
Forgetting Sarah Marshall (2008)
Friends (With Benefits) (2009)
Friends With Benefits (2011)
GI Jane (1997)
Ginger Snaps (2000)
Gone With the Wind (1939)
Hey Hey It's Esther Blueburger (2008)
Hungerjahre (Years of Hunger) (1980)
I Could Never Be Your Woman (2007)
I Love You, Beth Cooper (2009)
I'm Gonna Git You Sucka (1988)
In the Company of Men (1997)
Janghwa, Hongryeon (A Tale of Two Sisters) (2003)
Jennifer's Body (2009)

Juno (2007)
Just Looking (1995)
Keys to Tulsa (1996)
Kiss the Girls (1997)
Law Abiding Citizen (2009)
Man of the House (2005)
Manhattan Murder Mystery (1993)
Meaning of Life (1983)
Melancholia (2011)
My Girl (1994)
My Louisiana Sky (2001)
Osama (2003)
Overboard (1987)
Pitch Black (2000)
Possession (1981)
Prozac Nation (2001)
Psycho (1960)
Puberty Blues (1981)
Pups (1999)
Rango (2011)
Return to the Blue Lagoon (1991)
Sex and the City 2 (2010)
Sexy Beast (2000)
Shame (2011)
She's the Man (2006)
Showgirls (1995)
Silence of the Lambs (1991)
Sixteen Candles (1984)
Snow White and the Seven Dwarfs (1937)
South Park: Bigger, Longer, and Uncut (1999)
Stonewall (1995)
Submarine (2010)
Superbad (2007)
Teeth (2007)
Ten Inch Hero (2007)
The Adventures of Priscilla, Queen of the Desert (1994)
The Aristocrats (2005)
The Blue Lagoon (1980)
The Darkness Within (2009)
The Exorcist (1974)
The Hangover Part II (2011)
The Killer Inside Me (2010)
The Legend of Billie Jean (1985)
The Magdalene Sisters (2002)
The Misadventures of Margaret (1998)
The Proposal (2009)
The Rage: Carrie 2 (1999)
The Reaping (2007)
The Runaways (2010)
The Sitter (2011)
The Tall Guy (1989)
The Whistleblower (2010)
The Wizard of Oz (1939)
There's Something About Mary (1998)
To Sir With Love (1967)
Towelhead (2007)

Uncommon Women (1978)
Viskningar och rop (Cries and Whispers) (1972)
Weekend (2011)
Where the Heart Is (2000)

Music

"Only Women Bleed," Alice Cooper (1975)
"Strange Phenomena," Kate Bush (1979)
"I'd Do Anything for Love," Meat Loaf (1993)
"Blood in the Boardroom," Ani DiFrandco (1993)
"Codine Blues," The Charlatans (1966)
"Marry Me," Emilie Autumn (2006)
"Beautiful Red Dress," Laurie Anderson (1989)
"Dog in Heat," Missy Elliott (2001)
"Red Hot in Black," Rod Stewart (1986)
"Baby Baby Please (Just a Little More Head)," 2 Live Crew (1991)

Plays

Wasserstein, Wendy, Uncommon Women and Others (1977)

Bibliography

Aaronovitch, David. "Come on Baby, Let Me Know." *Independent*, March 10, 2001, www.independent.co.uk/news/uk/this-britain/come-on-baby-let-me-know-695464.html (accessed September 29, 2009).
Abraham, Suzanne F. "The challenges of adolescence." In *Handbook of Psychosomatic Obstetrics and Gynaecology*, edited by Lorraine Dennerstein and Graham D. Burrows. New York: Elsevier Biomedical Press, 1983.
Agrawal, Nisha. *Indonesia: Labor Market Policies and International Competitiveness*. Policy Research Working Paper, Washington, DC: World Bank, 1995.
Ahern, Emily A. "The power and pollution of Chinese women." In *Studies in Chinese Society*, edited by Arthur P. Wolf. Stanford, CA: Stanford University Press, 1978.
Albin, Rochelle Semmell. *Health and Beauty*. Philadelphia: Westminster Press, 1984.
Allan, Keith, and Kate Burridge. *Euphemism and Dysphemism: Language Use as Shield and Weapon*. New York: Oxford University Press, 1991.
Allen, Katherine R., and Abbie E. Goldberg. "Sexual Activity During Menstruation: A Qualitative Study. *Journal of Sex Research* 46, no. 6 (2009): 535–545.
Ames, Louise Bates. *Your Ten-to-Fourteen-Year-Old*. New York: Dell Publishing, 1989.
Anderson, Jami. "Bodily privacy, toilets and sex discrimination: The problem of 'manhood' in a woman's prison." In *Ladies and Gents: Public Toilets and Gender*, edited by Olga Gershenson and Barbara Penner. Philadelphia: Temple University Press, 2009.
Angier, Natalie. *Woman: An Intimate Geography*. New York: Random House, 1999.
Anthony, Kathryn H. *Designing for Diversity: Gender, Race, and Ethnicity in the Architectural Profession*. Urbana: University of Illinois Press, 2001.
Armstrong, Jolene. "Miss Information: Consumer Excess, Health Care and Historical Guilt in "Cherokee Hair Tampons.'" In *The Deep End of South Park: Critical Essays on Television's Shocking Cartoon,* edited by Leslie Stratyner and James R. Keller. Jefferson, NC: McFarland, 2009.
Avis, Nancy E. "Women's perceptions of the menopause." *European Menopause Journal* 3, (1996): 80–84.
Bahr, Nan, and Donna Pendergast. *The Millennial Adolescent*. Camberwell, Victoria: ACER Press, 2007.
Balint, Michael. *Problems of Human Pleasure and Behaviour*. London: Hogarth Press, 1957.
Ballard, Karen. *Understanding Menopause*. Hoboken, NJ: John Wiley and Sons, 2003.
Bandon, Alexandra. *Date Rape.* New York: Crestwood House, 1994.
Bark-Yi, Popho E. S. *Body That Bleeds: Menstrual Politics in Mala*ysia. Petaling Jaya, Selanor: Strategic Information and Research Development Centre, 2007.

Barnhill, Anne Clinard. *At Home in the Land of Oz: My Sister, Autism and Me*. Philadelphia: Jessica Kingsley Publishers, 2007.

Barr, Roseanne. "And I Should Know." *New York* magazine, May 15, 2011, nymag.com/arts/tv/upfronts/2011/roseanne-barr-2011-5/ (accessed November 6, 2011).

Bartky, Sandra Lee. "Foucault, femininity and the modernization of patriarchal power." In *Feminism and Foucault: Reflections on Resistance*, edited by Irene Diamond and Lee Quimby. Boston: Northeastern University Press, 1988.

Baumgardner, Jennifer. "Glamorous, but Not for Long, 1981." In *My Little Red Book*, edited by Rachel Kauder Nalebuff. New York: Twelve, 2009.

Bechtel, Stefan. *Sex Encyclopedia: A to Z Guide to Latest Info on Sexual Health Safety*. New York: Fireside, 1993.

Bepko, Claudia. *The Responsibility Trap*. New York: Free Press, 1985.

Bhatt, R. and Bhatt, M. "Perceptions of Indian women regarding menstruation." *International Journal of Gynecology and Obstetrics* 88, no. 2 (2005): 164–167.

Bordo, Susan. *Twilight Zones: The Hidden Life of Cultural Images from Plato to OJ*. Los Angeles: University of California Press, 1997.

Blue, Violet. *The Ultimate Guide to Cunnilingus*. Berkeley: CA, Cleis Press, 2002.

Blume, Judy. *Are You There God? It's Me, Margaret*. New York: Random House, 1970.

Bobel, Chris. *New Blood: Third-Wave Feminism and the Politics of Menstruation*. New Brunswick, NJ: Rutgers University Press, 2010.

"Bondage and Release," March 12, 2010, cmccrkn.thumblogger.com/home/ (accessed August 4, 2011).

Borich, Barrie Jean. *My Lesbian Husband: Landscapes of a Marriage*. Saint Paul, MN: Graywolf Press, 1999.

Bouchéz, Colette. *Your Perfectly Pampered Menopause*. New York: Random House, 2005.

Bourdieu, Pierre. *Distinction: A Social Critique of the Judgment of Taste*. Cambridge: Harvard University Press, 1984.

Boyd, Patricia A. "Blood on the Tracks, 1972." In *My Little Red Book*, edited by Rachel Kauder Nalebuff. New York: Twelve, 2009.

Brewis, Joanna. "How does it feel? Women managers, embodiments and changing public sector cultures." In *Transforming Managers: Gendering Change in the Public Sector*, edited by Stephen M. Whitehead and Roy Moodley. New York: Routledge, 1999.

Broadbent, Kaye. *Women's Employment in Japan: The Experience of Part-Time Workers*. New York: RoutledgeCurzon, 2003.

Brumberg, Joan Jacobs. *The Body Project: An Intimate History of American Girls*. New York: Random House, 1997.

Buckley, Thomas C. T., and Alma Gottlie. *Blood Magic: the Anthropology of Menstruation*. Berkeley: University of California Press, 1988.

Bullough, Vern L., and Bonnie Bullough. *Sexual Attitudes: Myths and Realities*. Amherst, NY: Prometheus Books, 1995.

Butler, Judith. *Gender Trouble: Feminism and the Subversion of Identity*. New York: Routledge, 1990.

Butler, Judith. *Bodies That Matter: On the Discursive Limits of "Sex."* New York: Routledge, 1993.

Byer, Curtis O., Louis W. Shainberg, and Grace Galliano. *Dimensions of Human Sexuality*. Boston: McGraw-Hill, 1999.

Callahan, Joan C. *Menopause: A Midlife Passage*. Bloomington: Indiana University Press, 1993.

Cambridge Academic Content Dictionary. New York: Cambridge University Press, 2009.

Campo, Natasha. *From Superwoman to Domestic Goddesses: The Rise and Fall of Feminism*. New York: Peter Lang, 2009.

Carroll, Janell L. *Sexuality Now: Embracing Diversity*. Belmont, CA: Wadsworth, 2010.

Caruso, Nancy L. "A Jealous Vajayjay, 1981." In *My Little Red Book*, edited by Rachel Kauder Nalebuff. New York: Twelve, 2009.

Cavendish, Richard, and Brian Innes. *Encyclopedia of World Mythology*. New York: Marshall Cavendish, 1994.

Cho, Margaret. "Let She Who Is Without Period Stains Throw the First Tampon," *Huffington Post* (January 22, 2008), www.huffingtonpost.com/margaret-cho/let-she-who-is-without-pe_b_82713.html (accessed August 4, 2011).

Chrisler, Joan C. "The menstrual cycle in a biopsychosocial context." In *Psychology of Women: A Handbook of Issues and Theories*, edited by Florence L. Denmark and Michele A. Paludi. Westport, CT: Praeger, 2008.

Chrisler, Joan C., Jennifer Gorman Rose, Susan E. Dutch, Katherine G. Sklarsky, and Marie C. Grant. "The PMS illusion: Social cognition maintains social construction." *Sex Roles* 54 (2006): 371–376.

Cohan, Steven. "Queer Eye for Straight Guise: Camp, Postfeminism, and the Fab Five's Makeovers of Masculinity." In *Interrogating Postfeminism: Gender and the Politics of Popular Culture*, edited by Yvonne Tasker and Diane Negra. Durham, NC: Duke University Press, 2007.

Cokal, Susan. "Clean porn: The visual aesthetics of hygiene, hot sex, and hair removal." In *Pop-Porn: Pornography in American Culture*, edited by Ann C. Hall and Mardia J. Bishop. Westport, CT: Praeger Publishers, 2007.

Cooper, Alice. *Alice Cooper, Golden Monster: A Rock 'n' Roller's Life and 12 Steps to Becoming a Gold Addict*. New York: Crown Publishers, 2007.

Cooper, Spring C., and Patricia B. Koch. "'Nobody told me nothin': Communication about menstruation among low-income African American women." *Women & Health* 36, no. 1 (2007): 57–78.

Coutinho, Elsimar M. *Is Menstruation Obsolete?* New York: Oxford University Press, 1999.

Creed, Barbara. *The Monstrous-Feminine: Film, Feminism, Psychoanalysis*. London: Routledge, 1993.

Curra, John. *The Relativity of Deviance*. Thousand Oaks, CA: Sage Publications, 2000.

Currie, Heather. *Menopause*. London: Class Publishing, 2006.

Dalton, Katharina. *The Menstrual Cycle*. New York: Pantheon, 1971.

———. *Once A Month: The Original Premenstrual Syndrome Handbook*. Claremont, CA: Hunter House, 1990.

Daniluk, Judith C. *Women's Sexuality Across the Life Span: Challenging Myths, Creating Meaning*. New York: Guilford Press, 1998.

Daugherty, Anne Millard. "Just a girl: Buffy as icon." In *Reading the Vampire Slayer: The Unofficial Critical Companion to Buffy and Angel*, edited by Roz Kaveney. New York: I. B. Tauris, 2001.

Davis, Rowenna. "What my period means to me." *Guardian*, October 2, 2009, www.guardian.co.uk/lifeandstyle/2009/oct/02/period-menstruation (accessed September 26, 2011).

de Beauvoir, Simone. *The Second Sex*. London: Vintage, 2011.

Dee, Richard. *The Pampered Black Queen*. 2007. books.google.com (accessed August 2, 2011).

De Freitas, Chrysta. *Keys to Your Child's Healthy Sexuality*. Hauppauge, NY: Barron's Educational Series, 1998.

Delaney, Janice, Mary Jane Lupton, and Emily Toth. *The Curse: A Cultural History of Menstruation*. New York: Dutton, 1976.

DePandi, Giuliana. *Think Like a Guy: How to Get a Guy by Thinking Like One*. New York: St. Martin's Press, 2006.

De Paulo, Raymond J., and Leslie Alan Horvitz. *Understanding Depression: What We Know and What You Can Do About It*. New York: Wiley, 2002.

Derting, Kimberly. *Desires of the Dead*. New York: HarperCollins, 2011.

Deutsch, Helene. *The Psychology of Women: A Psychoanalytic Interpretation*, Volume 2. New York: Grune and Stratton, 1945.

Devine, Ellen. "Hot Dog on a String, 1993." In *My Little Red Book*, edited by Rachel Kauder Nalebuff. New York: Twelve, 2009.

Devor, Holly. *FTM: Female-to-Male Transsexuals in Society*. Bloomington: Indiana University Press, 1997.

Dillaway, Heather E. "Menopause and misbehaving." In *Embodied Resistance: Challenging the Norms, Breaking the Rules*, edited by Chris Bobel and Samantha Kwan. Nashville, TN: Vanderbilt University Press, 2011.

Dirty Sanchez's Guide to Buck Nasty Sex. Berkeley, CA: Amorata Press, 2010.

Doyle, Tom. "I'm not some weirdo recluse." *Guardian*, October 27, 2005, www.guardian.co.uk/music/2005/oct/28/popandrock (accessed November 3, 2011).

Drelich, Marvin G., and Irving Bieber. "The psychologic importance of the uterus and its functions." *Journal of Nervous and Mental Diseases* 126, no. 1 (1958): 322–336, 330.

Edelman, Hope. *Motherless Daughters: The Legacy of Loss*. Cambridge, MA: Da Capo Press, 2006.

Ells, Alfred. *Restoring Innocence*. Nashville, TN: Nelson Publishers, 1990.

Elson, Jean P. *Am I Still a Woman? Hysterectomy and Gender Identity*. Philadelphia: Temple University Press, 2004.

Eskapa, Shirley. *Woman Versus Woman*. London: Heinemann, 1984.

Evans, Samantha. *Love Letters to Miscarried Moms*. Bloomington, IN: WestBow Press, 2011.

Fahs, Breanne. "Sex during menstruation: Race, sexual identity, and women's qualitative accounts of pleasure and disgust." *Feminism & Psychology* 21, no. 2 (2011): 155–178.

Farrell, Amy. *Yours in Sisterhood: Ms. Magazine and the Promise of Popular Feminism*. Chapel Hill: University of North Carolina Press, 1998.

Ferguson, Anthony. *The Sex Doll: A History*. Jefferson, NC: McFarland, 2010.

Ferguson, Kathy E. *The Man Question: Visions of Subjectivity in Feminist Theory*. Berkeley: University of California Press, 1993.

Ferguson, Michael. *Idol Worship: A Shameless Celebration of Male Beauty in the Movies*. Sarasota, FL: StarBooks, 2004.

Fey, Tina. *Bossypants*. New York: Little, Brown, 2011.

Fingerson, Laura. *Girls in Power: Gender, Body and Menstruation in Adolescence*. Albany, NY: State University of New York Press, 2006.

Fletcher, Anne M. *Eating Thin for Life: Food Secrets and Recipes from People Who Have Lost Weight and Kept It Off*. New York: Houghton Mifflin, 1997.

Flowers, Ronald B. *Female Crime, Criminals, and Cellmates: An Exploration of Female Criminality*. Jefferson, NC: McFarland, 1995.

Foeken, Ingrid. "Confusing realities and lessons learned in wartime: Supporting women's projects in the former Yugoslavia." In *Assault on the Soul: Women in the Former Yugoslavia*, edited by Sara Sharratt and Ellyn Kaschak. Binghamton, NY: Haworth Press, 1999.

Forbes, Gordon, Leah E. Adams-Curtis, Kay B. White, and Katie M. Holmgren. "The role of hostile and benevolent sexism in women's and men's perceptions of the menstruating woman." *Psychology of Women Quarterly* 27, no. 1 (2003): 58–63.

Fowles, Jib. *Advertising and Popular Culture*. Thousand Oaks, CA: Sage, 1996.

Franklin, Robert R., and Dorothy Kay Brockman. *In Pursuit of Fertility: A Fertility Expert Tells You How to Get Pregnant*. New York: Henry Holt, 1990.

Frayser, Suzanne G., and Thomas J. Whitby. *Studies in Human Sexuality: A Selected Guide*. Englewood, CO: Libraries Unlimited, 1995.

Freidenfelds, Lara. *The Modern Period: Menstruation in Twentieth-Century America*. Baltimore: Johns Hopkins University Press, 2009.

Freud, Hendrika C. *Electra Vs Oedipus: The Drama of the Mother-Daughter Relationship*. [Translated by Marjolijn de Jager.] New York: Routledge, 2011.

Freud, Sigmund. "The Taboo of Virginity." *The Standard Edition of the Complete Psychological Works of Sigmund Freud*, v. 11. London: Hogarth, 1953–1966.

Friday, Nancy. *My Mother My Self: The Daughter's Search for Identity*. New York: Dell, 1977.

Fulbright, Yvonne. *His Guide to Going Down*. Avon, MA: Adams Media, 2011.

Gammeltoft, Tine. *Women's Bodies, Women's Worries: Health and Family Planning in a Vietnamese Rural Community*. Richmond, Surrey: Curzon, 1999.

Gardner, Gerald. *The Censorship Papers: Movie Censorship Letters from the Hays Office, 1934–1968*. New York: Dodd, Mead, 1987.

Garrey, Matthew M. *Gynaecology Illustrated*. Edinburgh: Churchill Livingstone, 1972.

Gelder, Ken. *The Horror Reader*. New York: Routledge, 2002.

George, Demetra. *Mysteries of the Dark Moon: The Healing Power of the Dark Goddess.* New York: HarperCollins, 1992.
Giffin, Emily. *Baby Proof.* London: Orion Books, 2006.
Girshick, Lori B. *Transgender Voices.* Lebanon, NH: University Press of New England, 2008.
Glennon, Will. *200 Ways to Raise a Girl's Self-Esteem.* Boston: Conari Press, 1999.
Glover, Stephen. *Professional Idiot: A Memoir.* New York: Hyperion, 2002.
Good, Bryan J. "The heart of what's the matter: The semantics of illness in Iran." In *The Art of Medical Anthropology: Readings,* edited by Sjaak van der Geest and Adri Rienks. Amsterdam: Het Spinhuis, 1998.
Goodrich, Frances, and Albert Hackett. *The Diary of Anne Frank.* New York: Dramatists Guild Fund, 2000.
Graber, Julia A., and Jeanne Brooks-Gunn. "Adolescent girls' sexual development." In *Handbook of Women's Sexual and Reproductive Health,* edited by Gina M. Wingood and Ralph J. DiClemente. New York: Kluwer Academic, 2002.
Graham, Dee. *Loving to Survive: Sexual Terror, Men's Violence, and Women's Lives.* New York: New York University Press, 1994.
Greed, Clara. *Inclusive Urban Design: Public Toilets.* Jordan Hill, Oxford: Architectural Press, 2003.
Greer, Germaine. *The Female Eunuch.* London: Paladin, 1971.
———. *The Whole Woman.* New York: A. A. Knopf, 1999.
Gross, Rita M. *A Garland of Feminist Reflections: Forty Years of Religious Exploration.* Berkeley: University of California Press, 2009.
Halaby, Laila. *Once in a Promised Land.* Boston: Beacon Press, 2007.
Halberstam, Judith. *Female Masculinity.* Durham, NC: Duke University Press, 1998.
Hales, Dianne. *Just Like a Woman: How Gender Science is Redefining What Makes us Female.* New York: Bantam, 1999.
Hamkins, SuEllen, and Renée Schultz. *The Mother-Daughter Project.* New York: Hudson Street Press, 2007.
Hartmann, Margaret. "In historic moment, feminine hygiene ad shows blood." *Jezebel,* July 6, 2011, jezebel.com/5818826/in-historic-moment-feminine-hygiene-ad-shows-blood (accessed July 21, 2011).
Hatt, Michael, and Charlotte Klonk. *Art History: A Critical Introduction to Its Methods.* New York: Manchester University Press, 2006.
Healy, Erin. *The Baker's Wife.* Nashville, TN: Thomas Nelson, 2011.
Hewitt, Kim. *Mutilating the Body: Identity in Blood and Ink.* Bowling Green, OH: Bowling Green State University Popular Press, 1997.
Hill, Daniel Delis. *Advertising to the American Woman, 1990–1999.* Columbus: Ohio State University Press, 2002.
Himberg, Cathrine, Gayle E. Hutchinson, and John M. Roussell. *Teaching Secondary Physical Education: Preparing Adolescents to Be Active for Life.* Champaign, IL: Human Kinetics, 2003.
Hite, Shere. *The Shere Hite Reader: New and Selected Writings on Sex, Globalization, and Private Life.* New York: Seven Stories Press, 2006.
Hopson, Janet, and Anne Rosenfeld. "PMS: Puzzling monthly symptoms." *Psychology Today* (August 1984): 30–35.
Horney, Karen. "Premenstrual tension." In *Feminine Psychology.* New York: W. W. Norton, 1967.
———. "Psychogenic factors in menstrual disorders." In *The Unknown Karen Horney: Essays on Gender, Culture, and Psychoanalysis,* edited by Bernard J. Paris. New Haven, CT: Yale University Press, 2000.
Horowitz, Maya. "Behind Closed Doors: Take a ride on the red tide," February 17, 2009, flathatnews.com/content/70008/behind-closed-doors-take-ride-red-tide (accessed August 3, 2011).
hotpup. "Menstrual Love Doubled," June 26, 2004, www.literotica.com/s/menstrual-love-doubled (accessed August 4, 2011).

Houppert, Karen. *The Curse: Confronting the Last Unmentionable Taboo: Menstruation*. New York: Farrar, Straus and Giroux, 1999.
Howard, Amalie. *Bloodspell*. Minneapolis, MN: Langdon Street Press, 2011.
Howard-Bobiwash, Heather. "Feminist fields: Conversations to be continued." In *Feminist Fields: Ethnographic Insights*, edited by Rae Bridgman, Sally Cole, and Heather Howard-Bobiwash. Orchard Park, NY: Broadview Press, 1999.
Howe, James. *The Kuna Gathering: Contemporary Village Politics in Panama*. Tucson, AZ: Fenestra Books, 2002.
Hume, Scott. "'Most hated ads: Feminine hygiene." *Adverting Age* (July 18, 1988).
Isaacs, Susan. *Close Relations*. New York: HarperCollins, 2009.
Jack, Dana Crowley. *Silencing the Self*. Cambridge, MA: Harvard University Press, 1991.
Jaffe, Michele. "Going to X-tremes, 1982." In *My Little Red Book*, edited by Rachel Kauder Nalebuff. New York: Twelve, 2009.
Jeffreys, Sheila. *Beauty and Misogyny*. East Sussex: Routledge, 2005.
Jennifer Weigel Art. jenniferweigelart.com/Awareness/Identity/Menstruation.html (accessed September 24, 2011).
jimmy22990. "Breeding Lynn Ch. 01," March 23, 2008, www.literotica.com/s/breeding-lynn-ch-01 (accessed August 2, 2011).
Jong, Erica. *Parachutes and Kisses*. New York: Penguin, 1984.
———. *Fear of Fifty, A Midlife Memoir*. London: Chatto and Windus, 1994.
———. "Fear of Fourteen, 1991." In *My Little Red Book*, edited by Rachel Kauder Nalebuff. New York: Twelve, 2009.
Joyrich, Lynne. *Re-viewing Reception: Television, Gender, and Postmodern Culture*. Bloomington: Indiana University Press, 1996.
Jutel, Annemarie. "Cursed or carefree? Menstrual product advertising and the sportswoman." In *Sport, Culture and Advertising: Identities, Commodities and the Politics of Representation*, edited by Steven J. Jackson and David L. Andrews. New York: Routledge, 2005.
Kalbfleisch, Pamela J., Karen H. Bonnell, and Tina M. Harris, "Media portrayals of women's menstrual health issues." In *Evaluating Women's Health Messages: A Resource Book*, edited by Roxane L. Parrott and Celeste M. Condit. Thousand Oaks, CA: Sage, 1996.
Kane, Kate. "The Ideology of Freshness in Feminine Hygiene Commercials." In *Feminist Television Criticism*, edited by Charlotte Brunsdon, Julie D'Acci, and Lynn Spigel. New York: Oxford University Press, 1997.
Karo, Aaron. *I'm Having More Fun Than You*. New York: HarperCollins, 2009.
Katchadourian, Herant A., and Donald T. Lunde. *Biological Aspects of Human Sexuality*. New York: Holt, Rinehart and Winston, 1975.
Kato, Pamela, and Diane N. Ruble. "Toward an Understanding of Women's Experience of Menstrual Cycle Symptoms." In *Psychological Perspectives of Women's Health*, edited by Vincent J. Adesso, Diane M. Reddy and Raymond Fleming. Washington, DC: Taylor and Francis, 1994.
Kaufman, Gloria J., and Mary Kay Blakely. *Pulling Our Own Strings: Feminist Humor and Satire*. Bloomington: Indiana University Press, 1980.
King, Stephen. *11/22/63*. New York: Simon and Schuster, 2011.
Kipfer, Barbara Ann, and Robert L. Chapman. *American Slang*. New York: HarperCollins, 2008.
Kirshenbaum, Binnie. *Pure Poetry: A Novel*. New York: Simon and Schuster, 2000.
Kissling, Elizabeth A. "Bleeding out loud: Communication about menstruation." *Feminism and Psychology* 6 (1996): 481–504.
———. "When being female isn't feminine: Uta Pippig and the menstrual communication taboo in sports journalism." *Sociology of Sport Journal* 16 (1999): 79–91.
———. "On the rag on screen: Menarche in film and television." *Sex Roles* 46, no. 1–2 (January 2002): 5–12.
Klaits, Frederick. *Death in a Church of Life: Moral Passion During Botswana's Time of AIDS*. Berkeley: University of California Press, 2010.
Kushi, Gabriele. *Embracing Menopause Naturally: Stories, Portraits, and Recipes*. New York: Square One Publishers, 2006.

Landau, Carol, and Michele G. Cyr. *The New Truth About Menopause*. New York: St. Martin's Press, 2003.
Lane, Christina. *Feminist Hollywood: From Born in Flames to Point Break*. Detroit, MI: Wayne State University Press, 2000.
Laws, Sophie. *Issues of Blood: The Politics of Menstruation*. Houndmills, Basingstoke, Hampshire: Macmillan, 1990.
Lawson, Helen M. *Ladies on the Lot*. Lanham, MD: Rowman and Littlefield, 2000.
Lee, Abby. *Diary of a Sex Fiend: Girl with a One Track Mind*. New York: Ebury Press, 2007.
Lee, Janet. "Menarche and the (Hetero)sexualization of the Female Body." In *The Politics of Women's Bodies: Sexuality, Appearance, and Behavior*, edited by Rose Weitz. New York: Oxford University Press, 1998.
Lee, Shirley. "Health and sickness: the meaning of menstruation and premenstrual syndrome in women's lives." *Sex Roles* 46, no. 1 (2002): 27–35.
Leeming, David Adams, and Jake Page. *The Mythology of Native North America*. Norman: University of Oklahoma Press, 1998.
Legman, Gershon. *The Rationale of the Dirty Joke*. New York: Grove Press, 1968.
lesliejones. "Curing Cynthia's Monthly Misbehavior," www.literotica.com/s/curing-cynthia-s-monthly-misbehavior (accessed August 5, 2011).
Lessing, Doris. *The Golden Notebook*. New York: Simon and Schuster, 1962.
Letters to Penthouse IV: Erotica Unleashed and Uncensored. New York: Warner Books, 1994, books.google.com (accessed August 5, 2011).
Lewis, Zannette. "Loss and Gain of Responsibility, 1969." In *My Little Red Book*, edited by Rachel Kauder Nalebuff. New York: Twelve, 2009.
Lindsey, Shelley Stamp. "Horror, femininity and Carrie's monstrous puberty." In *The Dread of Difference: Gender and the Horror Film*, edited by Barry Keith Grant. Austin: University of Texas Press, 1996.
Linton, David. "Crossing the menstrual line." In *Embodied Resistance: Challenging the Norms, Breaking the Rules*, edited by Chris Bobel and Samantha Kwan. Nashville, TN: Vanderbilt University Press, 2011.
Llewellyn-Jones, Derek, and Suzanne Abraham. *Everygirl*. Oxford: Oxford University Press, 1999.
Logue, Alexandra W. *The Psychology of Eating and Drinking*. New York: Brunner-Routledge, 2004.
Loulan, JoAnn, and Bonnie Worthen. *Period: A Girl's Guide*. Minnetonka, MN: Book Peddlers, 2001.
Lundin, Mia. *Female Brain Gone Insane: An Emergency Guide for Women Who Feel Like They Are Falling Apart*. Deerfield Beach, FL: Health Communications Inc, 2009.
Lynch, Jane, *Happy Accidents*. New York: Hyperion, 2011.
MacDonald, John M., and David L. Michaud. *Rape: Controversial Issues: Criminal Profiles, Date Rape, False Reports and False Memories*. Springfield, IL: Charles C. Thomas, 1995.
MacDonald, Shauna M. "Leaky performances: the transformative potential of menstrual leaks." *Women's Studies in Communication* 30, no. 3 (2007): 340–357.
Macsai, Gwen. *Lipshtick*. New York: HarperCollins, 2000.
Maddux, Hilary C. *Menstruation*. New Canaan, CT: Tobey Publishing, 1975.
Madsen, Krista. "Ink blots and milk spots." In *My Little Red Book*, edited by Rachel Kauder Nalebuff. New York: Twelve, 2009.
Magistrale, Tony. *Hollywood's Stephen King*. New York: Palgrave Macmillan, 2003.
Malson, Helen. *The Thin Woman: Feminism, Post-Structuralism and the Social Psychology of Anorexia Nervosa*. New York: Routledge, 1998.
Mander, Anica Vesel. *Blood Ties: A Woman's History*. Berkeley, CA: Moon Books, 1976.
Marchand, Roland. *Advertising the American Dream*. Berkeley: University of California Press, 1986.
Marston, Stephanie. *If Not Now, When? Reclaiming Ourselves at Midlife*. New York: Warner Books, 2001.
Martin, Emily. *The Woman in the Body: A Cultural Analysis of Reproduction*. Boston: Beacon, 1987.

Martin, Karin A. *Puberty, Sexuality, and the Self: Boys and Girls at Adolescence*. New York: Routledge, 1996.
Marx, Patty. "Can I Just Skip This Period? 1971." In *My Little Red Book*, edited by Rachel Kauder Nalebuff. New York: Twelve, 2009.
Masters, William H., Virginia E. Johnson, and Robert C. Kolodny. *Human Sexuality*. New York: HarperCollins, 1995.
Matlin, Margaret. *The Psychology of Women*. Belmont, CA: Thomson Higher Education, 2008.
McConnell-Ginet, Sally. *Gender, Sexuality, and Meaning: Linguistic Practice and Politics*. New York: Oxford University Press, 2011.
McCoy, Kathy. *The Teenage Survival Guide*. New York: Simon and Schuster, 1981.
McFadden, Joyce T. *Your Daughter's Bedroom: Insights for Raising Confident Women*. New York, Palgrave Macmillan, 2011.
McGee Williams, Mary, and Irene Kane. *On Becoming a Woman*. New York: Dell, 1959.
McGeough, Danielle Dick. "Twilight and Transformations of Flesh: Reading the Body in Contemporary Youth Culture." In *Bitten by Twilight: Youth Culture, Media and the Vampire Franchise*, edited by Melissa A. Click, Jennifer Stevens Aubrey, and Elizabeth Behm-Morawitz. New York: Peter Lang, 2010.
McGilligan, Patrick. *Alfred Hitchcock: A Life in Darkness and Light*. New York: HarperCollins, 2003.
McLaren, Philip. *Scream Black Murder*. Sydney: HarperCollins, 1995.
McQuail, Dennis and Sven Windahl. *Communication Models for the Study of Mass Communication*. London: Longman, 1993.
Merriam-Webster's Dictionary of Synonyms. Springfield, MA: Merriam-Webster, 1984.
Messing, Karen. *One-Eyed Science: Occupational Health and Women Workers*. Philadelphia: Temple University Press, 1998.
———. "One-Eyed Science: Scientists, Workplace Reproductive Hazards, and the Right to Work." *International Journal of Health Services* 29, no. 1 (1999): 147–165.
Meston, Cindy M., and David M. Buss. *Why Women Have Sex: Understanding Motivations from Adventure to Revenge (and Everything in Between)*. New York: Times Books, 2009.
Meyer, Stephenie. *Breaking Dawn*. New York: Little, Brown, 2008.
Miller, Matthew. *Maybe Baby: An Infertile Love Story*. Deerfield Beach, FL: Health Communications, 2008.
Miller, William Ian. *The Anatomy of Disgust*. Cambridge, MA: Harvard University Press, 1997.
Millett, Kate. *Sexual Politics*. New York: Doubleday, 1970.
Milsom, Ian. "Dysmenorrhea." In *Urogenital Pain in Clinical Practice*, edited by Andrew Paul Baranowski, Paul Abrams, and Magnus Fall. New York: Informa Healthcare USA, 2008.
Molotch, Harvey. "Introduction: Learning from the Loo." In *Public Restrooms and the Politics of Sharing*, edited by Laura Noren and Harvey Molotch. New York: New York University Press, 2010.
Moore, Susan, and Doreen Rosenthal. *Sexuality in Adolescence: Current Trends*. New York: Routledge, 2006.
Morley, Patricia. *The Mountain in Moving: Japanese Women's Lives*. Vancouver: University of British Columbia Press, 1999.
Morris, Bonnie J. *The High School Scene in the Fifties: Voices from West LA*. Westport, CT: Bergin and Garvey, 1997.
Mouland, Michael. *The Complete Idiot's Guide to Camping and Hiking*. Indianapolis, IN: Alpha Books, 2000.
Moulder, Christine. *Miscarriage: Women's Experiences and Needs*. New York: Routledge, 1990.
Mulvey, Laura. "Visual Pleasure and Narrative Cinema." In *Movies and Methods*, edited by Bill Nichols. Berkeley: University of California, 1985.
———. *Visual and Other Pleasures*. London: Macmillan, 1989.
Murrin, John M., Paul E. Johnson, James M. McPherson, Gary Gerstle, Emily S. Rosenberg and Norman L. Rosenberg. *Liberty, Equality, Power*. Belmont, CA: Thomson Higher Education, 2009.

Museum of the Moving Image. "A Pinewood Dialogue with Kimberly Pierce." June 2, 2002, www.movingimagesource.us/files/dialogues/2/54906_programs_transcript_html_246.htm (accessed July 14, 2011).

Naharajan, Vijaya Rettakudi. "Threshold designs, forehead dots, and menstruation rituals: Exploring time and space in Tamil Kolams." In *Women's Lives, Women's Rituals in the Hindu Tradition*, edited by Tracy Pintchman. New York: Oxford University Press, 2007.

Nalebuff, Rachel Kauder. "Introduction." In *My Little Red Book*, edited by Rachel Kauder Nalebuff. New York: Twelve, 2009.

Nicholls, Dasha, Rose de Bruyn, and Gordon Isky. "Physical assessment and complications." In *Anorexia Nervosa and Related Eating Disorders in Childhood and Adolescence*, edited by Bryan Lask and Rachel Bryant-Waugh. New York: Brunner-Routledge, 2002.

Nichols, Dave. *One Percenter: The Legend of the Outlaw Biker*. St. Paul, MN: Motorbooks, 2007.

Nichols, Shana, Gina Marie Moravcik, and Samara Pulver Tetenbaum. *Girls Growing Up on the Autism Spectrum*. London: Jessica Kingsley, 2009.

NorthwestRain. "Sweet Gushing Pussies." January 15, 2002, www.literotica.com/s/sweet-gushing-pussies (accessed August 2, 2011).

Ogilvy, David. *Confessions of an Advertising Man*. London: Longmans, Green, 1963.

Ojeda, Linda. *Menopause Without Medicine*. Alameda, CA: Hunter House, 2003.

Oktay, Kutluk H., Lindsay Nohr Beck, and Joyce Dillon Reinecke. *100 Questions and Answers About Cancer and Fertility*. Sudbury, MA: Jones and Bartlett, 2008.

Orringer, Kelly, and Sheila Gahagan. "Adolescent girls define menstruation: A multiethnic exploratory study." *Health Care for Women International* 31 (2010): 831–847.

Paglia, Camille. *Sexual Personae: Art and Decadence from Nefertiti to Emily Dickinson*. New Haven, CT: Yale University Press, 1990.

Palmer, Rachel Lyn, and Sarah Koslow Greenberg. *Facts and Frauds in Woman's Hygiene: A Medical Guide Against Misleading Claims and Dangerous Products*. New York: Vanguard Press, 1936.

Parker-Pope, Tara. *The Hormone Decision*. New York: Pocket Books, 2007.

Parlee, Mary Brown. "The declining taboo against menstrual sex." *Psychology Today* 12 (December 1978): 50–52.

Perrotta, Tom. *Little Children*. New York: St. Martin's Press, 2004.

Petras, Kathryn. *The Premature Menopause Book: When the "Change of Life" Comes Too Early*. New York: HarperCollins, 1999.

Pharr, Susan J. "Status Conflict: The Rebellion of the Tea Pourers." In *Women and Women's Issues in Post World War II Japan*, edited by Edward R. Beauchamp. New York: Taylor and Francis, 1998.

Pheasant-Kelly, Frances. "In the men's room." In *Ladies and Gents: Public Toilets and Gender*, edited by Olga Gershenson and Barbara Penner. Philadelphia: Temple University Press, 2009.

Piercy, Marge. *Small Changes*. New York: Fawcett Crest, 1972.

Pinto, Sarah. *Where There Is No Midwife: Birth and Loss in Rural India*. New York: Berghahn Books, 2008.

Polak, Michele. "From the Curse to the Rag: Online gURLs Rewrite the Menstruation Narrative." In *Girlhood: Redefining the Limits*, edited by Yasmin Jiwani, Candis Steenbergen and Claudia Mitchell. New York: Black Rose Books, 2006.

———. "Menstruation." In *Girl Culture: Studying Girl Culture: A Readers' Guide*, edited by Claudia Mitchell and Jacqueline Reid-Walsh. Westport, CT: Greenwood Press, 2008.

Pollak, Otto. *The Criminality of Women*. Philadelphia: University of Pennsylvania Press, 1950.

Pondillo, Robert. *America's First Network TV Censor: The Work of NBC's Stockton Helffrich*. Carbondale: Southern Illinois University Press, 2010.

Pope, Alexandra. *The Wild Genie: The Healing Power of Menstruation*. Bowral, New South Wales: Sally Milner, 2001.

Preston, John. "The importance of telling our stories." In *Positively Gay: New Approaches to Gay and Lesbian Life*, edited by Betty Bergon. Berkeley, CA: Celestial Arts, 1992.

Price-Glynn, Kim. *Strip Club: Gender, Power, and Sex Work*. New York: New York University Press, 2000.

Rashid, Sabina Faiz. "Providing sex education to adolescents in rural Bangladesh: Experiences from BRAC." In *Gender and Lifecycles*, edited by Caroline Sweetman. Oxford: Oxfam, 2000.

Redmond, Geoffrey. *The Hormonally Vulnerable Woman*. New York: HarperCollins, 2005.

Reed, Jennifer. "Roseanne: A 'Killer Bitch' for Generation X." In *Third Wave Agenda: Being Feminist, Doing Feminism*, edited by Leslie Heywood and Jennifer Drake. Minneapolis: University of Minnesota Press, 1997.

Rempel, John K., and Barbara Baumgartner. "The relationship between attitudes towards menstruation and sexual attitudes, desires, and behavior in women." *Archives of Sexual Behavior* 32, no. 2 (2003): 155–163.

Richardson, Laurel. *The New Other Woman*. New York: Free Press, 1985.

Roberts, Tomi-Ann, Jamie L. Goldenberg, Cathleen Power, and Tom Pyszczynski. "'Feminine Protection': The Effects of Menstruation on Attitudes Towards Women." *Psychology of Women Quarterly* 26, no. 2 (2002): 131–139.

Robson, Ruthann. "Women's Music." In *The Struggle for Happiness: Stories*. New York: St. Martin's Press, 2000.

Rodgers, Joann Ellison. *Sex: A Natural History*. New York: Henry Holt, 2001.

Rogers, Kerry. *Women's Bodies: A User's Manual*. Cape Town: SchreiberFord Publications, 2006.

Root, Janet L. *Women's Perceptions of the Experience of Menstruation*. Unpublished PhD Dissertation. Salt Lake City: University of Utah, 1992.

Rosenbaum, Maj-Britt. "The Changing Body Image of the Adolescent Girl." In *Female Adolescent Development*, edited by Max Sugar. New York: Brunner/Mazel, 1993.

Rosewarne, Lauren. *Sex in Public: Women, Outdoor Advertising and Public Policy*. Newcastle: Cambridge Scholars Publishing, 2007.

———. *Cheating on the Sisterhood: Infidelity and Feminism*. Santa Barbara, CA: Praeger, 2007.

———. *Part-Time Perverts: Sex, Pop Culture and Kink Management*. Santa Barbara, CA: Praeger, 2011.

———. "Sweet charity, sleazy catfight," *The Drum*, November 9, 2010. www.abc.net.au/unleashed/40896.html (accessed September 6, 2011).

———. "The wilding of women: Why the media should ease up on girls." *The Conversation*, July 5, 2011, theconversation.edu.au/the-wilding-of-women-why-the-media-should-ease-up-on-girls-2114 (accessed October 26, 2011).

———. "Women can critique each other without the catfight." *The Punch*, March 1, 2011, www.thepunch.com.au/articles/women-can-critique-each-other-without-a-catfight (accessed September 6, 2011).

Roth, Philip. *The Dying Animal*. New York: Houghton Mifflin, 2001.

Rozin, Paul, Jonathan Haidt, Clark McCauley, Lance Dunlop and Michelle Ashmore. "Individual differences in disgust sensitivity: Comparisons and evaluations of paper-and-pencil versus behavioral measures." *Journal of Research in Personality* 33 (1999): 330–351.

Rubin, Gayle. "Thinking Sex: Notes for a Radical Theory of the Politics of Sexuality." In *The Lesbian and Gay Studies Reader*, edited by Henry Abelove. New York: Routledge, 1993.

Rumelt, Libby. "Men See Red—3 Men's Opinions on Period Sex." April 29, 2011, evolvedworld.com/sex/item/297?layout=item (accessed August 2, 2011).

Sanders, Theresa. *Approaching Eden: Adam and Eve in Popular Culture*. Lanham, MD: Rowman and Littlefield, 2009.

Scalzi, John. "Best personal hygiene products of the millennium." In *Your Hate Mail Will Be Graded: A Decade of Whatever, 1998–2008*, edited by John Scalzi. New York: Tom Doherty Associates, 2008.

Schaeffer, Neil. *The Marquis de Sade: A Life*. Cambridge, MA: Harvard University Press, 2000.

Schooler, Deborah L., Monique Ward, Ann Merriwether, and Allison S. Caruthers. "Cycles of shame: menstrual shame, body shame, and sexual decision-making." *Journal of Sex Research* 42, no. 4 (2005): 324–334.

Schulz, A. *Das Körperbild weiblicher Jugendlicher und seine Auswirkungen auf Erleben und Verhalten.* [*Body Image of Female Adolescents and Its Impact*]. Bonn: Friedrich-Wilhelms-Universitat, 1991.

Schwartz, Adam. *A Stranger on the Planet.* New York: Soho Press, 2011.

Seely, Megan. *Fight Like a Girl: How to Be a Fearless Feminist.* New York: New York University Press, 2007.

Shepard, Sara. *Flawless: A Pretty Little Liars Book.* New York: HarperTeen, 2007.

Shorter, Edward. *A History of Women's Bodies.* Plymouth: Basic Books, 1982.

Shutan, Suzan. "Burning Secret, 1996." In *My Little Red Book*, edited by Rachel Kauder Nalebuff. New York: Twelve, 2009.

Shvarts, Aliza. "The Ming Period, 1999." In *My Little Red Book*, edited by Rachel Kauder Nalebuff. New York: Twelve, 2009.

Siciliano, Elizabeth. "Silence, 1930s." In *My Little Red Book*, edited by Rachel Kauder Nalebuff. New York: Twelve, 2009.

Signorielli, Nancy. "Television and adolescents' perceptions about work." *Youth and Society* 24, no. 3 (1993): 314–241.

Sinatra, Stephen T. *Heartsense for Women: Your Plan for Natural Prevention and Treatment.* Washington, DC: LifeLine Press, 2000.

Slade, Joseph W. *Pornography and Sexual Representation: A Reference Guide*, Volume 3. Westport, CT: Greenwood Press, 2001.

Smith Greg M. *Beautiful TV: The Art and Argument of Ally McBeal.* Austin: University of Texas Press, 2007.

Smith, Mickey C., E. M. Kolass, Greg Perkins, and Bruce Siecker. *Pharmaceutical Marketing: Principles, Environment, and Practice.* Binghamton, NY: Pharmaceutical Products Press, 2002.

Snooks, Margaret Konz. "Expanding the academic knowledge base: Helping students to cross gender's great divide." In *Women in Higher Education: Empowering Change*, edited by JoAnn DiGeorgio-Lutz. Westport, CT: Praeger Publishers, 2002.

Somers, Suzanne. *Ageless: The Naked Truth About Bioidentical Hormones.* New York: Three Rivers Press, 2006.

Spencer, Scott. *Endless Love.* New York: Knopf, 1979.

Spiraling Moon blog. spiralingmoon.livejournal.com/2003/02/12/ (accessed September 24, 2011).

Spoto, Donald. *Dark Side of Genius: The Life of Alfred Hitchcock.* New York: Da Capo Press, 1999.

Stein, Elissa, and Susan Kim. *Flow: The Cultural Story of Menstruation.* New York: St. Martin's Griffin, 2009.

Steinem, Gloria. "If Men Could Menstruate." *Ms Magazine* (October 1978).

Stewart, Mary Lynn. "Sex education and sexual initiation of bourgeois French girls, 1880–1930." In *Secret Gardens, Satanic Mills: Placing Girls in European History, 1750–1960*, edited by Mary Jo Maynes, Birgitte Søland, and Christina Benninghaus. Bloomington: Indiana University Press, 2005.

Stover, Sara Avant. *The Way of the Happy Woman.* Novato, CA: New World Library, 2011.

Sullivan, Kate. "The Punk Pornographers." *Spin* 19, n. 2 (February 2003).

Sutherland, Max, and John Galloway. "Role of advertising: Persuasion or agenda-setting?" *Journal of Advertising Research* 21, no. 5 (1981): 25–29.

Teaff, Nancy Lee, and Kim Wright Wiley. *Perimenopause: Preparing for the Change.* New York: Random House, 1999.

Tedlock, Barbara. *The Woman in the Shaman's Body: Reclaiming the Feminine in Religion and Medicine.* New York: Random House, 2005.

Thompson, Clara, and Maurice R. Green. *Interpersonal Psychoanalysis: The Selected Papers of Clara M. Thompson.* New York: Basic Books, 1964.

Thompson, Hunter S. *Hell's Angels: A Strange and Terrible Saga*. New York: Modern Library, 1999.
Thornhill, Randy, and Steve W. Gangestad. *The Evolutionary Biology of Human Female Sexuality*. New York: Oxford University Press, 2008.
Tiffany, Sharon W. and Kathleen J. Adams. *The Wild Woman: An Inquiry into the Anthropology of an Idea*. Cambridge, MA: Schenkman, 1985.
Trobe, Kala. *The Witch's Guide to Life*. St Paul, MN: Llewellyn Publishers, 2003.
Tucker, Sherrie. *Swing Shift: "All-Girl" Bands of the 1940s*. Durham, NC: Duke University Press, 2000.
Turck, Mary. *Food and Emotions*. Mankato, MN: Capstone Press, 2001.
Ussher, Jane M. *Managing the Monstrous Feminine: Regulating the Reproductive Body*. New York: Routledge, 2006.
Ussher, Jane M., Myra Hunter, and Susannah J. Brown. "Good, bad or dangerous to know: representations of femininity in narrative accounts of PMS." In *Culture in Psychology*, edited by Corinne Squire. Philadelphia: Taylor and Francis, 2000.
Vachhani, Sheena J. "Vagina dentata and the demonological body." In *Bits of Organization*, edited by Alison Linstead and Malmo Rhodes. Sweden: Liber, 2009.
Valenti, Jessica. *He's a Stud, She's a Slut, and 49 Other Double Standards Every Woman Should Know*. Berkeley, CA: Seal Press, 2008.
———. *The Purity Myth: How America's Obsession with Virginity Is Hurting Young Women*. Berkeley, CA: Seal Press, 2009.
Van Gennep, Arnold. *The Rites of Passage*. London: Routledge, 2004.
Vertinsky, Patricia. *The Eternally Wounded Woman: Doctors, Women and Exercise in the Late Nineteenth Century*. Manchester: Manchester University Press, 1990.
Viljoen, Stella. "The aspirational aesthetics of 'Gentlemen's pornography.'" In *Sex, Gender, Becoming: Post-apartheid Reflections*, edited by Karin van Marle. Pretoria: Pretoria University Law Press, 2006.
von Krafft-Ebing, Richard. "Selections from Psychopathia Sexualis with Special Reference to Contrary Sexual Instinct: A Medico-Legal Study." In *The Transgender Studies Reader*, edited by Susan Stryker and Stephen Whittle. New York: Routledge, 2006.
Walker, Richard. *The Macmillan Encyclopedia of Sex and Relationships*. New York: Macmillan, 1996.
Wallace, David Foster. "The Suffering Channel." In *Oblivion*. New York: Little, Brown, 2008.
Walsh, Frank. *Sin and Censorship: The Catholic Church and the Motion Picture Industry*. New Haven, CT: Yale University Press, 1996.
Wasserman, Marlene. *Pillowbook: Creating a Sensual Lifestyle*. Cape Town: Oshun Books, 2007.
Watson, Chalmers. *Encyclopaedia Medica*, Volume 8. New York: Longmans, Green, 1901.
Weigle, Marta. *Spiders and Spinsters: Women and Mythology*. Santa Fe, NM: Sunstone Press, 2007.
Whatley, Mariamne H., and Elissa R. Henken. *Did You Hear About the Girl Who? Contemporary Legends, Folklore, and Human Sexuality*. New York: New York University Press, 2000.
Whisnant, Lynn, and Leonard Zegans. "A study of attitudes toward menarche in white middle-class American adolescent girls." *American Journal of Psychiatry* 132 (1975): 809–820.
Wilson, Carnie. *I'm Still Hungry: Finding Myself Through Thick and Thin*. Carlsbad, CA: Hay House, 2003.
Wilson, Natalie. *Seduced by Twilight: The Allure and Contradictory Messages of the Popular Saga*. Jefferson, NC: McFarland, 2011.
Women's Experiences and Understandings of Menopause. Dublin: Women's Health Council, 2008.
Woods, Gregory. "Fantasy Islands: Popular Topographies of Marooned Masculinity." In *Mapping Desire*, edited by David Bell and Gill Valentine. London: Routledge, 1995.
Woods, Nancy F., Gretchen K. Dery, and Ada Most. "Recollections of menarche, current menstrual attitudes, and perimenstrual symptoms." *Psychosomatic Medicine* 44, no. 3 (1982): 285–293.

Victor, Shalom. "The Lie, 1948." In *My Little Red Book*, edited by Rachel Kauder Nalebuff. New York: Twelve, 2009.

Young, Iris Marion. "Menstrual meditations." In *On Female Body Experience*. New York: Oxford University Press, 2005.

Index

101 Dalmatians, 193
2 Live Crew, 123
30 Rock, 22
3rd Rock From the Sun, 196
50/50, 143
7th Heaven, 9, 29, 44, 44–45, 54, 184, 185

abortion, 2, 182, 185, 210
Abraham, Suzanne, 197
absent period. *See* amenorrhea
absenteeism. *See* school; workplace
Absolutely Fabulous, 185
According to Jim, 20, 27–28, 32, 44, 106, 108, 109, 111, 112, 165
accusations (of menstruation; PMS), 2, 4, 93–102, 103, 104, 156, 208
activism, 3, 163–170, 208, 223
Adam Hills in Gordon St Tonight, 175n77
adolescence, 2, 3, 10, 11, 22, 57, 59, 121, 134, 168. *See also* coming of age; Fingerson, Laura; menarche rites of passage; school
The Adventures of Priscilla, Queen of the Desert, 96
advertising, 3, 4, 7, 28, 29, 52, 60, 69, 70, 71, 72, 73–75, 76, 87n12, 88n26, 99, 104, 105, 108, 109, 111, 115, 116, 124, 125–126, 127, 137, 147n17, 151–152, 153, 170, 187, 189, 205, 211, 216, 218, 223

aesthetics, 3, 13, 138, 170, 198; See also beauty
agenda setting, 74, 75
AIDS, 2, 115, 120n49, 133, 148n38
Albin, Rochelle Semmell, 197
All in the Family 188, 189, 192, 195
Allan, Keith, 113, 114
Allen, Katherine R., 77, 78, 115
Allen, Woody, 82, 97, 192, 217; See also *Annie Hall*; *Manhattan Murder Mystery*
allusion, 4, 70, 71, 72, 93, 105, 134, 137, 191, 197, 216
Ally McBeal, 212, 220n29
Along Came Polly, 212
alt-porn, 137, 138–140, 145
amenorrhea, 3, 197, 197–198
American Dad!, 48, 49, 79, 107
Ames, Louise Bates, 58
anal sex, 128, 143
Anchorman, 115, 141
Anderson, Jami, 34n11, 209
Anderson, Laurie, 125, 156
anger, 16, 46–48, 51, 54, 86, 96, 156
Angier, Natalie, 45, 50, 200n24
Annie Hall, 97, 217
anthropology, 5, 10, 11, 39, 61n2, 61n3, 86, 113, 118n19, 119n37, 122, 207, 217, 219n5
anticlimax, 22, 51, 54–56. *See also* disappointment; sadness

247

anxiety, 22, 29, 42, 43, 45, 50, 71, 110, 133, 165, 167, 168, 178, 180. *See also* fear
Apocalypse Now, 119n36, 158
Are You There God? It's Me Margaret 2, 12, 167, 170
The Aristocrats, 104, 105
art, 5, 11, 35n32, 130, 164, 168–170, 207–208, 218. *See also* aesthetics
artifice, 11, 15, 17, 152, 152–154, 157, 158, 163, 187, 198. *See also* femininity
audience, 9, 13, 22, 31, 42, 43, 45, 50, 71, 73, 83, 100, 123–125, 126, 127, 134, 135, 138, 140, 149n69, 149n71, 157, 161, 168, 171, 178, 179, 180, 182, 183, 185, 188, 189, 190, 191, 193, 204, 205, 206, 207, 210, 213, 214, 215, 217, 224
aunts, 9, 60, 64n78
Autumn, Emilie, 82

Bad Day, 97
Balint, Michael 80
Ballard, Karen 187
Barnhill, Anne Clinard, 46
Barr, Roseanne, 18, 41, 127, 153, 192; See also *Roseanne*
Bartky, Sandra Lee, 9
bathrooms, 7, 10–15, 16, 17, 24, 28, 35n23, 35n31, 35n37, 38n63, 40, 49, 99, 111, 112, 114, 119n35, 125, 133, 137, 143, 152, 167, 170, 179, 183, 211–212, 220n29
Baumgardner, Jennifer, 48, 180
Baumgartner, Barbara, 136, 137
Beaches, 162
beauty, 41, 75, 110, 138, 139, 152, 153, 163, 172n8, 178, 188, 189, 196. *See also* aesthetics; femininity
Bechtel, Stefan, 122
Bepko, Claudia, 154
Bérard, Carlota, 169
Beverly Hills, 90210, 179, 180
The Big Bang Theory, 30
Big Love, 200n16
biology, 3, 16, 17, 18, 25, 29, 38n63, 46, 52, 53, 67, 68, 96, 153, 187, 193–194, 195, 196, 209, 223
blindsided, 46, 49–50, 51, 54, 86
bloating, 45, 71, 75, 77

Blossom, 18, 21, 22, 44, 45, 47, 48, 52, 53, 56, 72, 73, 74, 110, 111
The Blue Lagoon, 8–9, 13, 46–47, 59, 124
Blue, Violet, 116
Blume, Judy, 12, 167; See also Are You There God? It's Me Margaret
Boardwalk Empire, 215
Bobel, Chris, 5n3, 8, 35n32, 61n2, 164, 166, 200n24
Body Double, 135
bondage, 145. *See also* sadomasochism
bonding, 7, 16–23, 33, 200n31
Borat, 215
Borden, Lizzie, 155
Bordo, Susan, 151
Borich, Barrie Jean, 169
Bouchéz, Colette, 195
Bourdieu, Pierre, 205
Boyd, Patricia A., 51
Boys Don't Cry, 48, 53, 58
Braceface 50
Brecht, Bertolt, 216
Brewis, Joanna, 159
Bridesmaids, 72, 73
Broadbent, Kaye, 207
Broken Flowers, 215
Brothers and Sisters, 25, 200n16
Buffy the Vampire Slayer, 134, 156
bullying, 74, 98, 107, 109, 117, 118n9
burden, 36n54, 48, 55, 77, 89n41, 127, 158, 178, 187, 210. *See also* inconvenience
Burridge, Kate, 113, 114
Bush, Kate, 225n1

Californication, 3, 12, 15, 27, 28, 43, 69, 81, 82, 89n34, 101, 112, 120n50, 128, 131, 132, 136, 167, 179, 195, 209, 213, 214
Callahan, Joan C., 187
Camillagate, 88n29, 76, 144, 149n81
Campo, Natasha, 126, 127
Carefree, 73, 125, 151, 153. *See also* menstrual products
caricatures, 7, 25, 28, 193. *See also* stereotypes
Carrie, 4, 13, 50, 74, 85, 86, 87n5, 98, 106, 107, 118n9, 124, 214
Caruso, Nancy L., 46

Index

catfight, 24–25, 37n55
celebrations, 10, 19, 20, 39–45, 46, 56, 60–61, 73, 140, 163, 166, 169, 170, 177, 178. *See also* congratulations
Center Stage, 97
Chambers, Christina, 126
Charlatans, 53
Charmed, 19, 22, 24, 118n8
Chasing Amy, 100
Cheers, 59
Chelsea Lately, 78
Chicago, Judy, 11, 35n32, 168, 170
childhood, 39, 45–56, 60, 62n32, 84, 85, 197
Cho, Margaret, 140
choice, 3, 52, 151
Chrisler, Joan C., 7, 147n20
Churchill, Winston, 216
circumlocutions, 164, 165, 179, 185
class, 4, 34n11, 157, 209, 209–210
cleanliness. *See* hygiene
The Closer, 158, 184, 188, 189, 191
Clueless, 160, 162
Cocoon, 2
Cokal, Susan, 138
comedy. *See* humor
coming of age, 9, 17, 39, 46
Community, 11, 15, 23, 30, 44, 163
compartmentalization, 156, 172n25
concealment, 4, 7, 8, 34n11, 48, 68, 70, 73, 98, 130, 138, 152, 204, 216. *See also* privacy; secrecy
conception. *See* pregnancy
congratulations, 1, 8, 18, 39, 40, 42, 43, 44, 45, 51. *See also* celebrations
consciousness-raising. *See* activism
consent, 4, 31, 53, 81, 90n57
Cooper, Alice, 3, 167
Cooper, Spring C., 67
The Cosby Show, 19, 33, 42, 56, 71, 163, 178, 190, 191, 194
Coupling, 183
Coutinho, Elsimar M., 217
Cox, Courteney, 29, 126
cramps, 30, 41, 69, 74–75, 76, 85, 160, 161, 163, 195, 204
cravings, 17, 162–163, 184
craziness, 95, 125, 127, 156, 163, 192–193, 194, 195, 196. *See also* moodiness

Creed, Barbara, 37n61, 86, 87n5
cunnilingus, 116, 140, 142, 128, 134
Curb Your Enthusiasm, 13, 105, 111, 112
Curra, John, 67
Currie, Heather, 187
curse, 20, 41, 46, 61, 67–69, 80, 84, 129, 178
Cybill, 165, 186, 188, 192, 194
Cyr, Michele G., 193

Dalton, Katharina, 81, 159
Daniluk, Judith C., 7, 17
The Darkness Within, 94
Daugherty, Anne Millard, 134
Davis, Rowenna, 160
Dawson's Creek, 100–101, 179
de Beauvoir, Simone, 48, 54, 55, 62n32, 63n56, 71, 88n17
De Freitas, Chrysta, 197
de Rossi, Alessandra, 126
de Sade, Marquis, 138
Dee, Richard, 143
defecation, 10, 12, 90n57, 140, 211, 212. *See also* excrement
Degrassi: The Next Generation, 15, 21, 25, 129, 165, 167
Delaney, Janice, 80, 135, 169
demonic possession, 67, 84, 85
demonizing, 3, 23, 60, 82, 86; See also evil
deodorizing, 34n11, 115, 152, 209; See also odor
DePandi, Giuliana, 130
depression, 21, 36n52, 39, 52, 55, 63n56, 84, 182, 190
Derting, Kimberly, 160
Designing Women, 160
Desperate Housewives 7n16
Deutsch, Helene, 55, 64n66
Devine, Ellen, 47, 48
Devor, Holly, 54
Dey, Susan, 126
DiFranco, Ani, 16, 116, 159
Dillaway, Heather E., 191
dirtiness, 71, 77, 82, 113, 114, 131, 136, 138, 142. *See also* messiness
Dirty Dancing, 2
Dirty Love, 62n27, 141, 149n80, 212
disappointment, 20, 46, 51–53, 54, 56, 180, 203. *See also* anticlimax; sadness

disgust, 3, 8, 10, 12, 22, 27, 35n28, 63n56, 77, 82, 87, 89n45, 93, 102–107, 111, 113–117, 118n19, 122, 132, 141, 143, 145, 155, 162, 205–206, 212, 224
disposal, 11, 12, 13, 48, 53, 224
dissociation, 53, 188
Dr. Pepper, 28, 29, 109
Dr. Quinn Medicine Woman, 50
Dumb and Dumber, 212
dysmenorrhoea, 158–159, 160. *See also* pain

Edelman, Hope, 34n12, 36n44, 36n52, 56, 120n47, 211
education, 2, 9, 11, 14–15, 18–19, 20, 36n45, 44, 47, 48, 49, 57, 62n33, 71, 76, 168, 169
Ellen, 181, 199n10
Elliott, Missy, 123
Elson, Jean P., 38n64, 119n35, 186, 189
emasculation, 7, 25, 28, 28–29, 69, 100–101, 103, 104, 107–109, 110, 112
embarrassent, 7, 10, 17, 27, 34n15, 42, 43, 44, 46, 60, 63n37, 74, 101, 104, 105, 109, 110, 144, 159, 161, 164, 165, 224
Emin, Tracey, 130
empowerment, 3, 126, 151, 163, 166
Entourage, 79, 82, 94–95
eroticization, 4, 130, 132, 136; of blood, 140–141; of humiliation, 142–144; of products 144–145; of smell, 141–142
Eskapa, Shirley, 205
essentialism, 9, 19, 118n9, 153, 181
Everybody Loves Raymond, 95, 157, 196
evil, 68, 84, 86, 193, 224. *See also* demonization
excitement, 19, 22, 29, 44–45, 52, 54, 134, 170, 180, 203, 204
excrement, 13, 114, 140. *See also* defecation
excuses, 4, 10, 36n54, 80, 81, 90n57, 114, 121, 151, 154, 154–163
The Exorcist, 85, 86
expense, 48, 62n27, 115, 132
Eyes Wide Shut, 212–213, 214

Fab Five: The Texas Cheerleader Scandal, 97
Fabianova, Diana, 170

Fahs, Breanne, 76, 78, 89n34, 114
faked menstruation, 68, 82, 140, 154, 156, 158
Family Guy, 43, 93, 141
fathers, 4, 8, 9, 10, 11, 15, 17, 18, 20, 24, 25, 27, 29, 34n15, 38n64, 39, 43–44, 45, 51, 72, 99, 101, 109, 111, 112, 113, 119n35, 144, 155, 165, 167, 195
fear, 1, 8, 10, 14, 17, 22, 25, 28, 42, 57, 68, 70, 71, 73, 75, 76, 86, 101, 105, 132, 140, 144, 157, 178, 179, 180, 188, 189, 191, 204, 207, 208, 218; of dying, 1, 50; of leakage, 70, 71, 72, 73, 75. *See also* anxiety; leakage; paranoia
fellatio, 110, 143
feminine hygiene products. *See* menstrual products
femininity, 9, 18–19, 28, 37n61, 39, 53, 56–57, 58, 68, 69, 70, 74, 87, 96, 101, 106, 114, 115, 142, 151–154, 156, 158, 163, 172n8, 181, 186, 186–190, 193, 196, 197, 198, 200n31, 204, 205, 209. *See also* artifice
feminist filmmaking, 4, 171, 206, 207, 208
feminist media theory, 3, 4, 123, 223
feminist theory, 5, 8, 36n54, 151, 187
feminization, 28, 55, 109, 145, 166, 171, 177, 187, 178, 185, 186, 189, 189–190. *See also* emasculation
Feng kuan de dai jia (*The Price of Frenzy*), 13
Ferguson, Michael, 124
fertility, 14, 22, 42, 178. *See also* mothers; pregnancy
Fetching Cody, 74, 98, 109, 111, 113, 214
fetishization, 4, 81, 96, 120n49, 121, 134, 140, 141, 143, 144, 189
Fey, Tina, 36n45, 62n33, 118n17. *See also* eroticization
Fingerson, Laura, 7, 11, 17, 19, 20, 21, 25, 32, 36n54, 37n55, 37n57, 39, 40, 45, 63n37, 68, 80, 94, 102, 114, 115, 116, 124, 138, 141, 156, 161, 162, 163, 165, 168, 186, 203, 206, 217
First Blood, 1
first period. *See* menarche
Fletcher, Anne M., 162
Flowers, Ronald B., 155
folklore, 10; *See also* myth

Forbes, Gordon, 77
forgetfulness, 191, 194–195, 196
Forgetting Sarah Marshall 215
Fowles, Jib, 157
Frank, Anne, 59, 170
Frasier 84
Frayser, Suzanne G., 86
Freidenfelds, Lara, 11, 15, 17, 20, 34n11, 35n23, 49, 76, 80, 89n45, 115, 116, 209
freshness, 72, 73. *See also* hygiene
Freud, Hendrika, 52
Freud, Sigmund, 85
Friday, Nancy, 161
Friends (With Benefits), 78
Friends, 29–30, 183
friends, 21–22; See also school
Friends with Benefits, 78
Fulbright, Yvonne, 116

Gahagan, Sheila, 20, 49, 51, 54, 56–57, 68, 203
Gammeltoft, Tine, 217
Garrey, Matthew M., 186
Gavin and Stacey, 183
Gelder, Ken, 86
George Lopez, 161
George, Demetra, 85
Gerbner, George, 216
GI Jane 106, 198
Giffin, Emily, 181
Ginger Snaps 42, 85
Glee, 101, 123, 198
Glover, Stephen, 127–128
Goldberg, Abbie E., 77, 78, 115
The Golden Girls, 68, 163, 184–185, 188–189, 190, 195, 204
Gone With the Wind, 163
grandmothers, 9, 13, 20–21, 36n47, 40–41, 60, 64n78, 68
Greenberg, Sarah Koslow, 155
Greer, Germaine, 8, 48, 155, 167, 172n17, 174n67
Grey's Anatomy, 16, 22, 23, 28–29, 108, 183, 184, 200n16, 213
Grious, Françoise, 187
gym class, 4, 160–161

Halaby, Laila, 214
Hales, Dianne, 188

The Hangover Part II, 215
Hatt, Michael, 168
Healy, Erin, 84
Helffrich, Stockton, 211, 213
hemorrhaging, 13, 26, 50
Henken, Elissa R., 10
heterosexuality, 58, 60, 90n60, 118n18
Hewitt, Kim, 170
Hey Hey It's Esther Blueburger, 15
A History of Violence, 215
Hitchcock, Alfred, 134, 211; See also *Psycho*
Hite, Shere, 116, 128–129
homosexuality, 2, 24, 58, 117n5, 208
Hooperman, 200n16
hormones, 27, 59, 95, 96, 97, 181, 187, 192, 193, 194, 195
Horney, Karen, 80
horniness, 121–123, 128, 129, 140, 158
horror, 13, 26, 42, 47, 48, 58, 85, 87, 93, 95, 102, 106, 107, 115, 116, 124, 134, 135, 139, 196, 224
hot flashes, 184, 188, 190, 191–192, 193, 194
Houppert, Karen, 11, 16, 59, 62n33, 147n17, 152, 153, 156, 166, 215, 218
House, 24, 31–32, 96, 97, 103–104, 105, 123, 162, 163, 197–198, 217
How I Met Your Mother, 183
Howard, Amalie, 55
Howard-Bobiwash, Heather, 207
humiliation, 49, 62n27, 62n32, 88n17, 107, 140, 141, 142, 142–144, 145, 149n78, 149n80, 165
humor, 7, 10, 21, 26, 28, 32, 43, 62n27, 69, 72, 90n57, 108, 112, 118n17, 126, 133, 147n24, 160, 161, 162, 165, 166, 179, 185, 188, 193, 196, 198, 211, 212, 224. *See also* mockery
Hungerjahre (Years of Hunger), 13
hygiene, 10, 12, 13, 15, 34n12, 36n52, 107, 138, 211

I Could Never Be Your Woman, 17–18, 40, 59, 84, 125
I'm Gonna Git You Sucka, 23, 33, 85, 159
idealization, 19, 44–45, 56, 137, 138, 196, 206, 216–217

identity, 39, 53, 56, 58, 60, 82, 121, 125, 136, 156, 158, 185, 186, 186–190, 218
In Living Color, 105
In The Company of Men, 68
In Treatment, 194
inconvenience, 23, 55, 61, 67, 97, 115, 191. *See also* burden
inequality, 46, 47, 54
Internet, 2, 5, 44, 139, 164, 167–168, 169
intimacy, 16, 17, 19, 20, 37n57, 110, 121, 132, 133–134, 135, 144, 146, 214
intuition, 9, 15, 58, 84, 85
Isaacs, Susan, 214

Jack, Dana Crowley, 58
Jaffe, Michele, 50, 203
Janghwa Hongryeon (*A Tale of Two Sisters*), 19, 22
jealousy, 20, 22. *See also* sibling rivalry
Jekyll, 95
Jennifer's Body, 95, 97
Jersey Shore, 79, 81
Jong, Erica, 45, 98, 134, 143, 196
Joyrich, Lynne, 181–182, 200n16
Judaism. *See* religion
Juno, 94, 95
Just Looking, 107
Jutel, Annemarie, 73, 74

Kalbfleisch, Pamela J., 191
Kane, Irene, 52
Kane, Kate, 151, 153, 205
Karo, Aaron, 154
Keys to Tulsa, 68
The Killer Inside Me, 135
The Killing, 94
Kim, Susan, 52, 164
King of Queens, 200n16
King of the Hill, 13, 27, 50, 68, 72, 73, 129
King, Stephen, 112, 148n44
Kirshenbaum, Binnie, 114, 134
Kiss the Girls, 32
Kissling, Elizabeth A., 17, 19, 35n33, 164, 179
Klonk, Charlotte, 168
Koch, Patricia B., 67
Kotex, 52, 99, 108, 109, 115, 118n17, 126, 142. *See also* menstrual products
Kushi, Gabriele, 190

Landau, Carol, 193
Lane, Christina, 207
late period, 2, 25, 132, 177, 178–179, 180–181, 182, 183, 185, 190, 198
Law Abiding Citizen, 123
Law and Order, 32, 131
Laws, Sophie, 8, 26, 29, 35n28, 80, 81, 90n57, 102, 104, 112, 113–114, 116, 128, 136, 149n78, 159, 189–190, 208
Lawson, Helen M., 98
leakage, 21, 46, 70, 71, 72, 73, 74, 75, 111, 151, 160. *See also* staining
Lee, Abby, 132
The Legend of Billie Jean, 171
Lessing, Doris, 52, 84
Lewis, Zannette, 8, 9, 199n4
Libra, 72, 73, 104, 105, 111, 137. *See also* menstrual products
Life Goes On, 2
Lindsey, Shelley Stamp, 124
Linton, David, 29
Llewellyn-Jones, Derek, 197
Loulan, JoAnn, 9, 20, 64n78, 110, 166, 203
Lundin, Mia, 156
Lynch, Jane, 101, 109, 111, 198
Lynley, Carol, 126

MacDonald, Shauna M., 71
Macsai, Gwen, 14, 15
Mad Men, 94, 179
Maddux, Hilary C., 48
Madsen, Krista, 59
The Magdalene Sisters, 48
magic, 41, 86, 166
Malson, Helen, 163
Man of the House, 108
Mander, Anica Vesel, 214
Manhattan Murder Mystery, 192
Marchand, Roland, 75
Married with Children, 24, 97, 156, 196, 217
Martin, Emily, 11, 122
Marx, Patty, 47, 48
masculinity, 7, 25, 27, 28, 58, 69–70, 82, 96, 102, 108, 110, 112, 117n5, 128, 133, 166, 198
masturbation, 47, 85, 123, 139, 143
Matlin, Margaret, 217
Maude, 185

Index

McConnell-Ginet, Sally, 100
McFadden, Joyce T., 55
McGee, Williams, 52
McGilligan, Patrick, 211
McGraw, Ali, 126
McLaren, Philip, 55
The Meaning of Life, 162
Meat Loaf, 28, 109
media effects, 60
Melancholia, 212
men: as creepy, 29–32; as dolts, 25–28; as ignorant, 50; as inconvenienced, 23; as suffering, 23. *See also* fathers; masculinity
menarche, 1, 2, 3, 4, 8, 10, 12–13, 14, 15, 17, 18–19, 20, 21, 22, 27, 33, 36n44, 38n64, 39–56, 57, 58, 59, 61, 61n2, 62n33, 63n56, 64n66, 68, 69, 71, 72, 74, 84, 85, 90n61, 98, 99, 109, 110, 112, 115, 118n9, 121, 124, 125, 129, 159, 160, 163, 165, 166, 167, 168, 170, 177, 178, 180, 182, 197, 199n4, 203, 204, 206, 223, 224
menopause, 5n3, 49, 96, 132, 152, 158, 163, 165, 171, 177, 178, 184, 184–197, 200n24, 200n26
menstrual leave, 158–159, 161, 208
menstrual products, 8, 11, 12, 14, 15, 16, 16–17, 23, 26, 27, 28, 29, 34n11, 35n23, 35n28, 48, 52, 56, 62n27, 87n12, 72, 73, 74, 75, 87, 93, 99, 101, 102, 103–113, 115, 117, 125, 126, 137, 142, 143, 144, 145, 147n17, 151, 153, 164, 168, 169–170, 203, 204, 205, 209, 210, 218. *See also* Carefree; Kotex; Libra; Tampax; Vagisil
messiness, 41, 53, 77, 86, 104, 114, 114, 119n35, 131, 138, 139, 149n69, 151, 153, 168, 178, 187. *See also* dirtiness
Meyer, Stephenie, 35n30, 179
Midol, 74, 75. *See also* pain relief medication
Miller, Matthew, 183–184, 214
Millett, Kate, 36n54, 89n41
The Misadventures of Margaret, 192
miscarriage, 36n44, 181, 181–183, 200n16, 210
Misfits, 212
misogyny, 2, 28, 68, 117, 117n5

missed period. *See* amenorrhea
Mitchell, Joni, 207
mockery, 10, 15, 44, 61n8, 84, 86, 94, 96, 99, 100, 105, 126, 174n66, 191, 224; *See also* humor
Molotch, Harvey, 14–15, 35n27, 35n37
Momsen, Taylor, 70, 205, 215
moodiness, 4, 20, 24, 30, 37n55, 84, 93–94, 97, 101, 153, 155, 156–157, 158, 163, 187, 190, 191, 192, 194, 195, 210. *See also* craziness; PMS
Moonlighting, 181–182, 200n16, 210
Moore, Susan, 121
Morris, Bonnie J., 160
mothers, 4, 8, 9, 11, 16, 17–19, 20, 21, 24, 33, 34n12, 36n44, 36n45, 36n52, 39–43, 45, 49, 52, 53, 54, 55–56, 57, 58, 59, 60, 62n33, 64n78, 69, 71, 84, 94, 97, 99, 100, 107, 109, 110, 112, 119n35, 120n47, 125, 156, 161, 162, 166, 167, 178, 181, 182, 185, 186, 188, 190, 194, 195, 197, 211. *See also* fertility; pregnancy
Mouland, Michael, 48
Mulvey, Laura, 3, 123
Murphy Brown, 32
My Family, 107
My Girl, 8, 9, 13, 18, 46, 47, 48, 49, 50, 52, 53, 56, 57, 58, 59, 60, 71
My Louisiana Sky, 20, 40, 41, 46, 50, 68, 178
My Own Private Idaho, 2
My Wife and Kids, 24, 33
mythology, 10, 69, 70, 74, 76, 77, 78, 81, 86, 87n13, 113, 117, 140, 193, 224. *See also* folklore

nagging, 24, 99–100
naiveté, 45, 50, 54, 99, 216
Nalebuff, Rachel Kauder, 110, 206
The Nanny, 160
The New Adventures of Old Christine, 24, 141
new-age literature and writings, 84, 86
new-age rituals, 44, 61n8
Nicholls, Dasha, 197
No Strings Attached, 24, 33, 79, 83, 153, 154, 159, 163
Notes on a Scandal, 212, 213, 214

odor, 9, 34n11, 67, 70, 71, 73, 75, 77, 85, 99, 105, 106, 114, 115–117, 128–129, 140, 141–142, 143, 145, 149n71, 151, 153, 209, 204
offense, 10, 29, 68, 81, 93, 102, 105, 114, 115, 146, 165, 169, 179, 209, 212, 215, 224
The Office, 23, 61n8, 160, 174n66
Offspring, 183
oppression, 117n5, 151, 168, 200n31
original sin, 68. *See also* religion
Orringer, Kelly, 20, 49, 51, 54, 57, 68, 203
Osama, 53
osmosis, 28
Overboard, 82
over-eye, 58
overreaction, 50

Packed to the Rafters, 185
Paglia, Camille, 68
pain, 24, 47, 71, 74, 75, 135, 158, 159, 170. *See also* dysmenorrhea
pain relief medication, 74–75, 88n26. *See also* Midol; Pamprin; Premesyn
Palmer, Rachel Lyn, 155
Pamprin, 69, 75. *See also* pain relief medication
paranoia, 72, 75; See also fear
Parenthood, 69, 183
Parker, Suzy, 126
Parker-Bowles, Camilla, 76, 88n29, 144, 149n81
Party of Five 36n44, 71, 109, 160, 182, 210
Passions 194
patriarchy, 36n54, 58, 89n41, 118n9, 153
Peirce, Kimberly, 53
penis envy, 47
Penthouse, 145
Perrotta, Tom, 132, 183
perversion, 28, 29, 81, 149n71
Petras, Kathryn, 188
Piercy, Marge, 82
Pippig, Uta, 70, 205
Pitch Black, 54, 85, 115, 141
Playboy, 121, 139, 140
PMS, 2, 20, 32, 35n33, 36n54, 73, 75, 88n26, 93, 94, 95, 95, 96, 97, 100, 101, 127, 130, 147n20, 153, 155, 156, 157, 158, 159, 160, 173n27, 192, 193. *See also* moodiness
Polak, Michele, 167–168, 170
Pollak, Otto, 68
Pondillo, Robert, 211
Pope, Alexandra, 7, 154
pornography, 4, 83, 120n49, 121, 123, 130, 135, 136, 137–145, 149n71, 215
Possession, 4
pregnancy, 2, 3, 14, 23, 25, 27, 32, 57, 58, 132, 156, 171, 177–186, 188, 195, 197, 199n10, 204, 213. *See also* fertility; mothers
Premesyn, 75. *See also* pain relief medication
pride, 1, 10, 20, 41, 43, 128, 139, 165, 168
Prince Charles, 76, 88n29, 144, 149n81
prison, 34n11, 143, 149n78, 209
privacy, 7–9, 10, 11, 12, 15, 17, 21, 32, 35n27, 39, 54, 70, 98, 106, 123, 144, 158, 159, 167, 169, 170, 171, 186, 204, 205, 211, 212, 214. *See also* concealment; secrecy
prophesy, 36n54, 67, 84
The Proposal, 108
Prozac Nation, 84
psychiatry, 56, 90n61, 197
Psycho, 13, 212
psychoanalysis, 47, 52, 55, 80, 85, 105
psychology, 5, 7, 34n12, 58, 59, 76, 102, 120n47, 121, 134, 138, 147n20, 155, 156, 163, 191, 193, 197, 200n31, 211, 217, 223
psychotherapy, 9, 64n78, 70, 110, 166, 203
puberty, 8, 48, 54, 59, 63n56, 121
Puberty Blues, 13, 171
public space, 1, 3, 7, 11, 12, 13, 14, 35n27, 35n37, 39, 70
punishment, 46, 74, 121, 143, 149n78
Pups, 15
purity, 74, 121. *See also* hygiene; religion
Pushing Daisies, 186

Queen Victoria, 155
queer theory, 90n60, 118n18, 148n52, 153

race, 4, 11, 33, 107, 126, 209–210
radical feminism, 96, 151
The Rage: Carrie 2, 100

rags, 29, 41, 99–100, 165
Rango, 210
rape, 13, 32, 158
Ready or Not, 13, 15, 22, 44, 48, 49, 50, 51, 52, 53, 54, 55, 57, 58, 60, 99
The Real Housewives of Atlanta, 71
The Reaping, 85
Red Dwarf, 26, 28, 179
Redmond, Geoffrey, 155
Reed, Jennifer, 157
religion, 4, 46, 68, 76, 85, 86, 87n9, 133; Judaism, 20
Rempel, John K., 136, 137
Rescue Me, 24, 108, 109, 200n16
resentment, 46, 47, 52, 53, 58, 82, 99, 102, 104, 145
Retton, Mary Lou, 73
Return to the Blue Lagoon, 8, 13, 46–47, 59, 124
Richardson, Laurel, 60
Rigby, Cathy, 73
rites of passage, 3, 33
Robson, Ruthann, 131
romance, 39, 59–60
Ron White: You Can't Fix Stupid, 79
Roseanne, 17, 18, 27, 40, 41–42, 43, 51, 52, 53, 55, 57, 58, 60, 71, 99–100, 119n36, 127, 156–158, 166, 178
Roseanne's Nuts 192
Rosenbaum, Maj-Britt, 56
Rosenthal, Doreen, 121
Roth, Philip, 133
Rozin, Paul, 102
Rumpole of the Bailey 155
The Runaways 15, 19, 84, 167

sadness, 51, 51–52, 181. *See also* anticlimax; disappointment
sadomasochism, 107, 142–144. *See also* bondage
sanitary. *See* hygiene
sanitary napkins. *See* menstrual products
Saturday Night Live, 162
Scalzi, John, 25–26, 86, 110
Schaeffer, Neil, 138
school, 1, 15, 20, 21, 47, 48, 49, 50, 63n37, 71, 74, 99, 106, 109, 110, 158, 159, 159–160, 161, 165, 206. *See also* friends

Schooler, Deborah L., 76
Schwartz, Adam, 78, 183
Scrubs, 101, 183
secrecy, 3, 4, 7, 8, 9, 16, 42, 43, 54, 85, 110, 124, 154, 164, 165, 168, 170, 173n32, 199, 204, 205. *See also* concealment; privacy
Seely, Megan, 71
self-esteem, 4, 24, 42, 44, 76, 89n34, 118n8, 134, 151
self-surveillance, 9, 58, 63n56, 154
separation, 7–15, 57, 185
Sex and the City, 16, 22, 23, 25, 104, 105, 114, 132, 166, 180–181, 185, 188, 189, 190, 196
sex drive, 81. *See also* horniness
sexiness, 4, 77, 116, 121–130, 134, 138, 139, 141, 146, 152, 153, 154, 181, 188, 189, 190, 206, 216, 218, 224
sexual corveé, 154, 163
sexual intercourse, 76–83, 177
sexual preference, 4. *See also* heterosexuality; homosexuality
sexuality, 3, 10, 17, 29, 59, 60, 68, 80, 84–86, 117, 121, 124, 129, 137–139, 140, 146, 161, 178, 197, 216, 223. *See also* horniness
sexualization, 124, 127, 144
Sexy Beast, 103
shame, 7, 8, 9, 34n11, 35n28, 63n56, 110, 164, 165, 208, 209
Shame, 212
She's The Man, 106, 111
Shepard, Sara, 166
Shepherd, Cybill, 126, 165, 181, 186
shock, 2, 13, 47, 49, 58, 62n33, 139, 145, 169, 188, 214
Shorter, Edward, 113
Showgirls, 79, 81
Shutan, Suzan, 50
sibling rivalry, 19. *See also* jealousy; sisters
Siciliano, Elizabeth, 46
Signorielli, Nancy, 217
Silence of the Lambs 141
The Simpsons 100, 159
Sinatra, Stephen T., 154
sisterhood, 4, 16, 42, 98, 166

sisters, 8, 9, 15, 16, 17, 18, 19–20, 24, 25, 29, 53, 58, 60, 64n78, 71, 79, 109, 118n8, 142, 156, 160
The Sitter 103, 104
Sixteen Candles 79
smell. *See* odor
Snooks, Margaret Konz, 70
social work, 5, 48
sociology, 7, 8, 14, 35n27, 35n28, 35n37, 38n64, 39, 54, 60, 67, 68, 71, 73, 94, 102, 119n35, 124, 128, 157, 159, 186, 189, 191, 203, 209, 217
Something So Right 27, 28, 43
The Sopranos 16, 99, 100, 192, 194
South Park 68, 94, 106, 107
South Park: Bigger Long and Uncut 68
Southland 94
Spade, Kate, 17, 104, 105
Spears, Britney, 70, 205
Spencer, Scott, 133–134
The Spice Girls, 147n17, 218
sports, 5n3, 18, 48, 51, 57, 58, 67, 69–75, 76, 82, 88n14. *See also* swimming
staining, 1, 4, 12, 21, 40, 48, 51, 70, 71, 73, 74, 75, 77, 114, 126, 130, 132, 135, 141, 142, 143, 145. *See also* leakage
Stein, Elissa, 52, 164
Steinem, Gloria, 166
stereotypes, 3, 4, 20, 32, 53, 56, 58, 75, 95, 96, 98, 99, 100, 121, 127, 137, 146, 147n20, 153, 155, 156–157, 158, 162, 191–193, 204, 209, 210. *See also* caricatures
Stewart, Mary Lynn, 49
Stewart, Rod, 123
stigma, 3, 7, 43, 74, 75, 105, 111, 113, 167
Stonewall, 100
storage, 11, 12, 35n23, 35n28
Submarine, 133
substitution, 135
subtext, 90n60, 118n18, 135, 137
Superbad, 10
supernatural, 19, 67, 86, 87, 90n61, 166
swimming, 46, 47, 70, 72, 73, 74, 160, 161; See also sports
synchrony, 4, 7, 17, 19, 22–25, 33, 36n54, 153, 159, 163
synecdoche, 93, 102, 191

taboo, 2, 3, 4, 12, 70, 74, 75, 76, 77, 78, 81, 83, 87n12, 93, 100, 113, 117, 134, 136, 139, 141, 144, 145, 161, 164, 165, 170, 171, 186, 198, 199, 203, 206, 208, 210, 211–216, 219, 224
The Tall Guy, 103
Tampax, 7, 16, 21, 72, 73, 102, 104, 108, 111, 134, 144. *See also* menstrual products
tampon run, 2, 16, 21, 28, 29, 32, 56, 104, 107–111, 128, 141, 212, 223
tampons. *See* menstrual products
taste, 56, 162, 205–206
Teaff, Nancy Lee, 49
Teeth, 105
telekenesis, 85
Ten Inch Hero, 72, 73, 104, 105, 106, 110, 113
That '70s Show, 184–185, 186, 188, 190, 195
There's Something about Mary, 212
third-wave feminism, 164–165
thirtysomething, 200n16
Thompson, Clara, 47
Thompson, Hunter S., 128
Tiegs, Cheryl, 126
Tiegs, Vanessa, 169
To Sir With Love, 8, 34n11, 70, 106, 115, 204
toilet, 10, 12, 13, 21, 29, 35n31, 83, 113, 123, 131, 171, 183, 211–214, 215, 224. *See also* bathroom
tomboys, 18, 39, 51–53, 56–58
Towelhead, 13, 33, 59, 113, 144
transgenderism, 5n3, 48, 145
transsexualism, 53, 58, 96
trust, 16, 67–68, 80, 110, 133, 195
Two and a Half Men, 72, 73
Two Pints of Lager and a Packet of Crisps, 180

Ugly Betty, 130
Uncommon Women and Others, 167
The United States of Tara, 103, 104
universality, 4, 117, 118n19, 208
The Unusuals, 111–112
urination, 10, 12, 14, 114, 140, 145, 211, 212
Ussher, Jane M., 7, 155, 156

Vaccaro, Brenda, 126
vaginas, 2, 35n32, 53, 67, 76, 80, 93, 99, 108, 109, 116, 124, 129, 143, 215, 216, 2; vagina dentata, 105; vaginal dryness, 191; vagina size, 17, 103, 104, 105, 107, 112, 161, 168
Vagisil, 99, 116
Valenti, Jessica, 96, 121, 173n27
vampires, 35n30, 134–135, 156
The Vicar of Dibley, 91n70
vicarious menstruation, 135–136
Victor, Shalom, 170
violence, 2, 85, 135, 155
virginity, 78, 116, 121, 132, 135, 161
Viskningar och rop (*Cries and Whispers*), 82
von Krafft-Ebing, Richard, 59
voyeurism, 124, 140, 124
vulnerability, 13, 15, 53, 104, 163

A Walk on the Moon, 9, 13, 20, 40, 41
Walker, Richard, 76
Wallace, David Foster, 114
Wasserman, Marlene, 122
Weekend, 195
Weideger, Paula, 161
Weigel, Jennifer, 169

Whatley, Mariamne H., 10
Where the Heart Is, 14, 180
The Whistleblower, 215
Whitby, Thomas J., 86
Whitney, 196
Wiley, Kim Wright, 49
Will and Grace, 30, 183
Williams, Serena, 73
Wilson, Carnie, 121
Wilson, Natalie, 134
Wilson, Robert, 187
Without a Trace, 200n16
The Wizard of Oz, 193
womanhood, 8, 17, 18, 44, 46, 47, 56, 58, 59, 61, 84, 85, 96, 103, 121, 138, 153, 168, 178, 193, 198, 208, 212
women's stories, 4, 21, 40, 57, 168, 171, 206–210
Woods, Gregory, 46–47
Woods, Nancy F., 49
workplaces, 23, 37n57, 38n63, 116, 158, 159, 161, 208, 217
Worthen, Bonnie, 9, 20, 64n78, 110, 166, 203

Young, Iris Marion, 95–96, 147n27
The Young Ones, 26–27, 28

About the Author

Dr. Lauren Rosewarne is a lecturer in the School of Social and Political Sciences at the University of Melbourne, Australia. She has degrees in political science, cultural studies, public policy, and education, and is the author of *Sex in Public: Women, Outdoor Advertising and Public Policy* (2007), *Cheating on the Sisterhood: Infidelity and Feminism* (2009), and *Part-Time Perverts: Sex, Pop Culture and Kink Management* (2011). More information can be found at www.laurenrosewarne.com.